Everything you need to know about the world's coolest range of computers

Hello...

WELCOME TO THE SECOND EDITION OF THE INDEPENDENT GUIDE to the Mac. A lot has changed in the world of Apple since the first edition was published, and you'll find details of every change here.

Whether you're new to the platform or you're looking to upgrade a trusty iMac or Power Mac you've had for some time, there has never been a better time to explore Apple's current line-up. The latest updates to its mobile computers are particularly exciting, with two brand new 13in models added to the MacBook Pro line-up. This will please anyone looking for a compact replacement for their trusty 12in PowerBook, which has been sorely missed by many.

But it's not just in the world of desktop and notebook computers that Apple is grabbing headlines these days. Less than three years ago it unveiled its audacious plan to launch its own mobile phone – the iPhone –and while half of the world expected great things of the company that had single-handedly taken over the market for portable media players with the iPod, many industry 'experts' talked of a long, hard uphill battle.

Well, that battle was won and now, on the basis of reported sales, Apple is among the world's 10 biggest mobile phone producers. Not bad for a company that didn't even have a single product a few years back. That first iPhone has evolved over time, spawning the iPhone 3G and, more recently, the iPhone 3GS. If you're wondering which one is right for you, here's where you can find out.

Over the next 260 pages, we'll guide you through Apple's complete consumer hardware line-up and show you how to get the most out of the applications they run. We'll focus on cross-platform suites like Microsoft Office and Adobe Creative Suite, so refugees from the world of PCs can see how similar the two platforms are, and we'll also be highlighting gems of the Mac, like RapidWeaver and iLife.

The Mac has long been considered one of the most desirable computers, and as Apple continues to evolve each model in the range, it makes that desire ever stronger. So, come with us as we explore the Mac and the add-ons and software that surround it as we guide you through the hardware and software that make these remarkable machines such a pleasure to use.

Nik Rawlinson

EDITOR Nik Rawlinson
ART EDITOR Camille Neilson
PRODUCTION EDITOR Jon Lysons
DEPUTY EDITOR Kenny Hemphill
CONTRIBUTORS Ian Betteridge, Christopher Brennan, Tom Gorham, Rod Lawton, Keith Martin, Howard Oakley, Christopher Phin, Misha Sakellaropoulo, Alan Stonebridge
IMAGES Danny Bird, Pio Blanco, Linda Duong, Peter Mac, Faissal Otmani, Chris Robson, Stephen Savage and some images courtesy of Apple

ADVERTISING
020 7907 6000, Fax 020 7907 6600
ads.macuser@dennis.co.uk
ACCOUNT MANAGER Alexandra Skinner 020 7907 6623
AD PRODUCTION EXEC Anisha Mogra 020 7907 6067
DIGITAL PRODUCTION MANAGER Nicky Baker
US ADVERTISING MANAGER Matthew Sullivan-Pond
++1 646 717 9555 *matthew_sullivan@dennis.co.uk*

PUBLISHING & MARKETING
020 7907 6000, fax 020 7636 6122
MANAGING DIRECTOR Ian Westwood 020 7907 6355
ASSOCIATE PUBLISHER Paul Rayner 020 7907 6663
BOOKAZINE MANAGER Dharmesh Mistry 020 7907 6100
LIST RENTAL INSERTS EXECUTIVE John Perry
020 7907 6151 *john_perry@dennis.co.uk*
MARKETING MANAGER Claire Scrase 020 7907 6113

DENNIS PUBLISHING LTD
PRODUCTION DIRECTOR Robin Ryan
DIRECTOR OF ADVERTISING Julian Lloyd-Evans
NEWSTRADE DIRECTOR Martin Belson
CHIEF OPERATING OFFICER Brett Reynolds
GROUP FINANCE DIRECTOR Ian Leggett
CHIEF EXECUTIVE James Tye
CHAIRMAN Felix Dennis
Typography Neue Helvetica © Heidelberger Druckmaschinen AG, licensed by Linotype *linotype.com* Collis © 1993 The Enschedé Font Foundry *teff.nl/fonts/collis*
Printed in England by BGP Print Ltd, Chaucer International Estate, Launton Road, Bicester, Oxon OX6 7QZ

MAGBOOK
The 'Magbook' brand is a trademark of Dennis Publishing Ltd. 30 Cleveland Street, London W1T 4JD. Company registered in England. All material © Dennis Publishing Ltd, licensed by Felden 2009, and may not be reproduced in whole or part without the consent of the publishers. *The Independent Guide to the Mac* is an independent journal, not affiliated with Apple Inc. 'Apple' and the Apple logo, 'Macintosh', 'Mac' and the Mac logo are the trademarks of Apple Inc.
The Independent Guide to the Mac ISBN 1-906372-65-9

PERMISSIONS AND REPRINTS
Material in *The Independent Guide to the Mac* may not be reproduced in any form without the publisher's written permission. *The Independent Guide to the Mac* is available for licensing overseas. For details contact Winnie Liesenfeld, International Licensing Manager,
00 44 (0) 20 7907 6134, *winnie_liesenfeld@dennis.co.uk*

LIABILITY
While every care was taken during the production of this Magbook, the publishers cannot be held responsible for the accuracy of the information or any consequences arising from it. Dennis Publishing takes no responsibility for the companies advertising in this Magbook.

HOW TO CONTACT US
MAIL MACUSER, 30 Cleveland Street, London, W1T 4JD
EMAIL *mailbox@macuser.co.uk* **WEB** *www.macuser.co.uk*
PHONE 020 7907 6000 Fax 020 7907 6369

CONTENTS

Welcome to the Mac....... 006
Whether you've just bought your first Mac or you're on the verge of making the leap, start here, as we run through the complete line-up, and dispel the most common Mac myths.

Mac OS X 030
The Mac's rock-solid operating system is crammed full of clever tricks and hidden features. Come with us as we explore the most exciting innovations that keep Mac OS X streets ahead of the competition.

iLife 048
Photos, videos and music all have a home in iLife, the easy, powerful media management and editing tools that ship with every new Mac. We'll show you how to get the best out of every application.

iWork 072
Who said the Mac wasn't a serious business machine? Apple's own office suite, iWork, sports a first-class word processor, spreadsheet and presentation application, all capable of outstanding results.

Software for the Mac 086
Look beyond Apple's own software: design cool websites with RapidWeaver, spend your working day with Microsoft Office, tweak your photos with Photoshop and chat with friends online.

Features 110
The 20 must-have Mac tools. How to build a website in a weekend. Getting better results from Google. Getting to grips with social networking. All this and much, much more.

Masterclass 176
Do everything you want more easily and in less time with our bumper bundle of Masterclasses. These step-by-step workshops cover everything from editing movies to producing revealing spreadsheets.

260 PAGES OF MAC KNOW-HOW

Welcome to the Mac

Welcome to the Mac, the most extraordinary and groundbreaking computer ever conceived.

It's more than 30 years since Steves Wozniak and Jobs got together to found Apple, and while the company enjoyed early success, it really only came to the public's attention with the launch of the revolutionary semi-transparent iMac. This squat, by today's standards, conventional device was to revive the company's fortunes, and inspire a whole range of follow-ups, including the MacBook, Mac mini, iPod and iPhone.

Whether you've just bought home your first Mac or you're a beginner just finding your feet, you'll find plenty here to help you get the most out of your new machine. Before that, though, we'll take a look at Apple's current line-up to help you understand where your computer sits or, if you've not yet taken the plunge, decide which is the right Mac for you.

Why should you buy a Mac?	008
Mac myths exposed	010
iMac	012
Mac Pro	014
MacBook	016
MacBook Pro	018
MacBook Air	020
Mac mini	022
Apple TV	023
iPod line-up	024
iPhone	028

Why should you buy a Mac?

If you're still considering making the leap from a PC or if you're about to buy your first Mac then fear not because it is one of the easiest computers to use. It also comes pre-loaded with a great software bundle so you can be up and running in no time at all, and once you've taken the plunge you'll never look back.

If you've not yet bought your first Mac, you're probably wondering why you should. Maybe you've never had a computer before, or perhaps you're on the cusp of making the switch from a PC, and you have a few concerns about compatibility, ease of use and value for money. Either way, there are good reasons to invest in a Mac rather than a computer running Windows and we're sure that once you've taken the plunge you'll never look back.

Macs, as you'll already have noticed, look great on the outside, and if you've ever opened one up you'll know that they look just as good on the inside, too. Apple's own operating system, Mac OS X, is the most beautiful and intuitive operating environment money can buy. It is also stable and secure, being built on top of the industry-standard Unix environment, which greatly reduces its vulnerability to virus, spyware and other harmful infections.

The Mac is the ultimate start-and-go machine. With a single company controlling both the hardware and the operating system, you can be sure that the two will work together without any glitches. If you want a computer you can use from the off and that is reliable, buy a Mac. If you want a computer you can fix and diagnose on a regular basis, buy a PC. How do we know? Because the team that put together this book uses both Macs and PCs, and while we often have to tweak our PCs to keep them happily chugging along, the last time we did any serious Mac maintenance is lost in the mists of time. The last time any of us had a system crash can be counted in terms of months, not days and weeks.

There is less confusion over what you should be buying when you invest in or upgrade a Mac. Unlike Microsoft, Apple doesn't make myriad versions of its operating system. It has only two: one for servers, which will be of no interest to most consumers, and one for desktop and portable machines, which we can all use.

This means that you have to pay only one price to get every available feature offered by Mac OS X, not look at your budget and decide what you can afford. Compare that to Microsoft's Windows Vista range, where there are no less than five different editions: Ultimate, Business, Home Premium, Home Basic, Business and Enterprise. Which one is right system for you? Who knows. Be warned, though, that if you opt for the cheapest, Home Basic, you'll be missing a lot of key features.

But it's not just the operating system that you get when you buy a Mac. PC users will already be familiar with getting a load of applications pre-installed on their machines when they arrive, but these are usually trials, which either expire after a certain period, or have had many of their most impressive features trimmed to encourage you to upgrade to the full edition.

Macs are different: they come pre-loaded with a fantastic software bundle. The included iPhoto (see page 50) makes photo editing, organising and printing simple, with professional features for making books and web sites from your galleries. iMovie (see page 64) grabs video footage from the best camcorders and lets you transform it from a series of shaky shots into a coherent film of which you can be proud. Don't believe us?

Images Courtesy of Apple

American Mac user Jonathan Caouette made a movie called *Tarnation* using iMovie, which was shown at the Sundance Film Festival and invited to both the New York Film Festival and the Directors' Fortnight at Cannes. Once you've edited your movie, you can burn it to disc using iDVD (see page 68).

iTunes (see page 54) does for music what iPhoto does for your pictures. It keeps everything organised, lets you build playlists to suit any mood, and download music and podcasts from its integrated online store. It also connects seamlessly to the iPod, the world's best-selling portable music player. GarageBand lets you create your own tunes the easy way – by dragging and dropping pre-recorded snippets in the order in which you want them to play – and iWeb (see page 60) does much the same for websites, greatly simplifying the process of getting your pages up online.

Beyond these, you'll find a first-class media player in the shape of Front Row, messaging tools, a web browser, email and calendar applications, and a range of third-party software tailored to whichever Mac you've bought.

Macs last, too. Apple's advertising team could also be forgiven if it took a leaf out of Volkswagen's book and highlighting how many of its machines go on and on and on, and how many get re-sold online, or passed on to friends. Take a look at the Macs for sale on eBay (*ebay.co.uk*) and you'll see that for many, there's very little difference in the prices between buying new and picking one up second-hand. This may be bad news if you were hoping to save a bit of money by nabbing some slightly older technology, but it's good news should you later decide to sell up and switch back to the PC, not that we think you will. Invest in a Mac today and you could still be enjoying its benefits in 10 years' time.

This is a great environmental benefit, as it means less of them will end up in landfill sites, leaching their dangerous components alongside all the dead PCs. In the US, Apple runs an extensive recycling scheme, taking back old machines you have bought through its stores and handling its safe disposal for you, leaving you feeling better about moving on to your next great machine.

At the start of their lives, new Macs are built with the environment in mind, too. The aluminium casings of the MacBook Pro, MacBook Air and Mac Pro are easily recycled and, following encouragement from environmental groups, Apple no longer uses many harmful chemicals in the production of its products and, by the end of 2008, it had eliminated PVC, brominated flame retardants and arsenic from all of its products, despite the fact that these harmful chemicals, which some other manufacturers continue to employ, make the production process easier and cheaper.

It has slimmed down the size of the boxes in which it ships its computers, saving on packaging and the fuel consumed in shipping them, and its portable products, ranging from notebooks to iPods and iPhones, have excellent power management, allowing their batteries to run for longer than most PC equivalents on a regular charge, saving on energy consumption.

All-in-all, there are many good reasons to choose a Mac instead of a PC, and with excellent compatibility between the two you shouldn't be scared of making the switch. Mac applications are great at reading Windows files, and the same is true in reverse, making it easy for you to continue working on the documents, such as spreadsheets, that you've already produced on your PC, and share work with your PC-using colleagues and friends.

Mac myths exposed

Time and time again you come across a range of arguments against buying a Mac, whether they're from family, friends or work colleagues who all use Windows-based computers. We take you through some of the most common myths to debunk them, so you can make a more balanced judgement about buying a Mac.

MACS ARE EXPENSIVE

No they're not. They may have a higher up-front price than some equivalent PCs, but in the long run Macs often work out cheaper. When Windows Vista launched it required up-to-date hardware – so up-to-date, in fact, that many users found they couldn't run it at all without a major upgrade. It was the same story for Windows XP, and 2000 and Me before it.

With Apple producing both the hardware and the software, it can ensure that this doesn't happen. The two are so finely crafted to work hand-in-hand that when Mac OS X 10.4 Tiger shipped, it was compatible with machines up to seven years old.

There are countless tales of people still using Macs 10 or more years old, either because they've been handed down through the years or because they bought them new and have never stopped using them. When you average the up-front cost of such a machine over such an extended working life, it usually ends up much cheaper than an equivalent PC, which would have become cluttered, fragmented and ground to a halt.

MACS HAVE A LIMITED RANGE OF SOFTWARE

What exactly do you want to do with a Mac that you think might not be possible? Every Mac sold ships with a browser (Safari), email client (Mail) and basic word processor (TextEdit). iLife provides video and photo editing tools (iMovie and iPhoto), a web design application (iWeb), DVD burning software (iDVD) and iTunes for downloading, buying and playing back music and podcasts.

There are dozens of office suites, including Microsoft Office, which is compatible with its Windows equivalent, and high-end design tools like Photoshop, InDesign and Dreamweaver, all from Adobe, are arguably better on the Mac than they are on PC.

We'd defy you to find a mainstream task that a Mac can't perform just as well as a PC, if not better. Plus, the Mac is far easier to program than a PC thanks to the great development software Apple and other publishers have put together. This has encouraged an army of third-party coders to knock out some great applications – at very low prices – that you simply can't get for Windows.

MACS ARE INCOMPATIBLE WITH MOST PERIPHERALS

While it's true that some devices still don't work with the Mac, it's unfair to say that most peripherals are incompatible with the Mac. Pretty much every printer, scanner and multi-function device will work with a Mac straight out of the box, and although other gadgets like webcams have had difficulty working on the Mac, shareware and open source projects are plugging the gap for drivers. And when it comes to printers, the Mac's Unix-based printing system has been tried and tested for many years on a wide range of non-Mac operating systems, allowing you to use a range of generic drivers if the one for your printer has never been ported to the Mac.

A wide range of ostensibly Windows-only products, like Microsoft keyboards with a Windows key beside the space bar, and of course two-button mice (Apple used to only make mice with a single button) work just fine without any drivers.

As the Mac gets more popular, more and more hardware developers will write Mac drivers for their peripherals, giving Mac users everywhere a bigger choice of add-ons than ever before.

MACS DON'T RUN WINDOWS

Oh yes they do. Since Apple started using Intel processors in its computers they've been more like regular Windows PCs than ever before. As such, you can actually install Windows on your Mac. There are two ways to do this, namely dual-booting and virtualisation. It's not as difficult as it sounds, and it means you can effectively have two computers in one. We cover this in more detail on pages 98-105, Windows on the Mac.

▲ Both the same MacBook, but one is running Windows and the other Apple's native operating system Mac OS X.

MACS ARE INCOMPATIBLE WITH A LOT OF WEBSITES

No they're not. A good, efficient, compatible website should be coded in such a way that it complies with guidelines set down by the World Wide Web Consortium – the so-called W3C. The Mac's default web browser, Safari, is written to interpret these pages, and should have no problems with any website that is properly written. Even if it does have problems with some sites, there are alternatives like Firefox and Opera, both of which also available for Windows PCs.

Unfortunately, however, lazy developers sometimes block Mac browsers from viewing their sites because they think there's a remote possibility they could be a security risk. This is untrue, of course, but the online banks can sometimes be the worst culprits here, and it's usually because they don't have the time, resources or simply inclination to even bother checking.

How do we know? Because simply telling the browser to fib about what it is, and pretend to be something more widely-used, such as Internet Explorer running under Windows, will often let you access the site. And guess what? No problems.

So websites aren't incompatible with Macs, but perhaps some Windows-based web designers are.

▲ Most online banking websites work just as easily in Safari as they do in Firefox or Internet Explorer.

▲ The BBC website is a perfect example of a website that complies with the guidelines from W3C.

MACS ARE ONLY FOR DESIGNERS

That would be true if designers were the only people who ever wanted to create spreadsheets, word process documents or write PHP code. But they're not, so it isn't.

The Mac is just a computer, like any other – technically a PC – and the fact that it appeals to designers dates back to the days when it was the first consumer PC to ship with a graphical user interface driven by a pointer and a mouse. All of the rival PCs at the time had text-based interfaces, which were great for writing and doing your sums, but no good for design.

So if you wanted to be a designer you bought a Mac, then recommended Macs to the next generation of designers who the did the same, all the way down the line to the present day.

While it's true that many designers buy Macs, it's not true that they're the only ones who buy them. Or indeed that they're the only people for whom they're built.

MACS DON'T CRASH

Well, much as we'd like to hold this one up we have to admit that there is a whisper of a lie in it. Macs do crash, but not nearly so often as Windows PCs. You can safely expect to go many weeks, or even months, without a crash on a properly maintained Mac and, as a bonus, should one of your applications throw a fit and break down, it is unlikely to bring down the whole of the operating system, so the data in your other applications should remain safe.

▲ Commonly called the spinning beachball of death, fortunately you don't see it that often.

MACS AREN'T PCS

PC stands for Personal Computer. The Mac is a computer, used by one person at a time; that is personally. Thus it's a PC.

iMac

With its all-in-one design, the latest incarnation of the iMac, a descendant of the computer that revitalised Apple's fortunes, looks fantastic. However, it isn't just the looks that are impressive, the specs are also very formidable, making the iMac a very powerful machine to have on your desktop whether you choose the 20in or 24in model.

DESKTOP MAC
iMac

Price £949 (£825 ex VAT) for 2.66GHz 20in; £1199 (£1043 ex VAT) for 2.66GHz 24in; £1499 (£1304 ex VAT) for 2.93GHz 24in; £1799 (£1565 ex VAT) for 3.06GHz 24in
Pros Looks gorgeous + Superb 1080p HD-compatible screen + Excellent performance + 3.06GHz option
Cons None

In August 2007, Apple pulled a rabbit out of the hat: a sleek new line of iMacs guaranteed to wow the world. Gone was the trusty white plastic, to be replaced by brushed aluminium, glass and black detailing. It was a whole new generation of desktop computers, and one that the company has updated since. In every sense these are things of rare beauty that make the previous flat-panel models look plump and even a touch garish. We're no stranger to Apple's design unveilings, but we weren't expecting to feel this much desire for the new iMacs.

The iMac's body is now a sleek matte aluminium shell with a matte black rear. The 20in or 24in LCD flat screen is set inside a black frame and protected with flush-fit, high-impact, scratch-resistant glass. Unlike Apple's 17in notebook, gloss is the only option. But before you get on your high-horse about this, it is worth noting that Apple's glossy screens give a noticeably better contrast ratio than the non-glossy designs. The result is richer, deeper blacks that improve the appearance of all kinds of content.

The 20in iMacs have a display resolution of 1680 x 1050 pixels, while the 24in models have 1920 x 1200 pixels. The larger size is perfect for playing high-end 1080p HD video; the 20in screens can handle 720p HD videos with ease. There were reports that some of the early aluminium 20in iMacs had 'washed out' displays, and this was attributed by some as being the result of using a panel that uses dithering to display millions of colours. However in everyday use we have found this and later versions to be fine for detailed, day-long use.

All the models include the same embedded iSight camera, which, set into the black frame that runs around the display, is even more discreet than before. About the only thing we missed from previous models was the side magnet that held the remote control. It was a nice touch that kept the tiny device from getting lost and it's a shame it's gone, but that's a minor quibble. In terms of overall physical design, these are effectively flawless. There are LCD displays more bulky on their own than this iMac is with the complete computer packed inside.

So has anything been compromised in the effort to squeeze everything inside the slim-line chassis? According to our tests, the answer is an emphatic 'no'. It isn't a match for a beefy Mac Pro, of course, but the 2.66GHz and 2.93GHz, and 3.06GHz Intel Core 2 Duo processors perform very well. The 3.06GHz processor is an option that is only available on the 24in model.

The graphics hardware for the entry-level model is now an Nvidia GeForce 9400M processor with 256MB of DDR3 SDRAM, which is shared with the main system memory. This will confidently take applications like Photoshop in its stride, but shared system memory is slower than dedicated chips.

The 24in model with 2.93GHz processor comes with a choice of three graphics processors, each with their own memory chips: the Nvidia GeForce GT 120 and GT 130, with 256MB and 512MB of GDDR3 memory respectively, or the ATI Radeon HD 4850, again with 512MB of GDDR3 memory. Upgrading to the 3.06GHz processor leaves you with just the Nvidia GeForce GT130 and ATI Radion HD to choose from.

Every model comes with an 8-speed SuperDrive that supports 4-speed double-layer DVD burning, so the optical drive is no longer a decision point.

The entry-level iMac comes with a 320GB Serial ATA hard drive, while the 24in models are graced with 640GB drives, all spinning at a decent 7200rpm. The high-end 3.06GHz iMac comes with a 1TB drive as standard but, of course, build-to-order drive options for up to 1TB can be selected for most models.

The bundled mouse is the Mighty Mouse scrollerball, but the keyboard is a new and slightly strange slimline design.

▶ The latest iMacs come in just two screen sizes – 20in and 24in. Both have a glossy screen to give deeper blacks.

◀ You can't help but be impressed by the iMac's looks – even the keyboard is super slim.

It is exceptionally low, which is a good thing, ergonomically speaking. Opinions around our office and elsewhere are divided. Those who use desktop keyboards, particularly with Windows PCs, tend not to be that happy with it, preferring a bigger, more noticeable distance of travel for the key caps. Those who have used MacBooks, however, will feel right at home as this keyboard looks and feels exactly the same as the portable model. The default choice is also the same in terms of size, as Apple ships the iMac with a cut-down keyboard missing the numeric keypad. You can opt for the full-size board at no extra cost. We think that most people who aren't keen on it now will come to like it after a little while; when we used it for regular work we found it to be comfortable and responsive.

The keyboard's USB ports are now USB 2 ports; earlier keyboards used USB 1.1-speed ports, which made them not much use for anything more demanding than a mouse. The controller keys along the top are arranged slightly differently from previous designs. The brightness controls (F1 and F2) are standard but the F3 key is the All Windows Exposé trigger and F4 kicks Dashboard into life and back again. F5 and F6 are unadorned with extra functions, but keys F7 through F9 are generic reverse, play/pause and forward controls, and F10 to F12 are now the volume control keys.

Curiously, there are F keys right up to F19 on the full-size keyboard. All this feels pretty logically organised, although it may take current users a little while to get used to things being in different places. If you use these F keys for anything else you'll need to hold down the Fn modifier key to get the traditional F key trigger behaviour. Notebook users will automatically look to the lower left of the keyboard for this, which is exactly where they'll find it on the smaller keyboard, but it has been moved to take the place of the Help key in the home/end block on the full-length option.

Finally, the one small, but clearly potential problem with the keyboard design is the recessed USB ports tucked below the keyboard's edge on either side. If you plan to use USB memory sticks, you'd better make sure these have slim profiles or be ready to fiddle round the back of the iMac to plug them into the USB ports located there.

These ports on the back are arranged horizontally rather than vertically. The analog audio out and in ports are near the right-hand edge, followed by four USB 2 ports, a FireWire 800 port, gigabit Ethernet and Apple's now-standard (for consumer Macs anyway) mini-DVI port for connecting a second display or projector. There is no FireWire 400 port any more.

Down at the bottom of the iMac, positioned centrally between the two downward-firing speakers, is a grille that is held in place by a single screw. This provides access to the memory slots – still just two, but still enough to allow a maximum of 8GB of Ram to be installed.

The stereo speakers are driven by a 24-Watt amplifier and their downward orientation spreads the audio effectively without requiring physically separate units. While no computer speakers are going to out-perform a proper hi-fi setup, or even a good set of powered speakers, these are rich, responsive and clear, and have enough power to fill a room with music without straining. They may not keep a party going, but they're more than enough for casual music enjoyment while you and your colleagues get on with your work or play.

So, which iMac is right for you?

If you have the space for it, the 24in screen is simply amazing and well worth the extra cost. Whichever model you choose, though, these are seriously powerful Macs. Demanding users may automatically be drawn towards the Mac Pro, but to skip past the iMac without giving it serious consideration would be a mistake. These machines have the muscle to hold their own in a creative environment, yet are slim and good looking enough to not look out of place in a home environment. As such, they're a great all-round choice.

Mac Pro

The configure-to-order Mac Pro is Apple's heavyweight desktop computer aimed at creative professionals who need power to handle large files, such as video and high-resolution photographs, as well as simultaneously open several high-end applications. As such the Mac Pro forms that backbone of Apple's range of Macs.

DESKTOP MAC
Mac Pro

Price £1899 (£1651 ex VAT) for Quad-Core + £2499 (£2173 ex VAT) for Eight-Core
Pros Fast + Easy to upgrade + Lots of expansion options
Cons No Blu-ray option + Wifi not included as standard

The Mac Pro represents the peak of Apple's desktop computer line-up. It is the most traditional-looking of all the machines that it produces, shipping in a conventional upright case that can be stood on or below your desk, separate from the monitor.

There are two configurations available off the shelf, with quad- or eight-core processor set-ups, each of which can be customised with a range of optional add-ons.

The Quad-Core machine, which represents the entry-level point unless you choose to downgrade, features a single 2.66GHz Intel Xeon 3500 processor with 8MB of shared Level 3 cache. The Eight-Core machine ships with twice as many processors, each running at 2.26GHz on an Intel Xeon 5500 chip, again with 8MB of shared Level 3 cache. Upgrade options on the two machines run to 2.93MHz processors in each case and, on the Eight-Core machine, a 2.66MHz Xeon 5500 processor.

The basic memory configuration is 3GB in the Quad-Core machine, upgradable to 8GB, and 6GB in the Eight-Core, with an option to upgrade to 32GB. Each of the default configurations is supplied as a combination of 1GB chips. You should consider your memory needs very carefully before choosing one Mac Pro over the other. Each sports only four slots per processor, so the Eight-Core machine has twice as many physical locations for installing memory. Further, it can address 4GB chips, whereas the Quad-Core machine can't; its abilities extend only to 2GB modules at best.

Unfortunately, upgrading memory at the time of purchase is expensive when compared to buying the modules from a third party and fitting them yourself. Opting for 8GB on the Eight-Core Mac Pro – an increase of 2GB over the default – will cost an additional £80.01. However, sticking with the base 6GB and adding a further 4GB in the form of two 2GB sticks from Crucial will cost an additional £71.29, including VAT, and in the process increase your total memory allocation to 10GB. There is no longer any need to install Mac Pro memory in pairs, and you can mix the capacities in each slot.

It's a similar story with the Quad-Core machine: taking it up from 3GB to 6GB costs an additional £120 when done at the point of purchase, whereas buying an additional 4GB from Crucial and fitting it yourself would cost just £71.29 and give you the benefit of an extra gigabyte to boot.

The Mac Pro's smart aluminium case, which has changed little since the arrival of the G5-based Power Mac, has bays for four 3.5in Serial ATA hard drives. These are cable-free, allowing the drives to attach directly as they are slid into place on sleds. The standard install in all models is a single 640GB unit spinning at 7200rpm, accompanied by an 18-speed SuperDrive with support for double-layer burning.

This can be upgraded to 1TB for £80.01, with further 640GB or 1TB drives fitted to the remaining bays for £160 and £240.01 apiece. An additional £80.01 will also buy you a second SuperDrive.

One curious omission, however, is built-in wifi – particularly when you spot that Apple has chosen to include Bluetooth 2.1 + EDR, an arguably less useful wireless technology for the majority of users. However, the explanation could be that while the lack of wireless Ethernet may encourage an upgrade at the point of purchase (for an extra £40), throwing in Bluetooth at no charge makes the £14 wireless Mighty Mouse and £20 wireless keyboard more tempting than they might be had it not been included.

Post-purchase upgrades are easily accommodated by the three available fill-length PCI Express 2.0 expansion slots with support for 16-lane cards, and for many buyers these are what will swing a buying decision, pushing them towards Apple's professional product line, rather than an equally competent iMac. For particularly demanding users, these will be put to good use with an optional Raid card upgrade, giving a choice of data capacity, speed or resilience, or a mix of the three.

The standard graphics controller is an Nvidia GeForce GT 120 with 512MB of GDDR memory. This is memory is dedicated to the card, rather than being shared with the system allocation, and so should deliver better results. This supports Mini DisplayPort and dual-link DVI output, and can be supplemented by three additional cards to support multiple monitors, or swapped out entirely for an ATI Radeon HD 4870 with 512MB of GDDR5 memory. Obviously, installing additional graphics cards uses PCI Express slots, restricting your upgrade options elsewhere.

There is no denying that the Mac Pro is a supremely powerful machine, and a creative user's dream, but unless you need to make use of its expansion features, consider the iMac, too.

▲ As its name would suggest, the Mac Pro is the ideal professional user's machine. Unlike the iMac it requires an external monitor.

◄ The innards of the Mac Pro are easily accessible, making the upgrading of hard disks incredibly easy. Drives slide into the case on a series of sleds, which you can see at the top of the open space in the middle of the case. The slots below them are for expansion cards, while the memory sits at the bottom. Here the memory chips are blue.

MacBook

The entry-level MacBook is Apple's budget laptop and is the cheapest Mac you can buy with everything included to get you up and running. But don't think that just because this is a budget machine Apple has skimped on the parts; despite the price, it compares favourably with the professional line of MacBook Pros.

NOTEBOOK
MacBook

Price £749 (£651 ex VAT)
Pros Good value + Good performance
Cons Only one screen size option

The MacBook is starting to look very lonely. Once there were three polycarbonate machines in the range: two white and one black. Then there was one white and two aluminium. Now there's just a solo white model, sitting alone and marking many users' entry-point into Apple's portable range of Macs.

In comparison to its siblings, it looks chunky, unsubtle and decidedly low-tech. The white plastic case has rounded corners that contrast sharply with the more refined edges of its aluminium brethren. And from using earlier models of this product, we know that it also has a tendency to get dirty, either from your fingers on the keyboard and trackpad, or from general daily use.

But don't write it off right away. This remains the cheapest all-in-one Mac, and the neatest way to run Mac OS X on the go.

Looking beyond its outward appearance, the specs are actually very good. For your £749, you get a 2.13GHz Intel Core 2 Duo processor with 3MB on-chip Level 2 cache. This is running in parity with the processor speed, so it certainly won't be the weak point when it comes to performance.

Neither will the 1066MHz frontside bus. However, the memory, which is 2GB by default, but can be upgraded to a maximum of 4GB at the time of purchase, is a disappointment, running at only 800MHz on account of being DDR2, not the DDR3 chips found in the MacBook Pro.

It's not only the speed of the memory that concerns us, though: it's also the way it's been configured. The MacBook has just two memory slots, and Apple has chosen to fill each with a single 1GB chip. That means that if you want to upgrade after purchase by buying third-party chips from a supplier like Crucial you'll have to throw away what you already have. Even so, we'd still recommend taking this course of action, as it'll cost you £40.24 including VAT, rather than the £69.57 charged by Apple. These prices will fluctuate, but they were correct at the time of writing.

The standard hard drive is a 5400rpm Serial-ATA drive of 160GB. This should be enough for most users of a low-end machine like this, but if you plan on building up an extensive music – or more importantly video – library, perhaps with downloads from the iTunes Store, then you could find this getting tight fairly quickly.

Fortunately it is another upgradable option, either at the point of purchase or afterwards, as swapping it out is a simple matter of removing the battering to access its housing. Again, you would be well advised to shop around for the best prices, with Apple charging between £40 and £160 for its upgrades of 250GB to 500GB. The £40 option isn't bad, but the £160 is steep for a 500GB unit.

Sadly Apple doesn't bundle its Remote with MacBooks any more, so if you do want to use your machine for watching movies and would rather not control it using the keyboard and mouse, you'll have to budget an additional £15 there, too.

Optical storage is handled by an 8-speed slot-loading SuperDrive, which can read and write double-layer discs, making this machine suitable as an on-the-go movie authoring system. However, its screen, the resolution of which tops out at 1280 x 800 pixels, still can't handle 1080i or p HD video natively. Maximum resolution on an external monitor is a more suitable 1920 x 1200 pixels.

Graphics are driven by an Nvidia GeForce 9400M chip, which shares 256MB of DDR2 memory with the system Ram. This isn't ideal, so if you have particularly demanding graphics requirements, such as rendering 3D scenes, you may benefit from instead choosing a MacBook Pro with the optional dedicated graphics memory and saving yourself a lot of processing time.

There's an iSight camera in the lid, mounted above the screen and, apart from the optical drive slot, a quick tour of the edges reveals a MagSafe power port, Gigabit Ethernet, Mini-DVI (adaptors for Mini-DVD to DVI or VGA are optional extras), two USB 2 and one FireWire 400 port, audio in and out and a slot for a security lock. All in all, a fairly comprehensive selection. Less evident are the connection options on the inside, which run to Bluetooth 2.1 + EDR and 802.11n wifi, using the as-yet unratified draft specification.

Unlike the MacBook Pro, the MacBook still features a removable battery, allowing you to replace a dud cell or take spares when you're travelling. Apple claims a five-hour life for wireless productivity.

All in all, the white MacBook adds up to a neat, well-specced and keenly-priced package and an ideal entry point. It has some shortcomings, but for less demanding users who will likely be looking for a workhorse that will spend most of its days handling email and web pages, with a little bit of photo editing thrown in, it's as good a buy today as it ever has been.

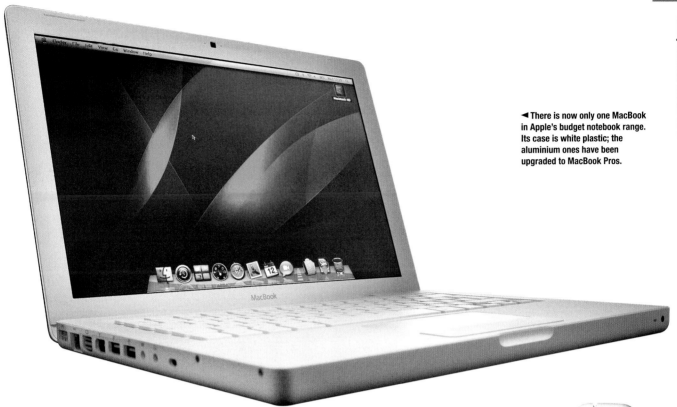

◄ There is now only one MacBook in Apple's budget notebook range. Its case is white plastic; the aluminium ones have been upgraded to MacBook Pros.

IS THIS ONE RIGHT FOR YOU?

A MacBook is kitted out well in terms of hardware and extra features – it has all of the essential networking options and plenty of ports for connecting peripherals over USB and FireWire.

Aside from the Air, the MacBook is the most portable of all Mac notebooks with its small but functional screen and full-size keyboard. It's suitable for desktop use when space is limited.

The MacBook is a real winner for Apple. With the notebook market increasing and Apple's market share on the up, it's an ideal way for newcomers to jump platforms. Without specific application needs to warrant extra expense, the MacBook should have wide appeal. And it's a solid workhorse, too.

3 REASONS TO BUY

Easy way in: If you're looking to make the move to the Mac, the MacBook is a great way in, giving you everything you need in a small bundle, with no need for additional monitors, keyboards and mice, meaning it can be stored in a drawer if you also have a PC taking up your valuable desk space.
Generous features: The MacBook is well kitted out. Just make sure that it has enough disk space and Ram to cope with the tasks you'll throw at it. Remember that it benefits from wifi, Bluetooth and a built-in iSight camera.
Price: As Apple's cheapest laptop, it is ideal for those after a solid Mac that can handle everyday tasks without needing to be at the cutting edge of performance and style.

► The MacBook's ports are on its left-hand side. From top to bottom, they are the Kensington cable lock slot, audio line out, audio line in, two USB ports, FireWire 400, Mini-DVI, Gigabit Ethernet and a MagSafe power port.

PRICES AND SPECIFICATIONS

13.3in glossy widescreen + 1280 x 800 pixel display + Nvidia GeForce 9400M graphics processor + 8-speed SuperDrive + Quoted battery life of 5 hours of wireless productivity

Price £749
Specifications 2.13GHz Intel Core 2 Duo + 2GB DDR2 memory + 160GB hard disk + white polycarbonate body

3 REASONS TO THINK AGAIN

Restrictive screen: The 13.3in screen crams in 1280 x 800 pixels and Spaces makes it easy to manage. A 15in MacBook Pro is comfier for prolonged use at a desk though, and its higher resolution leaves plenty of space for iChat and other small windows at the screen's edge.
Shared graphics memory: Sharing memory with the main system leads to poorer performance when compared to the more ably-equipped MacBook Pro.
Portability: The MacBook weighs 2.27kg and is considerably thicker than the MacBook Air.

MacBook Pro

While the white MacBook is the budget model in Apple's line-up, the MacBook Pros sport the latest aluminium livery of the range. Only the 13in model could be truly classed as a computer for the road as the 15in and 17in editions are at the limit of comfort where portability is concerned and, as such, are more akin to a desktop replacement.

NOTEBOOK
MacBook Pro

Price £899 (£782 ex VAT) 13in 2.26GHz; £1149 (£999 ex VAT) for 13in 2.53GHz; £1299 (£1129 ex VAT) for 15in 2.53GHz; £1499 (£1303 ex VAT) for 15in 2.66GHz; £1699 (£1477 ex VAT) for 15in 2.8GHz; £1849 (£1607 ex VAT) for 17in 2.8GHz
Pros Dual-link graphics chip + LED on all models + Hi-res display on 17in models
Cons In the 13in models, the processor is only moderately more powerful than the white MacBook

The importance of mobile computing to Apple's strategy is best demonstrated by the size of the MacBook Pro range. With six machines in the line-up, it represents the largest section of Apple's inventory.

The 13in models are effectively upgraded MacBooks, which were bumped up from the bottom end of the portable range to leave the white MacBook sitting on its own. Off the shelf, they come with a choice of two processors: 2.26GHz or 2.53GHz Intel Core 2 Duo with 3MB of on-chip L2 cache. Like the MacBook, they have a 1066MHz frontside bus but, unlike the MacBook, their memory runs at this speed, too, being supplied as 2GB or 4GB of DDR3 chips.

The machines themselves have two memory slots which are filled upon arrival, whatever configuration you choose, so if you want to upgrade them to their maximum possible level – 8GB – you're going to have to dispose of what's already in place. Sadly it's the same story with the 15in and 17in models: although they come with 4GB as standard and have the same 8GB limit, their default install is supplied as a pair of 2GB sticks.

Apple has thought carefully about the line-up's processor range, with the fastest processor in each screen size leading directly into the next size up. So, while the processors in the 13in MacBook Pros are clocked at 2.26GHz and 2.53GHz, the 15in model picks up at 2.53GHz and adds in 2.66GHz and 2.8GHz variants. The default speed for the 17in model is also 2.8GHz.

While it's not possible to take the 13in model beyond 2.53GHz, the 15in and 17in models give you the option of upgrading to a 3.06GHz chip for enhanced performance. Obviously this is one upgrade that can only be performed when you place your order.

Other upgrades are not so simple: swapping out the hard drive requires that you remove the bottom plate of the machine, while the battery is strictly off limits. You can swap it out in the MacBook, and even travel with a spare, but in the MacBook Pro it's a sealed unit that can only be replaced by an Apple technician.

The standard-issue graphics processor in each of the MacBook Pros is an Nvidia GeForce 9400M with 256MB of DDR3 memory, shared with the main system Ram. However, in the 17in and the 2.66GHz and 2.8GHz 15in models this is supplemented by a GeForce 9600M GT with a further 512MB of memory (256MB in the 2.66GHz edition). Apple claims that by building in two chips it can deliver performance increases of up to 2.5x when compared to integrated processors. Games players, take note.

The native screen resolution of the 13in body is 1280 x 800. As you might expect, this is the same as the 13in MacBook. However, it can support a more impressive 2560 x 1600 pixels on an external display, which compares favourably with the 1920 x 1200 supported by the MacBook. The maximum external display resolution is the same for the 15in and 17in models, but the native resolutions of their integrated screens are 1440 x 900 and 1920 x 1200 pixels respectively.

Hard drives run in size from 160GB on the lowest-specced 13in model to 500GB on the 17in edition and upper-end 15in device. Impressively these are all upgradable to 128GB and 256GB solid state drives found in the MacBook Air – including the one found in the 13in MacBook Pro.

The same 8-speed slot-loading SuperDrive is found in all of the MacBook Pros, allowing CD and dual-layer DVD reading and writing, and they all boast 802.11n wireless networking and Bluetooth 2.0 + EDR for communicating with mice, keyboards and headsets.

When it comes to ports and expansion options, there are some slight differences, though. All have MagSafe power ports, Gigabit Ethernet, Mini DisplayPort and a single FireWire 800 port. However, while the 13in and 15in models have two USB 2 ports, the 17in model has three. Moreover, while the 17in model has an ExpressCard/34 slot, which allows you to slot in hardware add-ons, such as dial-up modems, the 13in and 15in MacBook Pros boast an SD card slot for directly downloading images from digital camera cards.

When it comes to choosing between the 15in and 17in models, the size of the screen will undoubtedly be your guiding force. While a 17in display is great on your desk, it is a hefty slab to travel with – particularly if you plan on balancing your MacBook Pro on your lap on the daily commute.

Within the 15in line-up, though, it's less clear cut. The steps between each processor speed aren't great, in terms of percentage increments, so our best advice would be to start your deliberations with the 2.66GHz model and work up or down from there. If, on the other hand, you find yourself drawn to the 13in model, then don't immediately discount the white MacBook, which could do all you need for less.

◄ The MacBook Pro is a good desktop replacement, particularly when paired with an external monitor, to give you the best of both worlds.

3 REASONS TO BUY

Raw power: The dedicated graphics processor makes the Pro models the only contenders for running certain applications such as Premiere Pro CS4 and Motion 3. These notebooks – especially the 17in one – are closest to a portable Mac Pro.

Better dual-monitor support: All Pro models are sensibly outfitted with a dual-link DVI port that can power the 30in Apple Cinema Display. It provides enough space to edit 1080p content without having to constantly hide and reveal tool palettes.

Expansion ports: Only the 13in and 15in MacBook Pros feature an SD card slot. FireWire 400 devices can be attached to the FireWire 800 port with a suitable cable. The ExpressCard/34 slot allows even more to be added.

IS THIS ONE RIGHT FOR YOU?

Though we've already mentioned it, it's worth emphasising that the MacBook Pro occupies a privileged position: it's the only portable Mac that's able to run certain applications. It's also a good choice if you're reluctant to install an iMac or Mac Pro and don't want to be tied to a desk. Even the bulkier 17in model is still good for anyone who likes to move around the home – it's just too uncomfortable for regular carriage.

In a professional capacity, the 17in model is best for those working with HD video, high-resolution photos and graphic design that demands a lot of screen space. These apart, the 15in model is fine for most tasks, while remaining comfortably portable – it weighs only a little more than the MacBook.

PRICES AND SPECIFICATIONS

13in MODELS
Both feature Nvidia GeForce 9400M graphics processor + SD card slot + Quoted battery life of 7 hours
Price £899 (£782 ex VAT)
Specifications 2.26GHz Intel Core 2 Duo + 2GB DDR3 memory + 160GB hard disk
Price £1149 (£999 ex VAT)
Specifications 2.53GHz Intel Core 2 Duo + 4GB DDR3 memory + 250GB hard disk

15in MODELS
All feature 4GB DDR3 memory + SD card slot + Quoted battery life of 7 hours
Price £1299 (£1129 ex VAT)
Specifications 2.53GHz Intel Core 2 Duo + 250GB hard disk + Nvidia GeForce 9400M graphics
Price £1499 (£1303 ex VAT)
Specifications 2.66GHz Intel Core 2 Duo + 320GB hard disk + Nvidia GeForce 9400M and 9600M GT graphics processors
Price £1699 (£1477 ex VAT)
Specifications 2.8GHz Intel Core 2 Duo + 500GB hard disk + Nvidia GeForce 9400M and 9600M GT graphics processors

17in MODEL
Price £1849 (£1607 ex VAT)
Specifications 2.8GHz Intel Core 2 Duo + 4GB DDR3 memory + 500GB hard disk + ExpressCard/34 slot + Quoted battery life of 8 hours

3 REASONS TO THINK AGAIN

Cost: The MacBook Pro is a powerful piece of kit, but you certainly pay for it. Consider the white MacBook if you are a less demanding user, and balance the Pro's features against your needs.

Portability: The 15in model approaches the comfort limits of portability. The 17in is heavy to carry at almost 3kg.

Desktop replacement: If you're considering a MacBook Pro as a desktop replacement, consider a real desktop machine instead and you could make some serious savings.

Images Courtesy of Apple

MacBook Air

Apple claimed that the MacBook Air was the world's thinnest notebook on its launch in early 2008 and, when experienced in the flesh, it doesn't fail to impress any friends or colleagues. It's also unbelievably light, making it the ideal machine for those who spend a lot of working life on the road and have to lug around their computer.

NOTEBOOK
MacBook Air

Price £1149 (£999 ex VAT) for 1.86GHz 120GB hard disk; £1349 (£1173 ex VAT) for 2.13GHz 128GB solid state drive
Pros Beautifully engineered + Very light
Cons Expensive for specification + No optical drive + Few expansion ports

The star attraction at Steve Jobs' January keynote in 2008 was undoubtedly the MacBook Air. Greeted with huge interest by the industry and the public alike, its light weight and lean looks impressed many. Despite an update since then, the lean looks and light weight remain.

The sleek lines are achieved by dispensing with unnecessary bloat. Gone are most of the expansion ports and the optical drive, which has allowed Apple to reduce the height of the machine to 0.4cm at its thinnest point. Yet the Air is comfortable to use as it retains the screen and keyboard size of the MacBook, making it feel like a regular MacBook rather than the cramped and cumbersome sensation of some ultraportables.

The MacBook Air uses Core 2 Duo processors like the rest of the line-up, though the available clock speeds are the slowest of all. It's even further removed from the MacBook Pro's performance than the cheapest MacBook, which is a better-suited machine to handling a barrage of tasks throughout the day. The hard disk and Ram are quite easy to replace in the MacBook and MacBook Pro but with the Air, all components are sealed inside the case, which is screwed shut. Anyone brave enough to open it would find that only the hard disk and battery can be replaced. By necessity of the design everything else is part of the logic board.

This impacts on the Ram, which is limited to the 2GB fitted as standard, whereas other MacBooks can be upgraded to 4GB. The 1.6GHz model's 4200rpm Serial ATA hard disk will have more impact on general performance though; it's the slowest in any Mac. This used to be upgradable to the same solid state drive that is found in the 2.13GHz model, but this option has now disappeared. If you want a speed boost, therefore, you'll have to opt for a more expensive machine altogether.

The Air's battery is also fixed inside the case. Apple can replace it at the end of its life but it can't be swapped on the move. Replacements cost £99 and you will be without the unit for up to five days. If you need power for longer consider the MacBook and buy a second battery.

A slimline USB SuperDrive is available for ripping CDs to iTunes, watching DVDs and installing software that comes only on a disc. Fortunately the iTunes Store is now featuring more movies for rent or download in the UK now, so it's no longer so important to invest in a drive if you want to watch films on the go. However, you will need a USB hub to plug in more than one device at a time. Note that there's neither a FireWire port for connecting a DV camera nor an Ethernet port for locations that offer only a cabled network connection unless you buy an optional dongle.

The MacBook Air makes many compromises to achieve its slim stature but it stands head and shoulders above the rest of the range on portability and Apple's famed design aesthetics. Even its nearest competitor, the 13in MacBook Pro appears bulky and heavy by comparison. However, there's no overlooking the MacBook Air's limitations. The build-to-order options are even fewer than those of the MacBook, so it's even more important to choose the right spec in the first place because it's a closed box and upgrading it later is not an option you can take. All upgrade options are external – apart from pre-installed software – and run to a SuperDrive, Remote and different keyboard layouts.

The cheaper model comes with the slowest Core 2 Duo processor of all Mac notebooks, clocked at 1.86GHz. Sadly the option to upgrade this to the same processor as used in the solid state model, but without the solid state drive, has now disappeared, meaning that if you want anything faster you'll have to pay considerably more

There are no real upgrades for the 2.13GHz model, either – only extra peripherals like the USB SuperDrive. It includes everything in the box, which is just as well since it costs £1349 – a cut of about £350 on its previous price, but still a considerable sum. It's a shame that price doesn't include the external SuperDrive, though the extra £64 that the drive costs will mean little to anyone who is seriously considering the solid state drive option.

The Air isn't an ideal notebook if you're reliant on external devices. There's only one USB port, so you're left to carry a USB hub too, which works a little against the Air's portability. If you need to use more than one USB device and portability isn't such a big issue, a MacBook is a far better option.

The MacBook Air uses the same Nvidia graphics processor as the plain MacBook, again sharing the system memory, which will limit some video-intensive applications. As such, serious video professionals should skip over this and look at the Pro range for maximum performance.

▼ MacBook Air's three ports from top to bottom are the Mini DisplayPort, USB and a headphone jack.

IS THIS ONE RIGHT FOR YOU?

The MacBook Air's hardware features are lean. When it was introduced, much attention was lavished on its multi-touch trackpad but this has already filtered across to the pro range; if it is to garner support and flourish, expect to see it on the regular MacBook at some point. It certainly shouldn't sway a buying decision until that happens.

The lack of expansion opportunities means it's unsuitable as a main computer except for infrequent users, who would be better off with the cheaper MacBook. The Air is capable enough to run Photoshop but is best suited to those who already own a capable Mac and who crave a lightweight Mac notebook on the road – provided that there's a mains power source to charge it every few hours.

PRICES AND SPECIFICATIONS

Width 32.5cm
Depth 22.7cm
Height 0.4 to 1.94cm
Weight 1.36kg

Specifications 2GB DDR3 memory + 13.3in glossy widescreen LED + 1280 x 800 pixel display + Nvidia GeForce 9400M graphics processor + Quoted battery life of 4.5 hours of wireless productivity

Price £1149
Specifications 1.86GHz Core 2 Duo processor + 2GB DDR3 memory + 120GB hard disk

Price £1349
Specifications 2.13GHz Core 2 Duo processor + 2GB DDR3 memory + 128GB solid state drive

3 REASONS TO BUY

Weight: The Air is almost a kilo lighter than the plain MacBook yet the case feels reassuringly durable – just as well since you could forget that you're carrying it.
Full-size screen and keyboard: Despite its portable aspirations, the Air features the same screen size and resolution as the MacBook – and doesn't lose anything when it comes to the physical interface.
Abandon physical media: Music, video and software downloads take up a lot less space than discs and printed manuals. The lack of a built-in optical drive will mean little if you've adopted the download culture. If the Air will play second fiddle to a desktop Mac, it can share the optical drive for those increasingly rare instances when software ships only on a disc – these days, even Adobe CS4 is available as a download.

3 REASONS TO THINK AGAIN

Cables: Many of the missing features can be added to the Air but it means carrying cables. A hub is also needed to play music from your iPod – and there are no adaptors as standard for using an external mouse and hooking up to an Ethernet port.
Slower parts: The hard disk is slow by nature of its size. The 128GB solid state drive is faster, but the payoff is that it's also smaller and more expensive.
Integrated battery: Without mains power in easy reach, the Air isn't suitable for prolonged use. The battery is replaceable (by Apple) only when its life has expired.

Mac mini

If you have a Windows PC, complete with a monitor, keyboard and mouse then Apple's lowest priced desktop machine, the Mac mini, provides a cheap way of sampling the Mac environment. However, its hardware specs, packed into its small biscuit tin sized casing, does have its limitations, but then its price is unbeatable.

DESKTOP MAC
Mac mini

Price £499 (£434 ex VAT) for 2GHz, 120GB hard disk; £649 (£564 ex VAT) for 2GHz, 320GB hard disk
Pros Inexpensive + Compact
Cons Poor graphics performance + Not a significant upgrade

◄ Same look – all the changes to the new Mac mini take place on the inside.

Apple's Mac mini really grabbed people's attention when it launched back in January 2005. But when the cheapest model rose to about £400 its relevance was questioned, and it has been regarded as a product line on the way out, which is why the launch of the new Mac minis came as such a surprise to industry observers.

Now the cheapest Mac mini costs £499, a figure easily beaten by several budget PCs, Apple still believes it has a market and has kept it up to date with the recent advances. The new line uses the same Intel Core 2 Duo processors found in other Macs, with both models running at 2GHz, upgradable to 2.26GHz; the only significant difference between the two models being the size of the hard disk. They both have the same 3MB of Level 2 processor cache memory, shared between the two cores.

Considering that the Mac mini is Apple's smallest desktop Mac, it should come as no surprise that both models use a mobile graphics chip, the Nvidia GeForce 9400M. However, each model has a slightly different amount of shared DDR3 SDRam with the low-end machine accessing 128MB and the top-end model accessing 256MB.

The standard Ram allocation is better than before. The £499 model comes with 1GB of Ram, while the £649 model has 2GB; both can be upgraded to 4GB. Hard disk space is a little better, with 120GB or 320GB rather than 80GB or 120GB capacities in previous models – the maximum hard disk size in the mini is now 320GB. These are still the slower 5400rpm models, but most Mac mini users won't be bothered by the difference between these and the more expensive 7200rpm drives. The difference in optical drives has now disappeared, with both models featuring an eight speed SuperDrive for reading and writing both CD and DVD media.

And that's it. You'd be right to think the difference between the new and previous generations of Mac minis is not exactly staggering. It's a welcome upgrade but a small one, more an exercise in keeping the minis in their place in the Mac pack than grabbing customers' attention.

Performance was in line with what we would expect from a Core 2 Duo-based Mac running at these speeds with no extra hardware support. Graphics performance was roughly equivalent to the white MacBook: more or less identical for Cinebench 3D rendering times and fractionally faster with the OpenGL lighting routines. We got similar results from Xbench, although the CPU-specific tasks inched ahead, allowing for differences in processor speed, and the graphics-based tests just about kept up.

With these comparisons in mind, it should be obvious that the Mac minis are the desktop equivalent of MacBooks. If you've considered getting one of those portables but would rather spend less on the hardware, perhaps a Mac mini is the answer. But don't forget to factor in the cost of buying a screen, keyboard and mouse if you don't have one already. Sure, these are pretty cheap these days, but it all adds up.

What about using a Mac mini as a media centre? That's one logical use, but now that the Apple TV is available, and works so well, this alternative use for Mac minis is no longer such an attractive idea.

There is one yardstick where it wins out over other desktop Macs and probably virtually any desktop PC as well. Although you'll need to factor in the screen, the Mac mini itself remains a very low-power device, peaking at about 110W (similar to a regular lightbulb) compared with up to 280W for the iMac and a staggering 1440W (at peak power usage) for the Mac Pros. This means that a Mac mini has a much smaller impact on your carbon footprint, which is handy if you just need Internet access and basic office tools.

The Mac minis are cheap (although not quite as cheap as they first were), they use impressively little power, and they're still attention-grabbingly small. But they're not particularly well suited to those with even moderately demanding needs. Don't dismiss them by any means, but do think carefully before handing over your cash.

Apple TV

When the iPod was released it marked a significant departure for Apple as it branched out from making computers. And now Apple TV marks another departure as it takes its hardware and software into the living room by giving you the ability to watch film and TV shows, play music, view photos on Flickr and video on YouTube.

MULTIMEDIA HARDWARE
Apple TV

Price £195 (£170 ex VAT) for 40GB; £263 (£229 ex VAT) for 160GB
Needs High-definition TV capable of 1080p 60/50Hz, 1080i 60/50Hz, 720p 60/50Hz, 576p 50Hz or 480p 60Hz; HDMI or Component input
Pros Buy music and TV shows from your living room + Works seamlessly with or without iTunes
Cons Limited connectivity options + No movie downloads or rentals + Lacks PVR functionality + Expensive

◀ After the initial disappointment over lack of movie rentals in the UK, Apple TV now has a sizable selection in both HD and SD to rent.

When Steve Jobs announced that the Apple TV had failed, it was an unusual admission that sometimes Apple doesn't get it right. The first version failed for several reasons, so Apple has re-focused its living-room offering with take two of Apple TV. If you had invested in a first generation Apple TV, you'll be glad to know that this improved Apple TV is simply a software upgrade, which can be downloaded for free.

A 40GB and 160GB model are available for £195 and £263 respectively. However, the Apple TV software has been radically remodelled and now it can be used without the aid of a Mac. Setup is a breeze and if you want to tie your Apple TV to your Mac the process is as simple as it was with the original software.

The main menu has lost the Front Row styling and is simply a table with content types on the left and the options within these are displayed on the right. The movies option is there but it only allows you to watch trailers or view movies that you've copied to an iTunes library. After initial difficulties in negotiating international movie licences limited film downloads or rentals in the UK were resolved, the mix of content to rent has steadily grown and now covers a wide range of films and TV shows that can be downloaded.

Navigating the download options is simple and elegant. When you choose a show to download, you're asked for your password and then the transfer begins. We chose an episode of *The West Wing* and it was ready to watch within a few seconds of the download beginning. That's quite impressive if you bear in mind that this is a 50-minute programme. Image quality is very good, though it's not exceptional; we'd say it's on a par with DVD content – no better no worse.

Buying music on your Apple TV is a simple process. You can navigate through with a selection of hand-picked albums that Apple thinks you'll enjoy. If Morrissey and the soundtrack to *Juno* aren't to your liking though, you can search for alternatives. This requires that you use the Apple remote to select individual characters but the predictive search does a good job of narrowing down the choices. We only had to type 'eme' to get to Emerson, Lake and Palmer for instance.

Podcasts, Photos and YouTube navigation are all much the same. The Flickr integration is a nice touch and being able to add multiple contacts increases the appeal of the photo aspect of the Apple TV. Watching video of teenagers dancing to the latest chart topper doesn't yet hold a mass appeal but the Apple TV does offer a good method of transferring this online technology to the living room. When the quality of the video and the production values improve, however, the YouTube content will be really worthwhile.

We're still a little hesitant to recommend the Apple TV even in this much improved second coming, although the changes to the interface and the ability to purchase music and TV shows is really excellent. However, there are still a few insurmountable failings. The lack of PVR functionality, or ability to add one is disappointing as is the function to stream replay services, like the BBC iPlayer, would be a bonus.

If this had been the Apple TV take one, there's no doubt we'd have been raving over it but this is the second swing of the bat for Apple and though it's not the miss of Apple TV 1 it's not the home run we wanted either. ✪

iPod line-up

The iPod, arguably, kick-started the resurgent Apple as it has attracted millions of devotees with its stylish looks, while its halo effect has pulled in many more computer users who bought their first Mac after buying an iPod. The current line-up of iPods means that there's one that will match every budget and pocket.

MEDIA PLAYERS
iPod range

Price shuffle 1GB second generation: £31 (£27 ex VAT), 4GB third generation: £59 (£51 ex VAT); nano 8GB: £107 (£93 ex VAT), 16GB: £146 (£127 ex VAT); classic 120GB: £175 (£152 ex VAT); touch 8GB: £165 (£143 ex VAT), 16GB: £214 (£186 ex VAT), 32GB: £283 (£246 ex VAT)

The iconic white iPod, which has existed in one form or another since its launch in 2001, has gone. In its place is the iPod classic, now only available in silver and black. Rather than a lonely device in a range of its own, it's just one of many music players, with a model to suit every user.

The iPod has been replaced at the pinnacle of the line-up by the iPod touch, a widescreen, touch-sensitive, wireless media player. The touch takes its cues from the iPhone but completely redefines what constitutes a portable music player by allowing you to download music directly from the iTunes Store.

Further down the line-up is the iPod nano, now in its fourth incarnation, and the third edition shuffle, which announces your tracks and playlists as they come up.

iPod touch

The announcement of the iPod touch wasn't exactly a surprise: rumours of a widescreen, touch-sensitive iPod with built-in wifi had been circulating for more than a year before it finally arrived. And given that Apple already had the bones of the device in the iPhone, the touch seems a natural and logical move. Despite the lack of surprise, though, the confirmation of the new iPod was greeted with great enthusiasm, particularly as it can be used as a mobile web browser and web email device wherever there's a wifi network.

The iPod touch features the same multi-touch interface as the iPhone, and includes Cover Flow — Apple's visual metaphor for flipping through record sleeves in a stack. In addition to playing music, it has built-in applications for viewing photos, watching movies, connecting to YouTube, and a version of Safari for web browsing. PDA-type applications include a calendar, contacts book, clock and calculator.

With one push of a button on the touch's screen, users can connect directly to the iTunes Store whenever they're connected to a wireless network. This means that for the first time, iPod users don't need a Mac or PC to download music.

The iPod touch's screen is the same 3.5in widescreen, 480 x 320-pixel display seen on the iPhone. But the device itself is thinner than the iPhone, presumably due the absence of a phone and camera inside. However, it does feature a receiver for the Nike + iPod system that tracks your training and lets you upload your performance to the web through iTunes.

The built-in wifi adaptor supports 802.11b and 802.11g standards but not the draft n specification supported by Apple's Macs. This shouldn't be too much of a problem in a handheld device though – particularly as your download requirements will be less demanding.

Battery life has been a thorn in Apple's flesh since it shipped the very first iPod. So its reassuring to note that even with such a large screen, Apple quotes 36 hours of playback for music and six hours for video.

The touch, like the iPhone and the nano, uses flash memory. That's why it's so thin and is able to run for a reasonably long time on one charge. But it also seriously limits its capacity. The three available capacities, 8GB, 16GB and 32GB, fall far short of the capacities of the hard disk-based iPod classic.

For those of us with large music libraries, who've become accustomed to copying everything from iTunes to the iPod, this presents a problem: either choose a classic, or start to be very strict about what music you copy to your iPod and how often you sync it with your Mac.

This dilemma was unavoidable – it wouldn't have made sense for Apple to swap the flash memory for a hard drive:

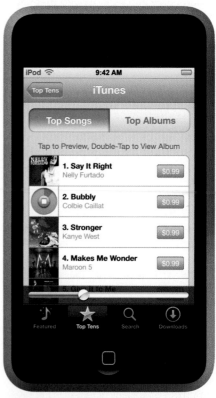

▲ The iPod touch uses the same touch-screen display as the iPhone as well as having wifi capability.

◀ Apple's current line-up of iPods comes in four flavours, which means there's one for every different-sized pocket.

doing so would have meant a fatter case and shorter battery life. Yet there must be thousands of potential touch users who will be put off by the low storage capacity. Storage is even more limited when you consider that one of the touch's main attractions is the ability to play video on a reasonable (for a handheld) sized screen.

VIDEO FORMATS
The touch supports the same audio and video formats as other iPods. That means there's still no support for Windows Media Audio or Video. While this is unlikely to be an issue for most Mac users, it remains a bone of contention among consumer groups who believe that the cost to Apple of licensing Windows Media would amount to a few pence per iPod, and that the reason for its exclusion is to lock iPod owners out of the stores that sell music in Windows Media-protected formats.

Supported video formats on the touch are H.264 and Mpeg-4, with a maximum resolution of 640 x 480 pixels (which is scaled down to the touch's display resolution of 480 x 320 pixels).

Despite being a small device, and dwarfed by rivals like the PSP, the touch remains a good option for viewing video on the move, and that screen – once you get used to using it for moving pictures – isn't as small as you might first think.

ONGOING UPDATES
The iPod touch runs the same operating system as the iPhone, albeit without the phone and SMS features activated. As such, it receives regular updates from Apple, delivered as downloads through iTunes. Unlike the iPhone, though, these updates are not free because of regulations governing the way that Apple accounts for its income from the two devices. As such, each update generally costs about £12 for iPod touch users.

Updates are not compulsory, and the iPod will continue to work without it, but they are usually worth buying as they open up new features. The first update, for example, opened up the App Store to iPod touch users. This lets you buy applications to bolster the ones that ship on the device for added functionality.

IS IT THE RIGHT iPOD FOR YOU?
The touch is a fully-featured, great fun device. If you can live with the low storage capacity, then the only decision you have to make is whether to buy the 8GB, 16GB or 32GB model.

However, if you need a higher capacity device, perhaps because you plan on travelling and will be unable to refresh your music collection on the road, the more traditional iPod classic may be a more appropriate choice.

It may therefore be easier to think of the iPod touch as a very portable computer with email, web browsing, contact and calendaring features, or as a traditional touch-screen PDA with exceptional media playback tools.

▶ The touch is skinnier than the iPhone, but then it lacks most of its innards.

iPOD TOUCH VS iPHONE
The 32GB touch costs almost as much as a 16GB iPhone. Of course, there are contract costs to pay for the iPhone, but that's true of any mobile phone bought on a contract. So assuming an iPod touch owner would also have a separate mobile phone and pay a similar monthly fee for the contract, it's a straight comparison between the iPhone and touch.

The advantage of buying the touch is that it has more storage, it's smaller and allows you greater flexibility in choosing a contract for your mobile. There is also a benefit in keeping devices separate – if you lose one or it gets broken, you haven't lost everything.

The benefits of the iPhone are that you get a camera and phone included in the price, but then you lose storage capacity. Advocates of a single device would say that carrying only one device around is a definite plus. There are other, less obvious benefits to the iPhone, though. It now has the volume rocker that was missing from the first edition, but it still doesn't get free software updates like the phone does. This is because of the way that Apple accounts for the revenue from the iPod product line as opposed to the iPhone, so don't forget to factor in a minimal charge – about £12 every year or so – to keep it up to date. There's no Bluetooth on the touch, although this is barely an issue given that syncing and file transfer through the Dock is fast and straight-forward. The iPhone buys you quite a lot. If you find a contract you're happy with, it's probably well worth it.

▲ The iPod nano comes in a choice of nine colours – one to match every outfit.

iPod nano

The iPod nano was, briefly, a squat flat device, as wide as it was tall, and somewhat reminiscent of an after dinner mint. It was quite a shock after several years as a tall, slim player. The change was to enable it to play video, though, and make use of Cover Flow, Apple's graphical interface for leafing through your album covers. Now in its fourth incarnation, though, it is once again a portrait-orientated device, and in switching back to its old dimensions it has kept hold of the video features.

The nano is now a slightly barrel-shaped device constructed entirely of aluminium and glass. It's sensitive to its orientation, sporting an accelerometer like the iPod touch, and so switches between menu and Cover Flow modes as you twist it, and builds random playlists every time you give it a shake. It's a smart feature.

Unlike the shuffle – the smallest iPod in the range – the nano has always sported a click wheel, and it is with this that you scroll through the albums in your collection as there is, sadly, no touch-sensitive screen. However, it is responsive and easy to use, and you quickly learn to use it without needing to look at it.

Also new on the fourth edition model is Genius, which builds smart playlists of songs that go well together. The same feature is found on the iPod classic and in iTunes, and the more you use it, the more intelligent it gets as it works out which songs complement each other.

The new nano comes in nine different colours stretching from silver to black and taking in pretty much every colour of the spectrum between. They sport 2in, 320 x 240 pixel displays with an impressive 204ppi resolution for crisp photos and movie playback.

Capacities are 8GB and 16GB in the form of flash storage, thus eliminating moving parts and maximising potential battery life. Apple claims maximums of 24 hours for audio playback and four hours for video on every charge. This is the same as its predecessor for audio, but represents a 20% cut for video.

Charging the nano fully over USB takes about three hours, while charging to 80% of the battery capacity takes an hour and a half, according to Apple. Although the USB cable plugs into a standard Dock connector, allowing you to use a wide range of third-party add-ons including, perhaps most importantly, speakers.

The 8GB model, which costs £107, can store 2000 tracks; the £146 16GB model will happily double that.

Over the time of its short existence we grew to love the squat, square nano that this new model has replaced, but the new features seen here more than compensate for its demise. If you want to watch video on the move using the smallest practical device, the nano is an excellent choice, and you'll be surprised at just how watchable that video is on such a small screen.

That said, if you are a serious movie buff, then think carefully about investing in an iPod touch.

iPod classic

The iPod is dead. Long live the classic. Ditching the white iPod makes sense for Apple now that it seems to be moving away from white as its favoured colour scheme for consumer products (the MacBook is now the only white Mac in Apple's range of computers).

Apple hasn't just changed the colour scheme though; the classic has ditched its ancestor's plastic and stainless steel

Images Courtesy of Apple

▼ Turning the iPod nano on its side lets you use the screen to view movies or navigate your albums using Cover Flow.

▲ The iPod shuffle now comes in two colours and has lost its body-mounted controls. These have now moved to the earphone cable.

casing for a metal shell, and is now slimmer than ever.

The classic is the only iPod in the range to use a hard drive rather than flash memory for storage. For many users this will be enough to sway the decision of which iPod to buy in its favour. Using a hard drive means that its storage capacity is significantly higher than the flash-based nano and touch. The two classics currently available – silver and black – have only one storage capacity: 120GB.

Despite this capacity, and the fact it can store an impressive 30,000 songs, 25,000 photos or 150 hours of video, it's still just 10.5mm thick – a little over a centimetre and still slim compared with, say, a fourth-generation iPod. It is the highest capacity iPod in Apple's range, so it is a shame to see that the former king of the hill – the 160GB device – went the same way as its smaller 80GB stablemate.

Sadly, the classic's screen is nowhere near as good as the touch's for watching video. At 2.5in across its diagonal, it's bigger than the nano's, but well short of the touch. And its 320 x 240-pixel resolution is the same as the nano's, but due to the larger surface area the pixels don't need to be crammed in quite so tightly. The resolution is a respectable 163 pixels per inch. The interface makes full use of the colour display for Cover Flow, while the menu items such as the graphic equaliser have been spruced up.

The battery lasts for an impressive 36 hours on a single charge when listening to audio, and runs for 6 hours when you're watching video, according to Apple's own figures. Overall, the classic is a worthy update to the hard disk iPod line. It will have to compete with the touch for attention, and there's no doubt that with the iPhone, both it and the touch will get nearly all the publicity, but the classic has plenty of life left in it and could yet prove itself to be the iPod for grown-ups.

◀ The iPod classic is now the media player of choice for those users with a large music library.

▶ The headphone socket is on one side of the 2nd generation shuffle, and the on/off and shuffle switches on the other.

iPod shuffle

If the iPod classic is the iPod for grown-ups, the shuffle is the iPod you can give your kids without worrying too much about them losing it. It starts at £31, for which you can buy the second-edition model in a range of five colours, and with a capacity of 1GB. This lets you store up to 240 tracks. The new third-generation shuffle, available alongside its predecessor, costs £59, has a capacity of 4GB, and lets you load about 1000 tracks at a time. It is available in silver and black.

Neither shuffle has a screen, but the third-generation model has VoiceOver features that enables it to speak the names of tracks and playlists as you reach them. Both have a clip so that you can attach it to your clothing, and in the second edition model this is hinged around the headphone socket in a perfect example of Apple's trademark considerate engineering.

The second-generation model also has a four-way rocker switch on the front, allowing you to play, pause and navigate tracks, as well as changing the volume. This has been removed from the third-generation device, with all controls now located on the headphone cable.

The shuffle isn't for everyone, but if you don't mind syncing regularly and want an inexpensive iPod, it's perfect. We were, however, pleased to see Apple retain the earlier model as an option.

iPhone

Unveiled to the world in January 2007, the iPhone quickly became one of the most talked about electronic product announcements. It's had several updates since then and, with the arrival of the App Store, users can now install their own choice of software. The iPhone certainly looks amazing, but does it manage to live up to the hype?

SMARTPHONE
iPhone

Price From free to £96.89 for 8GB iPhone 3G; from free to £184.98 for 16GB iPhone 3GS; from free to £274.23 for 32GB iPhone 3GS. Prices include VAT and depend on monthly contracts. Pay-as-you-go options are also available.
Pros Great design + Innovative touch-screen + Best Internet experience on a phone
Cons Sealed battery

The iPhone was a long time coming, and expectations were understandably high when it was finally unveiled. Competitors tried to talk it down, but the public was in no mood for listening, and by mid-2009, Apple had become the world's eighth largest mobile phone maker.

Rumored to be in development for more than five years – and some accounts suggest it actually was – the iPhone's long-awaited arrival marks a significant milestone not only for Apple aficionados, but for anyone who relies on that most common piece of digital kit.

With six months of hype between its first announcement and delivery, did it live up to expectations? The simple answer is yes, the iPhone really is as cool as the ballyhoo that preceded its launch suggested it would be.

At the first glance, it's apparent that Apple has delivered a level of elegance and class never before seen in the mobile market. Even ignoring the iPhone's two most impressive accomplishments, its innovative touch-screen display and Mac OS X-based operating system, the iPhone trumps the design of every other handset we have held. It simply looks and feels terrific in hand.

The iPhone's dimensions resemble that of a fat iPod touch, with a more pronounced bulge at the back. Earlier editions had a silver bezel running around the edge, but in the latest models this had disappeared, with the back now wrapping right around the edges. Overall, it is less than half an inch thick, making it stunningly thin for a smartphone. The iPhone also feels remarkably solid due to its plastic, metal and glass construction.

Apple has learned from its experience with the iPod – that while consumers may love a sleek finish, they abhor the scratches that accompany them. Accordingly, the glass front is very durable, like the face of a good watch that can take a beating and still emerge unscathed.

Without being activated, the iPhone passes only for an elegant paperweight: out of the box, not even the non-mobile features will work without signing up for service through iTunes. Those who envisioned tapping their wifi network for Internet access on the iPhone and taking advantage of its iPod capability without some kind of cellphone payment plan are out of luck. However, it is now available on pay-as-you-go deals, as well as regular monthly contracts.

On the bright side, Apple has taken an ingenious route in delegating activation to iTunes, so you can have your phone up and running in under a minute by completing just a few screens of required information.

► The latest generation of the iPhone, the 3GS, comes in two sizes, 16MB and 32MB, with a choice of two colours, black and white.

The iPhone's touch-screen feels immediately natural to use, although it can take some practice to discover what part of your finger actually makes contact with the screen first. Perfecting your pointing instrument is made easy on account of the instantaneous response that the iPhone delivers, and the animated interface elements Apple has sprinkled throughout the iPhone only make the experience better (delete an email and watch it get sucked down into the trash can).

Like a laptop's trackpad, the touch-screen magic works by sensing the change in capacitance created by your finger, meaning it needs only to contact the screen, not actually 'press' it. This makes operating the iPhone an extremely light-weight task that won't tire your fingers and hopefully will mitigate some of the stress injuries that repetitive thumb typing can create among

► The touch-screen is the iPhone's most prominent feature. All the iPhone's features are accessed through touching it.

smartphone users. It also makes the iPhone useless in the hands of a gloved operator, a potential point of inconvenience when using the device during the winter.

Typing on the iPhone's virtual keyboard is easy, despite the fact that your digit will dwarf the miniature key caps. When a key is pressed, the iPhone responds with the audible click of a typewriter and the pressed key momentarily expands above your finger, allowing you to easily verify that it was the one you wanted.

It takes little time to familiarise yourself with typing on the iPhone, although typos will always be an inevitable fixture. Fortunately, Apple has that mostly covered with its clever error-correction algorithm, which monitors what you're typing and automatically corrects misspelled words, eliminating the need to make corrections yourself. If you see a mistake in your typing, carry on and the iPhone will likely fix it for you.

The iPhone ships with most of the functionality expected in a smartphone, including a calendar, address book, and email client that can be synchronised across multiple systems via iTunes or over the air. Of those three, the iPhone's capabilities best shine through with Mail, which like Safari on the iPhone looks and acts much like Mail on Mac OS X.

Rich HTML email is fully supported and attached photos can be viewed directly in Mail. A selection of other documents, including PDF, Word and Excel can also be viewed when sent as attachments or downloaded from Safari.

While both Mail and Safari are miles ahead of most competitors' mobile apps, they aren't quite fully featured desktop replacements. Flash and Java are not supported and any files not compatible with the iPhone's document viewer can't even be saved for viewing later on your computer.

Fortunately Apple is addressing omissions all the time, such as copy and paste, which was added with a software update.

The iPhone makes it a breeze to take photos with a 2-megapixel camera in the 3G edition and 3-megapixel sensor with VGA-resolution video recording in the 3GS. The iPhone 3.0 software update finally made it possible to send photos and videos by MMS. SMS text messaging is deployed in the form of iChat-like conversations with each contact you have, but iChat itself is missing unless you download the AIM application from the iTunes App Store.

The iPhone's iPod functionality exhibits more of this give-and-take. Apple has packed the best iPod ever into the iPhone, with features like wide-screen video viewing and Cover Flow, but in the process has crippled the iPhone's versatility by mandating that its media library be tied to a single computer.

Content can only be managed through playlists on that computer, so forget about popping that new tune on your iPhone that you bought at work through iTunes if your iPhone is linked to your computer at home. Fortunately you can now download tunes directly from the Store to the phone.

One aspect of the iPhone that owners of the first-generation will never be able to improve is the Edge wireless data support, which is considerably slower than the more modern 3G standard featured on the second- and third-generation models.

Edge is roughly two-to-three times faster than a 56K dial-up connection and is perfectly suited for email and casual Web browsing, but it wasn't uncommon to wait at least 30 seconds or more for a page to load. With the switch to 3G, reception and speed are improved, to the point where it may be worth early adopters considering an upgrade.

The iPhone supplements its mobile network connectivity with wifi features, something that only a minority of smartphones on the market currently feature. If you have a wifi access point at work, school, or home like many people now do, chances are the iPhone will spend more time connected to the Internet that way than over phone network. Some applications can only work over a wifi connection, such as the Skype client, which can be downloaded from the iTunes App Store. This stops it being a competitor to a traditional mobile contract.

The iPhone does a commendable job of managing its wireless connectivity to conserve battery life, but even more so in the iPhone, whose battery can't be removed and replaced with a fresh one. Apple claims the iPhone 3G and 3GS offer up to 5 hours of continuous talk time on 3G or 24 hours of music playback on a single charge and our own testing with the 3G came very close to those numbers.

Most owners will regularly use their iPhone for a mix of voice, data and media functions, and they'll want to make it a habit to charge the iPhone at least every night to ensure ample juice for the day ahead.

Apple does make charging more convenient by including a USB lead that can draw power from either your Mac (or PC) or a wall socket, using the bundled plug. Sadly the Dock that was included with the first generation iPhones was removed when Apple upgraded to 3G connectivity.

The iPhone exemplifies the marvels of modern technology. Like the iPod before it, Apple opted not to pioneer the market that the iPhone now finds itself in but, to the benefit of consumers, has blazed a trail that is simply miles ahead of competitors. With the introduction of the 3GS and retention of the 3G it has now made iPhone ownership more affordable than ever.

Mac OS X

Apple doesn't only build computers: it also makes the software that runs them. Mac OS X, Apple's equivalent to Windows, is stuffed full of useful features that make your life easier and Macs more fun to use.

With an industrial strength email application, a speedy web browser, organisational tools like iCal and Address Book, there is plenty built in to get you up and running from day one.

Over the next 14 pages we'll run you through all of the key features of Mac OS X, explain its smart, clean interface and show you how to make changes through System Preferences to have it running just the way you need it.

Interface	032
System Preferences	034
Keyboard shortcuts	036
Mail	038
iCal	040
Address Book	041
iChat	042
Spaces	044
Time Machine	045
Dashboard	046

Interface

The Mac OS X interface is composed of windows, icons, menus and pointers, making it a classic Wimp environment. That's why it's so easy to use.

INTERFACE

1 The **Menubar** runs across the top of the screen. At the moment it is showing the options associated with managing your files. However, it will always tailor itself to your current application, with the bold word on the very left indicating which application that is.

2 The **Dock** is where you'll store your most common applications. You can drag applications icons on and off it to add or remove them. When an application needs attention, its icon will bounce.

3 Stacks are special Dock icons found in Mac OS X 10.5 Leopard, which fan out to reveal the contents of a folder on your hard drive. By default it will show your Documents and Downloads folders, but you can create new Stacks by dragging folders onto the Dock to the right of the vertical dividing bar.

4 The **Trash Can** holds all of your deleted documents so that you can rescue them if you didn't mean to erase them. Files, applications and folders can be sent to the Trash by dragging them to it from the Desktop or any Window. To empty the trash, right-click (or click while pressing Ctrl on the keyboard) on the Trash icon and select Empty Trash from the menu.

5 This icon shows your currently active **Space**. Spaces are virtual screens (see page 44) that allow you to run several applications at once. Switch between spaces using Ctrl and 1, 2, 3 or 4 as appropriate.

6 The **Desktop** is your main working area. It is the backdrop to all of the open windows on your Mac, and is also a place where you can temporarily drop files you are working with. However, you should never use it for permanent file storage.

7 The **red button** on a window closes it, the **amber button** minimises it to the Dock, and the **green button** switches between a full-size and shrunken view of the document. Note that this is different to the maximise button in Windows, as while that fills the whole screen with your application, the Mac's green button simply makes the application the largest appropriate size for your work.

8 The **lozenge** on the top right of a window shows and hides an application's toolbar, allowing you to hide distracting buttons that you may no longer need once you have learnt each application's keyboard shortcuts.

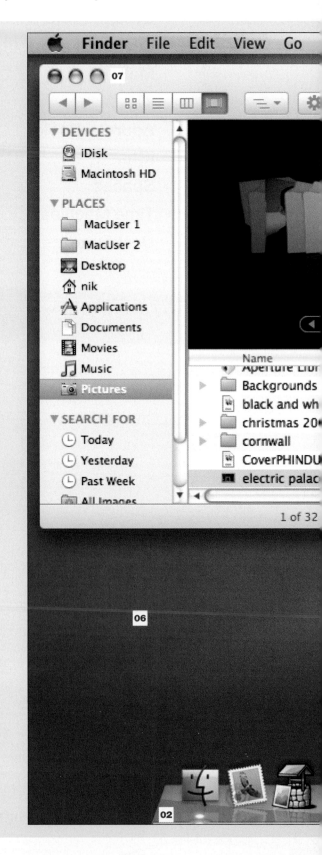

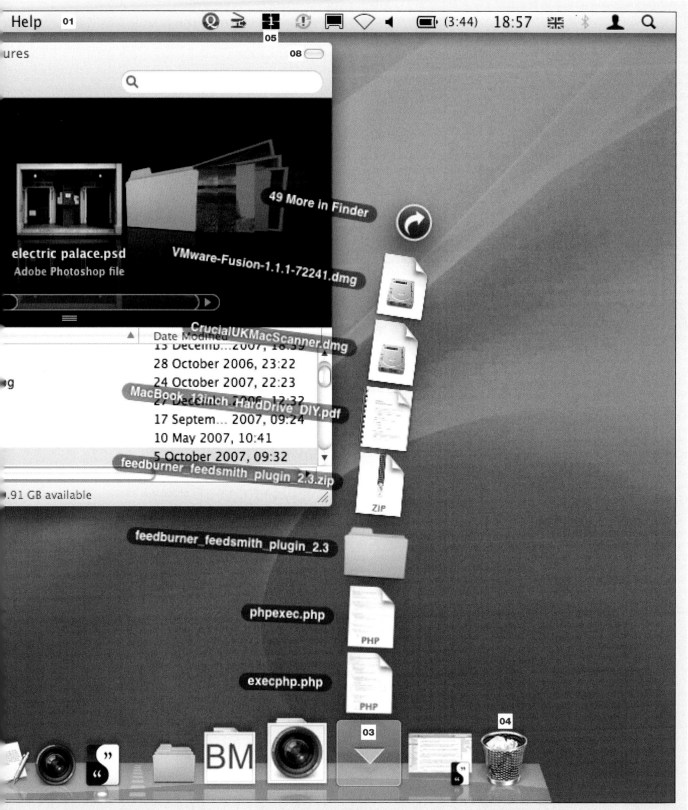

System Preferences

When you need to tweak your settings in Mac OS X, turn to System Preferences, found in the Apple menu. It's the fastest way to tailor your Mac to your needs.

INTERFACE

System Preferences is the part of Mac OS X that lets you control how it works. The closest equivalent on a PC is Windows Control Panel. In Mac OS X 10.5 Leopard, System Preferences is represented by a set of grey cogs. In Mac OS X 10.4 Tiger and earlier it is a white light switch with an Apple logo. It can also be accessed through the Apple menu in the top-left corner of the screen.

System Preferences is split into logical sections, with each feature represented by an icon. You can also search for features using the box at the top of the panel, and it is intelligent enough to understand Windows terms, so while the picture on your Desktop is called the Desktop Background and accessed through the Desktop & Screen Saver option, typing Wallpaper (the Windows equivalent) into the search box will highlight that option in System Preferences.

1 Accounts is used to add new users to your computer, allowing several members of one household to share a single computer while keeping their documents, email and bookmarks separate.

2 International controls the languages and formats used by your Mac. This is where you could add new language options for the spell checker, or change the date and currency symbols.

3 You add new printers through **Print & Fax**, which will search the ports on your Mac or a network to which you are connected and lets you specify an appropriate driver file. The driver file tells the Mac how to communicate with the printer.

4 You can change the resolution of your screen through **Displays**, and control how your Mac spans the Desktop and its applications across multiple screens attached simultaneously.

5 .Mac is Apple's Internet service for synchronising contacts and calendars across multiple Macs, backing up your files, publishing websites and accessing email online. You control what it synchronises and how it manages your allocated space here.

6 Mac OS X's **Parental Controls** were expanded in version 10.5 Leopard to allow you to specify how long your child can use the computer, who they can chat to and email, and what websites they can visit, all the while logging what they do.

7 The bottom row of **System Preferences** will gather together all of the extra settings tools for any third-party applications you install.

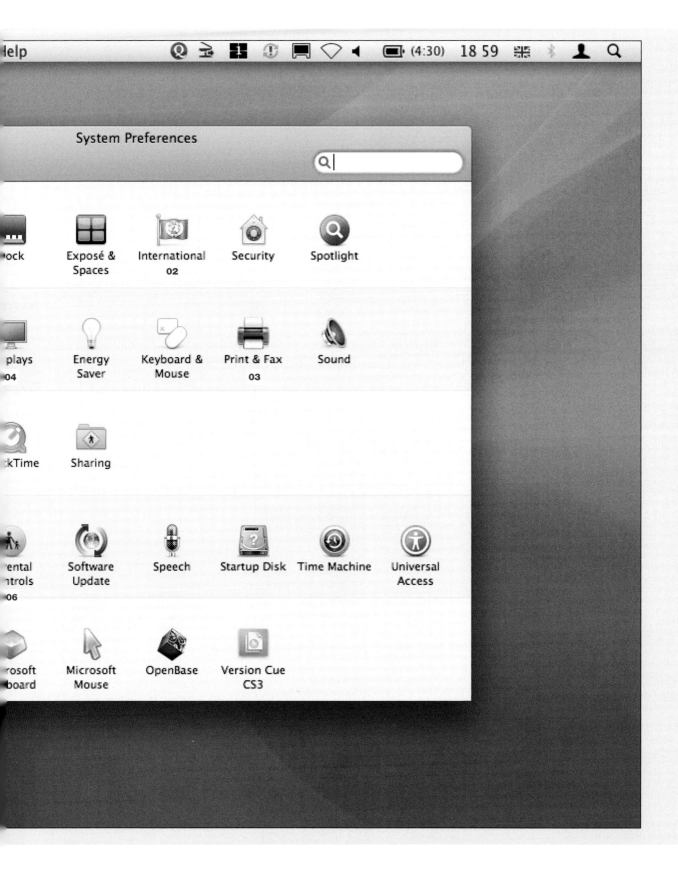

Keyboard shortcuts

You'll get a lot further in a lot less time by learning a few handy keyboard shortcuts. These let you perform common tasks without having to hunt through your menus using the mouse or trackpad. The longer you use your Mac, the more you'll learn, but it's worth keeping this list of the most common – and most useful – shortcuts handy as you get to know your Mac better. Remember that the more shortcuts you know the less time you'll spend mousing, and the more time you'll save.

MAC OS X	
Show all active Spaces	F8
Show all windows in Exposé	F9
Show all windows in the current application	F10
Move all windows off the desktop	F11
Show the Dashboard Widgets	F12
Hide or show the Dock	alt-command-d
Show Spotlight search box	command-space
Close current window	command-w
Quit current application	command-q
Force quit	alt-command-escape
Log out	shift-command-q
Undo last action	command-z
Select all	command-a
Copy selection	command-c
Paste selection	command-v
Cut selection (remove to clipboard for later pasting)	command-x
Open Computer in Finder	shift-command-c
Open Home folder in Finder	shift-command-h
Open Desktop in Finder	alt-command-d
Open Applications folder in Finder	alt-command-a
Open Utilities folder in Finder	alt-command-u

FILE MANAGEMENT	
Open a new Finder window	command-n
Create a new folder	shift-command-n
Create a new smart folder	alt-command-n
Get a file's info	command-i
Open a file	command-o
Duplicate a file	command-d
Quick Look a file	space
Find a file	command-space
Add file to favourites	shift-command-t
Send file to the trash	command-backspace
Empty the trash	shift-command-backspace
Eject a disc	command-e

ZOOMING	
Turn zoom on and off	alt-command-8
Zoom in	alt-command-=
Zoom out	alt-command-- (dash)
Zoom in and out with the mouse	by scrolling the wheel or ball while holding ctrl

(Note that universal access must be enabled before you can zoom the screen, adjust the contrast or reverse out the screen display. Do this by opening System Preferences and navigating to Universal Access where you'll find the necessary checkboxes to enable it.)

APPLICATIONS	
Open Preferences	command-,
Hide this application	command-h
Hide all other applications	alt-command-h

DISPLAY	
Save screen shot to the desktop	shift-command-3
Save selection to desktop	shift-command-4, then select area using the mouse
Save window to the desktop	shift-command-4, then space. Position mouse pointer over the window and click.
Send screen to the clipboard	ctrl-shift-command-3
Send selection to clipboard	ctrl-shift-command-4, then select area using the mouse
Send window to the clipboard	ctrl-shift-command-4, then space. Position mouse pointer over the window and click.

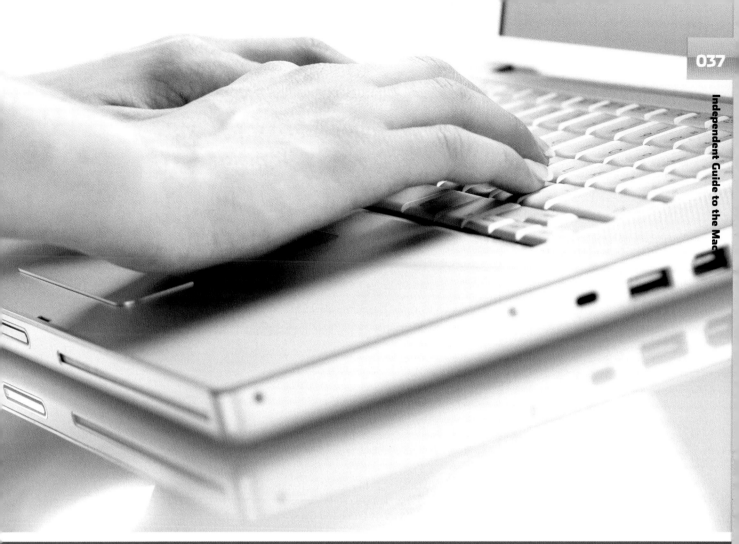

SAFARI	
New window	**command-n**
New tab	**command-t**
Switch to next tab	**command-}**
Switch to previous tab	**command-{**
Open location (web or network address)	**command-l**
Send page contents by email	**command-i**
Automatically fill out form	**command-a**
Re-load page	**command-r**
Enlarge text	**command-+**
Reduce text size	**command-- (dash)**
Bookmark current page	**shift-command-d**
Show bookmarks	**alt-command-b**

(Note that use of tabs requires tab features to be switched on through Safari's preferences pane.)

TEXTEDIT	
Show document properties	**alt-command-p**
Print	**command-p**
Check spelling	**command-;**
Paste text but match current style	**shift-alt-command-v**
Bold	**command-b**
Italic	**command-i**
Underline	**command-u**
Show fonts	**command-t**
Enlarge font	**command-+**
Reduce font	**command-- (dash)**
Left align	**command-{**
Right align	**command-}**

MAIL	
New message	**command-n**
Reply to message	**command-r**
Reply to all recipients	**shift-command-r**
New note	**ctrl-command-n**
Delete message	**command-backspace**
Bounce message	**shift-command-b**
Forward message	**shift-command-f**
Mark message as spam	**shift-command-j**
Erase spam	**alt-command-j**
Paste as quotation	**shift-command-v**
Show or hide BCC field	**alt-command-b**
Get new mail	**shift-command-n**

Mail

One of the best email applications on any computer is Mail, which found only on the Mac. It is bundled as part of the operating system, and as such it integrates well with the other key components, including Address Book, iCal, iChat and the downloads folder found in Mac OS X 10.5 Leopard. An extensive set of built-in tools lets you define rules that help cut down on unwanted commercial email (spam) and route incoming emails to specific folders based on their content.

Apple couldn't have chosen a better name for its email application than Mail. Its closest equivalent on Windows PCs is Outlook Express. Microsoft makes an equivalent of the full-blown Outlook for the Mac called Entourage, which is available as part of Microsoft Office for Mac (see page 114). However, we think you're better off sticking with Mail rather than switching to Microsoft's rival for two reasons: many people feel it works in a far more logical and smooth way than Entourage, and it integrates better with other applications in the operating system. Plus, of course, it's free.

The first time you start it up, you'll be walked step-by-step through the process of adding your first account, using the details supplied by your Internet Service Provider (ISP). Mail will run through a series of checks to make sure that it can connect to their servers and download your messages and, all being well, you'll be sent to the inbox from which you can start messaging your friends and colleagues.

Mail connects with Address Book, so even if you don't remember your contacts' email addresses, you can still send them messages by just typing their name. Mail will immediately start to sort through your address lists, and as soon as it finds a match, will fill it in. If it's the wrong one keep typing and it will try again.

JUNK MAIL
The Internet is now plagued with junk emails – so-called Spam. Mail is good at recognising these and filtering them out, so if you find that your inbox is creaking under the weight of irrelevant incoming messages, go to Mail > Preferences > Junk Mail and check the box beside Enable junk mail filtering.

You have several options here, and we would recommend choosing to move junk mail to the junk mail box, which will keep your inbox nice and tidy while still allowing you to pop into the junk mail folder now and then to check that it's not filtering out anything you really ought to read.

Mail doesn't always get it right the other way, too; it sometimes drops junk mail in your inbox. Every time it does this you should correct it, as the more times you put it right, the less often it will make the same mistake in the future. Click on the erroneous message and then tap Command-Shift-j, or the Junk button on the main Mail toolbar.

CREATING MAILBOXES AND SMART MAILBOXES
Maintaining an efficient mailbox means sorting through your messages as they arrive. The temptation, of course, is just to leave them in the inbox where the list of communiques will grow to almost unmanageable proportions in no time at all. You should therefore set up separate mailboxes in which you can file your messages according to subject or sender and, once they're in place, rules to do this for you.

Mailboxes are added by clicking on the '+' button at the bottom left-hand corner of the Mail interface and selecting New Mailbox… Give it a name and click on OK and you'll see that it appears in a new section of the sidebar called On My Mac. If you can see this section, but not your new mailbox, click on the disclosure triangle to the left and it should drop down.

You will also have seen the option to create a Smart Mailbox when pressing the '+' button. This lets you define rules that will automatically sort matching messages. Try creating one now. Again, give it a name, then use the input boxes and drop-down menus to define the criteria that, when matched, will redirect a message to your new folder.

You can combine multiple criteria by adding new lines to the box by pressing the '+' button to the right of each line to add a

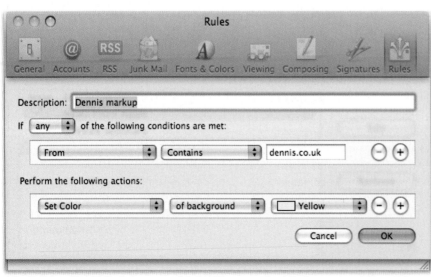
▲ Use the Rules setting (Mail > Preferences... > Rules) to filter your email and direct messages matching certain conditions to specific mailboxes.

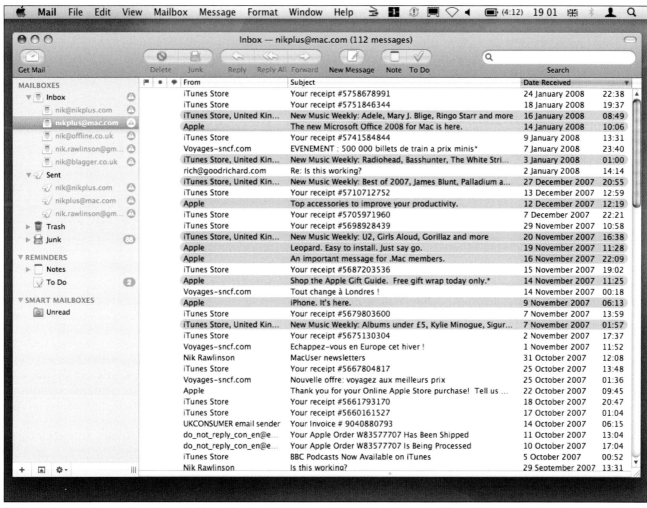

▲ A simple but very effective way of handling your Mail inbox is to set up a Rule. Here, we added a rule that colour codes all the emails from a particular sender, in this case Apple.

new one below it. You can also, usefully, define criteria that should not be matched. For example, if you worked for Dennis Publishing, had set up Mail to pick out both your home and work emails, and wanted to route all non-internal messages to another mailbox, you would select From in the first drop-down and Does not contain in the second, then enter dennis.co.uk in the third box.

Click on OK to create the new smart mailbox and you'll be given the opportunity to run the filter on all messages in the presently open mailbox.

Note that no message sent to a Smart Mailbox is actually taken out of your inbox. You should therefore think of a Smart Mailbox as a lens through which you can see just a selection of all of the emails in your main inbox. If you have set up a mailbox to display only unread messages, therefore, they will not be counted as part of that mailbox when read, but remain within your main inbox for future reference.

Note that Smart Mailboxes don't always automatically update. For example, when reading messages in a folder that only contains unread messages, you may notice that the now read message remain in place despite the message count decreasing. To get around this quirk, click out of the mailbox – say onto your Inbox – and then back into the Smart Mailbox.

CREATING RULES

Rules work in a similar way to Smart Mailboxes, but offer greater flexibility and don't always have the ultimate goal of moving your messages from one place to another. Although you can divert messages to various locations within or outside the Mail application (you can automatically delete, redirect or bounce unwanted messages, for example), they are most powerful when used to mark up incoming emails for easy identification.

For such a powerful tool, it is surprising that Apple has hidden away the Rules function in Mail's preferences pane. Click on Mail > Preferences > Rules and then Add Rule to define one of your own.

As with the mailboxes, you'll need to give each new rule a name. It doesn't matter what you call it, as it will never appear in the Mail interface, but you should choose one that you will understand next time you come back to edit it. We're going to call our example rule Dennis Markup, as we're going to use it to re-colour all messages received from Dennis Publishing, but leave them in the inbox rather than putting them into a Smart Mailbox.

Now skip down to the line below 'If any of the following conditions are met' and ensure that the drop-down boxes and input lines match the ones we set up for our Smart Mailbox above, so that reading across the line we get 'From' 'Contains' 'dennis.co.uk'. Now move to the box below 'Perform the following actions', and select 'Set Color of Message' in the first drop-down, 'of background' in the second, and then a colour in the third. We'd select yellow as it's sufficiently different from the standard white background, but not so pronounced that it clashes.

Click on OK and then select the option to apply the rule to all messages in the open mailbox. All messages from the domain dennis.co.uk will now be clearly visible because they have a yellow background.

iCal

What's the point of hanging a kitten-adorned calendar on your wall when you have a Mac? iCal, Mac OS X's integrated calendaring application, can track all of your appointments and tasks, flashing up alarms when things become due so you never miss a meeting or deadline. It integrates perfectly with Mail to capture incoming meeting requests and, if you have a .Mac account, it will let you publish your calendar online so that colleagues can keep tabs on where you might be.

When you want to track your appointments and jobs in Mac OS X, the first place to turn is iCal. It's a sophisticated calendaring application that ties in with Mail to automatically add appointments and invite attendees to meetings.

When you first fire it up, you'll have two calendars: work and home. Clicking on each one in the left-hand column switches between them, while checking and unchecking the boxes beside each name will show and hide each one, so you can have just the most relevant calendar at any one time visible on the screen, or everything at once if you so wish.

You'll notice that each calendar is colour coded, and these colours are replicated on any entries you create so that you can see at a glance whether they relate to your personal or professional life.

In Mac OS X 10.5 Leopard, there is a third calendar: Birthdays. This draws its data from contact cards in Address Book, assuming you have entered your contacts' birthday details.

Of course, there are times when two (or three) calendars simply isn't enough. You might want a separate calendar to track fixtures in your local football league, remind you when your recycling is due to be collected and when to put the bins out. In that case you would click on the '+' button at the bottom of the screen, give your new calendar a name and start adding entries.

There are three display modes in iCal – day, week, and month view – and you switch between using the buttons at the top of the window. The arrows to either side of them will step you one increment forwards and one backwards from wherever you are, so if you're displaying whole months, the right-hand arrow will take you to the next month. If you're showing days, the left-hand arrow will take you one day back.

You can move more quickly between different days using the small calendar view that appears in the lower left-hand corner of the iCal window. Clicking on any day here will take you to the appropriate place in the main window, while clicking on the Today button will take you back to the current date.

Once you enter an item in your calendar, by double-clicking in the appropriate day in the main part of the screen, it will be displayed as a coloured box (matching the colour of the calendar on which it is entered) taking up as much of the day as is relevant. If it is an all-day event, it will be displayed as a more discrete bar at the top of that day's entry. If you got the date or time wrong then don't go to the hassle of re-entering them manually – just click and hold on the entry and drag it to a new point in the calendar.

For more substantial edits, such as changing meeting venues or adding alarms so that you'll be reminded of an event before it begins, click once on an event and press Command-i to open up the editing dialog.

TO-DO LISTS
iCal is also the best bundled application for managing your to-do lists, as it will track due dates and display them beside your appointments. Press Command-k to create a new to-do job and, once entered, Command-i to create a due date and priority, which will allow you to sort your jobs in order of importance of impending deadline.

To-dos created using Mail will also appear in iCal, and when checked off as being completed in Mail they will also be marked as done in iCal. If your to-dos don't show, click on the thumbtack, bottom right.

▲ In iCal, each of the calendars are colour coded. Home and Work are there as standard but you can add your own.

Address Book

Ever since the earliest days of computers, they have been used to store and manage contact details. Indeed some of the earliest applications were little more than digital versions of the old Rolodex address books found in offices nationwide in the days of rotary telephones and manual typewriters. It's only natural, then, that the Mac should sport a first-class, attractive address book that works flawlessly with its email application and even helps you track your contacts' birthdays.

The address book built into Mac OS X is more important than you might imagine. No mere store of names and email addresses, it integrates with other key applications, such as iCal, though which it maintains a calendar of your contacts' birthdays, and iTunes, which will send its contents to an iPod or iPhone. It works with iChat, Mac OS X's IM tool (see page 42) to automatically populate your contacts list, and tell you who is online.

The main window is divided into three panes handling groups, names and full contact details. The first of these – Group – lets you organise your contacts logically by dragging them from the Name section into sections that you define by clicking on the '+' button at the foot of the window.

No actual change is made to any contact card when it's placed in a Group, and all contacts remain both searchable and corralled in the All group. The benefit of organising them in this way, though, is that you can then restrict which contacts are synced to different devices rather than taking all of your contacts with you.

In this way, you can set up lists of purely personal or business contacts, and sync the business contacts to your mobile phone using iSync, and the personal contacts to your iPod or iPhone using iTunes.

In its default state, Address Book is a perfectly usable and flexible piece of software. However, by giving it a few simple tweaks you can tailor it to your precise requirements. Click on Address Book > Preferences > Templates and you can specify the exact fields that are displayed on each card, allowing you to add such business essentials as a phonetic pronunciation of the first and family names of each contact, job titles, departments and even maiden names and nicknames.

You can have it automatically format phone numbers to comply with specific country customs through the Phone tab, and specify which country that should be using the General tab.

YOUR OWN PERSONAL CARD

Business cards and email signatures may still rule the day when it comes to passing on your own details, but electronic cards, or vCards, are an increasingly important tool for keeping contacts updated with your various moves and developments.

These are standard data files that conform to an internationally-agreed standard and can thus be passed from one computer to another with relative confidence. Your first job when setting up Address Book should therefore be to input your own card. Do this by creating a new record, filling in all of the details you want to pass on. Bear in mind that it is not necessary to complete every field, and that leaving out your mobile number or personal email address won't throw up any errors.

When complete, click on the Edit button at the bottom of the window to close off the record (you can go back and change things later by clicking that button again) and then click on Card > Make this my card.

Now, every time you want to send your details to a contact click on Card > Go to my card, and drag your name from the Name column into an email, which you then send.

Even if you don't plan on emailing your details to family and friends, it's worth setting up a card for yourself, as various applications, such as email, business card creation and financial tools use it as a fast and efficient way to automatically populate various fields about yourself.

▲ Address Book is more than a store for contact details as it integrates with a host of other applications to share data.

iChat

Sometimes even lightning-fast email is just too slow. On those occasions when you need an answer right now you have to revert to either the phone or an instant messaging application. While the Mac can't help greatly with the first of those options, it is well tooled for the latter with a first-class messaging client called iChat. This can handle regular written notes, alongside audio and video conferencing using the Mac's integrated iSight camera, speakers and mic.

iChat is Mac OS X's integrated messaging application. The closest equivalent on the PC is AOL Messenger with which it is totally compatible. The most popular PC equivalent, however, is MSN Messenger or Windows Live Messenger, thanks to a bundling deal with Windows.

Microsoft's messaging applications also work on the Mac, so if all of your contacts use them they may suit you better, as you'll not be able to talk to them using iChat. However, iChat is very closely integrated with the operating system as well as being very attractive.

The first time you run iChat, you'll be taken through the set-up process, during which you'll need to enter an existing AOL or .Mac username. If you don't already have one, you can get a free AOL address from *aol.co.uk*, and a .Mac username from *mac.com*.

You will also be taken through setting up any built-in or attached webcam, microphone and speakers, which will allow you to use iChat as a simple video conferencing system with other users on the same system.

Assuming you are using Mac OS X 10.4 Tiger or later, you can video conference with up to two other people. If you are using Mac OS X 10.3 Panther, you can video conference with just one person, but nothing earlier than that can use video conference features at all.

BONJOUR

You will be asked if you want to use Bonjour messaging. This lets you connect to other users on the same network as yourself. If you are using your Mac at home, or you're the only Mac user in your office then you can safely decline, but if you work with other Mac users then enabling this will allow you to send messages to each other without them passing over the Internet.

Contacts with messenger details in Mac OS X's Address Book will automatically be added to your iChat contacts list – assuming they are AOL or .Mac Buddy details. To add your own, click on the '+' button at the bottom of the window and enter the necessary details, remembering to select Aim or .Mac as appropriate from the account-type drop-down.

To chat with any of your contacts, simply double-click their name and start typing. The two sides of your conversation will appear as speech bubbles within the iChat window. To video conference, click on the green video icon to the right of their name. If it looks like there are more than one of these icons for any one person stacked up on top of each other, then they are capable of taking part in multi-party conferencing. Anyone showing a telephone symbol can chat using audio, but will be unable to take part in video chats because they do not have a compatible camera connected.

Between your name at the top of the window and the contacts list that takes up the major part of the interface you'll see a status line, which most likely says Available. Clicking on it drops down a list of alternatives, with whichever one you select being reflected in your contacts' own contact lists. A wide range of default options have already been entered, including one to post the name of the current song playing in iTunes as your status, but by selecting either 'Custom Available' or 'Custom Away' you can write your own, such as 'Here, but busy, so only chat if it's urgent'.

You can also monitor your contacts' statuses and change your own online, offline and do not disturb settings through the menubar if you have activated this option through iChat's Preferences.

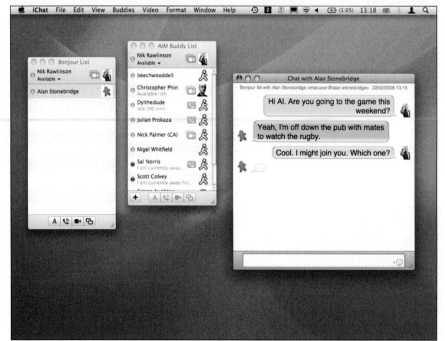
▲ iChat is the IM application that comes with Mac OS X and is a great way of getting in contact with your friends.

All new Retrospect 8.0 for Mac

- **Easy and Automatic**
  Retrospect is simple to use. Makes a complete and reliable backup strategy easy. Works in a mixed Macintosh/ Windows environment.

- **Powerful and Flexible**
  Retrospect is packed with features that business and network users require for protecting critical data. Media management benefits make media rotation easy.

- **Reliable and Secure**
  Retrospect saves a complete point-in-time file listing with every backup, and then verifies the data copied during the backup process - ensuring an accurate restore every time

BETTER, STRONGER FASTER.

The backup software that Mac experts recommend.

EMC Retrospect 8.0 backup and recovery software for the Mac provides small and midsize businesses with the reliability, ease of use, power and flexibility they need to protect critical data on their Macs and Windows PCs.

EMC Retrospect includes a state-of-the-art Mac user interface and enterprise-level features - Including remote management of one or more backup servers and disk-to-disk-to-tape backups - at a fraction of the cost of other products.

With more than two decades of field-tested expertise and millions of users worldwide, EMC Retrospect is the most trusted name in Mac backup.

For more information visit your local APR Store. For a full list of APR stores visit www.apr-stores.com

Distributed by:

EMC^2 retrospect

Spaces

Spaces is a radical feature of the latest edition of Mac OS X that lets you have several 'virtual' screens running at the same time. It has been common in Linux and Unix operating systems for several editions now, and it allows you to either group similar applications together in discrete working environments, or run several applications in full-screen mode. It saves both the cost and environmental impact of buying multiple monitors, which may not work with older machines anyhow.

Spaces is new to Mac OS X 10.5
Leopard. It allows you to have as many as 16 different working areas, each able to run several applications at once, or display a single application in full screen. It is activated through Exposé & Spaces in System Preferences.

You can display all active Spaces, including those with no applications running inside them by pressing F8, or switch between spaces using Ctrl and the number of the Space (Ctrl-2 for Space 2, for example). Of course, this means you can only access up to nine Spaces using the keyboard. If you have between 10 and 16 Spaces active, you'll have to use the cursor keys or the Spaces drop-down on the menubar. This is a four-paned icon with the number of the current Space in the middle. Clicking it drops down a list of all available Spaces from which you can pick the one you want. If this menu is not visible on your menubar, it must be activated through System Preferences. Click on Exposé & Spaces, then the Spaces tab, and check the option for Show Spaces in menu bar.

If you have a good visual mind, you can skip straight to the Space you need using the cursor keys – the four arrow buttons at the bottom of the keyboard to the right of the space bar. Combine these with Ctrl to move through the Spaces in turn. This allows you to quickly navigate to screens beyond the first nine. In a 16-Space configuration, for example, you could step from Space 1 to space 10 by pressing Ctrl and down twice, then Ctrl and right once.

There are times when the Spaces shortcuts can interfere with key combinations in other applications. Version 1 of Apple's own Aperture, for example, uses control and the number keys for rating photos, and this will take precedence over Spaces' controls. You may therefore need to change the default key combinations by using the drop-down menus in System Preferences.

But Spaces is more than just a clever way of expanding your Desktop without paying for extra monitors and graphics cards: it is a neat way to organise your working environment by having your most commonly-used applications open on different screens.

SPACES AND APPLICATIONS
Once an application is up and running you can drag it to different Spaces by holding down on its title bar and pulling it to the edge of the screen in the direction of the Space you want. So, to move Word from Space 1 to Space 2, you would take it to the right-hand edge of your screen and hold it there for a second until the new Space slides into view.

However, the Application Assignments section of Spaces' preferences pane lets you specify where applications should open by default. If you therefore always open Mail, Safari and Address Book each morning, you may want to assign each one to a different space, rather than having to drag them there once they've already been opened.

Click the '+' button below the Application Assignments panel and select the first application from Finder window that pops up. Click on Add to return to the pane and then assign it to a Space using the drop-down menu to the right of the panel. Repeat this for every other application you want to assign and then try launching them, either from the Dock or from your Applications folder to see how each one is immediately sent to its allocated Space.

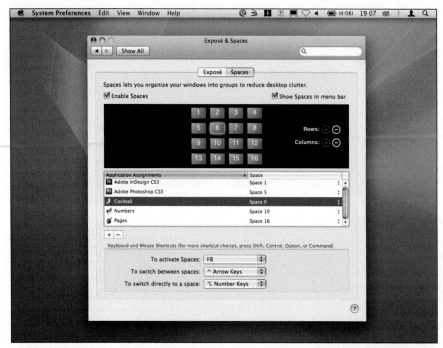

▲ Spaces, which was added to Mac OS X 10.5, allows you to easily switch between applications as you work.

Time Machine

Time Machine is Apple's radical backup software. Built into the heart of the operating system, it takes all of the pain out of creating backups of your work, by automating the whole process. Switch it on and attach a drive, and every hour your Mac will quietly set to work saving any changes you have made to your files in the last 60 minutes. If disaster strikes, it's easy to roll back these changes and recover your data. If there's only one reason why you upgrade to Mac OS X 10.5, make it this one.

If you're like most computer users, you won't back up your work nearly so often as you should. It's not that backing up is complicated or hard work; it's just that you need to remember to do it and, when you do, set by enough time for it to complete.

Fortunately in Mac OS X 10.5 Leopard, Apple has significantly simplified the process through the introduction of Time Machine, its automated, entirely passive backup software.

Time Machine takes all the responsibility for backing up your work away from yourself. It identifies which files should be copied, and every hour writes any changes you have made to your system to an attached external drive. These changes could be as major as creating and deleting documents, or as minor as changing a contact's phone number in Address Book.

If you do any of this inadvertently and decide you need to roll back to a previous version, you simply open Time Machine and navigate backwards through time using its graphical display of system windows.

The first time you plug in a large external hard drive, Mac OS X will spot it and offer to use it as a backup destination using Time Machine. However, you can also invoke Time Machine manually – if, for example, you've previously dismissed the automatic offer – by opening it through System Preferences and sliding the large activation switch to On. You'll need to select the drive you want to use for backups, and then Time Machine will start to create its first backup set, taking a copy of your computer's whole internal drive in its current state.

Although it depends on the amount of data on your drive, this will take quite some time, so it's fortunate that you can keep using your Mac while it completes the task.

Thankfully this lengthy backup only takes place once, and when complete it will be used as the basis for all future backups,

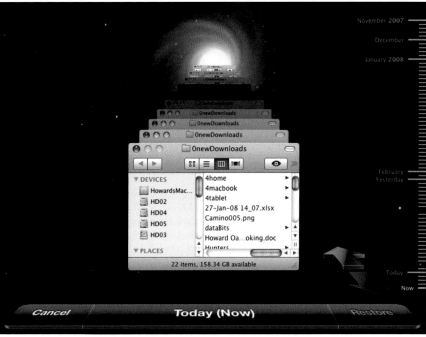

▲ Time Machine backs up the data on your Mac every hour, allowing you to go back in time to recover particular files.

allowing your Mac to send just the changed files to the drive on an hourly basis.

TIME CAPSULE
If you use a desktop Mac then these subsequent backups will be quite passive. The external drive will likely stay permanently connected to your Mac and, assuming you don't suffer some chronic failure, you'll never have to think about backup again. However, if you have a portable Mac, such as a MacBook or an older PowerBook, you'll have to manually connect the drive every time you start up to ensure that the backups are carried out on schedule.

This is a hassle, and almost guaranteed to see you missing the odd backup here and there. However, Apple has come to the rescue with Time Capsule, a wireless networking device that includes a built-in hard drive. If you use this to share your Internet connection around your home or office, then all of the Macs on your network will be able to use it as a Time Machine backup destination simultaneously.

There are two different versions of Time Capsule, featuring drives of 500GB and 1TB (1 terrabyte or 1000GB). The size of drive you need will be determined by the contents of your hard drive, but our advice would be to buy as much as you can afford, always bearing in mind that a USB port on the back of the Time Capsule will allow you to add more external drives later on should you find that the smaller drive was just too small.

While wireless features are common on modern routers, and several have ports for drives, it is not possible to replicate the Time Capsule features on them.

Dashboard

Dashboard is the Mac's best-kept secret. It first appeared in Mac OS X 10.4 Tiger, but even if you're running this operating system – or its successor, Leopard – you'll barely ever see it. It is a secondary layer of small applications that sits below your regular working environment and is only ever called into use when you have a specific need. It is home to a wide range of tiny tools, called Widgets, that do everything from converting currencies and languages to tracking traffic and weather.

The Dashboard is a hidden layer of Mac OS X on which you can run a series of small applications called Widgets. It is invoked by pressing F12 on your keyboard (F4 on newer Macs) or, if you've set it up right, by rolling your mouse to one corner of the screen. To turn this on, and define the active corner, open the Expose & Spaces section of System Preferences and use the drop-down menus in the Active Screen Corners panel.

Although some only ever reference information on your Mac – such as the Stickies Widget – most Widgets draw in data from the Internet, and so work best with a broadband or dial-up connection.

Activate Dashboard now and if you've never used it before you'll see that there are four default Widgets already in place. You can close them by holding down Alt while you hover your mouse over each one. You'll see that a cross appears in the corner which, when clicked, sucks in the Widget to close it.

To open new Widgets, click on the '+' button at the bottom of the screen to open the Widgets Bar, and then drag the ones you want into the shaded Dashboard area. If you have a new Mac with an up-to-date graphics card, you should see ripples splash out from the edge of the Widget as you drop it.

Most Widgets will need a little information from yourself before they can work properly, such as your home location for the Weather Widget, or which companies you want to track in the Stocks Widget. To enter this, move your mouse to the bottom-right corner of the Widget and click on the 'i' icon. This will flip the Widget around like a playing card to show you the options on the back. Use these to tailor it to your specific needs

ADDING AND REMOVING WIDGETS

If you only ever use three or four Widgets, then you may want to disable the ones that don't interest you. You can do this by clicking on the Dashboard's '+' icon followed by Manage Widgets. This brings up a grey panel listing all of the Widgets installed on your system. Unchecking a box beside the ones you don't need removes them from the Widgets Bar at the bottom of the screen, regardless of where they came from.

Any that you have downloaded by clicking on the More Widgets... button at the bottom of this panel can be uninstalled entirely by clicking on the red bar symbol to the right of each one. The ones that already come as part of Mac OS X can't be entirely uninstalled in this way.

Since their first appearance in Mac OS X 10.4 Tiger, Widgets have proven to be an attractive focus for programmers. They work in a very similar way to intelligent web pages, and so it's not difficult to learn how to make your own.

Apple maintains a large database of available third-party Widgets, which cover everything from blog posting to monitoring the status of your Mac's hardware, on its site at *apple.com*.

WIDGETS FROM THE WEB

Safari 3 added a new button to the browser toolbar for creating simple web-monitoring Widgets. Visit any page and click on the fourth button from the left, with the box and scissors on it. Now move your mouse pointer over the active page until the area you're most interested in is highlighted. Click, and it'll be added to the Dashboard as a constantly-updating Widget, allowing you to monitor news headlines, weather reports or sports results without returning to that page each time.

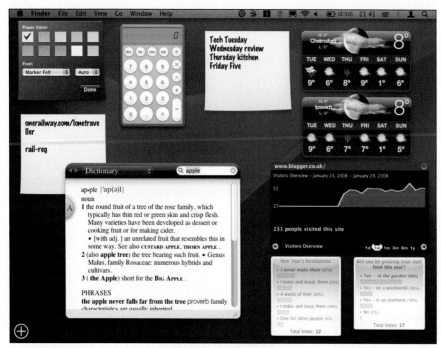

▲ This is the Dashboard and it is home to a wide variety of Widgets, everything from calculators to dictionaries.

FASTER DRIVE...PERIOD.

VERTEX SERIES
SOLID STATE DRIVE

- 64MB Cache
- RAID Support
- Maximum Performance*:
    Read Up to 250MB/s
    Write Up to 180 MB/s
- Sustained*:
    Write up to 100MB/s

*based on Vertex 120GB

Put your system in high-gear! OCZ Technology, a pioneer in Solid State Drives, leaves hard drives in the dust when it comes to performance. The all-new Vertex eries takes it to a whole new level with a trailblazing design that delivers superior sysem responsiveness, unparalleled speed, and a price that seals the deal. For an SSD that lives up to your performance standards, park nothing less than the Vertex in your system.

OCZ Technology
www.ocztechnology.com

OCZ Europe
Kleveringweg 23
2616 LZ Delft, The Netherlands
+31 (0) 15 219.10.30 Phone
+31 (0) 15 213.67.85 Fax
oczeuro@ocztechnology.com

AVAILABLE AT:

iLife

Whatever you want to do with your personal media, you should do it with iLife. Apple's suite of lifestyle applications, incorporating iPhoto, iMovie, iTunes, GarageBand, iWeb and iDVD, handles movies, music and photos and helps you create web pages without any prior technical knowledge.

They take care of the underlying standards and managing libraries of your media, freeing you to spend your valuable time being creative. But how do you get the most out of the applications, and of your media? Over the next 20 pages we'll explain which application is the best for you, and how you can use them to your best advantage.

iPhoto	050
iTunes	054
iWeb	060
iMovie	064
iDVD	068

iPhoto

iPhoto is a superb way to manage your photos, and if you've mastered iTunes then you'll be up and running within minutes, since it uses Apple's familiar interface design and concepts like Smart Albums. It's more than just a photo library though. There's a whole range of tools to help salvage photos from common flaws such as red-eye. When you're ready you can share photos, send them via email, publish to the web, or showcase your photographic skills by publishing your own photobook or calendar.

We've reached a point in consumer electronics where you're probably carrying a digital camera as part of your mobile phone, even if you've never purchased a dedicated camera. Over the years, even a casual snapper will build up a sizable collection of photos of friends and family. It's important to keep them organised, but you could do that with folders. So why use iPhoto?

If you take photos of a many different people and places, iPhoto gives you the ability to attach keywords to each photo in the library so you can quickly find the one that you want at a later date. Make a habit of doing this from the start and it'll be easy to find the photos that you want many years down the line. There's no need to pore through photo albums by hand, as you'd have to do with printed photos. Make good use of your Mac's ability to process information quickly and let it do the hard work of weeding out a handful of photos from hundred or thousands of others, leaving you with a much easier job of pinpointing the exact photo that you want.

iPhoto's selection of editing tools is just right for the majority of us, addressing common flaws like red-eye, tilted images where a camera wasn't held level, and incorrect white balance where a camera's automatic mode has failed to live up to expectations. The basic tools are complemented by a range of special effects and adjustment tools.

One of the standout features is the ability to make your own photobooks, calendars and cards, and to have them printed and bound professionally. iPhoto provides a great deal of control over the look of each page, with plenty of alternative page layouts, cropping and scaling of photos on the page, and captions to annotate events or other details for a photography portfolio. They make wonderful gifts and a superb creative outlet to make you proud of your handiwork.

The first of our workthroughs details how to make a web gallery that only family and friends can see. It also demonstrates one of the excellent benefits of hosting your website on Apple's MobileMe service: other people can contribute their own photos to the gallery. The second workthrough shows you how to create a calendar featuring your photos; the same skills can be used to create books and cards.

The iLife Media Browser lets you use any photo from iPhoto in iWeb, iMovie and iDVD. Don't forget to check out the workthroughs for those applications that cover other ways to share your photographs.

ALSO CONSIDER...

APERTURE 2
apple.com/aperture
Apple's professional equivalent of iPhoto costs a modest £129 and it integrates with the Media Browser so your photos can still be used in the other iLife applications.

PHOTOSHOP LIGHTROOM
adobe.com/lightroom
Lightroom carries the Photoshop brand name. It also provides extensive tools for managing large photo collections and improving the look of your photographs.

▲ Editing in full-screen mode gives a lot more room for manoeuvre, with tools hidden off the bottom of the screen until needed.

INTERFACE

1 Flag photos if you want to reorganise them into a new event (Events > Create Event From Flagged Photos) or to keep track of shots that need work – such as colour correction – before they're usable. Flag a photo by selecting it and choose Photos > Flag Photo.

2 Items deleted from the library aren't really gone for good. iPhoto has its own trash can, and photos sit here until you either restore them to the library or select Empty Trash Can on iPhoto's application menu.

3 Events display a range of dates during which photos were taken, and a count of how many photos are visible and hidden. Hide and show their contents by clicking on the triangle next to their names. Change the size of thumbnails by dragging the slider at the bottom right.

4 Photos belong to one event, but can appear in as many albums as you choose. This button adds an album. Hold Alt while pressing the button to create a Smart Album that uses keywords, ratings and other information to gather photos, such as your favourite ones.

5 This group of buttons lets you create a web gallery or email selected photos. Choose the quality at which they're sent; print photos with optional titles, borders and other presentation features; and order prints of your photos through the online Kodak Print Service.

6 Click on the magnifying glass next to the search box to choose whether to search on photos' dates, keywords or ratings, or all data including event and photo names. Just type in the box and the photos shown are updated to only those matching your criteria.

Creating a private MobileMe web gallery

▲ **STEP 01 IMPORTING PHOTOS** Save people downloading large email attachments with a password-protected gallery on MobileMe. Friends and family can upload their own photos using a browser or email. If you haven't already done so, import some photos into iPhoto, and make any necessary corrections such as red-eye removal, blemishes and colour enhancements.

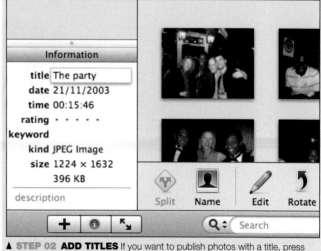

▲ **STEP 02 ADD TITLES** If you want to publish photos with a title, press the information button at the bottom left to show a panel where the title can be changed. Select View > Titles to preview them in the library and check for mistakes before uploading. Once you've selected the photos to upload, press the MobileMe button; in future, you'll email photos to the gallery.

▲ **STEP 03 ADD A PASSWORD** Protect your site by adding a password. Click on the first option to choose who can view the album: Everyone or Only me. Select Edit Names and Passwords, then the + button and enter a new username and password; these are needed to view the web page and the RSS feed. Go back to the first page and choose the new user.

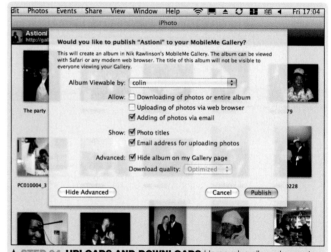

▲ **STEP 04 UPLOADS AND DOWNLOADS** Here we've allowed users to upload via email. Since visitors need a username and password, there's no harm publishing the email address on the page itself. Check the relevant box under advanced settings then click on the Publish button. Keep an eye on the progress indicator shown next to the gallery name.

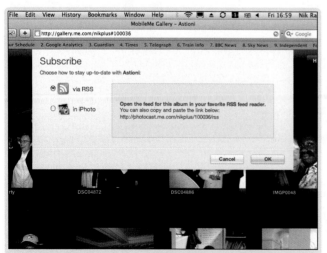

▲ **STEP 05 VIEW IN A WEB BROWSER** Select your web gallery in iPhoto's left pane. Near the top of the window is the gallery's address and email address for uploads. Click on the address to visit the page. Above the photos are links to upload photos and to subscribe to the photo feed. Viewing options below the photos include the trendy Cover Flow-like carousel.

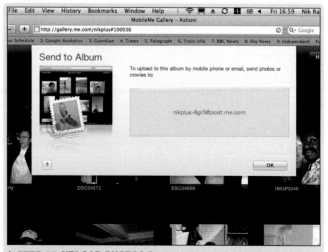

▲ **STEP 06 UPLOAD PHOTOS** Email people to let them know about the gallery. As well as the address, don't forget to supply the username and password, and tell them how to upload by email. All they have to do is create a regular email and attach a photo. MobileMe creates photo titles from the subject header, so it's best to upload just one photo per email.

Publishing a calendar

▲ STEP 01 **CREATE A CALENDAR** Select some photos in the library, then press the Calendar button in the toolbar and choose a style for it. Calendars can be between 12 and 24 months. National holidays can be added along with birthdays from Address Book and iCal calendars. Turn these off for now as we'll concentrate on the look of the calendar before personalising it.

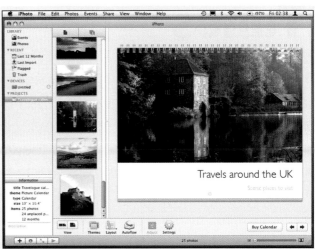

▲ STEP 02 **ADD PHOTOS** A pane containing your photos is shown alongside the calendar's cover page. Drag a photo to the placeholder on the cover. Click on the photo on the page to display a toolbar. The slider zooms in and out, and the hand repositions the photo within its frame. If you run out of photos to use, drag more from the library onto the project in the left pane.

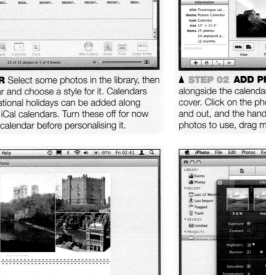

▲ STEP 03 **CHANGE PAGE LAYOUTS** Add photos to the rest of your calendar. Press the layout button to choose a different page style. Some have a second version with space for a caption. Don't worry if your photos don't match the orientation of boxes; iPhoto tries to rearrange them. Photos are also easily swapped between placeholders just by dragging one to another box.

▲ STEP 04 **ADJUST PHOTOS** Beware of double-clicking a photo on the page, which edits the original in the library. Press the Adjust button to show a panel for changing saturation and other settings. Changes made here affect only the instance on the page. Keep an eye open for alert icons on photos. Those photos are low resolution and may not print well at the size chosen.

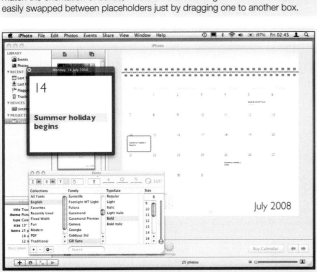

▲ STEP 05 **PERSONALISE DATES** Switch the page view to a single page instead of a full spread, then to a calendar page. Add iCal calendars, holidays and birthdays through the Settings button, or add information directly by clicking on a date. If you want to highlight some events, select their text and press Command-t to show the fonts palette to customise colours and more.

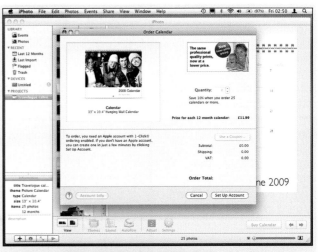

▲ STEP 06 **BUY OR PRINT A CALENDAR** The Buy Calendar button purchases professionally printed copies of your calendar, photobook and card projects. Proofread your project first to avoid any embarrassment. iPhoto doesn't let you do this in full-screen mode. For a bit more room, select File > Print and save to a PDF file and open it in the more streamlined Preview.

iTunes

The iPod is undoubtedly a work of engineering genius that has made Apple a household name, but its success owes plenty to iTunes, which is an integral part of the experience. A digital music library means no more searching through a stack of CDs, just type in its name to find the track you want. Rediscover long-forgotten classics using Smart Playlists and Party Shuffle. Abandon physical music altogether in favour of the iTunes Store, where you can pick up tracks for 79p each.

iTunes is far and away the best known iLife application. Apple released a Windows version a few years ago for iPod users on that platform and as a taster of the Mac experience. In unison, the iPod and iTunes have drawn some people to switch from Windows. Anyone doing so will be relieved to know that iTunes has the same look and feel on the Mac as it does on Windows. The majority of features on iTunes, such as ripping CDs, buying music from the iTunes Store and transferring music to an iPod, all work in the same way.

However, you may already have a large iTunes library on a PC. Our first workthrough shows you how to transfer it to the Mac using an external hard disk. There are also some essential tips on ripping CDs and browsing the library for absolute beginners. Adding genres, ratings and other details to tracks in the library lets you harness the power of Smart Playlists to find your least or most popular music, and automatically create mix CDs for long car journeys.

That's just the surface of iTunes; it's more than just a music library. Our second workthrough demonstrates the power of playlists. You'd be forgiven for thinking that they're just a convenient way to make your own compilations. iTunes can do more than just play their contents thanks to a nifty feature called an iMix.

By the end of this article you'll know how to share playlists with other music lovers by using the iTunes Store's handy iMix feature to publicise your favourite tracks. iMixes can be published on the iTunes Store for everybody to see, and they're easily added to a website, complete with links back to the store, so that others can preview the tracks and purchase them.

Publishing iMixes as a widget on a website or as an RSS feed is much more exciting for visitors than a static page that talks about your favourite tracks of all time. iMixes are dynamic; even after a playlist has been published to the iTunes Store, its contents can be updated and republished. If you're a .Mac subscriber, put an iMix on a blog entry to encourage visitors to discuss your selection, making for a much richer website with two-way interaction. These two dynamic features will keep visitors flocking to your website as they'll feel involved.

Music is the perfect subject matter to make your website a hub of interesting conversation. After all, who doesn't have an opinion about music?

ALSO CONSIDER...

LAST.FM
last.fm
This social network is for dedicated music fans. The free software publishes your listening habits to your profile. It's all about bringing together people with similar tastes, and it's a great way to learn about new artists and bands.

EYETV
elgato.com
The iTunes Store has a limited range of TV shows. Get an EyeTV digital tuner to watch TV on your Mac. The accompanying software also puts shows on your iPod.

▲ The iTunes Store offers over 6 million songs and thousands of podcasts, audiobooks and TV shows from the likes of the BBC.

INTERFACE

1 The Library is divided into several categories. Unless you own an iPhone, ringtones are irrelevant. Likewise, iPod Games won't be of interest to everybody. Open iTunes preferences and you'll find options to show or hide categories under the general settings.

2 After signing up for an account, you can purchase music from the store. Purchases are made with a single click, or you can switch to a shopping cart system in preferences pane. The Store can also be disabled under the parental controls settings.

3 Regular playlists (shown with a blue icon) are a good way to make your own compilations, while smart playlists (with purple icons) offer a refined version of Party Shuffle to help you become re-acquainted with long-forgotten friends.

4 In List and Album views, the button marked with an eye shows and hides three columns: Genre, Artist and Album. With a well-categorised music library, these columns make it very easy to find music to match your mood. The other button here simply ejects a CD, if one is present.

5 The view buttons switch between a long list, tracks grouped by album and Cover Flow. Clicking on these buttons changes the area below the view. Here Cover Flow is shown, whereas the other two views would show columns for selecting Genre, Artist and Album.

6 The search box works like any other in Mac OS X. Clicking the magnifying glass lets you search by album, artist, composer, song or everything. Just click in the box and type what you're looking for. The areas below immediately changes to show only matching tracks.

▲ **STEP 01 TRANSFER YOUR PC'S LIBRARY** Use an external hard disk to transfer an iTunes library from a PC. Ensure there's enough free space (library size is shown in the status bar) then create a new folder. Select Edit > Preferences then Advanced > General. Set the library location to the new folder then press OK. Select Advanced > Consolidate Library to gather all items.

▲ **STEP 02 IMPORT ON THE MAC** Disconnect the hard disk from the PC and connect it to the Mac. When it appears on the Mac's desktop, open iTunes and make sure the option to copy imported files to the library is enabled (Preferences > Advanced > General) then choose File > Add to Library and point at the folder on the external disk. Wait while the library is imported.

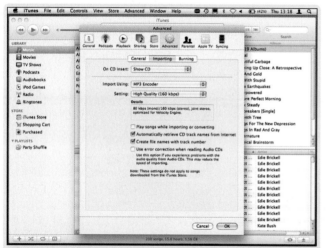

▲ **STEP 03 CHANGE IMPORT SETTINGS** Press Command-comma to open iTunes' preferences and select Advanced > Importing. AAC plays on iPods and some other devices, but MP3 plays on a wider range of non-Apple hardware. If yours has limited capacity, choose a lower quality like 128Kbit/sec to fit more tracks onto it, otherwise you can choose a higher quality.

▲ **STEP 04 RETRIEVE CD DETAILS** Insert an audio CD and it appears under Devices. iTunes will retrieve information about CDs from the Internet. This can be switched off in preferences under Advanced > Importing. Sometimes there will be several possible matches. If the wrong one is selected, choose Advanced > Get CD Track Names to try again, or enter them manually.

▲ **STEP 05 MANUALLY ENTER CD DETAILS** The cursor keys move between tracks and Enter on the keypad edits names and confirms changes. Press Command-a to select all tracks and Command-i to edit common information such as the album title. Save others the bother by selecting Advanced > Submit CD Track Names then press the Import CD button.

▲ **STEP 06 ADD ALBUM ART** In List and Album views, Command-b shows genre, artist and album columns. Columns on the right are affected by selections to their left. Select Advanced > Get Album Artwork to download artwork for the whole library. Copy artwork to the clipboard from a website, then edit the tracks, click the artwork field and press Command-v to paste it.

Softline

Premier Macintosh Distributor

Available from:

www.amazon.co.uk

 Apple Store
www.apple.com/ukstore

ATcomputers
www.atcomputers.co.uk

CANCOM
www.cancomuk.com

PLAY.COM
www.play.com

MICROLINK PC
www.microlinkpc.co.uk

iansyst
www.iansyst.co.uk

Western Computer - Bristol
Temple Gate
01179 225 661

Western Computer - Cheltenham
Beechwood Shopping Ctr
01242 234700

Scotsys - Glasgow
164 Great Western Rd
0845 606 2641

Albion Computers - London
112 The Strand
0207 212 9090

Apple Store - Birmingham
West Bullring Shopping Ctr
0121 260 1900

Apple Store - London
235 Regent St
020 7153 9000

Apple Store - Manchester
Arndale Ctr
0161 216 4570

Cancom - Brighton
110 Queens Rd
01273 748 083

Cancom - Cambridge
58 Regent St
0845 686 3300

Solutions Inc - Brighton & Hove
255 Old Shoreham Rd
0870 3898610

Scotsys - Edinburgh
95-97 Nicolson St
0845 606 2641

Square Group Ltd - London
78 New Oxford St
020 7692 9990

GBM - Manchester
One Piccadilly Gardens
0161 605 3838

Apple Store - Kent
Bluewater Shopping Ctr
01322 640100

Apple Store - London
Brent Cross Shopping Ctr
0208 359 1050

MacSpeech Dictate
Speech Recognition for Mac OS X
Better. Stronger. Faster.

New Version 1.5

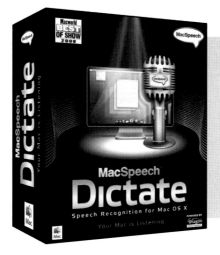

**Introducing MacSpeech Dictate 1.5.
Better accuracy. Stronger recognition.
Faster performance.**

**Premier speech recognition
for the Macintosh.**

£176.12 RRP INC VAT

MacSpeech Dictate provides a whole new way to interact with your Mac. Instead of typing, use your voice to input text; rather than clicking your mouse, just speak commands. With MacSpeech Dictate, it's easy.

FREE Headset*

MacSpeech Dictate includes a certified, noise-cancelling microphone headset. Or you can choose from other high-quality microphone options to suit your needs.

Amazing Accuracy
Right out of the box, MacSpeech Dictate will astonish you with its accuracy. You simply talk and leave the recognition to MacSpeech Dictate.

Built Especially For The Mac
Mac users expect only the best from the applications they use on their Macs. MacSpeech Dictate was built from the ground up to ensure the ultimate experience on Mac OS X.

* Plantronics DSP-400 headset included (Note: actual colour & design may vary)

Minimal Training Required
MacSpeech Dictate provides astounding accuracy and productivity. With just minutes of training, you'll be using MacSpeech Dictate's superior capabilities.

Essential Command Capabilities
Instead of using your mouse to select menu commands or your keyboard to type shortcuts, just speak a command. MacSpeech Dictate executes it for you. What could be easier?

Works With The Apps You Already Have
Microsoft Word, Adobe Photoshop, QuarkXPress, and more. And MacSpeech Dictate works great with Apple's applications as well, including iChat, Mail, iPhoto, and Keynote, among others.

Even Greater Recognition
MacSpeech Dictate boasts robust Phrase Training capabilities allowing it to learn as it goes based on your voice input. That means even greater accuracy that more fully integrates into your Macintosh experience.

System Requirements
Intel-based Mac, Mac OS X 10.5.6 or greater (Leopard)
Internet connection required for product registration.
MacSpeech-certified noise-cancelling microphone included with new purchase.

Visit www.softlineuk.com for more product information
All prices include VAT and correct at time of going to press. All images copyright of their respective owners. E&OE

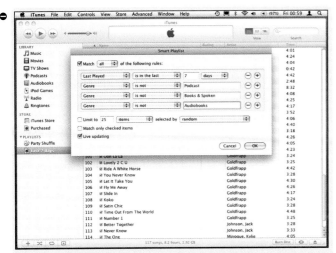

▲ **STEP 07 CREATE A SMART PLAYLIST** Press Alt-Command-n to create a smart playlist. Set the first rule to Last played is in the last and 7 days. Click on the + button at the end of the row to add a rule and choose Genre is not and type Podcast. Create additional rules to exclude the Books & Spoken and Audiobooks genres. The playlist shows songs played in the last week.

▲ **STEP 08 LIMIT THE PLAYLIST'S LENGTH** There's no limit on how many items our smart playlist contains. Ctrl-click it and edit it. Beneath the rules, you can limit the playlist using various criteria. Tick the adjacent box and set the options to 10 items selected by most often played. This short list of the most popular songs will look more presentable on a website.

▲ **STEP 09 PUBLISH AN iMIX** Playlists can be shared on the iTunes Store and a website. Sign into an iTunes Store account, then select File > Create an iMix. Enter a title and description. Tracks may be missing if track information doesn't accurately match an item in the store or it's unavailable. Click on Publish. An email confirmation will arrive when the iMix is available online.

▲ **STEP 10 SHARE ON THE WEB** Click on the arrow next to the playlist and choose View. At the store page, press Publish to the Web. On the web page, choose a size for the widget, select the code, and press Command-c to copy it to the clipboard. Make a blank page in iWeb. Select Web Widgets > HTML Snippet and paste the code into the floating toolbar. Click Apply to preview it.

▲ **STEP 11 SHARE BY RSS** Click on the arrow next to the playlist and click View again. Further down the page is an address to an RSS feed that can be read in Apple Mail. FeedDemon (newsgator.com) is a free reader for Windows. Email the address to your friends and they'll be able to preview and buy tracks from the iTunes Store, and they can always share their own iMixes too.

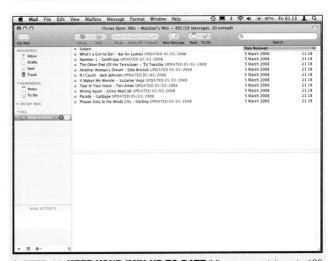

▲ **STEP 12 KEEP YOUR iMIX UP TO DATE** iMixes can contain up to 100 tracks and can be updated too. Add some new tracks to the playlist then click on the arrow next to it. Click Update in the window. Check the changes are okay, and click Update to submit them. The iMix takes a while to update, but the widget and feed update without intervention, keeping friends up-to-date.

iWeb

There's nothing quite like the thrill of seeing your own website live on the Internet. Technical jargon and difficult-to-use tools put many people off the idea, long before any pages have even been designed. iWeb takes away the pain of website creation by hiding technical details so that you can concentrate on the important details of designing a site and filling it with compelling content such as a blog, photo galleries and podcasts. Make your mark on the web without going through hours of frustration.

So you've already got a profile on a social networking site, and you're sharing photos in an online gallery. Maybe you already have a blog too, but have you got your own website that keeps all of this information in one place and makes it easy for everyone to keep up to date with all the interesting things that are happening in your life?

iWeb comes with a range of themes and page templates that help you to create an attractive website that visitors will want to keep coming back to over and over again. The tools it provides genuinely make a pleasure of adding new information to your site because you can rest assured that iWeb is taking care of the technical side of things in the background. Of course, you're not limited to the existing page layouts. It's possible to create your own and add text and photos and arrange them however you want.

Subscribers to Apple's .Mac service get a few extra features, such as a searchable blog and the ability to make private pages that are protected by passwords. But you don't have to subscribe to .Mac to benefit from the really important features that will impress visitors, such as beautiful photo galleries that look and feel like a professional website, rather than something that looks and feels outdated.

Our workthrough covers building all of the essential types of page. You'll see why iWeb is the ideal application for building your first website and you'll want to keep using it because it's such a doddle. Integration with other iLife applications makes it easy to add photos to a page using drag and drop, then crop and adjust them to fit the website using simple techniques that don't require you to jump back and forth between applications.

Although it buries technical details out of sight, don't think iWeb is too limited. We'll also show you how to use widgets – HTML code – from sites such as Google Maps and last.fm to integrate compelling web applications into your site. If you're concerned that no one will visit your site then send your friends a link to it. They can subscribe to your RSS feed, which iWeb also builds on your behalf – so Apple Mail users (and other RSS readers) are kept informed every time you update the website.

ALSO CONSIDER...

FREEWAY 5
softpress.com
Softpress's website software lets designers ignore the code behind their site. The latest version makes it easier than ever to add Web 2.0 effects and menus to a site.

RAPIDWEAVER
realmacsoftware.com
RapidWeaver has all the benefits of iWeb including a selection of themes. It's ideal for anyone that wants to learn about professional web development.

◀ The Inspector contains a lot of tweaks for your website's appearance. You can set how many blog postings are shown before they're archived, add links to other websites, and control what can be downloaded from your online photo galleries.

▼ To add photos to a page, just drag them from the Media Browser. Enter keywords, ratings or other information stored in iPhoto into the search box. The browser makes it easy to find exactly the right photograph.

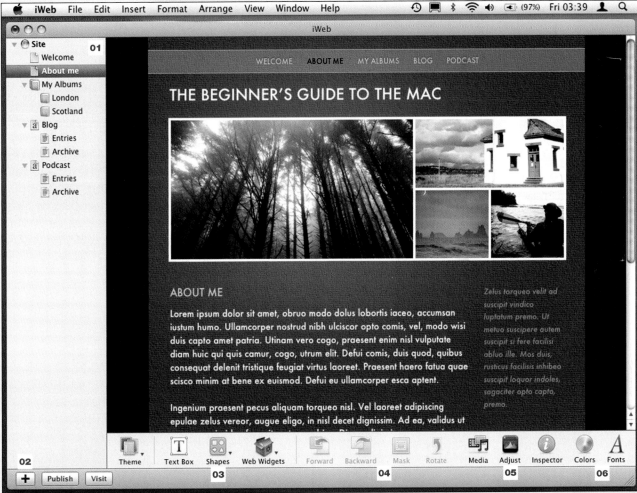

INTERFACE

1 The left-hand pane shows your website's structure. Pages that haven't yet been published to the web appear in red, while blue pages have already been published to the web. Cream pages – like the blog and podcast archive – are automatically kept up-to-date by iWeb.

2 Press the + button to add a new page to your website. A panel displays the available themes and page templates. The page's placement in the left-hand pane is reflected in the site's navigation bar. Click and drag a page in the list to change its order in the bar as well.

3 As well as adding photos by dragging them from the Media Browser, you can add shapes and boxes for text by clicking these buttons. Add other interesting elements to the page, like Google Maps, Google Adsense and HTML snippets (also called widgets) from other websites.

4 Objects on the page can overlap, so use the Forward and Backward buttons to choose the order in which they're stacked. Photos appear without a mask when they're dropped onto the page, so click on the Mask button and edit the mask to show only part of the photo.

5 The Adjust button lets you tweak a photo's appearance on the page. It provides the same controls as iPhoto, allowing you to adjust exposure, contrast and other factors. This lets you tweak images so they fit with the tone of your page. Changes made within iWeb only affect the photo on the page, not the original.

6 The Colors and Fonts buttons bring up the standard Mac OS X dialog boxes for controlling the appearance of text. Although you can use any font on your Mac, other people won't see them unless they have they are installed on their computer too.

▲ **STEP 01 CREATE A PAGE** Open iWeb and choose the Darkroom theme, then create a Welcome page. It's automatically added to the navigation bar, which appears throughout the site. Double-click page names on the left to rename them there and in the bar. Open the Inspector (Alt-Command-i). Pages can be excluded from the bar and it can be turned off too.

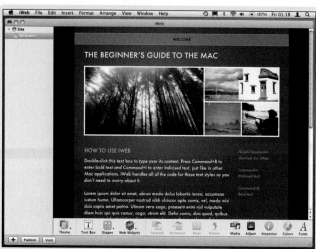

▲ **STEP 02 CHANGE TEXT** Click once on text to resize and move its box on the page. Click again to edit the text. Press Command-b and Command-i to add bold or italicised text, respectively. If you've prepared text in another application, Edit > Paste and Match Style keeps the template's style. iWeb creates the code behind the site. Replace all of the text on this page.

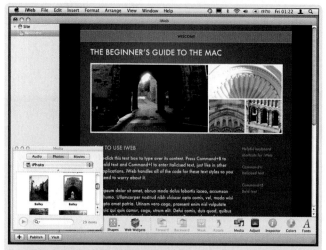

▲ **STEP 03 ADD AND REPLACE IMAGES** Select View > Show Media Browser to use media from other iLife applications. Go to the photos tab to see your iPhoto library, which can be searched using keywords, ratings and other information. Drag a photo to the page to add it, or onto a placeholder to replace its contents. Add some of your photos to the boxes on the page.

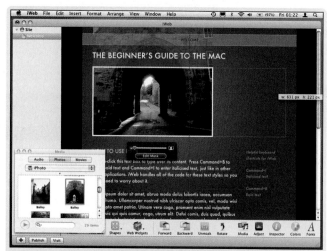

▲ **STEP 04 CHANGE SIZE AND POSITION** Delete all but the largest placeholder. Drag a photo from the media browser onto it. To better fit the page's width, click on the placeholder and select Edit Mask on the toolbar. Drag its right handle until a blue line cuts through vertically. On the toolbar, drag the slider to resize the photo. Click and drag it to reposition within the frame.

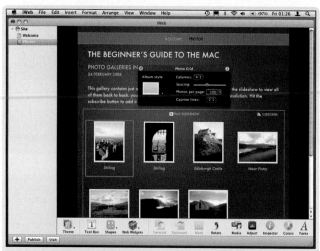

▲ **STEP 05 CREATE A GALLERY** Select File > New Page and create a Photos page. Replace its text and drag photos to the grid. Click it to customise the thumbnail size, number of columns and more. The floating toolbar's 'i' button shows the Inspector, which lets you choose whether downloads are allowed, publish an RSS feed and, for .Mac subscribers only, invite comments.

▲ **STEP 06 CREATE AN ALBUM** Add a new page and select the My Albums template. In the left-hand pane, drag the gallery inside the album. Click on the albums grid and the toolbar again lets you tweak the layout. Create and drag more photo galleries into the album. Change their names on the left and they change in the album too. Drag galleries in the grid to reorder them.

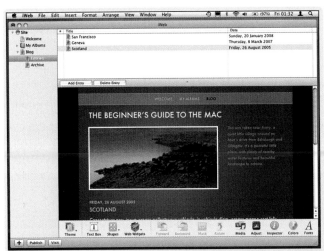

▲ **STEP 07 ADD A BLOG** Add a blog page this time. Three pages are added to the site: the blog summary and Entries and Archive pages. On the entries page, a list of them appears at the top of the window. Double-click a title or date to change it, which allows entries to be written retrospectively. Replace the entry's text and images, then add more entries and do the same.

▲ **STEP 08 CHANGE THE BLOG SUMMARY** Select the main blog page. Change the text and photo at the top of the page, then click on the list of blog entries below. A toolbar appears, as in the photo gallery. Open the Inspector and select the RSS button. Choose how many excerpts appear – between five and 10 is reasonable. Older entries will be available through the archive link.

▲ **STEP 09 ADD GOOGLE MAPS** Add a Google Map to blog entries that talk about places. Create a new blog entry, click on the main text box and make it narrower. Click on Web Widgets and select Google Map. When it appears on the page, click and resize it. Enter a location in the address bubble and hit apply. The location shown will appear when someone visits the page.

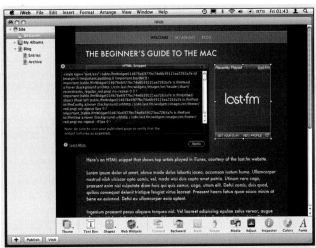

▲ **STEP 10 ADD HTML SNIPPETS** The iTunes workthrough shows how to add iMixes from the iTunes Store. HTML snippets aren't limited to Apple's own services though. Widgets (HTML code) can be used to embed video from YouTube or use a site like *last.fm* to show what you've just listened to in iTunes. Here we've added one that shows our most played artists.

▲ **STEP 11 VIDEO PODCASTS** Add a podcast page; it's structured like a blog. Edit a movie in iMovie and share it in the Media Browser. In iWeb, drag it onto the entry's placeholder. In the Inspector, choose RSS then Podcast to set details of the series or individual episode. Podcasts can be submitted to the iTunes Store from the File menu, though they are reviewed before going live.

▲ **STEP 12 PUBLISH YOUR SITE** .Mac subscribers only need to select File > Publish to .Mac to upload a page. For other website hosts, use the Publish to a Folder option and save to your hard disk. Your hosting company will provide details of how to connect and upload to their server. Many use FTP (File Transfer Protocol) and you just need to drop the files onto the server.

iMovie

iMovie is a great application for editing movies, whether they've been recorded on a DV camera, the iSight camera built into some Macs, or one of the new generation of AVCHD video cameras. It handles the technical side of video while you concentrate on the creative part. It's much simpler to use than professional applications, but don't be fooled into thinking that equates to poor results. With a little effort, you'll be able to publish superb video podcasts and DVDs that are far from amateurish.

iMovie 09 is a radical departure from earlier versions and more traditional video editing tools. Its interface is less tricky for non-professionals to master, and all of the essential tools for producing video podcasts and movies for the web and DVD are provided. However, you'll need to know exactly where to look to get the most out of the many useful tools in order to produce stylish and impressive movies.

The baggage of professional applications is stripped away, leaving a clear view of your projects. Video, audio and other elements on the timeline are colour coded in a single timeline that is always uncluttered and easy to understand at a glance.

When it comes to finding footage, just roll the mouse cursor over a video and a preview is continuously updated in the viewer; it's much faster than dragging a playhead around a timeline. This interface was first introduced in iMovie 08 and proved controversial for some existing users of previous editions of iMovie, but rest assured that they are intended to make life much easier for you. You can get great results from iMovie 09 as it brings back some important features, such as DVD chapters and advanced audio editing, that were missing from the previous version.

Our workthrough shows you how to add footage to the timeline and put together a cut of your movie. Most movies include titles of some sort, so you'll also find out how to add them to your project. They're essential for documentaries, podcasts and any movie that needs end credits. Apple provides a solid list of common titles that can be customised with different font styles to suit the movie's subject matter. Along with transitions, they're key to making an eye-catching production.

On the audio side, there are plenty of options. iLife's Media Browser gives access to music from GarageBand, allowing budding musicians to build their own score. There's also a library of sound effects in the iLife and iMovie effects libraries and, most excitingly, there's the opportunity to follow in the footsteps of all good documentary makers by recording a voiceover. Again, iMovie's simplicity betrays excellent features that mimic professional productions, like the ability to lower background audio while your spoken commentary plays.

You'll also find out how to add Ken Burns-style effects to still images. It's a treatment that you'll have seen countless times before in documentaries because it adds a subtle but effective motion to otherwise static photos to keep the viewer's interest, typically with a voiceover playing on top. It's an essential technique whether your project is a fully-fledged documentary or a simple commentary about holiday snaps.

iMovie is also great for creating DVDs complete with chapter markers. It's well worth the effort of adding them because the final result will look far from amateurish. When people receive your DVD, they'll be impressed by your film-making and DVD-authoring skills, and they're unlikely to guess that it was produced with software that came free with your Mac.

▲ The Video Adjustments panel contains controls for adjusting the look of a video clip. So if your video is underexposed, press 'v' to call up the panel and try to improve the situation.

ALSO CONSIDER...

FINAL CUT EXPRESS
apple.com/finalcutexpress
Final Cut Express is a trimmed-down version of Final Cut Pro. At £126, it still includes more than 200 transitions, titles and effects. That's enough creative potential to satisfy aspiring film makers.

FINAL CUT STUDIO
apple.com/finalcutstudio
After mastering Final Cut Express, move up to Final Cut Studio. Alongside the renowned Final Cut Pro, it includes other professional applications including DVD Studio Pro to replace iDVD, and Motion for creating stunning graphical effects.

PREMIERE PRO CS4
adobe.com/premiere
Premiere Pro isn't just the basic editing application. It also includes Encore DVD for DVD and Blu-ray authoring. It's a strong rival to Final Cut Pro's throne as the king of video applications.

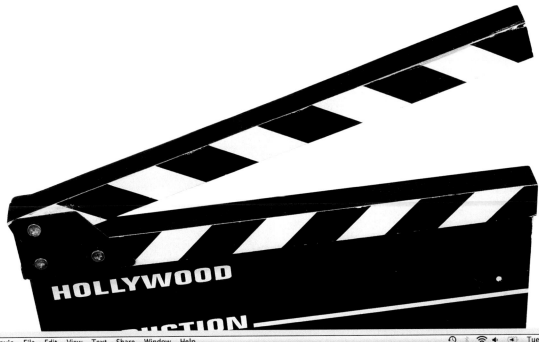

INTERFACE

1 This button switches the position of the Project and Events libraries. Give yourself more editing space by placing the Project Library on the bottom half of the window. Use shortcuts (Command and a number from 1 to 4) show and hide the Media Browser, titles and transitions panels so they don't get in the way too.

2 The Events Library shows footage that has already been imported from a camera onto your Mac. Portions of this footage can be selected in the timeline on the right. Click and drag several pieces of footage to assemble a cut of your movie.

3 With a selection made in the Event Library, these three buttons let you mark a clip as a favourite, mark a piece of video as a reject, and clear videos of marks. At the bottom of the library, you can then choose which videos you want to show. Like iPhoto's ratings, it lets you find the footage you're looking for more quickly.

4 The Project Library holds multiple projects, each with its own timeline for combining video, audio, titles and transitions into a movie. Projects can be organised into folders (File > New Folder). The button at the bottom left hides the list of projects, giving even more editing space.

5 The viewer shows a preview of your video, including titles, transitions and video adjustments. Hold down the Command key and 8, 9 and 0 to change its size. At its smallest size, it lends more space to editing your project.

6 These three buttons call up essential tools for polishing the look and sound of your movie. The first calls up the voiceover recording panel; the second crops video in the view; and the other one let you adjust various aspects of the audio and video in the Inspector.

▲ **STEP 01 IMPORTING VIDEO** Create a new project and choose the aspect ratio that matches your material – iMovie's help file details how to capture from specific types of camera, such as DVD, hard disk and DV tape. During import, you can add clips to one or more events. Footage already added to a project's timeline has an orange bar along its bottom.

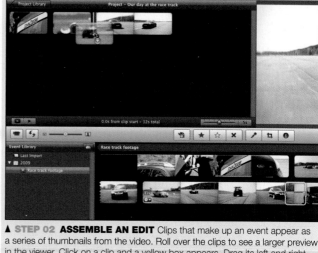

▲ **STEP 02 ASSEMBLE AN EDIT** Clips that make up an event appear as a series of thumbnails from the video. Roll over the clips to see a larger preview in the viewer. Click on a clip and a yellow box appears. Drag its left and right edges to set in and out points. Click inside the box and drag to the timeline to add it. Keep adding clips until you've assembled a rough edit.

▲ **STEP 03 TRIM CLIPS**
To trim a clip on the timeline, roll over it and press the cog icon that appears on top of the clip. The Clip Trimmer appears below; drag the left and right handles of the yellow box to trim. Allow some footage either side for use in transitions. If you trim too much, just drag outwards to reinstate footage.

▲ **STEP 04 ADD TRANSITIONS**
Press Command-4 to show transitions. Drag one between two clips; a green bar shows where it'll be inserted. Once placed, double-click it to see the Inspector, where you can change its duration. Just drag another transition on top to experiment with styles. The duration will remain unchanged.

▲ **STEP 05 ADD TITLES**
Press Command-3 to show title styles. Drag one on top of a clip to superimpose it, or between them to set a title slate with a choice of backgrounds. Just click text in the viewer to change it, and click on Show Fonts to choose from preset styles, or to access the System Font Panel for full control.

▲ **STEP 06 TITLE DURATIONS**
Titles are show as a blue bar in the timeline. Their duration is changed by rolling over the left and right edges and dragging them. Click and drag on the middle to adjust where the title's position. Overlap a title between clips or a transition to produce subtle fades, whose duration can be adjusted in the Inspector.

▲ **STEP 07 ADD MUSIC**
Press Command-1 to browse iLife's sound library. Drag and drop music tracks at the edge of the timeline to set a soundtrack, shown as a green box around your clips. Ctrl-click it and choose Arrange Music Tracks to reorder them. Add sound effects by dropping them on top of clips and dragging to position them.

▲ **STEP 08 KEN BURNS EFFECTS**
Press Command-2 to see your iPhoto library. Drag a photo into your project, then select it and click the Crop button in the toolbar. Green and red boxes indicate the start and end points of the motion, which you can reposition. Press play at the top right to preview it and, when you're happy, press Done.

▲ **STEP 09 VOICEOVERS** The microphone button shows the Voiceover panel for recording a commentary. Select your Mac's built-in microphone (or an external one) and run some tests to tweak volume and noise reduction levels. Wear headphones if you need to refer to existing audio. Click where you want to record audio; iMovie counts down. Click away from the clip to finish.

▲ **STEP 10 EDIT AUDIO** Voiceovers appear in the project as purple bars. Close the Voiceover window then click on the purple bar. Drag and trim it in just the same way as for titles. Press 'a' to show the Audio Adjustments panel, where other audio can be ducked (lowered) while the voiceover plays and reduce the distraction. Fade audio in and out for smoother results.

▲ **STEP 11 MAP TRANSITIONS**
Press Command-5 for iMovie's map transitions. Drag one into your project and use the Inspector to set start and end positions of a journey. The animation is automatically generated. Names on the map can be changed, and you can add locations using decimal coordinates. Maps can be cropped to zoom in.

▲ **STEP 12 ADD DVD CHAPTERS**
To add DVD chapter markers, turn on the advanced tools (iMovie > Preferences > General). Marker controls appear at the top right of the timeline. Drag the orange one (on the right) to add a chapter wherever you drop it. Click on the chapter number to replace it with a more meaningful name.

iDVD

You've already created a masterpiece with iMovie and posted it on the Internet so that family and friends around the globe can enjoy it. However, a physical gift will be much more appreciated, and this is where iDVD comes in to action by helping you to make a professional, slick-looking disc that your loved ones can play in their living room DVD player. iDVD gives you all the essential tools to make DVDs that feature chapters, extras, menus and photographic slideshows.

iDVD is the perfect companion to iMovie, so it comes as no surprise that they are both part of the iLife suite. Publishing movies on DVD allows your friends and family to enjoy them in stunning quality on their television in their living room, rather than huddling around a computer to watch them online.

There's a huge selection of menu themes bundled with the application. Apple has built this collection with each release of iDVD over the years so that you have dozens of stylish designs at your fingertips. Many of them are customisable by dropping photos and videos into drop zones to tailor the menu's appearance to your content. Some of the more recent templates include motion graphics that create a subtle mood for themes like wedding discs.

Adding content to a disc couldn't be easier. Once you've prepared a movie in iMovie, open the Media Browser and drag it onto a menu to add a button. iDVD automatically links everything together. Photos from iPhoto or Aperture can be made into slideshows in the same manner, and menus are enhanced by adding music and ambient sounds from GarageBand, which is also part of the iLife suite.

DVDs are much more personalised gifts for friends and family. If your website goes down or if they don't have access to the Internet, they'll be unable to view your movies, while a DVD is always to hand when the recipient wants to look back at happy memories. A physical disc elicits a better reaction.

Best of all, making discs doesn't require hours of painful, intensive work to get brilliant results. That's because iDVD uses the Media Browser to make it easy to gather media from other iLife applications.

Follow our workthrough to learn the basics of adding menus and movies. It also covers the advanced features like adding slideshows and photo galleries, and adding other files to the disc, such as high resolution copies of photos.

Authoring a professional DVD isn't just about flash menu graphics, though. That's why we've also covered a few essential tips that will save you the hassle of burning duff DVDs. By the end of this workthrough, you'll know how to make good use of the huge capacity of space available on a DVD. Despite it being free with every Mac, iDVD still makes the most of the format to produce brilliant results.

ALSO CONSIDER...

DVD STUDIO PRO 4
apple.com/dvdstudiopro
It's only available as part of Final Cut Studio 2, but DVD Studio Pro provides access to the full range of DVD authoring features. The advanced scripting capabilities can take some mastering, but they're ideal for making complex DVDs like interactive quizzes.

ENCORE DVD
adobe.com/encore
Adobe gets one up on the competition by providing DVD and Blu-ray authoring. Although burners and blank discs are expensive, more movies can be placed on a single disc.

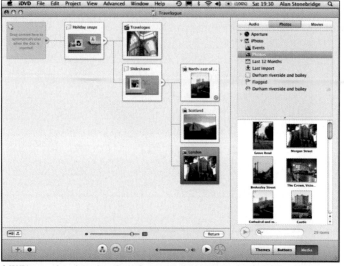

▲ iDVD's map view shows how the various parts of your DVD are linked together. If you want a movie to play as soon as the disc is inserted, switch to this view and drag it to the first box. Drag the slider beneath the map to shrink the boxes and see more of your disc's structure.

▼ The Project Info window (Command-Shift-i) shows a breakdown of space on your DVD. By default, iDVD encodes movies in the background as you work. You can check how it's progressing here.

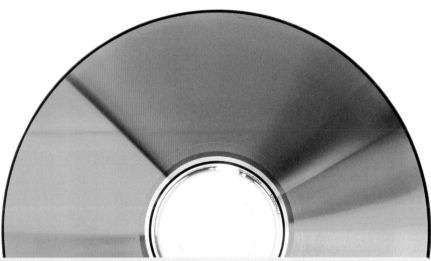

INTERFACE

1 The largest area of iDVD's window shows your DVD menu in all its glory, with menu effects like reflections and motion graphics conveniently animated without the need to burn to a disc. Press the loop button beneath it to preview the menu.

2 Use this to reveal the floating Inspector window. Its contents change depending on what is currently selected. For buttons, it shows font options. Click on a menu background to change its duration, background audio and the colour of button highlights.

3 The DVD map is a tree-like overview of the DVD's structure. It shows how all of your menus, movies and slideshows are linked together. You can see where work is needed as broken links are highlighted with a clear alert symbol.

4 The play button takes you to a live preview of your project, as it will appear on a disc. Details like transitions aren't visible in iDVD's editor, so use this to check that they're correctly set and that you're happy with their appearance before burning a disc.

5 The right column in iDVD provides a wide range of menu themes and button designs. It also encapsulates the Media Browser so that you can gather photos, music and movies from other iLife applications.

6 Click on the burn button when you're ready to write your disc. iDVD checks for problems with your project, such as unlinked buttons on menus. That saves on the unnecessary waste of burning a disc only to discover that a simple mistake means redoing the work.

▲ **STEP 01 CREATE A NEW PROJECT** Create a project and choose the aspect ratio that matches your footage. Open iDVD's preferences found under iDVD in the menubar and ensure the video mode matches your camera (Pal for the UK). Changing this setting requires you to create a new project – TVs in some countries use NTSC. Your disc will play on computers worldwide.

▲ **STEP 02 CHOOSE A THEME** The column on the right will already show DVD themes. Each consists of main menu, a chapters menu and an extras menu. You don't have to add the latter two but the main menu always exists. From the list at the top of the window, we've chosen 5.0 Themes and then Travel Cards.

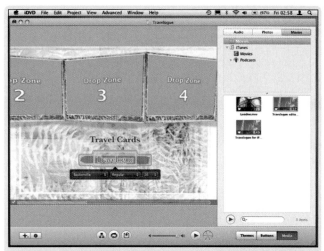

▲ **STEP 03 ADD A MOVIE** iDVD's media browser is integrated into the main window. Press the media button and find a movie you've prepared in iMovie, then drag it onto the menu. iDVD creates a button and links it to the movie. Click on the button and open the Inspector to change font settings; don't use thin ones as they will flicker on a TV. Click again to edit the text.

▲ **STEP 04 FILLING DROP ZONES** Click on the Edit Drop Zones (the box with an arrow pointing inside it) button to see all the Drop Zones. Drag some photos into a box beneath the menu to set a drop zone's content. Click on the box to see the drop zone in the animated menu. Open the Inspector, then click on menu background to change options like duration.

▲ **STEP 05 CHANGE A MENU'S AUDIO** Prepare some music or record a voiceover in GarageBand, then select Share > Send Song to iTunes. In iDVD, select Media then Audio and locate the track. Open the menu's Inspector by clicking on the 'i' button and drag the track to the audio box. When making audio, take into account the menu's duration, as audio will stop briefly when it loops.

▲ **STEP 06 ADD A SLIDESHOW** Select two photos in the media browser and drag them to the menu. The new button links to a slideshow. Double-click it to add more photos or movies. Drag items up and down the list to reorder them. Set a uniform duration at the bottom of the window; five seconds is a good starting point. Fade Through Black is one of the more tasteful transitions.

▲ **STEP 07 ADD AUDIO TO YOUR SLIDESHOW** Drag an audio track from the media browser onto the speaker icon beneath your slideshow. The slideshow's duration is adjusted to match the audio. Press the play button to check the pace of the slideshow and the music. If it's not right, just drag the track out of the box or drag another one into the box to replace the existing track.

▲ **STEP 08 ADVANCED SETTINGS** Click on the Settings button. You can add copies of original photos to the disc, so recipients can print a high resolution copy. Choose whether to loop the slideshow indefinitely, and include photo titles and comments. Adding navigation arrows gives manual control of the slideshow; don't use them with a soundtrack as this will skip when moving between photos.

▲ **STEP 09 ADD OTHER FILES** The Advanced menu has an option to add other files to the disc. Slideshow photos shown here can only be removed in the slideshow's settings. In iMovie, prepare an iPod version of your movie (Share > Export Movie) to include on the disc. It's easier to gather files and folders in the Finder than adding folders here and adding the files individually.

▲ **STEP 10 PREPARE MENUS FOR TV** DVD menus are visible all the way to the edge on a computer, but TV sets cut off the border. All text on a menu needs to fall within the TV safe area. On the View menu, turn off the crop area option, then turn on the TV safe area. The grey area outside the red line is likely to be cut off on a TV set. Move all text inside this area on all of your menus.

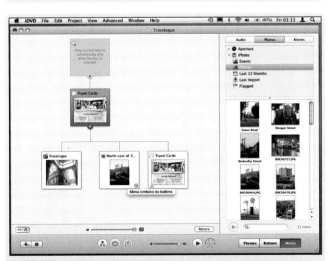

▲ **STEP 11 CHECK FOR ERRORS** Switch to the Map view. If any alert icons are shown in the map, roll over them to see what the problem is. It could be an empty slideshow or empty drop zones on a menu. iDVD will also warn you if a button on a menu isn't linked to anything. Menus also need at least one button. Fix these issues before attempting to burn a disc.

▲ **STEP 12 BURN A DISC** To burn multiple copies of a DVD, choose File > Save as Disc Image. Wait a while for iDVD to compile the DVD. When it's finished, browse to Applications/Utilities and open Disk Utility. Drag the disc image into the pane on the left. Click on the image in the pane and press the Burn button. Once it's done, press the Burn button again to make another copy.

iWork

You don't need to spend a fortune to buy an office suite for the Mac. Apple's excellent iWork family comprises a word processor, spreadsheet and presentation application, which are called, respectively, Pages, Numbers and Keynote.

They boast excellent compatibility with Microsoft Office, the leading suite on both the Mac and PC, and go further than the de facto choice in many areas by enhancing its layout tools to greatly simplify the task of creating attractive, effective documents.

Over the next 20 pages, we'll walk you through each application in the suite, and show you how you can step beyond the basics to produce persuasive output that will really impress.

Pages	074
Numbers	078
Keynote	082

Pages

On every new Mac you'll find a copy of iWork, and part of that is Pages, Apple's word processor. It replaces the much-admired equivalent in Apple Works, but expands greatly on its feature set to offer basic page layout tools. They may not rival the kind of software used to design newspapers and magazines, but for home users who need to knock up a quick birthday card, poster or invitation they are both flexible and easy to use. We take a look at Pages' key features and show you how to use its styling tools.

Pages is Apple's word processor. It's not quite a full replacement for Microsoft Word on the PC, but the two do share many common features, such as the ability to track changes, check your spelling and format documents. However, while Pages may be lacking some key Word features – and by default uses its own file format – it boats some impressive features that put it ahead of its competitor, such as a desktop publishing (DTP) style layout mode that performs many of the same tasks as Microsoft Publisher.

Pages looks and works very much like an application from iLife. A large, simple toolbar at the top of the interface gives you access to its most common features, and an Inspector palette (accessed by clicking the blue 'i' on the right) lets you make changes to your document and pull in resources from iPhoto, iTunes and so on.

It is a highly organised application, which works on the basis of applied styles. Styles are collections of attributes, such as text colour and size, font, alignment, spacing and so on. While you can change each of these individually – you can pick a new font using the drop-down menu on the toolbar, for example – it is much more efficient to either tweak the editing styles or define new ones of your own.

You can see this in practice by opening a new Pages document (Command-n) and clicking the circular blue button on the far left of the toolbar. It looks like it has a back to front P in it (actually a paragraph mark). This opens up the Styles drawer. Now type a few words in your document, and then pick a new font from the toolbar's menu.

Notice how the downward-pointing arrow beside Normal in the drawer, which was once black, is now red to indicate that you have made some changes. Click it and select Redefine style from selection. Your previously-entered text will change to your new font, and any other text styled up as Normal elsewhere in your document will also be changed.

If a plain typed document is just a bit too bland for you, there is a wide range of pre-defined layouts already built in. Click File > New from Template Chooser… (Command-Shift-n) and all of the available templates will be displayed, ready for you to pick one.

These are divided by type, and cover everything from envelopes to reports. Some of them will be pre-populated with important information, such as your name and address, which is drawn from your own card in Address Book (see page 41 for more on setting this up). Be wary, though, that some forms will be US-orientated, and you may want to think carefully before using something like a standard CV template (or resume, as it calls it) to apply for a job.

Once you have completed your document, you can obviously save or print it from the File menu. You can also send it to iWeb for use on a web page. Be aware that when saving, though, Pages uses its own file format by default, and so if you want to share your documents with other people – especially those on a Windows PC – they may have some trouble reading them. The answer is to export them rather than save them. Choose File > Export… and then pick PDF, Word, RTF or plain text from the menu that pops up. Plain text is the most compatible of all, but you'll lose all of your formatting. To both retain your formatting and maximise compatibility, choose RTF (Rich Text Format). For Word-native files, pick Word, and for use on the web, pick PDF (Portable Document Format).

▲ The look and feel of your documents is controlled by the Styles palette, where you define how text should appear.

ALSO CONSIDER…

NISUS WRITER PRO
nisus.com
Heavy duty, yet inexpensive rival to Pages, if you only want to do regular writing. A cheaper Express edition boasts many similar features.

MICROSOFT WORD 2008
microsoft.com/mac
Industry standard word processor, which now incorporates layout tools. Best bought as part of the Microsoft Office 2008 bundle, alongside PowerPoint, Entourage and Excel.

TEXTEDIT
apple.com
Basic word processing tool built into Mac OS X, which nevertheless has some very impressive text formatting options.

▼ It's often missed, but Pages includes an impressive word count tool. To use it, open the Inspector and click on the first tab, followed by Info.

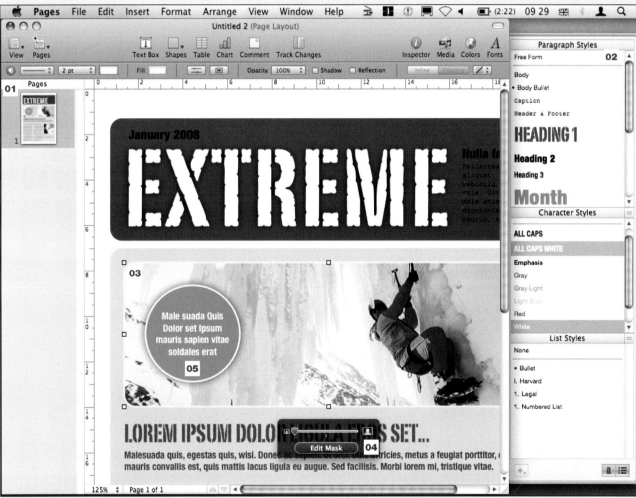

INTERFACE

1 The Pages panel shows you thumbnail views of the pages in your document, allowing you to quickly skip back and forth between them.

2 The Paragraph Styles drawer organises the various typefaces used on your pages. They can be defined by changing the instance on the page and then updating the saved style.

3 Images are held in boxes, which define where they appear on the page.

4 The slider enlarges or reduces the size of the image inside the box, showing more or less of it in the available space.

5 Shapes added to the page can be dragged to new positions, and used either as containers for text, or as masks for images.

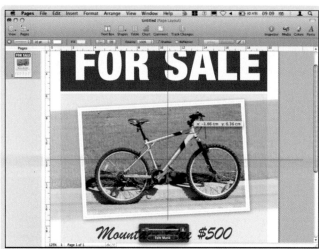

▲ **STEP 01** Pages gives you the opportunity to create new documents from a template, saving you a lot of work. In iWork 08, Pages' templates are split into two sections for plain word processing and laying out more complex documents. Pick Flyers > For Sale Flyer and click on Choose.

▲ **STEP 02** Pages may be a word processor, but it includes some sophisticated tools. The bike photo, for example, is much larger than the section you see, but masked out so that only the part in the frame is visible. Double-click and drag it to reposition it within the white border.

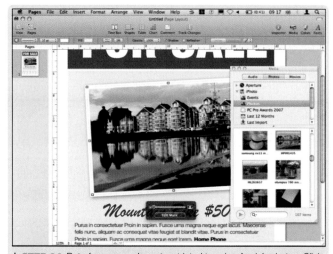

▲ **STEP 03** Now we'll change the look of the photo. Click on the Image Adjustments button on the toolbar (sixth button in) and use the head up display that appears to reduce the level of colours by dragging Saturation all the way to the left. Increase the contrast by dragging its slider to the right.

▲ **STEP 04** But of course you're not restricted to using Apple's photos. Click on Media in the toolbar and use the panel that pops up to browse through the photos on your Mac. Once you've found the one you want, drag it out of the media browser and drop it on the page in place of the bike.

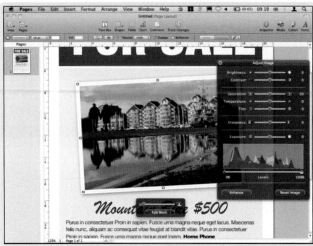
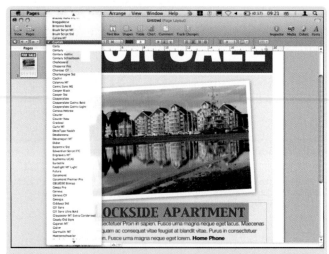

▲ **STEP 05** Notice how even if you used a colour photo it will be converted to black and white when dropped on the page. That's because the settings we applied to the bike photo are attached to the frame holding it. To get your colours back, click on Reset Image on the Image Adjustments panel.

▲ **STEP 06** We're not selling a bike any more, so change the text under the photo to something more appropriate, then choose a suitable font from the drop-down menu on the toolbar. You have now performed the most fundamental tasks in the layout mode, so it's time to look at plain word processing.

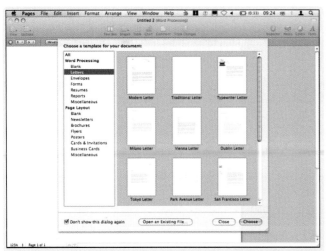

▲ **STEP 07** Close the Flyer and pick File > New from Template Chooser… Pick Letters > Modern Letter and Pages will open a far plainer document than the Flyer we have just been working on, ready for you to edit. Here we'll take you through character styles, which are used to format text on the page.

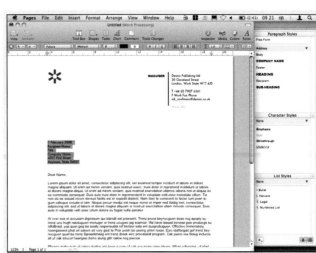

▲ **STEP 08** Select the recipient's address, then click on View > Show Styles Drawer. This opens a panel through which you can manage the look of your document. Click on Address to change the recipient address font to match the one used on your own address at the top of the page.

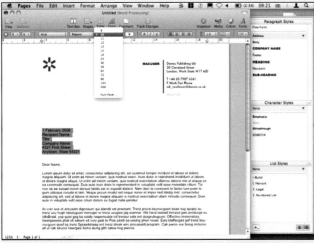

▲ **STEP 09** Without deselecting the address on the page, use the drop-down menus below the toolbar to choose a new font and size, such as Arial, 10pt. When you apply them they will change only the selected text, but in the next step we'll automatically apply them to our own address, too.

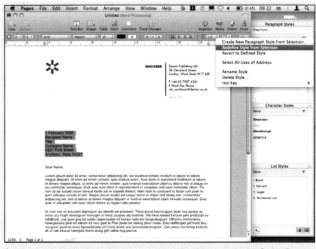

▲ **STEP 10** Notice how the arrow to the right of Address in the Styles Drawer is red. This indicates that you have made changes to a piece of text that uses it. Click on the arrow and select Redefine Style from Selection, and see how, because this style has now changed, your own address at the top of the page matches the recipient address.

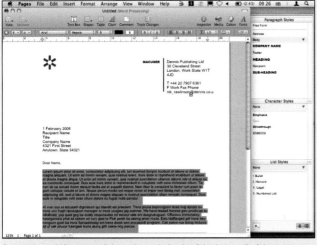

▲ **STEP 11** When you click on the main body of the letter, all of the text is highlighted. This is because it is only there as a placeholder and used as guidance. Start typing your letter and you'll see that as you press the first character all of the text is removed. Templates are a very speedy way to create documents in Pages.

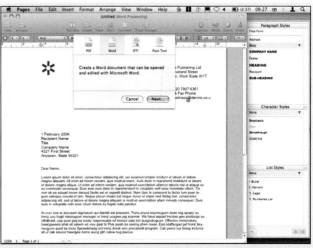

▲ **STEP 12** Once you have finished your letter, you can obviously print it from the File menu, and save it by tapping Command-s. However, you can also save it as a Microsoft Word document. Do this by choosing File > Export > Word.

Numbers

If you want to work with numbers, you need Numbers. Well, that's what Apple would like you to believe. It's a spreadsheet application, and it took a long time to make it into iWork. A radical departure from other spreadsheet tools, it lets you work on several tables side by side on a single sheet, so you can directly compare your figures and make references between them for more dynamic and meaningful analysis. Here we'll show you how to create and style your tables and charts.

The best-looking spreadsheet application on any platform – bar none – is Numbers. It took a long time for Apple to add a spreadsheet to its office suite, but once it arrived it was well worth the wait. It has great layout tools, produces the smoothest, most engaging charts, and lets you put more than one table on any sheet. This last feature is the ace in its hand. It's not until you've used it and then switch back to something like Excel that you realise how innovative and useful it is. Why did nobody think of it before?

The first time you start Numbers, you'll be presented with a blank spreadsheet. To the left is a column showing the number of sheets in the document, and the tables in each sheet, and below that the styles that can be applied to the sheets. You'll see that there are grey cells running across the top and down the left-hand edge of the current active table – which takes up the whole of the sheet.

The easiest way to understand the relationship between sheets and tables is to right-click on Table 1 in the sidebar and select Delete. The cells will disappear, but you'll see that Sheet 1 stays active in the sidebar.

▲ The range of colours and styles that can be applied to charts is impressive, and includes realistic marble and wood finishes.

Click on the Tables button in the toolbar and select Basic to insert a new table into the sheet. By default it will have 10 rows and four columns, but you can make it larger or smaller by dragging the fat corner handle at the bottom right. Click on Tables again and select Sums Checklist. A new table will appear in the same sheet, this time with checkboxes that let you mark off different items in a list. Note how both tables can exist side by side and you can work on them both at once. You can't do this in Excel.

Add some details to columns B and C in your new spreadsheet, and then check a few of the boxes to the left. Note how the total at the bottom of column C doesn't start to rack up until you have checked the boxes in column A. This is an example of the pre-defined functions Apple has built into Numbers.

Try moving your tables around by dragging the dimpled area above row one and to the left of column A. Notice how blue guidelines appear to help you line them up with other tables and elements on the Sheet, making Numbers one of the best spreadsheet applications for laying out attractive sheets of data.

To add new tables on a separate page you need a new Sheet. Right-click in the top half of the sidebar and select New Sheet to create one. You can now click backwards and forwards between them, with each one showing only the tables it contains.

Elsewhere, Numbers works in a similar way to Excel, and if you have any familiarity with Excel's formulas, you should have no problem making the switch. =SUM(D3:D9) would add together all of the cells between D3 and D9. =SQRT(C2) gives you the square root of the value in cell C2. =AVERAGE(B1:B4) will give you the average of those cells. A trick for checking the validity of your functions as you type them is to always use lower case, and watch how the case changes as you type your opening bracket. Thus =average(will jump to upper case, showing you the function is correct. =avg(will remain in lower case, indicating a problem you need to resolve.

ALSO CONSIDER...

MICROSOFT EXCEL
microsoft.com/mac
The world's best-known spreadsheet also works on the Mac, giving good cross-platform compatibility. Excellent though it may be, though, it's missing some key features found in Numbers, including multi-table sheets.

MARINER CALC
marinersoftware.com
Mariner claims that its spreadsheet, which ships with more than 150 functions, uses less disk space and memory than any rival on the Mac, making it a good choice for less well-specced machines.

GOOGLE SPREADSHEETS
docs.google.com
Free online spreadsheet application that lets you collaborate with other members of your team, no matter how remote they may be, and access your data from any Internet-connected computer in the world, so it's a good option for travelling workers. If you like the idea of online spreadsheets, be sure you also check out the features on offer through Zoho Office at zoho.com.

▼ Highlight a range of values and Numbers performs these quick sums in the sidebar. You can drag them into cells on your spreadsheet.

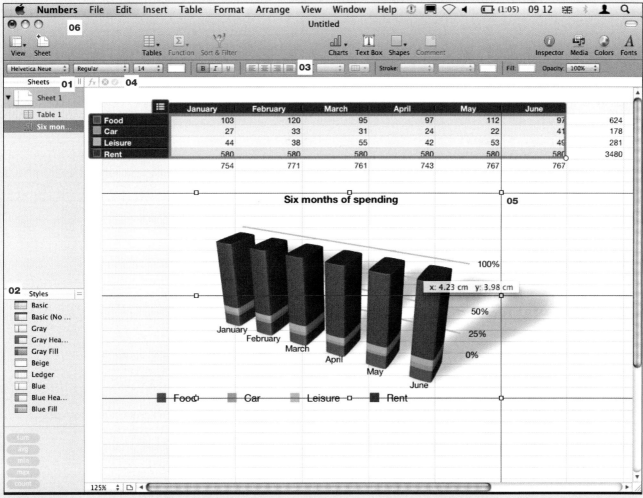

INTERFACE

1 The Sheet panel holds all of the pages in your spreadsheet. Each sheet can contain several tables and charts, allowing you to present diverse data side by side.

2 The Styles panel lets you quickly format your spreadsheets. However, as this is a context-sensitive area, which changes depending on what you have clicked in the spreadsheet, it can also show quick automatic calculations if you have selected a range of numbers.

3 The formatting toolbar above the working area works in the same as at that in a word processor, allowing you to change font and sizes, and background colours.

4 The input bar is where you input the data to be displayed on the spreadsheet.

5 Guide lines help you to line up the edges of tables and charts with other elements on a spreadsheet page.

6 Turn to the toolbar to perform the most common tasks in creating a spreadsheet, including adding charts, shapes and notes.

▲ **STEP 01** The first thing you see in numbers is an empty spreadsheet. We're going to use it to track some spending, so enter the months January to June in the grey boxes at the tops of columns B to G, and Food, Car, Leisure, Rent in the grey boxes down column A, from rows 2 to 5.

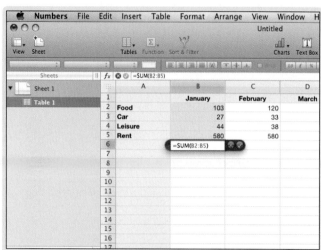

▲ **STEP 02** Enter some numbers for each category and month so that you have a total of 24 values on your spreadsheet. The first thing we're going to do is total each month. Click in the cell below the numbers in column B and type =sum(B2:B5) then press return.

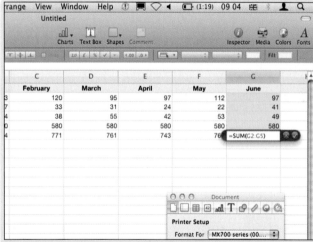

▲ **STEP 03** Numbers adds up the values for January and puts the answer in cell B6. Do the same for the remaining columns, noticing how the case of 'sum' changes to capitals to indicate that Numbers understands the command.

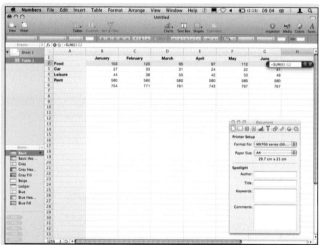

▲ **STEP 04** Now click in cell H2 and type =sum(and rather than finish off the sum, click on cell B2, then with the mouse button held down drag to H2 to highlight every cell in the Food line. Type the closing) and hit return and Numbers performs the calculation without us typing the formula.

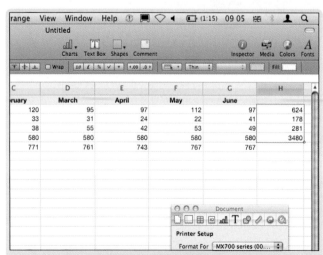

▲ **STEP 05** We'll use that formula again for the other categories, but without typing at all. Click on H2 again and then on the small circle in the bottom-right of the cell. Keep the mouse button held down and drag this circle down to H5. As you move it, Numbers fills in the totals spent on Car, Leisure and Rent.

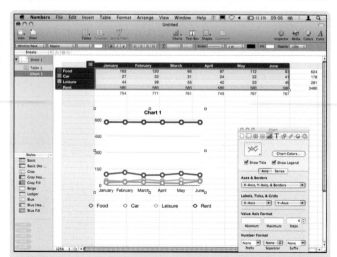

▲ **STEP 06** Let's make a graph. Click and hold the mouse in cell A1, then drag it to cell G5 to highlight all of our values and category names, but not the totals. Now click on the Charts button in the toolbar and pick the fifth chart down in the left-hand column. Numbers puts a line chart under the data.

▲ **STEP 07** Notice how the categories are given colours to match the lines on the chart. It will also have opened an Inspector palette, which we'll use to customise the chart, starting by changing the chart type. Click on the large square button to the left of chart colours and pick the style shown one down in the right-hand column.

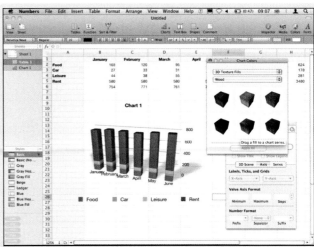

▲ **STEP 08** We now have a 3D bar chart. Click on Chart Colors and pick a new colour scheme by clicking on the drop-down menu and choosing from the list that comes up. Press Apply all to apply the colours to your chart. Try a few colours, including Wood, which gives a realistic veneer.

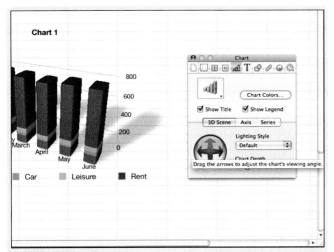

▲ **STEP 09** Close the colours palette and click on the Inspector's 3D scene button. Here you can change the 3D depth of the chart. You can also swivel it around by clicking on the circular blue button to the left and dragging it in various directions. Try this.

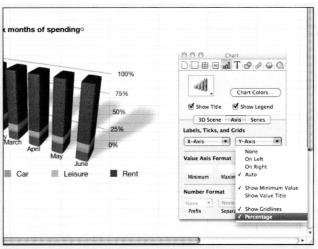

▲ **STEP 10** Our chart is simply called Chart 1, which would be no good in a presentation. Click this in the chart itself and change it to 'Six months of spending'. Now click on the Inspector's Axis button, then Y-Axis, and pick Percentage from the menu that pops down.

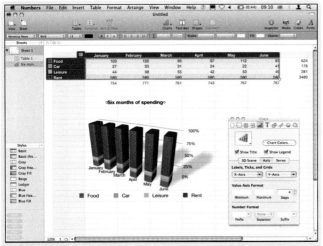

▲ **STEP 11** All of your bars now extend to the full height of the chart, allowing you to see what proportion of your total spending for each month went on each category in our spreadsheet, helping you identify your major cost areas.

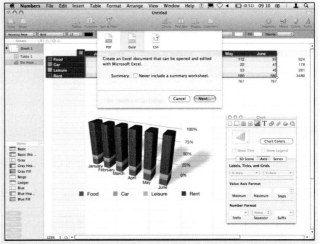

▲ **STEP 12** Close the chart Inspector. It's time to save our spreadsheet. You could simply press Command-s to save in Numbers' native format, but for maximum compatibility, you should save as Excel. Do this by picking File > Export… > Excel.

Keynote

Apple's CEO, Steve Jobs, is well known for his stunning presentations. Relaxed and casual, he steps up on stage twice a year to announce the company's new product offerings, against a backdrop of smart, impressive graphics. It was obvious he wasn't using industry-standard PowerPoint, so when Apple came out with Keynote the world was impressed, but not surprised. Since then it has matured to become one of the best, easiest presentation composers you could ever hope to use.

If there is one thing for which Apple CEO Steve Jobs is famous, it's his keynote addresses every January and September. At these he steps up on stage with the minimum of props, always wearing his trademark blue jeans and black polo-neck jumper, and announces what products the company will be launching in the next six months. His only prompts are a series of impressively slick slides that pop up behind him as he prowls the stage.

For years, it was obvious that he was not using PowerPoint, Microsoft's industry-leading presentation software, so it came as no surprise when the company finally released Keynote, a rival Mac-only presentation package.

Keynote is a gift for anyone lacking design experience. It ships with 36 pre-designed themes, each of which can be created in one of five different screen sizes. The themes boast a wide variety of master slides, allowing you to drag different designs onto pages you have already produced to change their layouts. If you change your mind about the theme altogether, you can even switch themes half way through, and Keynote will re-layout all of your sides to match the new design.

Keynote takes the best of Pages and Numbers, giving you access to first-class layout tools and powerful graphing features. It also integrates chunks of your iTunes and iPhoto libraries, allowing you to directly place media within your presentations, and can even incorporate QuickTime movies to create some truly compelling output. These are controlled by the Inspector palette which, as in Pages and Numbers, is split into different areas, each of which focuses on a specific task, such as changing fonts, adding tables and changing the size of images.

Beyond this, the most important button of all is the View menu found on the toolbar. This lets you skip between slide creation and navigation modes, a light-table on which you can re-organise and re-order your slides, and the essential presenter notes view. Presenter notes are additional points you write for yourself to help you through your presentation. They only come into play if you're running your presentation on two monitors, or a monitor and a projector. The slides will be shown on the projector for your audience, while the presenter notes will be shown on your own screen, along with a preview of the next slide.

As with any presentation tool, though, the rule by which you should live when creating your slides is to keep them simple. Don't be tempted to put so much content on your slides that you end up reading them out wholesale when you come to make your presentation, make sure your text is large enough to be seen from the very back row of your audience, and if you can ever use a picture instead of words, do so. Let it illustrate what you're saying while you speak the words yourself.

You should also avoid using too many transitions. We would suggest sticking to just two wherever possible; a subtle motion from one slide to the next, and a more obvious choice, such as the rotating cube, to move between sections or groups of slides. Combine these with slide builds to introduce the various parts of a single slide in succession and you'll quickly build an engaging presentation that holds your audience's attention from beginning to end.

> **ALSO CONSIDER...**
> **MICROSOFT POWERPOINT**
> *microsoft.com/mac*
> So ubiquitous has PowerPoint become that it is now a byword for presentations in general, and 'Death by PowerPoint' is a euphemism for being stuck in a room as inept presenters flash slides up before your eyes. Nonetheless, it's just about the only standard the business world has for sharing presentations, so a familiarity with the world's leading presentation software is a must. Fortunately, Keynote can import and export PowerPoint files with a good degree of accuracy, so even if you would rather not use the software you can still read its files.

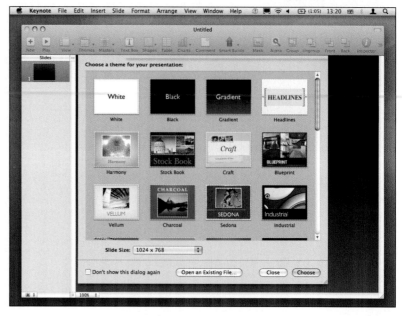

▼ The easiest way to start a new presentation is to select a template from the Gallery that pops up when you start the application. This includes a blank template if you're feeling creative.

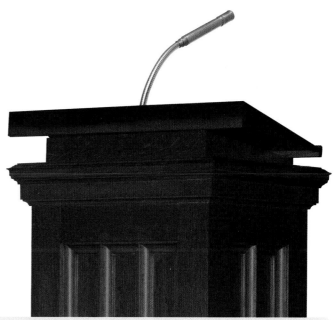
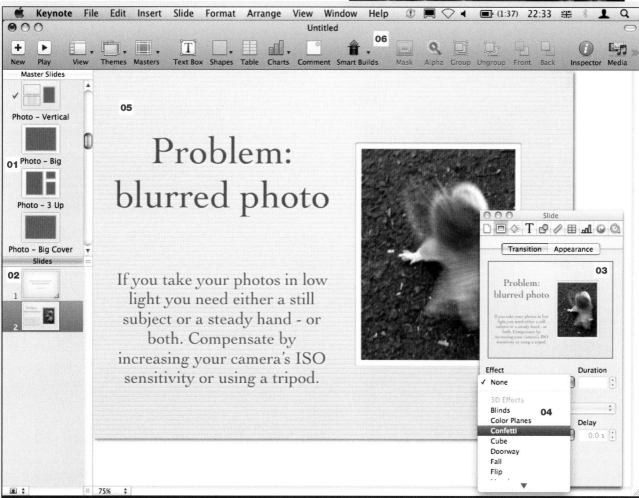

INTERFACE

1 The Master Slides panel contains all of the pre-set style layouts in your chosen theme. You can drag them onto blank slides to create quick layouts.

2 The Slides panel contains your work, and shows thumbnails of every slide in your presentation

3 The Inspector controls every aspect of your slides and their contents, including images, text and transitions.

4 Use the Effects menu to choose a transition style, allowing you to apply fades and motion to the switch from one slide to the next, as well as introduce a little bit of interactivity to your presentations.

5 The main part of the screen is taken up by your working space, which is where you'll do the work of the layout of your slides. This slide contains two text boxes and a single image box.

6 The Toolbar gives you quick access to the most common tasks you'll need to perform, such as adding a chart, placing a shape, building a table or defining a text box. All text must be placed inside a box.

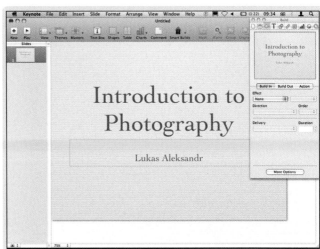

▲ **STEP 01** Every time you start Keynote, you'll be given the opportunity to choose a pre-defined slide type. Scroll down the list until you find Formal, which we'll use as the basis of our presentation. Click it and then click Choose.

▲ **STEP 02** Keynote creates your first slide. Double-click where indicated, and replace the main headline text with the words 'Introduction to Photography'. Double-click the line below and replace it with your name to give yourself a credit.

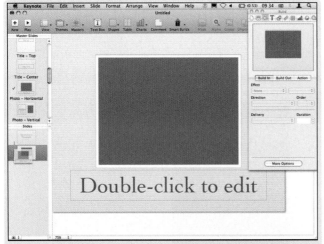
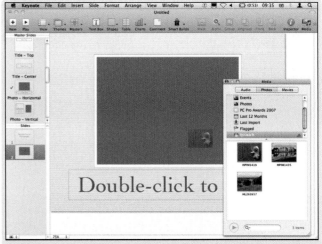

▲ **STEP 03** Time to add another slide, by right-clicking in the Slides pane on the left, and picking New Slide. Click on the View button on the toolbar and select Show Master Slides, then scroll down the list in the panel that appears and drag Photo Horizontal down onto your new slide.

▲ **STEP 04** Notice how your new slide changes its appearance. Open the Media Browser from the View menu and scroll through any existing photo libraries on your Mac. Pick an image you like, and drag it into the large grey square to place it on your slide.

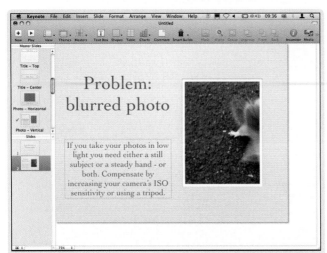
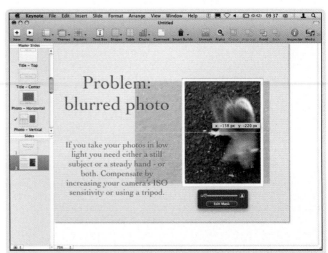

▲ **STEP 05** Give your photo a caption using the space below. Now let's imagine we need more space for a secondary caption explaining our point. Drag Photo – Vertical from the Master Slides pane and notice how the slide's layout automatically reformats. Use the new space to expand your caption.

▲ **STEP 06** Changing the slide's layout means our photo no longer fits its holder. Clicking and dragging moves it around the box holding it, but double-clicking shows a ghost of its full contents, allowing you to drag these around to re-centre the image on the main focus – in this case, the squirrel.

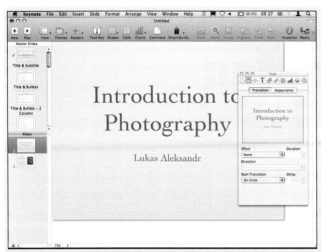

▲ **STEP 07** Try playing your presentation and you'll see that the slides make a straight switch. Not very exciting. Spice things up a bit by clicking on your first slide, then in the Inspector, click on the Slide button (the second one along the button bar, with a blue square on it).

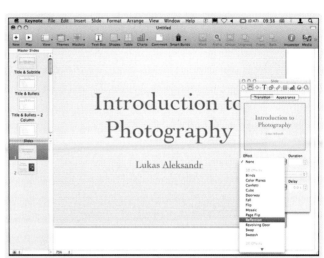

▲ **STEP 08** Use the Effect menu to choose a transition style you like, remembering that you should only choose two for your whole presentation: a low key one to take you between slides in the same section of your presentation, and a more impressive one to transition between distinct sections.

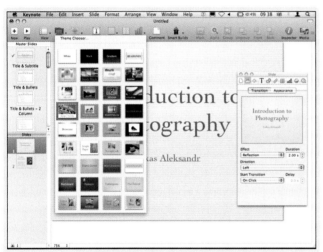

▲ **STEP 09** Nice though this theme is, you might think it doesn't quite work for our chosen subject, photography. It's a bit too formal and over-designed. You can change this quickly, by clicking on Themes on the main toolbar and picking a new one. Try Vellum or Modern Portfolio.

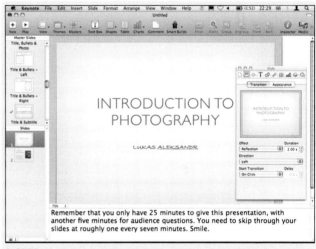

▲ **STEP 10** Continue building your slides until the presentation is complete, then click on View in the toolbar and select Presenter notes. This opens a small pane at the bottom of the interface, where you can type notes to which you can refer when making your presentation. These will show up on your screen, but not the one seen by your audience.

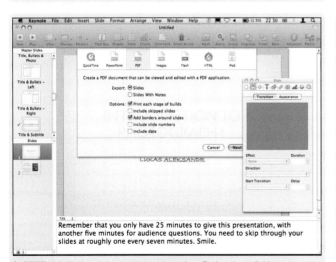

▲ **STEP 11** It's time to save your presentation. Rather than clicking on Save, go to File > Export, where you can choose a specific format, including PowerPoint, PDF or HTML, for outputting your slides for the web. This allows you to publish presentations for viewing when you're not around.

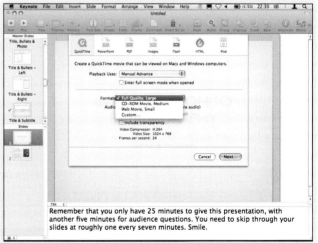

▲ **STEP 12** The most advanced presentation type is QuickTime. Compatible with both Macs and PCs, it is rendered as a small movie that can be played back in the QuickTime application, embedded in a Web page, or used in another Keynote presentation.

Software for the Mac

Whoever said the Mac doesn't have a wide range of software clearly never used a Mac. Many of the key applications on Windows, including Microsoft Office, Photoshop and Dreamweaver also run on the Mac. So, come to that, does Windows itself, assuming you have a fairly up-to-date machine.

But how do you know what is the best application to meet your needs? And what should you do with it when you've installed and launched it for the first time? Those questions can be tough to answer for the novice Mac user.

Here we'll walk you through the task of choosing the best software for your Mac, and then installing and using Microsoft Office, web development applications, messaging clients and even Windows for those times when you simply can't find a Mac-native application to meet your needs.

Windows on the Mac	088
Adobe Creative Suite	098
RapidWeaver	100
Messaging Clients	102
Online video	104
Microsoft Office	106
MobileMe	108

Windows on the Mac

Just because you've bought a Mac, it doesn't mean that you are only limited to applications specifically built for the Mac. By using emulation software or Boot Camp, you can turn your Intel Mac into a Windows PC to run Windows software. Why would you want to do that? Because regardless of how wide the range of software you can run on the Mac might be, there are some notable exceptions that are PC only. And besides, you may just want to test a website you've designed on both platforms.

Much as you may love your Mac, there may be times when you have to run an application that is only available for Windows. Perhaps this is because you still need tools like Visio and Access that simply don't run on a Mac (although there are Mac equivalents that you should try), or maybe it's because you need to check that a website you've designed works across all platforms and browsers. Either way, you have two choices: you either hang on to your old PC, or you install Windows on your Mac.

Since Apple started using Intel processors in its Macs, it's been making some of the most versatile computers on the market. They are the only machines that can simultaneously run three operating systems: Mac OS X, Windows and various flavours of Linux, both natively and in so-called virtualisation mode.

Virtualisation is a means of poking a virtual hole in the Mac's main operating system, Mac OS X, so that other operating systems, such as Windows, can share the hardware inside your computer.

Before this was possible, you had to run a third application called emulation software, of which Microsoft Virtual PC was the most popular. This ran on top of Mac OS X, and Windows ran on top of Virtual PC. Virtual PC would then capture every instruction sent by Windows and translate it into a language understood by Mac OS X, rather like a translator, and the Mac operating system would then perform the necessary function.

As you can imagine, it was a slow, tedious and unpleasant way to work, which is why viruallisation has proven such a boon. Microsoft is no longer actively developing Virtual PC for the Mac.

A CHOICE OF TWO
There are two leading contenders in the virtualisation market: Parallels and Fusion. Both works in pretty much the same way and in terms of performance, for everyday tasks, there's little to choose between them. Once installed they will walk you through the steps necessary to install Windows, leaving you to go off and do something more productive in the meantime.

Under both systems, Windows applications can be made to act as though they are native Mac OS X software, appearing in their own distinct frames, rather than being trapped inside a Windows environment, which in turn is inside a Mac window of its own. If you prefer, however, you can minimise the impact of Mac OS X and running two operating systems at once by running Windows in full-screen mode, with OS X in the background. Performance will be noticeably improved.

Parallels ships in two editions: Desktop (£49.99) and Desktop Premium (£59.99). Both let you access your Windows files without starting Windows, open Mac files with Windows applications (and vice versa), offer support for Windows games, let you run Windows and Mac applications side by side in a single environment, and have a snapshot tool for saving known working configurations of your Windows machine, effectively freezing it in time so that you can come back to it at a later point.

Opting for the Premium edition adds in Kaspersky virus protection, Acronis Disk Director for adjusting the size of the Windows portion of your hard drive if you find it's too small, and Acronis True Image Home, which backs up your whole Windows installation, including all of your settings so that should it all come crashing down at some future point you can recover the lot. It's well worth the extra £10.

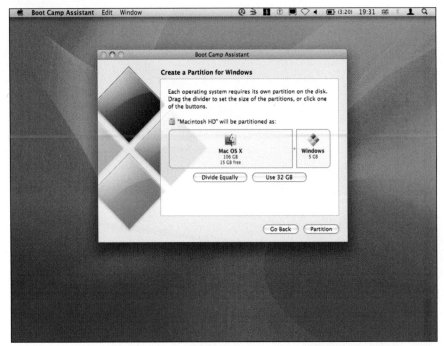
▲ Boot Camp comes with Mac OS X 10.5 Leopard and it allows you run a version of Windows on your Mac.

▲ Windows Vista appears in a window on your Mac when its run under emulation. Here we've used VMware Fusion.

VMWare ships only one version of Fusion, which costs £44. It boasts many of the same features as Parallels, allowing you to run PC games with support for DirectX 9, and the ability to run Mac and Windows applications side by side. It will also detect Boot Camp installations, and let you run their copies of Windows without rebooting, which brings us to Apple's solution to the question of running Windows on the Mac…

THE APPLE OPTION
There is a third option for anyone running Mac OS X 10.5 Leopard, called Boot Camp. This isn't quite the same as virtualisation, as rather than simply poking a hole in the Mac's native operating system, it pushes it out of the way altogether, allowing Windows to have 100% of the Mac's hardware resources.

It is by far the most efficient way to run Windows on the Mac, but does require that you reboot your machine every time you want to switch from one operating system to the other. The benefit is that with Boot Camp there is only ever one operating system working at once, so no need to share resources, unlike running Windows full screen in either Parallels or Fusion, which may occasionally feel a little bit sluggish because the Mac is still having to devote resources to its own native operating system at the same time.

The Boot Camp Assistant, which helps you install Windows on your Mac, is found in the Applications > Utilities folder. It examines your hard drive, identifies the necessary free space for installing Windows, and then partitions off a section to keep the two operating systems separate.

You next insert your Windows disc and, once that's finished installing, re-insert your Mac OS X 10.5 Leopard DVD to install all of the drivers for your Mac's internal hardware. This is much easier than installing Windows on a PC, where you may have to spend time trawling the Internet for the necessary drivers for your computer's components.

It is important to note that whatever technology you choose to help your run Windows on your Mac – Parallels, Fusion or Boot Camp, you'll still have to buy a fully-licensed copy of Windows to go alongside it, as none of these applications come with a bundled copy. You'll also have to activate it, which means you can't use a copy you've already installed on a PC somewhere, or indeed on another Mac using the same copy of Parallels or Fusion. Windows treats every instance of virtualisation software as a new virtual machine, so you'll be subject to the same restrictions as anyone who was foolishly hoping to buy one copy of Vista and install it on a dozen PCs.

Fortunately, it is now possible to use any version of Windows Vista with each of these three methods. Previously, Microsoft would only licence the more expensive Ultimate and Business editions for use under Parallels or Fusion.

Combined, these three ways of running Windows – or pretty much any other modern operating system – on the Mac makes Apple hardware far more versatile than a PC, contrary to most peoples' expectations. PCs may let you run various editions of Windows, Linux and Unix, but they don't open up the world of small developers available to Apple users, and they don't give you access to what many people consider the world's best, most stable operating system – Mac OS X.

Windows on the Mac

You have chosen a Mac, but there are times when you need to run Windows, be it for testing purposes or to be compatible with PC-using colleagues. But you don't need a PC to do so, as it's easier than ever to install and run Windows on a Mac, as we explain here.

When you buy a Mac, you've chosen more than just your hardware, as it comes bundled with the world's best operating system. For most people, that's as much of a draw as the computer itself.

Yet sometimes you have to test your work on alternative operating systems. While we may believe the Mac is the best platform for web design, failing to check that your pages display properly in a PC browser can be commercial suicide. And while we may love the Mac and be perfectly satisfied with the range of software at our disposal, there are times when a client may send you something that just won't run under Mac OS X. It's at times like these that you have no choice but to run Windows, but rarely will investing in a PC be a cost-effective option.

Fortunately, now that Apple builds its machines around Intel chips, it's easier than ever to install Windows – or Linux – on Apple hardware, as we'll show you here.

Hardcore fanboys aside, traditional Mac users should welcome this development with open arms. It brings to the Mac the ability to run applications that are developed only for Windows. As well as creatives who can take advantage of the benefits we've outlined above, IT professionals should also take note, not just because it means Macs can now access hitherto denied corporate applications such as Access and Visio, but also because it means the decision over whether to buy Mac or PC hardware is much simplified: buy Mac, because it can run both operating systems.

This is particularly true when buying hardware for hotdesking or other sharing techniques – the stereotypical designer can boot up the Mac into OS X, while 'the office worker' can boot into Windows.

And PC users? Well, they get access to Apple's beautiful hardware. It's not just about aesthetics with Macs: it's about care and an attention to detail, plus a certain panache.

In this feature, we'll explain the different ways in which you can install and run Windows on a Mac, highlight each approach's strengths and weaknesses, and walk you through the process of installing the latest version, Vista.

One important thing to remember before we begin, however, is that you should ensure you're properly licensed. Installing Windows on a Mac is no different to installing it on a PC – literally as well as conceptually – and Windows will have to be activated as it is on a PC. Note, too, that you'll need full versions of the operating system; upgrade discs won't work, and while OEM install discs are likely to work in practice, using them would contravene your End User License Agreement (EULA).

CHOOSING THE RIGHT SOFTWARE

When it comes to installing Windows onto a Mac, you essentially have two options.

One comes from Apple, and it's the company's Boot Camp utility. More on this later, but for now you just have to be aware that this works by partitioning off a chunk of your Mac's hard disk for a fresh Windows install. If you want to run Windows, you have to boot the Mac from this partition, and Windows completely takes over the computer. Boot Camp comes free with Mac OS X 10.5 Leopard, previously it was only available as a beta and has now ceased to be available as a standalone tool for anyone running Mac OS X 10.4.

The alternative to Boot Camp is virtualisation. Here, the Mac boots into Mac OS X, but you can run Windows and its applications alongside the host operating system. The advantage here is that you can move seamlessly from one operating system into the other, without having to reboot. If you're a web developer working in Dreamweaver on the Mac, for example, you can check how your site looks in Internet Explorer 7 simply by pasting a URL into the Windows browser.

To enable virtualisation, you'll need to get hold of some third-party Mac software. Parallels Desktop for Mac was the first solution available to allow this (£50 from *avanquest.co.uk*), but virtualisation giant VMware has now thrown its hat into the ring, recently releasing the second beta of its Fusion software for the Mac.

Virtualisation has the advantage of flexibility and convenience, but what it lacks is the power to run Windows natively. One obvious reason for this is that if you're running a virtual guest operating system alongside the host operating system, the hardware has to allocate resources across both at the same time. (Indeed, you can run many more than one guest operating system concurrently, compounding the problem at the same time as giving you more flexibility.)

More importantly, though, we have to understand the difference

▲ Boot Camp lets you create a Windows partition on your drive to install the operating system.

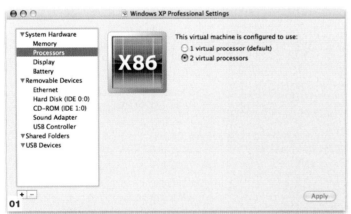

01 Virtualisation software can take advantage of one or both cores.

02 Windows Task manager lets you monitor how it is utilising your Mac's resources.

03 PCs boot using a bios – Macs don't have one.

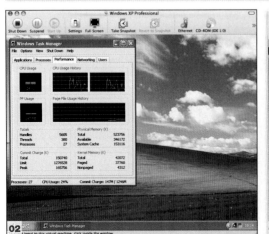

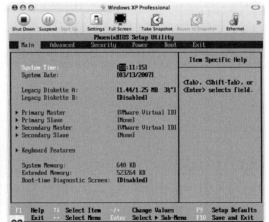

INSTALLING WINDOWS UNDER PARALLELS

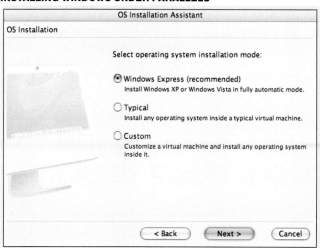

▲ **STEP 01 CHOOSE INSTALLATION** Pick your Parallels installation type. Express asks you for the serial number for Windows XP or Vista, and it will do the rest, picking default options for hardware configuration and dumping the virtual hard disk and configuration file in ~/Library/Parallels. Typical is similar, but gives you more control over where your virtual machine is stored. We'll pick Custom.

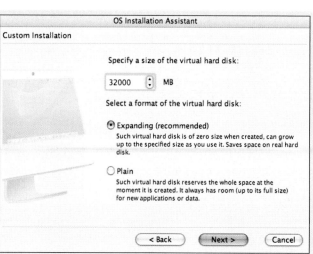

▲ **STEP 02 ALLOCATE RESOURCES** Specify how much of the Mac's resources you want to allocate to the guest operating system. Here, we're creating an expanding hard disk. It will start of at zero bytes in size and grow as the guest operating system makes demands of it, all the way up to the size specified, 32,000MB. You can store it anywhere, even on an external disk.

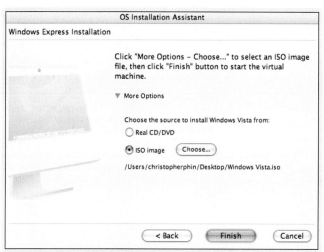

▲ **STEP 03 CHOOSE INSTALL DISK** When you come to pick the disk to install from, you can simply slot in the CD or DVD, but you'll find the install process works much more quickly if you work from a virtual disk image. Roxio's Toast on the Mac creates appropriate ISO images. Actually, they're .toast images, but you can rename them .iso and everything will be fine.

▲ **STEP 04 INSTALLATION** The installation process will begin, and the length of time it will take depends on the complexity of the operating system you have chosen. This process is usually fully automated, but some operating systems require you, for example, to eject the install CD manually following installation. If you're using an ISO, click the CD icon at the bottom right of the window.

▲ **STEP 05 INSTALL PARALLELS TOOLS** Once the install process has completed, you have to install Parallels Tools to activate such features as copying and pasting between host and guest operating systems. With newer versions, this should happen automatically, but if it doesn't, simply pick Install Parallels Tools from the Actions menu.

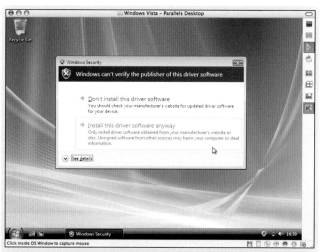

▲ **STEP 06 WINDOWS SECURITY** The drivers that allow network sharing and the like are unsigned. Under Windows XP, the installer can optionally suppress the warnings, but Vista's more robust security model insists on clearing every component's installation with you before going ahead. Remember to follow normal Windows patching and updating procedures.

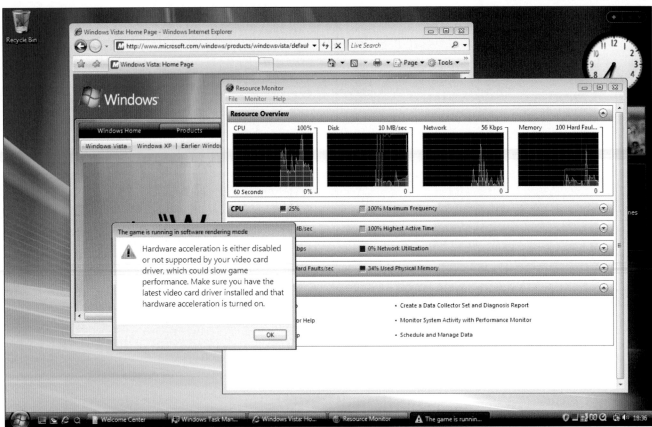

▲ Due to a lack of drivers for some Mac hardware you may find some incompatibilities under Windows Vista.

between emulation and virtualisation, and the limits of the latter. This is covered on the following page.

As such, the bottom line is that using Boot Camp to boot the Mac hardware exclusively into Windows will give you the best performance – although the Boot Camp drivers are still not perfectly optimised – while using virtualisation provides most convenience. Mac users in a corporate environment, for example, might choose to use Mac applications within OS X most of the time, but have Outlook running under Windows for richer Exchange integration than is offered in native Mac tools.

The good news is that you don't have to plump for one approach to the exclusion of the other. When Parallels was first launched, it followed the traditional approach for guest operating systems – that is, it generated a small configuration file, and created a ring-fenced, virtual hard disk not by partitioning the physical volume but by creating a virtual hard disk document (you can still opt for this approach, as it makes backup and restore very simple).

Now, though, it can also use a partition created by Boot Camp. This has two advantages. Most significantly, it enables you to boot the Mac into Windows when you want to give all the system resources to Windows, or to boot back into Mac OS X when you want to run the two side by side. Second, it can allow more complete access to the Windows partition. Formatted as Fat 32, Mac OS X can read and write to this partition with no difficulties, but if you decide to format the Boot Camp-created partition as NTFS, the Mac can only read the data that's held on it. Parallels, running from this partition, can give Mac users the ability to drag and drop to and from it.

And Parallels has one last trick up its sleeve: Coherence. 'Trick' is the right word, too, as it's just a sleight of hand, but a damned good one. Along with Full Screen and OS Window – the latter constraining the guest operating system within a window, say, set to 1024 x 768, or on a secondary screen – Parallels supports Coherence mode for the guest operating system, in which windows floating within the guest operating system environment are effectively cut out and stuck alongside windows from the host operating system. You can access the Start menu from Parallels' Dock icon, and Windows applications can be added to and launched from the Dock. All it does is mask out the Windows desktop.

ADDING LINUX

There are many Linux distributions that can run natively on older PowerPC Mac hardware as well as Intel hardware. Dual-boot systems (and more) are possible, too, although these require a little more mucking about in the command line than many users will be comfortable with.

A simpler option is to use virtualisation software to run a Linux OS alongside Mac OS X. This is very easy indeed, as most distributions are offered as downloadable ISO images, and both Parallels and VMware can install directly from ISOs on the Mac's hard disk without them first having to be burned to optical media.

Technically, any x86 Linux build will run under virtualisation. Parallels, for example, provides presets for Red Hat, Debian, Fedora, SuSE, Mandriva and Xandros, along with Other Linux kernel 2.4 and 2.6, and the über-generic Other Linux. You also have options to run even less mainstream operating systems, including Solaris, OS/2, FreeBSD and Dos.

Under Parallels, the experience isn't as rich in the Linux builds we've tried as when

MAC OS X ON A PC

Of course, this is all well and good if you want to run Windows on a Mac, but if you'd rather install Mac OS X on your PC, well, you're rather out of luck. It's not so much that it's impossible, rather that there are so many legal and technical hurdles in the way that it's just not worth it. Various projects – among them the well-known tutorials at tinyurl.com/y7z3cf – can walk you through the process, but it's simply not a practical option at the moment.

Fish and ...
Gilbert and ...
Fortnum and ...

 and

Mac without **Office for Mac?**

Unthinkable.

Macintosh and Office for Mac 2008 are the perfect pair. They combine creativity with outstanding productivity software to provide everything you need to produce superb documents, presentations and communications and share them with anyone on a Mac or a PC. Whether at home, in the classroom or in the office, now you can connect, communicate and collaborate with everyone on any platform.

Great Office for Mac deals are available now, when you purchase a new Mac. So there's never been a better time to connect with the rest of the world and get more from your Mac.

Just a selection of stores you will find around the country. For a full store listing, visit www.apr-stores.com

Basingstoke - iStore
Unit 72a Upper Level, Festival Place, RG21 7BF
call: 0845 521 2140   visit: www.albion.co.uk

Bath - FarPoint Developments
The Old Red House Bakery, 90c Wolcot Street, BA1 5BG
call: 01225 460 678   visit: www.farpoint.org.uk

Bournemouth - Solutions Inc Ltd
78 Old Christchurch Road, BH1 1LR
call: 0870 389 8610   visit: www.solutions-inc.com

Bradford - KRCS Computer Store
44 Kirkgate, BD1 1QT
call: 01274 743 338   visit: www.krcs.co.uk

Brighton - Solutions Inc Ltd
12-13 Brighton Place, The Lanes, BN1 1HT
call: 0870 389 8610   visit: www.solutions-inc.com

Cardiff - AT Computers
18 Morgan Arcade, CF10 1AF
call: 0870 863 5420   visit: www.atcomputers.co.uk

Chelmsford - CT Solutions
The Meadows, High Street, CM2 6FD
call: 01245 359 511   visit: www.ctsolutionsretail.com

Cheltenham - Western Computers
Beechwood Shopping Centre, High Street, GL50 1DQ
call: 01242 234 700   visit: www.western.co.uk

Chester - MCC
5/7 Watergate Row, CH1 2LE
call: 01244 304 060   visit: www.mccdigital.com

Derby - Square Group
21 Iron Gate, Cathedral Quarter, DE1 3GP
call: 0845 873 8215   visit: www.squaregroup.co.uk

Edinburgh - Cancom
95-97 Nicolson Street, EH8 9BY
call: 0845 686 3100   visit: www.cancom.com

Guildford - Cancom
Genesis House, Merrow Lane, GU4 7BN
call: 01483 500 500   visit: www.cancom.com

High Wycombe - Square Group
Eden Shopping Centre, HP11 2BY
call: 01494 492 000   visit: www.squaregroup.co.uk

Jersey - IQ Music Solutions
32 Burrard Street, St Helier, JE2 4WS
call: 01534 769320   visit: www.i-quipment.com

London - Albion
112 The Strand, WC2R 0AG
call: 020 7212 9090   visit: www.albion.co.uk

Manchester - GBM Digital Store
One Piccadilly Gardens, M1 1RG
call: 0161 238 8951

Peterborough - KRCS Computer Store
32 Long Causeway, PE1 1YJ
call: 01733 847 747   visit: www.krcs.co.uk

Plymouth - StormFront
Drake Circus Shopping Centre,
1 Charles Street, PL1 1EA
call: 0800 612 1044   visit: www.stormfront.co.uk

Swindon - Western Computers
Brunel Plaza, The Brunel, SN1 1LF
call: 01793 531 444   visit: www.western.co.uk

Tewkesbury - AT Computers
Unit 2E, Green Lane Business Park, GL20 8SJ
call: 01684 291 112   visit: www.atcomputers.co.uk

GREAT SAVINGS
AVAILABLE NOW

Visit **www.apr-stores.com**

Distributed by:

Office:mac 2008

Office for Mac. It's the Business.

© 2009 Microsoft Corporation. All rights reserved. Microsoft, the Microsoft logo and Microsoft Office for Mac are either trademarks or registered trademarks of Microsoft Corporation in the United States and/or other countries.

running Windows: the Parallels Tools set of utilities that, for example, allow you to sweep the mouse pointer across from the host into the guest operating system and out again aren't as fully featured for Linux. Basics such as shared networking are provided, but you don't get the same abilities in sharing files or changing screen resolution, and you certainly don't get Coherence mode.

Things are a little more consistent with VMware Fusion. However, as Coherence is a Parallels trick, you don't get it here, either.

There's little stopping you mixing and matching as many virtualised operating systems as you like. On a test 2GHz MacBook with 2GB of Ram, we've had Windows 98SE, XP Pro, Vista Ultimate, Ubuntu and Red Hat Linux running simultaneously under Parallels, plus XP Pro and Ubuntu running using Fusion. We're not claiming that performance was even particularly usable at this stage, but the Mac was taking it quite happily, and the only reason we stopped there was that boredom started to set in.

Indeed, the only real problem we've experienced of running any virtualised operating systems is when we flick from the Mac OS X user that's hosting the running instance of Parallels, either to another user or to the login screen. More often than not, we've successfully come back to the host user account smoothly, but it has occasionally hung.

THE LIMITATIONS

Emulation – the technology for running Windows on pre-Intel Macs – translates instructions from one processor architecture to another. In the case of PowerPC Macs running software such as Virtual PC, it was translating instructions given to the emulated Intel chip to the real PowerPC chip.

▲ Even when it's running on a Mac, Windows Vista requires that a valid activation code is entered on installation.

Virtualisation software, however, can dip into the processor and pass instructions to and from it directly, bringing commensurate performance. For virtualisation to work, however, it has to be supported in the hardware, as it is with the Intel Core chips that power the Mac line. Every other piece of hardware has to be emulated.

This is most evident with graphics performance. Support for DirectX is limited – and you can forget about getting Vista's Aero interface running under Parallels – and we strongly recommend against attempting to run any modern 3D games under a virtualised operating system.

That said, Parallels and VMware do a cracking job of network and USB support. Parallels, for example, gives you the option of bridged networking where the guest OS negotiates its own connection; shared, where it uses NAT to piggy-back onto the Mac's connection; or host-only, isolating the guest OS from the network. Both Parallels and VMware support USB 2.

VMware Fusion is ahead in some respects here. It allows for the guest operating system to access more than one of a multi-core Mac's cores, and already has experimental support for DirectX 8.1. Additionally, while Parallels can only virtualise 32-bit operating systems, Fusion enables you to install 64-bit versions on Core 2 Duo and Xeon-powered Macs.

Because Windows can't natively read or write the Mac's default disk format (HFS+), you have no access to the data held on the Mac partition when running Windows courtesy of Boot Camp without installing third-party applications such as MacDrive from *mediafour.com*.

This could be a good thing, mind you, as you're not making the data held on your Mac's hard disk vulnerable to attack through sloppily configured Windows installations. Mac data is held on a different (and differently formatted) partition in the case of Boot Camp, and in an entirely different way – a virtual C: drive rather than an actual volume – in the case of virtualised solutions.

You should be aware, too, that the EULA for Windows Vista prohibits its use with virtualisation software except with the Business and Ultimate editions; other versions will install fine, but you'll be contravening your licence agreement.

Finally, remember that if you install Windows using Boot Camp, you'll get no technical support from Apple, and may find it trickier to get support from software and hardware developers on the Windows side.

WINE

There's a third option if you want to run Windows applications within Mac OS X, and it's very cheap – you don't even have to pay for a copy of Windows. That's because the applications designed to run under Windows are recompiled to run natively under OS X. This is achieved thanks to Wine, a project that allows Unix-like operating systems such as OS X to execute Windows applications via the X Window System. Install discs for OS X also contain X11 to provide this X Window System, so all you need is a copy of Wine.

We should state clearly that the Wine system, originally designed to allow Windows applications to run under Linux, should be regarded at best as a beta software experience; it's not usually for the faint-hearted.

There are many concurrent Wine projects for the Mac as well as for other operating systems – among them Darwine, porting the Wine libraries to the Darwin layer that underpins Mac OS X; and Cider, a developer-only tool from TransGaming Technologies to begin to enable Windows games to run under Mac OS X – but the most end-user-friendly of these is CrossOver Mac from *codeweavers.com*. This $59.95 (about £30) piece of software will allow you to run many Windows applications within Mac OS X, and while our testing suggests that it's a feasible alternative for low-power and office applications, it's not without its flaws.

The company is commendably up front about this, however: in a statement from its CEO giving feedback on its real-world experiences of using CrossOver Mac, it says: 'If you decide to purchase CrossOver Mac [even without reading about these experiences], and feel that you did not receive a fair value, we will refund your money, no questions asked.'

You can check how well certain Windows applications fare at *codeweavers.com/compatibility*, but remember that if an application doesn't appear on the list, it just means that the company isn't aware of it, and hasn't yet tested it.

Adobe Creative Suite

The Mac is the computer of choice for many professional designers. In part this is because in the earliest days it was the only affordable machine to sport a graphical interface controlled by a mouse, and because it sported an excellent range of creative software. Today that's also true of the PC, but the Mac has nonetheless remained a key choice for arty pros. A lot of that is thanks to the continued existence of Creative Suite on the platform. But what exactly is it, and what does it do?

ADOBE CREATIVE SUITE 4

If one company – other than Apple – can be said to have ensured the continued production of Macs, it's Adobe. As the owner of Photoshop and page layout application InDesign, it has ensured a healthy stream of high-quality software that has made the Mac the computer of choice for creative users.

Of course, these applications are available on the PC, too, and Adobe sells more Windows editions of its software than it does for Mac OS X, but the continued availability of Creative Suite is key to the continued existence of the Mac.

Creative Suite 4 includes various applications covering design for print and the web, or movie creation.

PHOTOSHOP

Photoshop is unquestionably the headline application. It is a powerful image manipulation application with an extensive set of tools that cover everything from adding a heading to airbrushing out exes from photos. It used to ship with a separate application called ImageReady, which was largely designed to create compressed editions of your images for use on the web. These features have now been rolled into the regular Photoshop application, giving you direct web export options.

Photoshop can open an enormous range of file formats, including many native camera file types, allowing you to import your photos without first translating them using the software that came bundled with your camera. It also works with external peripherals, such as graphics tablets, and is extendable, allowing you to download or buy additional features from third-party publishers.

You can't deny that to get the most out of Photoshop you need to spend some time learning its features. However, there are some jobs for which it is not the best tool. Despite the fact that Creative Suite ships with a management application called Bridge, first-time users will find iPhoto better suited to storing and cataloguing their photo collections; particularly with Events and Faces features in later editions.

It is also not so hot on vector graphics, either. These are made up from specific coordinates, and lines and curves drawn between them, which is very different to photos, which are made up from a grid of coloured dots. Photoshop can offer some vector-style drawing features, allowing you to draw shapes, lines and so on, but depending on your edition of Creative Suite you may also have a copy of Illustrator, which is built specifically to handle these types of files.

INDESIGN

It's a long time since the only choice in high-end desktop publishing was QuarkXPress. At one time that application was used to lay out pretty much every newspaper, magazine, flier and newsletter you read, but then Adobe came along with InDesign and things changed for good.

Over the years many users have accused Quark of being slow to react to change and have criticised its price tag, and although this has changed in recent years you can't deny that it must have contributed – in some part, at least – to the speed at which Adobe found an audience for its rival application.

InDesign may be overkill for low-end home use, but if you do a lot of design work then you will find it a far more suitable application than Pages, which offers

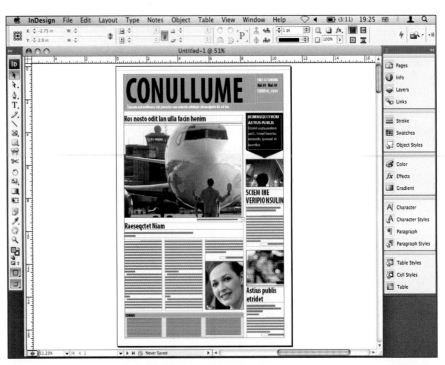
▲ InDesign is Adobe's heavyweight desktop publishing application and is commonly used to design magazines.

rudimentary layout tools for creating text boxes and positioning images.

Adobe also sells a companion application to InDesign called InCopy. This works in a similar way to a word processor, giving content creators a simple interface through which they can concentrate on writing the words without having to think about the look and feel of the page.

DREAMWEAVER
The majority of websites designed by professional web developers are built using Dreamweaver. It wasn't originally an Adobe application, but the company acquired it when it bought rival developer Macromedia. Before Adobe's acquisition of its rival, the company had its own web design tool called GoLive.

Dreamweaver lets you work in two ways: either code-based, where you directly type in all of the HTML underlying your pages, or design-based, in which you draw boxes on your pages like you would in InDesign, and then style them up to your own particular requirements.

Dreamweaver understands a wide range of online languages, can connect to the most common database types to create interactive sites, and has excellent error checking tools to make sure that the pages you create with it are compatible with the widest possible range of browsers.

However, it is a very high-level application, and its most powerful features are beyond even some of the most advanced users. As such, first-time web designers would do better to use an application like Real Mac Software's RapidWeaver (see page 108). Not only is this application inexpensive, it is very well supported by an active user community, and it works on the basis of templates, allowing you to create new pages in no time at all, and change their look in even less time.

We would not recommend Apple's own iWeb application as even in its latest iteration it is an immature application that needs some work to make it a serious rival to the likes of Dreamweaver.

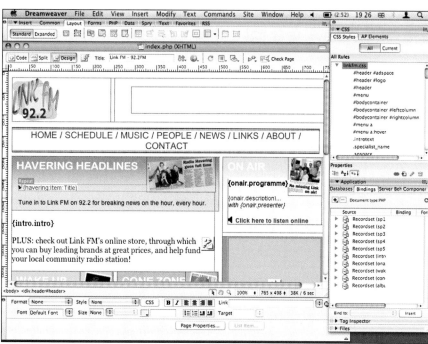
▲ Most professional web designers favour Dreamweaver and it is used for the vast majority of commercial websites.

FLASH
One of the most important technologies on the Internet is Flash. It was the basis of YouTube's original incarnation, where it was used to encode all of the videos in its library, and in many cases still is.

It's also the video mechanism that underpins the BBC's iPlayer, and it is the animation tool that we must thank for those countless addictive online games that waste many a Friday afternoon.

However, if Dreamweaver is a high-end application for professional users, this is in a different league entirely. It's easy to create new Flash files and put some shapes on the page, and even to make them move around on screen, but to do anything… well, 'flash' with it you need to understand a complex coding language that can take months to learn to any competent degree.

While it is bundled with many versions of Creative Suite, therefore, and is a tempting tool, it is beyond the reach of many inexperienced users on any platform.

PREMIERE
Adobe was once a big player in video on the Mac, and then along came Apple's own Final Cut, and Premiere disappeared from the platform. For a long time. But now it's back. On the PC it remains the leading application in its field, but on the Mac it's going to have an uphill battle to build itself a market. Again, it's a high-end application that will appeal to very few first-time users, who will naturally be drawn to iMovie, which ships as part of the iLife suite.

▲ Photoshop is a high-end application that is mostly used by professional photographers and graphic designers.

RapidWeaver

All new Macs ship with iWeb, a sophisticated tool for developing personal websites. The results are impressive, and by calling on features that form part of the .Mac hosting service, it can perform some pretty cool tricks, rivalling applications many times its price. However, it's not entirely friendly, and getting the best out of it can require jumping through some hoops. Fortunately, there is an alternative in the form of RapidWeaver, an approachable, powerful, template-based designer for everyone.

Unless you want to learn a powerful, complex tool like Adobe Dreamweaver, the best tool for consumer web design on the Mac is Real Mac Software's RapidWeaver. It may have a similar name as Adobe's high-end software, and it may perform the same function – designing pages for the web – but that is where the similarities come to an end.

It makes no assumptions about your knowledge of web design, allowing you to create everything using a series of templates, into which you then put your own words and pictures. It ships with a wide selection of templates in the box (or, more accurately, in the download package) and extras can be downloaded – usually for a fee – from both the Real Mac Software site and those of third-party developers.

When you first open RapidWeaver, you're presented with a very clean interface. There's a welcome screen in the middle and an empty column on the left. Clicking the '+' button at the bottom of this column creates a new page, allowing you to pick from a wide range of page types, such as a blog, a photo gallery or styled text, which gives you a word processor-like page into which you can enter your own content.

As you work on your pages you have a choice of three environments: Code, Edit and Preview. Code is used simply for inspecting the underlying HTML and can be largely ignored by novice users; Edit is where you do the work of creating your page; and Preview is the pane through which you can see the fruits of your labours. If they don't look right, you can quickly change their look and feel by clicking on the arrow button on the bottom row of the interface to call up the templates chooser. Here you can see thumbnail previews of every installed template, and click on a new one to apply it to your page. You'll see right away that the content you have created is immediately slipped into the new styling without any extra work from you.

▲ RapidWeaver is a powerful tool for designing websites, yet it is not as complex to learn as Adobe's Dreamweaver. The application comes with a wide selection of templates to choose from and creating web pages is very and simple.

Some elements of your pages can't be edited through the usual page creation interface because they're integral to the design, such as the name of your site and its slogan, which appears in a prominent position on your pages, along with your name and various copyright notices. These are changed through the Inspector, accessed by clicking the button marked 'i' on the bottom bar.

iWeb, which ships as part of the iLife suite, performs a similar function to RapidWeaver, but to our mind it doesn't do it nearly as well. For one thing, iWeb is very skewed to publishing on Apple's . Mac service, and although you can publish to your own domain you lose some of the smartest features. At least with RapidWeaver you know from the very beginning that whatever the design of your website then it will be compatible with pretty much any web host.

You will obviously need to sort out your own hosting deal before you can publish your pages with RapidWeaver, as web space is not included in the package price. We would recommend doing this after you have finished designing your pages so you know whether you need any specific features as part of your hosting deal, such as the language PHP, which is required to host RapidWeaver's contact form pages. Many hosts include this as part of their standard package, but some charge extra for it as an option.

684,703 NATURAL BEAUTIES

Woman Beauty #12 © Giorgio Gruizza
#5146371 / XL Standard / 6 Credits (£3.60)

NOW ALSO SELLING VIDEO

Images For All. 6 million stock images. Starting from 7p.
Phone 020 881 67284 | www.fotolia.co.uk

fotolia

Messaging clients

Like sending text messages on your mobile, instant messaging is a convenient way of having a conversation with a friend or colleague over the course of a day. Apple bundles an instant messaging client, iChat, with Mac OS X. This allows you to chat, have voice conversations, and even video conferences, but only with people on the Aim network. If you want to talk to friends on Yahoo! or MSN, you'll need to look further afield. Luckily there is a variety of clients available, so we take a look at the options available to you.

Instant messaging, once the preserve of teenagers who couldn't bear to be out of contact with one another for more than a few minutes at a time, is fast becoming a seriously useful tool for a variety of communication functions. These include video conferencing, voice over IP telephony, and sending and receiving files.

Although instant messaging clients have been around for more than a decade, it still has the feel of a technology in its infancy. For example, much like the early days of email, there's no standard protocol. And applications which use different protocols can't communicate with each other, with one or two exceptions. In some cases, protocols are proprietary, for example, both Microsoft and Yahoo! use their own protocols. Others, such as Jabber, are open.

Things are improving. Microsoft and Yahoo! clients can now talk to each other, although functionality is limited. And Google's adoption of Jabber for it's Google Talk application may encourage more organisations to adopt existing systems rather than use their own.

iChat, the instant messaging client that comes with Mac OS X and which was pre-installed on your Mac, uses AOL's Instant Messenger protocol. This means that as well as chatting with other Mac users on iChat, you can chat to PC users who have AOL's Instant Messenger.

That would be fine if most PC users had Instant Messenger as their instant messaging client of choice, but they don't. Most use either Yahoo! or Microsoft's Messenger systems. In order to talk to them, you'll either have to install the Mac versions of these two applications, or one of the multi-protocol messaging applications available for Mac OS X, such as Adium. Whichever route you take, you'll need to set up an account with the provider whose service you want to connect to.

There are other options. One is web messaging. These services work like Adium and its contemporaries in that you can connect to multiple services from one place. And like Adium, you'll need an account with each service you want to connect to. Web clients are particularly useful if you use different machines in different locations as you can elect to save chats on the host's server and have them available whenever you log-in through a web browser. Using a web client is also a useful way of connecting to an instant messaging client in a location where a firewall prevents you from using a desktop instant messaging client.

The final option is to access an instant messaging client from a mobile device, such as a phone, rather than your Mac. Sadly, the iPhone doesn't yet have an iChat client, but Yahoo! and Microsoft both have versions of their clients that work on mobile phones.

If you have friends or business contacts who use a number of different systems, you can choose to download and install an application for each and log into them separately each time you go online. This would mean you would have to launch and sign in to iChat, Yahoo! Messenger, Microsoft Messenger and Google Talk, and have windows for each application on your screen if you wanted to chat to different people on these networks during the course of a day.

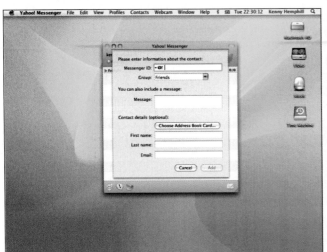 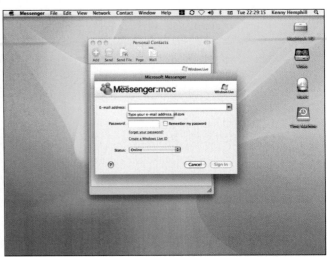

▲ **Yahoo! Messenger (left) and Microsoft Messenger (right), are the most commonly used instant messaging clients and each will need you to open a separate account to use.**

▲ Adium is a multi-protocol client that will allow you to log on to various systems.

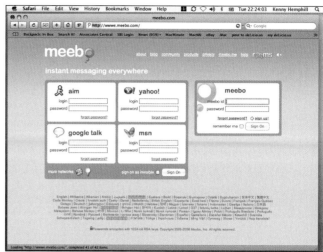
▲ Meebo is a Web-based instant messaging client that you can use on any computer.

The advantage of this approach is that you have access to the latest features of each system as soon as the application is updated and that you have more control over settings for each service. And you can be sure of having access to all the functionality of each system.

The disadvantage is that you have to log in to each account separately and then have multiple contacts windows cluttering your screen. If you choose this approach, the best option is to use the free applications available from the service provider, that is Yahoo! Messenger for Yahoo! and Microsoft Messenger for MSN or Windows Live as it is now called.

There are other clients available for these systems, but by using the official client, you ensure the best chance of compatibility with the people you chat to and will always have the latest available features for the system.

YAHOO! MESSENGER 3 BETA
Yahoo! Messenger 3 for Mac OS X is currently available as a beta download. This means that the program is not finished and is still being tested.

There are a few features missing from Messenger 3 when compared to its PC counterpart. The most obvious of these is the lack of voice chat on the Mac version. While the PC client allows you to make free voice calls to contacts in your list, just like iChat, the Mac client doesn't. You can, however, share video from a webcam and swap files. You can also tab conversations in Yahoo! Messenger 3, and its Dock icon displays the number of unread messages.

Message archiving is also listed as a feature, although we couldn't archive messages in our tests. You can also add contacts from Microsoft's Messenger and chat to them from Yahoo!.

MICROSOFT MESSENGER 6.0.3
Like Yahoo!'s application, Microsoft Messenger 6.0.3 lags behind its PC counterpart in a number of ways. However, you can exchange files, archive conversations and chat to contacts from both Microsoft and Yahoo!'s systems.

So far, so Yahoo!. But Microsoft's client also integrates with its Office suite of business applications. So if you're working on a Word document, you can use Messenger from within Word to share the document with a contact as well as have a Messenger conversation from within Word.

GOOGLE TALK
The desktop application for Google's Talk messaging service is currently Windows-only. However, Mac users can use the systems from within Gmail, Google's web email service. You invite contacts to chat, in a similar way to iChat and you click on a contact's name in the Gmail sidebar to chat to them. A small window opens up in the bottom-left of the Gmail window, allowing you to converse with the contact. If a contact is offline, that is not logged in, when you send them a message, it's stored like an email in a folder within Gmail called Chats.

ADIUM AND PROTEUS
Adium and Proteus are both multi-protocol clients. This means that you can log into all the systems for which you have accounts from one interface with all your contacts listed in one window, along with an icon which denotes the system they are connected to.

By setting Adium or Proteus to log in automatically on start-up, you can log into all your accounts simultaneously with one double-click. Although you still need multiple accounts, one for each system, this approach does take away much of the pain of incompatibility between protocols.

The downside is that if, for example, Yahoo! released the next version of Messenger tomorrow and it had the ability to make Mac-to-Mac voice calls, you'd have to wait for it to be implemented in Adium or Proteus before you could use it. And because both are made by small developers, there's no guarantee of a regular flow of updates.

MEEBO
Web-based instant messaging clients allow you to log into your account from any computer with a web browser — great if you are travelling or are away from your main computer. They are also useful if you want to chat on a computer on a network that is connected to a company firewall. Many companies set their firewall to block the ports used by instant messaging clients and so chatting using the client application is impossible.

Yahoo! Messenger has its own web messaging client, but there is no equivalent for the likes of iChat or Microsoft Messenger. Step-forward Meebo. An online messaging and chat application in its own right, Meebo also allows you to chat on most other protocols. So, by entering your log-in details for iChat, Microsoft Messenger and Yahoo! Messenger, you can connect to all three systems simultaneously and chat using your web browser.

Meebo supports avatars and emoticons and allows you to archive chats on its servers. It has all the usual functions you'd expect of an instant messaging client, such as the ability to exchange files and add contacts. There's also a Firefox plug-in that allows you to keep track of contacts and conversations in a browser sidebar.

Online video

The Internet is alive with audio and video content, with everything from teenagers miming to their favourite tracks on YouTube to the latest news bulletins available for viewing. Yet to the uninitiated, watching streaming content can be complex process. It needn't be, though. With the help of a few additional applications and plug-ins watching video, whether it is streamed or downloaded, is a simple as doing anything else on your Mac.

Watching video on the Internet used to be a frustrating experience. Postage stamp-sized clips, poor video and audio quality, and long download times made it a pastime for only those with bags of patience to spare. Add to that the various different formats for viewing downloads and streaming content and its little wonder that for most of the web's lifetime video has been little more than a curiosity.

Things have changed dramatically in the past couple of years however. YouTube has changed the streaming video landscape and made it possible for anyone with an up-to-date computer and an Internet connection to view and share video clips. Every news site worth its server space has it's own video content to accompany text and images, and you can view and download high-resolution movie trailers on your Mac. The BBC's iPlayer allows you to catch-up on up to seven-days worth of BBC TV content, and you can buy or rent movies and TV shows to download and watch on your Mac.

The most significant technological shift in video on the web, and the one which has allowed this video revolution to take place has been a de facto standardisation of formats. Just as MP3 became the standard for downloading audio, Flash has done the same for video.

The FlashPlayer, owned by Adobe, is bundled with Safari and Firefox, meaning that you don't have to download additional software to view content on YouTube or iPlayer. The only exception is when Adobe upgrades the FlashPlayer in between browser updates. However, in this instance a dialog box will open on your Mac and you'll be invited to download the latest version.

Sadly, not all video on the web is as easy to view, and there are still a number of different formats around. Many of these are viewable on the Mac without the need for additional software, while others need the help of browser plug-ins or QuickTime add-ons to work. The two most common are Real Media and Windows Media.

We'll deal with Windows Media first. Until recently, to view Windows Media content on a Mac, you needed the Mac version of Microsoft's Windows Media Player. That was problematic, because the Mac version was way behind the Windows version in the development cycle and suffered compatibility problems as a result. In addition, it meant you had to use the hideous Windows Media Player interface. Now, though, Microsoft has abandoned the Mac version of Media Player altogether and instead licensed a utility from Flip4Mac that allows you to view Windows Media video content in QuickTime Player. It's not perfect, and can be a bit sluggish, but it's a workable solution.

To download Flip4Mac, go to *microsoft.com/mac* and click on Other Products. Click on the third item down, Flip4Mac, and on the next page, click on Download Flip4Mac for free. Click Free Download on the next screen, and download on the screen after that. Double-click on the disk image which mounts on your desktop when the software has downloaded and follow the instructions. You'll now be able to play Windows Media format movies in QuickTime Player.

Although you can now play WMV files, you can't export them in a different format, or create WMV files from other video

▲ To view DivX movies, you first need to download its player from *divx.com*.

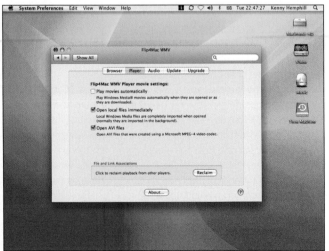
▲ Flip4Mac allows you to play Windows Media content in the QuickTime player.

formats. To do that you'll need WMV Player Pro and WMV Studio, which cost $29 (about £15) and $49 (about £25) respectively. To find out more, go to *flip4mac.com*.

Real Media is a different story. A pioneer in streaming audio and video over the web, Real has steadfastly clung to its proprietary format and although fewer and fewer sites stream content using Real, it's still used on high profile websites, such as the BBC. The basic RealPlayer plug-in is pre-installed with Safari and Firefox, so if you do come across a site that uses it, and there's no alternative, you should be able to view the content in a browser window.

To find out more about Real Player, go to *real.com*. Click on Download Free Real Player and install it. You will now be able to watch and listen to Real video and audio in a web browser or dedicated application.

These days most streaming and downloadable video content is encoded in Mpeg-4 (think of it as MP3 for video). That would be straightforward if there was only one version of Mpeg-4, but unfortunately for us, there are several. The two most common variants are H.264, Apple's preferred video format, and DivX, a format that gained significant support until the advent of H.264.

Apple encodes all the video downloads in iTunes, including movie trailers and the new video rentals in H.264 and so, unsurprisingly, support for the format is built into QuickTime.

Support for viewing and encoding DivX files doesn't come as standard with QuickTime, but can be added easily. Go to *divx.com* and click on the Free Download button. Once it's downloaded, installation will begin automatically. The free download allows you to watch DivX movies, and will install trial versions of software which will allow you to convert other movies to DivX.

As an alternative to the DivX player, particularly if all you want to do is watch DivX movies in QuickTime Player, download Perian. Perian is an Open Source QuickTime component which adds support for a whole host of file formats to QuickTime. It's free, takes only a few minutes to download and install and has been known to come up trumps when nothing else works. Go to *perian.org* to find out more and download it.

AUDIO FORMATS

Playing audio is almost as complex as video. The de facto standard for downloaded music is MP3. However, most of the major download stores don't use MP3. Apple uses another open standard, AAC, and a variant called protected AAC on iTunes, and many other download stores use a protected form of Windows Media Audio.

Some download sites, like Emusic, use MP3. If you have an iPod, your music must be either MP3, AAC or protected AAC. The iPod doesn't support Windows Media Audio. Similarly, MP3 players from other manufacturers, such as Creative, don't support Apple's protected AAC format. Microsoft's Zune has yet another proprietary audio format. For the widest possible compatibility, you should encode any

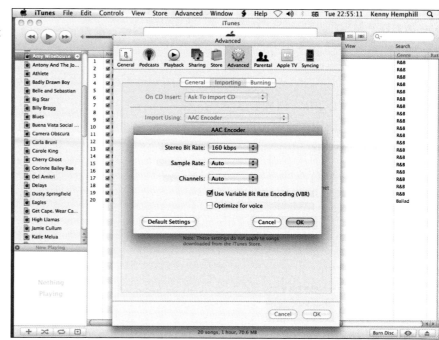
▲ To get the best quality when importing audio tracks, you adjust the bit rate – the higher the bit rate, the better quality.

CDs you import to iTunes as MP3. However, AAC offers higher quality audio at lower file sizes and is widely compatible. If you buy tracks from the iTunes Store, opt for the iTunes Plus version where available. This is a non-protected file and so will be playable on any device which supports the AAC format.

If you want to listen to radio programmes from the BBC's website, either live or using it's Listen Again service, you can choose between Real Audio and Windows Media Audio. As with video, whichever you opt for, you'll need to have the relevant plug-in installed in your browser.

When you convert audio CDs to play on your Mac or record your own audio, a good rule of thumb is the higher the bit rate, the better the quality of the resultant file. However, high bit rate files take up lots of room on your hard drive so you need to compromise between file size and audio quality.

The first thing to do is make sure variable bit rate is switched on. In Preferences in iTunes, click on the Advanced button, then the Importing tab. Select either MP3 or AAC and in Setting, select Custom. Tick the box labelled Use Variable Bit Rate Encoding and experiment with different bit rates to see which is the lowest that is acceptable to you. Variable bit rate encoding uses the maximum bit rate in passages where it is needed and where its not, uses a lower bit rate, keeping down the file size.

The sheer number of video and audio formats used on Macs and PCs can seem daunting. Gradually however, standards are emerging and by following these guidelines you should be able to play any audio or video file on a Mac.

▲ RealPlayer is one of the preferred methods for streaming video on the BBC website.

Microsoft Office

The lack of software compatible with Windows PCs is one of the most cited reasons for not switching to the Mac. Yet with the release of Microsoft Office 2008 for the Mac, this argument has little bearing in today's business environment. Office has been a key application in the Mac's software line-up for two decades now, and today it's stronger than ever. But is Microsoft's choice of business applications the best option for non-Windows users? In many cases, the answer is a hearty 'yes'.

One of the reasons people give for not switching to the Mac is that they can't get the same applications as they use on their Windows PCs. They worry about compatibility, but really they shouldn't. Why?

Because as we've already pointed out, Macs can run Windows on those rare occasions when you can't find a compatible equivalent on this platform. In addition, there are often direct translations of Windows software that are available for the Mac. Microsoft Office is a prime example. It was originally a Mac application that later made the switch to the PC, so in some ways you could argue that it wasn't the Mac that was made compatible with the PC, but the PC that was made compatible with the Mac.

The latest version for the Mac is Office 2008, and although it lacks some key features of the Windows edition, such as Visual Basic scripting, it does boast excellent file compatibility, ensuring the Mac and Windows users can share documents with ease. That should calm the worries of the Mac's biggest detractors, and may yet be enough for some business users to make the switch.

Yet there are some key differences, the biggest being the omission of Access, Microsoft's business and consumer database for Windows, from the Mac version. Fortunately, FileMaker, a wholly owned Apple subsidiary, produces two excellent products to plug the gap: FileMaker Pro for business users, and Bento for home users running Mac OS X 10.5 Leopard.

But it works both ways. Windows users have no built-in equivalent of Project Centre, the low-end project management tool built into the Mac version. Neither do they have access to My Day, a floating toolbox that keeps track of your appointments and tasks for the day ahead.

THE DRAW OF COMPATIBILITY

Word and Excel remain the world's most important word processor and spreadsheet. Their native file formats, .doc and .xls, are used by a wide range of other applications. While other formats such as plain text, rich text (RTF) and comma-separated values (CSV) may be more widely used, you can't play an active role in document sharing if you can't read .doc and .xls, particularly in business and academia. Simple as that.

This is complicated slightly by the fact that Microsoft changed its file types for its latest Office suite when it introduced the Office Open XML format. However, that still doesn't mean that you have to invest in Word or Excel to keep up with the Joneses of the business world. Pages – part of iWork – can read and write Word 2008 documents and Numbers can read and write files for Excel 2008. Other applications such as Nisus Writer Express do an excellent, although not quite perfect job of interpreting older Word files, offering you an inexpensive way into the format for simpler documents.

For those who choose to follow the crowd and stick with the Microsoft solution, though, here's a run-down of the suite's most salient features.

MICROSOFT WORD

Microsoft is selling Word, in part, on the basis that it simplifies creation of DTP-style documents. It ships with a wide range of templates on which you can change the default frame sizes, swap out images and re-style text. You can flow text into boxes, which moves from one box to the next as you edit it; you can drag images onto the page and, once they're there, re-size them.

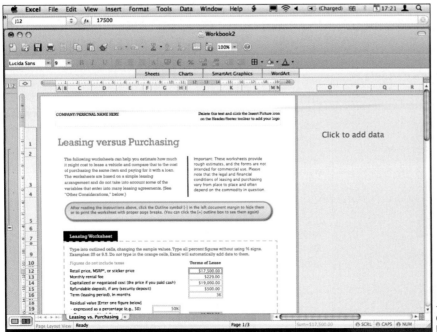

◀ If you've ever worked in an office environment then the chances are that at some point you will have come across Microsoft's spreadsheet application, Excel.

The 2008 edition is far better at doing this than any previous edition, as there is now a dedicated layout mode to complement the regular writing mode, so for home users there will be little to choose from here between Word and Pages.

One feature missing from Pages is the notebook view that Microsoft introduced with Office 2004. Used for taking notes with associated recordings, this has had a revamp, so you can now colour-code the pages it contains and create to-do items while you're taking notes. Word also has excellent outlining features, allowing you to quickly structure a document's outline, which you then flesh out later. For anything other than low-grade DTP or plain document writing, then, Word is the way to go.

MICROSOFT EXCEL
The world of business spreadsheets is ruled by Excel. Nothing else comes close. It took over from Lotus 1-2-3 on the PC a couple of decades ago, and has remained the dominant force ever since. If you want to use a Mac rather than a PC in a business environment, Office is a sensible move. However, it's no longer necessarily the best.

Since the removal of Visual Basic from Office 2008, which impacted compatibility, Microsoft has done much to dent its appeal, and you should be asking yourself whether switching to another third-party tool such as Mariner Calc, which also offers good, although not perfect, compatibility would be a financially astute move. Or, if you're feeling brave, make the switch to an online tool like Google Spreadsheets (*docs.google.com*).

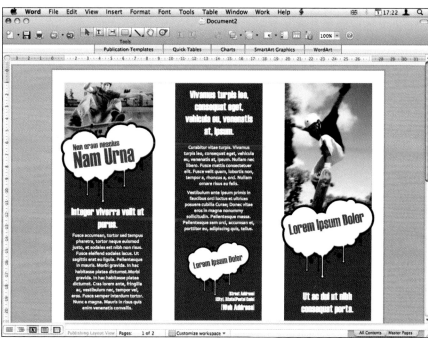

▲ Microsoft Word is the word processing application that most computer users will have used at some point.

However, if most of your spreadsheets are destined to be printed and used as evidentiary documentation, we'd recommend using iWork's Numbers. It's much easier to create a good-looking spreadsheet in Apple's own office suite than it is in Microsoft's offering, which could be just enough to swing a business proposal in your favour.

MICROSOFT POWERPOINT
PowerPoint is the industry standard for presentations, so it was a shame that the Mac version lagged behind Apple's Keynote for so long. Microsoft has rectified that with this release, which boasts improved transitions and better slide designs. However, as many users take their own computers to a presentation and plug them in before they speak, there's now little to choose between PowerPoint and Keynote since the latter became so well established and compatibility is now less of an issue.

MICROSOFT ENTOURAGE
Entourage offers the best compatibility with corporate email systems currently on offer. Microsoft's Exchange server technology dominates many businesses, and while Apple's own Mail application does offer good compatibility, it's not up to the standard of Entourage, which will see you running both server and client software from the same vendor.

Entourage doesn't have the contact and appointment sensitivity of Mail, but it does boast excellent tools for working with shared calendars and, thanks to its links to MyDay, it enables you to keep an eye on your appointments without launching your full-blown communications tool.

MICROSOFT MYDAY
MyDay is a Mac-only application for showing your appointments in one unified interface that floats within the Mac environment. If you want a constant reminder of what you should be doing next, rather than relying on iCal alarms, it's a neat solution, although there's a choice of Dashboard Widgets that will do the same for you by hooking into Mac OS X's centralised calendaring database.

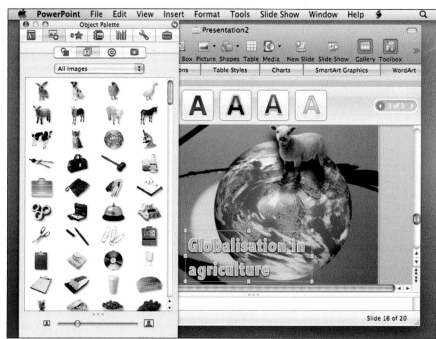

▲ Industry standard for presentations, PowerPoint for the Mac is now on a par with the Windows edition.

MobileMe

It's not cheap, but Apple's online service, MobileMe, really does help you to get more out of your machine. It's an excellent, pain-free way to share data between several machines, to get your photos and web pages up online, and to back up your files and keep them safe. As an added bonus, it also throws in calendar sharing and email features, and a steady stream of free software. So what exactly is this service that Apple tries to foist upon you the first time you switch on your Mac? And is it worth it?

MobileMe is Apple's online service for Mac users. It is closely integrated with many features of Mac OS X, and you will have been given the opportunity to sign up for it when you were first setting up your Mac. Note that it's not a free service, and you will have to pay an annual subscription to keep it running, but despite this it is a feature-packed, worthwhile service that will make your Mac far more useful – especially if you have more than one.

SHARING DATA

MobileMe is by far the easiest way to share data between several machines. Address Book and iCal are built from the ground up to synchronise their contents with a MobileMe account and, as you can sign in to an account from an unlimited number of Macs, you can use it as an easy way to keep your calendars and contacts at home and at work perfectly matched.

Synchronisation is set up through System Preferences, and here you can specify how often data is swapped with your MobileMe account (we recommend hourly) and what should be included. As you'll see, it goes well beyond contacts and appointments, even offering to back up your browser favourites, your Dashboard Widgets and your email account settings.

Once set up on every machine that you want to synchronise, you should not need to do anything else. Each Mac will take care of updating itself at the specified intervals and passing back any changes you have made to its records to the MobileMe servers.

Occasionally, however, there may be a conflict when, for example, you have made two sets of changes to a particular record on two machines between synchronisations. In this case, iSync will throw up the Conflict Resolver, highlight the differences between the two adjusted records and let you choose which one to keep.

PUBLISH WEBSITES AND GALLERIES

The Mac is often seen as a creative computer, so it is only right that Apple should provide some means of publishing your work online. MobileMe integrates well with iPhoto, iWeb and its professional photo processing application, Aperture, allowing you to upload websites and photo galleries to your public webspace on the MobileMe servers for all to see.

If you only made use of MobileMe for publishing web pages, it would be an expensive solution to a fairly simple problem, but when this feature is bundled in with everything else that the service offers, it's an added bonus – particularly when you see the quality of the galleries it produces. Different applications produce different galleries, with Aperture the most impressive.

Because Apple controls the hardware, the software and the online service, it is able to make sure that they all work together flawlessly, so MobileMe photo galleries are among the most impressive you could ever hope to browse. Even better, if you have an iPhone, you can post photos taken direct to your MobileMe gallery, meaning that even before you get home your friends can see what a great night out you've been having.

BACKING UP FILES

Mac OS X 10.5 Leopard may ship with Time Machine, a high-end backup system for copying your changed files to an attached hard drive, but it suffers from two fatal flaws. First, it doesn't run on anything earlier than Leopard, so if you're not running the latest operating system you're out of luck.

▲ A key feature of the MobileMe account is the ability to synchronise applications on one Mac with those on another.

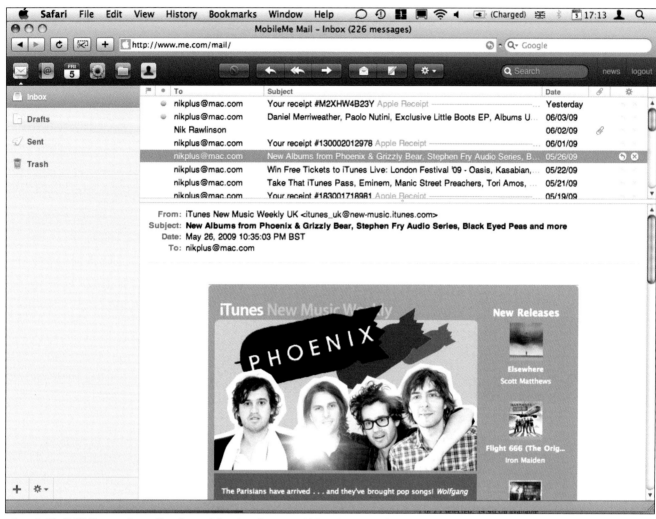

▲ As part of the MobileMe account you will receive a web-based email account, which can be accessed from any Mac and is synchronised with your Address Book.

Second, as your backup drive is connected to your Mac, your backups will probably be kept on the same site as your original files. Think what this means if you have a fire; not only will you lose your originals when your Mac goes up in smoke, but you'll lose your precious backup copies, too.

Fortunately all versions of Mac OS X include a backup application called, not surprisingly, Backup and found in the Applications folder. If yours isn't there, look for it in the software folder of your iDisk (see Free Software, right).

This lets you set up various backup sets – groups of files – that can be backed up to the iDisk on your MobileMe account. This is just a storage area in which you can keep files that you want to either have access to from multiple locations, or keep copies of off-site.

To simplify matters still further, it includes presets for backing up your important data and settings, such as addresses and calendars, or your iTunes library. To see these, simply launch Backup and press the '+' button at the bottom of the interface to start a new backup set. If none of them meets your needs, pick Custom from the list of available options and you'll be able to pick the precise files you want to back up.

AN ALWAYS-AVAILABLE CALENDAR

As well as backing up your appointments, MobileMe will publish your calendar online, so that even if you access it from a Mac not yet registered to your MobileMe account you'll still be able to get a quick fix on where you're supposed to be, and when. This is a boon for business travellers who may need to quickly borrow some airtime on someone else's corporate network, or log in at an Internet café, to check which appointment they should be attending next.

To publish a calendar online, open iCal and right-click (or hold down Ctrl while clicking) on its name in the left-hand sidebar. Choose what you'd like to publish from the dialog box that pops up. We recommend checking the box to publish changes automatically, which is left empty by default. In this way, every change that you make to the calendar, such as adding, deleting or altering an entry, will automatically be sent to the server.

Click on Publish and iCal will send your calendar to the MobileMe server and show you the address, giving you the option of visiting it directly or having the address emailed to you. Click on the button to see it right away (you can always come back and have the address sent on) and you'll be taken to an address starting *ical.me.com*, where a replica of your calendar should be on display.

FREE SOFTWARE

The final bonus of MobileMe, which is forgotten by many users, is a periodical supply of free software. It's not massively generous by any means, but if you use GarageBand in the iLife suite it's a good place to go for free loops to add to your library, and it's also the place to look for updates to the Backup application.

The free software can be found by opening a new Finder window (click the square face on the left-hand side of your Dock) and then navigating to iDisk (in the left-hand pane) and then Software. The applications and add-ons are organised here in individual folders.

Features

Want to uncover the coolest tools for your Mac? How about the most useful tools for your business? Do you want to become a Google power user, or build a website in a weekend?

All of these things – and many more – are possible with a Mac. All you need is a little bit of time, and a little bit more know-how. We may not be able to do the former, but in this section, we'll set out to do the latter, and include our ultimate tips guide to fast-track you from novice to know-all on the Mac.

Leopard books 112
Mac OS X secrets 114
20 cool tools 122
20 top business tools 128
Google power user 136
Website in a weekend 144
100 Mac tips 154
Make RSS work for you 166
Profit from social networking 170

Leopard Books

We review five books that are designed to help you make the most of all those mouth-watering features in the Leopard armoury.

Brilliant Mac OS X Leopard

Price £11.89 (RRP £16.99)
Author Steve Johnson
Publisher Pearson/Prentice Hall
ISBN 0273714408
Contact *pearson-books.com*
Available from *http://books.macuser.co.uk/leopardbooksbrilliant*

Mac OS X Leopard for Dummies

Price £10.49 (RRP £14.99)
Author Bob LeVitus
Publisher Wiley
ISBN 0470054338
Contact *eu.wiley.com*
Available from *http://books.macuser.co.uk/leopardbooksdummies*

Leopard has more features than any previous version of Mac OS X and whether you're a beginner or a more experienced user, you could almost certainly do with a helping hand when it comes to making the most of them.

The fact that Apple doesn't include a comprehensive manual with Leopard means that we have to turn to third-party books for help. Luckily, there are plenty of them on the market. From pocket-sized, monochrome productions to larger, more extravagant, full-colour publications, the titles covered here represent a broad, though by no means exhaustive, sample of those available in your local high street stockist and online.

Whether you need an author to hold your hand as you take your first steps with a brand new Mac or just want a reference book to dip in and out of occasionally, we're sure you'll find something here to meet your needs. The five publications reviewed range from £6.29 to £11.89 and are all available on *MacUser*'s online bookstore.

This is the only book here in colour and it's visually appealing. Tasks are presented as step-by-step guides down the side of the page, with crisp, annotated screenshots opposite. There's a brief discussion of each task, although it doesn't lend itself to the broader conversation found elsewhere.

The range of topics includes using TextEdit as a word processor and a description of what .Mac has to offer. But more specialist aspects, such as running Windows applications, aren't afforded much depth, with Boot Camp being the only proffered description. Uninstalling software is unfortunately simplified to just trashing the application – and some descriptions leave a great deal to be desired, being unhelpfully self-referential.

This isn't the book for those looking for in-depth discussion or hidden secrets, and keyboard shortcuts are a little thin on the ground. It's more suited to outright beginners who don't need these; those with intermediate skills should look elsewhere.

Living up to its name, this For Dummies title offers descriptions of the most basic terms – such as point, click and double-click – that only a total novice will find useful. On that level, it even provides a detailed walk-through of the system's Save dialog box.

In the page margin are markers to draw attention to tips and Leopard features. There are groan-inducing puns too, though talk in the third person is more off-putting. Nonetheless the language is suitably chatty to attract reticent technophobes who need easing into the subject matter.

In spite of this, the book admirably teaches a useful range of keyboard short cuts and provides a tear-out sheet of common ones. And when it comes to backups, coverage isn't simplified and biased towards Time Machine. Alternative applications and regimes are there as well.

Patience with the writing style is rewarded with a good introduction to the Mac. But those wanting to cut to the chase should seek a straight-laced option.

The Rough Guide to Macs and OS X 10.5 Leopard

Price £6.99 (RRP £9.99)
Author Peter Buckley & Duncan Clark
Publisher Rough Guides
ISBN 1843538733
Contact Roughguides.com
Available from http://books.macuser.co.uk/leopardbooksrough

Mac OS X Leopard Pocket Guide

Price £6.29 (RRP £8.99)
Author Chuck Toporek
Publisher O'Reilly
ISBN 0596529813
Contact oreillygmt.co.uk
Available from http://books.macuser.co.uk/leopardbookspocket

Mac OS X Leopard Phrasebook

Price £9.79 (RRP £13.99)
Author Brian Tiemann
Publisher Addison Wesley
ISBN 0672329549
Contact international@pearsoned.com
Available from http://books.macuser.co.uk/leopardbooksphrase

This Rough Guide doesn't just cover Leopard – it also devotes several chapters to the Mac and highlights reasons to switch to the platform. They serve as a simple buyer's guide, even dipping into the second-hand market and upgrades.

Each subject covered provides pointers to related sites, alternative applications and where to get more information, living up to the Rough Guide name. Asides, such as tips and useful short cuts, are presented in the margin and highlighted in cyan throughout, making for clear presentation, although the colour choice isn't very pleasing.

There's little technical detail, which is helpful for beginners. But it's too simplistic in places. Boot Camp is supplemented by talk of Virtual PC rather than more relevant options for Intel Macs, and a simple lack of power is offered as a reason to avoid the Mac mini for tasks such as gaming. However, the pointers to other sources should help even intermediates to expand their knowledge of particular subjects.

Despite the title, you'd need a pretty deep pocket to carry this guide around. Though the format is too small for tips to sit in the page margin, they're still clearly highlighted in main text so you don't skim over vital information.

Though it starts with a guide to Leopard's new features, this isn't the best option for an absolute beginner. Don't expect a discussion of alternatives to applications, while some bundled applications – such as Font Book – aren't explained in any useful depth. It works better to jog the memory of an existing Mac user, leaving those unfamiliar with .Mac services able to configure an iDisk, but having to infer its purpose for themselves.

Throughout the book are simple question-and-answer sections covering common scenarios, such as finding a MAC address, and thankfully they're indexed to save flicking through the guide. So for the space afforded to it, the guide is a useful reference for existing Mac users.

This isn't for those wanting walk-throughs of Time Machine and the more graphical side of the Mac, but it is a tamed introduction to the uglier side of Mac OS X. Tiemann cleverly garners enthusiasm for the daunting world of Terminal by immediately customising the appearance of Leopard's newly-tabbed Terminal window.

Normally fearsome Unix commands are explained in a frisky style that doesn't have you reaching for Command-Q. Plenty of reasons to use the command line are proffered, though the book also provides tips for the graphical side, highlighting integration between the two, as well as recommendations of tools for tasks such as scheduling cron jobs.

The focus upon the command line makes this a dryer offering, though there's also coverage of Disk Utility and network configuration. Thankfully it's well enough written to prevent you coming to a grinding halt, and it is a good route into the underbelly of OS X.

Mac OS X Secrets
34 hidden features

Whether you're a seasoned pro or testing the water with the latest cat to join Apple's family, there are dozens of hidden, undocumented features in Mac OS X 10.5 waiting to be discovered. This collection of essentials will quickly make your Mac much more productive.

Words Kenny Hemphill + Alan Stonebridge
Image Danny Bird

Whether you're a recent convert or you adopted Leopard as soon as it was released, you'll have settled into working with it and be familiar with the basics. You'll also have favourite features, tricks that you wonder how you ever lived without, and things that irritate you to the point where you feel like throwing your mouse out of the window.

Over the next eight pages, we've put together our favourite Leopard tips and hacks. Some of them will boost your productivity, others remove common irritants, such as the 3D Dock and translucent menu bar, and the rest show you how to use Leopard's new features in ways you may not have thought of.

Whether you've been wondering if it's possible to make a Time Machine volume bootable, want to know how to create a To Do task from a Mail message, use Screen Sharing in full-screen mode or highlight the contents of your Stacks as you hover over them with the mouse pointer, there's plenty in this feature that will be of use to you.

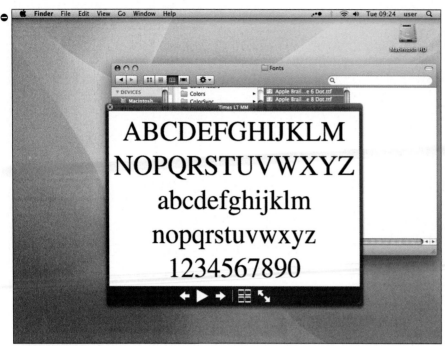

▲ Previewing fonts in Quick Look is a very effective way of quickly scanning through your font collection and selecting your favourite fonts, at full-screen size. Oh, and it looks great, too.

01 Make a bootable Time Machine Volume

Time Machine is fantastic and is rapidly becoming our favourite Leopard feature. But there is just one thing missing, though: the ability to boot your Mac from a Time Machine volume. If your hard drive fails catastrophically, you need to buy a new one, install Leopard from the original disc and then restore your Mac from the Time Machine volume. Not any more…

Take a new or re-formatted disk with enough space to use as a Time Machine volume, connect it to your Mac, insert your install DVD, open Disk Utility, and perform a Restore using the new disk as the source. Once that's done, go to System Preferences, click on the Time Machine pane and select the new drive as your Time Machine volume by clicking Choose Backup Disk. Time Machine only writes to free space, so it won't over-write your Leopard installation.

02 Use Quick Look efficiently

Quick Look is one of Leopard's most useful features, enabling you to view the contents of a supported file without opening its associated application.

In addition to viewing the contents, you can view a folder full of files as a slideshow and view files in a heads-up full-screen mode. The quickest way to activate Quick Look is to click on the file you want to view and hit the spacebar. You can also click on the eye icon in the Finder toolbar (if it's not there, then just add it from View/Customize Toolbar in the Finder). To invoke full-screen mode immediately, Alt-click the eye icon or use the keyboard shortcut Alt-Command-y.

03 Preview fonts with Quick Look

There are a number of ways to preview fonts in Mac OS X, but this is easily our favourite. Navigate to the Fonts folder in the Finder and select it. Press Command-a to select all the fonts and then hit Alt-Command-y to activate Quick Look full-screen mode. You will immediately see the upper case and lower case letters and the numbers in the first font, alphabetically, in the folder on the screen. Quick Look will play a slideshow of each font family, and you can also navigate or view thumbnails of each font using the controls at the bottom of the screen.

When you see a font you like or want to use, press Escape to go back to regular Quick Look mode and the name of the font will be displayed at the top of the Quick Look window.

04 Create a favourite System Preferences stack

Stacks has split Mac OS X users into three camps – those who like it, those who hate it, and those who have never used it. But it can be very useful. Here's a way to use it to quickly access System Preference panes you use regularly.

Create a new folder inside your user folder and give it a name like System Pref Favourites. Now navigate to System/Library/Preference Panes and, while holding down the Alt and Command keys (to create aliases), click and drag the panes you use most often to your new folder. Drag the folder to your Dock and you have easy access to the panes. To hide the file suffixes, select all the panes, click Command-i to open Get Info and click on the Hide Extension checkbox. The resulting stack can be viewed as a fan, grid, or in Mac OS X 10.5.2, as a list.

▲ Despite being much criticised, Stacks do have their uses. Creating a Stack for your most used System Preference panes saves you having to open System Preferences first.

▲ It's not the kind of tip you'll use every day but there's sure to come a time when you want to change the short name for an account. Luckily, it's very easy.

05 Create a new short name

In addition to the full name of your Mac OS X account, every user also has a short name. That short name is fixed and can't be changed once the account has been set-up. But what if you don't like it and feel a desperate need to use another short name instead? There is an answer: create an additional short name and use that instead. Here's how.

Open System Preferences/Accounts and Ctrl-click or right-click on your account name in the left-hand side of the window. Select Advanced Options. Don't change anything. Instead, click on the plus symbol at the bottom of the window. Now type in the name you want to add. Your account now has a new alias, which you can use as a new short name.

06 Ambient noise reduction

This one only works on Intel Macs. There's nothing worse than spending ages recording a podcast or a voiceover for a presentation or movie, only to discover that the noise of the builders across the street can be heard alongside your commentary.

Leopard has a simple way to eliminate this. Before you start recording, go to System Preferences/Sound and click on the Input tab. Select your audio input device and click on the Use ambient noise reduction checkbox. This turns your microphone into a noise-cancelling mic.

▲ iDisk is a convenient way of backing up files off-site and transferring them between work and home.

▲ Gone are the days when you had to erase the data on a hard drive before you could partition it. Now you can even partition your boot drive with just a few clicks. It's that simple.

07 Calculations in Text Edit

Mac OS X has a very powerful and versatile calculator and you can, if you don't want to open Calculator, also perform calculations in Spotlight, simply by typing the formula in Spotlight's search bar. But, if you're in Text Edit or any other application into which you can input text, there is another way. Just type your formula, highlight it, and press Command-Shift-8. The formula will be replaced by its result.

08 iDisk syncing

Copying files to and from your iDisk, if you have a .Mac account, can be a convenient way of backing up important files off-site and transferring files between Macs in different locations, for example, between work and home.

But copying files to and from an iDisk can be slow and tedious. The solution is to turn on iDisk Syncing. When it's running, Mac OS X creates a local copy of your iDisk on your hard drive and when you copy files to and from it, it's as fast as copying them to anywhere else on your hard drive. Mac OS X then copies the files to your real iDisk in the background. To turn on iDisk syncing go to System Preferences/.mac and click on the iDisk tab. At the bottom of the window, click on Start and check the Automatically radio button.

09 Ditching irritating dialog boxes

If, like us, you find yourself annoyed by the boxes that pop-up when you restart or shutdown your Mac and ask you if your sure that's what you want to do, then you can get rid of them. Hold down the Alt key when you select Shut Down or Restart and the dialog box will be banished. Note that this won't work if there are other users logged into the Mac as you will still have to authenticate in order to log them out and shutdown or restart.

10 Partitioning on the fly

If you have a capacious hard drive that you want to split into multiple volumes, you can now do it without erasing the data on the drive. Open Disk Utility and click on the icon of the drive you want to partition. Make sure you click on the drive and not the volume. Now click on the Partition tab and click on the plus symbol at the bottom of the screen. You can now drag the horizontal slider in the window to set the size of the new partitions. To add more volumes, simply click on the plus sign again.

11 Control Cups

Common Unix Printing System, or Cups, for short is the printing system used in Mac OS X. If the idea of tweaking Unix settings fills you with horror, this tip is not for you. But if you want more control over how your Mac communicates with the printers to which it is connected, it may be useful.

Open a web browser window and type http://127.0.0.1:631 into the address bar. You now have access to a range of options including the ability to view recent jobs sent to that printer, move jobs from one printer to another and configure a printer.

12 Get rid of translucency in the menubar

One of the biggest complaints about Leopard has been reserved for the newly translucent menubar. Whereas in previous versions of Mac OS X, the menubar was opaque, in 10.5 it allows your desktop background to apparently show through.

Apple clearly listened and in Mac OS X 10.5.2 there's an option in the Desktop System Preferences pane to switch off the translucent menubar. However, that leaves you with a dull grey menubar. For a more metallic looking menubar, open Terminal from Applications/Utilities and type following:

sudo defaults write /System/Library/LaunchDaemons/ com.apple.WindowServer 'EnvironmentVariables' -dict 'CI_NO_BACKGROUND_IMAGE' 0

Or for a white menubar:

sudo defaults write /System/Library/LaunchDaemons/ com.apple.WindowServer 'EnvironmentVariables' -dict 'CI_NO_BACKGROUND_IMAGE' 1

You'll be asked for your admin password, enter it and hit Return. Now quit Terminal and restart your Mac.

13 Make the Dock 2D

Many users who don't like the translucent menubar also complain about the new 3D Dock. We've never felt it was a problem and have learned to live quite happily with it. But if you really want to get rid of it, there is a way to replace it with a simpler, 2D version. Again it involves a small amount of work in Terminal, so open it from Applications/Utilities and type the following:

defaults write com.apple.dock no-glass -boolean YES

Now press Return and type:

killall Dock

This restarts the Dock and activates the new version.

If you decide to revert back to the 3D Dock, use the same commands but replace *YES* with *NO* at the end of the first string.

14 Change the volume in smaller increments

The ability to change the volume of your Mac's audio output from the keyboard is great. The problem is that there are only 16 steps, so the volume jumps up and down rather than rolling smoothly.

You can adjust it more finely from System Preferences by going to the Sound pane and dragging the slider pixel by pixel, but it's hardly convenient. A much better way is to hold down Shift and Alt and then use the keyboard volume control as normal. The modifier keys multiply the number of increments by four giving you much better control over the volume.

15 Make a recent applications Stack

Leopard, like every previous version of Mac OS X, keeps a list of recent applications that can be accessed by going to the Apple menu and hovering over Recent Items. This is rather counter intuitive, however, as the chances are your normal method of opening the applications you use regularly is to click on them in the Dock. You can create a Stack in the Dock for all recently used applications, making it easy to find those which aren't in your Dock. Open Terminal and type the following:

defaults write com.apple.dock persistent-others -array-add '{ "tile-data" = { "list-type" = 1; }; "tile-type" = "recents-tile"; }'

Now type

killall Dock

On the right-hand side of your Dock, next to your other Stacks, there will now be one for recent applications. To remove it, just drag it out of the Dock.

16 Use the Guest Account

Leopard makes it easy to allow guests to access your Mac to surf the web or check their email without having access to any of your files. To set up this feature, go to System Preferences and click on Accounts. Click on the padlock and enter your Admin password. Now click on the Guest Account icon in the left-hand window and tick the Allow guests to log into this computer checkbox.

Now, whenever a guest logs in using this account a new Home folder is created and is deleted when they log out again.

17 Create a To Do with associated Mail message

Leopard Mail includes the ability to create To Do tasks and share them with iCal. And you can also associate a task with an email message. Here's how: click on the Mail message you want to use to create the task and select the text within the Mail that relates to the task. Now click on the To Do button on Mail's toolbar and a drop-down window displays the new To Do. To edit, click on the right-hand arrow icon next to the task title, and set a priority and completion date. In the To Do window, you can view the associated Mail message by clicking on the arrow in front of the date.

18 Search Wikipedia from Leopard's Dictionary

Leopard's Dictionary application saves you the bother of wasting valuable space in Safari's tab bar, presenting the online encyclopedia's information in a beautiful

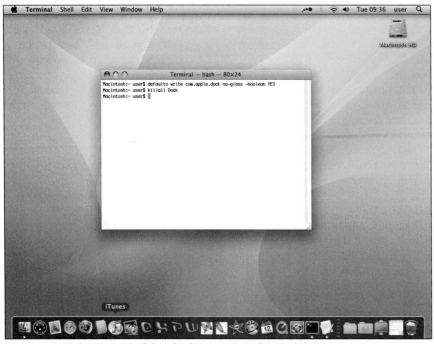

▲ If you're not a big fan of Leopard's 3D Dock then it's easy to change it to 2D, which looks much cleaner.

serif stylesheet. Ordinarily, its content appears last in the page beneath the dictionary, thesaurus and Apple-related definitions, but it can be moved further up in the application's preferences.

Once you've entered a search term, Dictionary pulls a list of matching pages from the Wikipedia website. If the results aren't helpful, just type a new search term; the search box retains the focus, so submitting another search is a very rapid process. It makes investigative searches – and those that are just for the sake of it – a real doddle.

19 Reopen the last closed window or last session

Safari's History menu has a couple of useful features designed to help you pick up where you left off in you previous session.

If you've accidentally quit Safari or need to restart your Mac after installing a software update, the option to reopen all windows from the last session will restore all windows and tabs.

The other option will reopen the last closed window, but there's no corresponding feature to reopen the last closed tab.

20 Clear specific data from Safari

Safari has been brought into line with other browsers like Firefox. The Reset Safari command in the application menu now displays a dialog with several categories allowing you to choose what goes and what doesn't in one fell swoop. So you can now clear the cache, remove cookies and site icons, previous searches and other sensitive data, all from one convenient place.

21 Force a Time Machine backup

It's easy to forget about the contextual menu of icons in the Dock. They come in handy when quitting applications without switching to them, but they typically offer features like switching windows and hiding an application's windows that are better served by Exposé and keyboard shortcuts.

In light of this, you would be forgiven for never having Ctrl-clicked on the Time Machine icon in the Dock, but it does offer a couple of useful options. There's an option to browse Time Machine disks other than your main one, but more important are options to begin and cancel backups regardless of Time Machine's schedule.

So if Time Machine begins to back up at an inconvenient moment, there is no need to dive into System Preferences to cancel it. Just Ctrl-click the dock icon and tell it to stop backing up. Conversely, if you're about to leave the office or home and want to ensure Time Machine backs up recent work ahead of schedule, there's an option to force an immediate backup.

22 Reduce delay when dragging between Spaces

Apple provides plenty of options for dragging windows between Spaces, but the most convenient is to simply drag a window to the edge of the desktop to move to an adjacent space. The short delay can be easily tweaked by entering into the Terminal:

defaults write com.apple.dock workspaces-edge-delay –float 0.1 then restarting the Dock will killall Dock

The default value is 0.75, but you can set it lower for a snappier feel, though very low settings run the risk of quickly jumping across multiple Spaces, or very high to prevent accidental jumps.

The zoomed out view that appears when F8 is pressed offers another useful way to drag windows between Spaces. Holding the Command key when dragging a window has two benefits.

First, all other windows from the same application follow it. Second, when released over another Space, the windows will drift back to the same coordinates that they occupied in the previous Space.

23 Stop printers hanging around in the Dock

The printer queue icon is a frequent annoyance in Leopard, as it hangs around in the Dock even when a print job is finished. Go to System Preferences and open the Print and Fax pane. Click on any printer in the left-hand window and then click on Open Print Queue to make its icon appear in the Dock, then Ctrl-click on it.

Tucked away in the contextual menu is an option labelled Auto Quit. In a strangely counter-intuitive move, enabling it for one printer does so for all, which makes it all the more surprising that the option isn't in plain sight in the preferences pane.

▲ We're not quite sure why Apple chose to place such a useful option here, especially when it affects all printers.

24 Separators in the Dock

Stacks are a good way to launch applications, but the fan and grid views only afford a limited number of items to be viewed at once. The main trouble with grouping commonly used applications on the left-hand side of the Dock is that it becomes cluttered even when you only have a couple of applications open.

Adding separators visibly breaks icons up into groups. Clever organisation of icons is also a good way to keep track of what's open in other Spaces. Type the following command into the Terminal to add a single spacer.

defaults write com.apple.dock persistent-apps -array-add '{ "tile-type" = "spacer-tile"; }'

Do this as many times as you need to create more separators, then enter *killall Dock* to restart it. Click and drag one of these blank separators to move it like any other icon, or drag it out of the Dock if you no longer want it.

25 A Stack of volumes

Thanks to Stacks, Spotlight and the recent items list, most things are just a couple of clicks away. However, volumes can easily get lost on an untidy desktop. You could browse in a Finder window instead or keep volumes in specific places on the desktop, as Leopard now remembers where they were positioned. However, Stacks offer a third option. Use the Finder's

▲ Visually grouping Dock icons is a great way to keep track of applications by function or which Space they're in, making it much easier for you to find the right application.

Go to Folder feature to browse to /Volumes – the folder is typically hidden, but you'll now be able to drag it from the Finder to the Dock to create a new stack.

The downside is that volumes can't be dragged from the stack to the trash to eject them. Instead you'll have to click on the icon to open the volume, then press Command-e to eject it.

Also volumes lose their visual identity in a stack as their own icons aren't displayed, but it could still save time on scanning a busy desktop.

26 More refined Spotlight searches

There are useful refinements to Spotlight in Leopard, such as the ability to use additional Boolean conditions rather than just matching all criteria.

From a Finder window, after entering a search term or from Spotlight's Show All window, Alt-click the '+' to add a Boolean condition to your search.

Beginning a search using Spotlight or by creating a new Smart Folder, the list of searchable locations is limited to the local Mac, shared volumes and folders and your user folder.

The trick is to fall back on the old Find command that still resides in the Finder's File menu. Browse to the folder or volume where you want to begin searching and press Command-f. Now, rather than searching wide and far, you can refine your searches to within a specific folder or local or networked volume.

27 Pruning language support

While previous versions of Mac OS X allowed you to remove foreign language support from applications, the size of a Leopard installation makes it an important feature for those with older Macs or notebooks, whose system drive may be tight on space.

Go into your Applications folder, select an application and press Command-i to show the Get Info panel. Then expand the Languages section, click in the list, and press Command-a to select all languages, then hold the Command key and deselect your preferred language. Click on the minus button below the list and the unwanted languages will be removed.

Particularly large applications may support many languages, which also happens to waste a lot of disk space as a result. Removing foreign languages could save anything from a few hundred megabytes to well over a gigabyte of valuable space. Also worth considering is trashing the Japanese dictionaries found in Library/Dictionaries as that will save another few hundred megabytes, after which they simply no longer appear in the Dictionary application.

28 Say Bonjour to Screen Sharing's browser

Leopard's Screen Sharing feature is a great way to administer other Macs if you don't need the full power of Remote Desktop. It's invaluable for small offices and even in the home to administrate those Macs without monitors that you've dedicated to one task in your home.

The Finder already indicates which Macs have Screen Sharing enabled, but it does so on a Mac-by-Mac basis. Screen Sharing is an application in itself, but it's tucked away in System/Library/CoreServices – browse there in the Finder and drag it to the Dock. Launch it and you'll be presented with an unfriendly dialog that requires you to know the network address of the Mac you want to connect to. Close Screen Sharing and open Terminal, then type:

defaults write com.apple.ScreenSharing ShowBonjourBrowser_Debug Yes

Open Screen Sharing again and it will present a list of all machines found using Bonjour on which Screen Sharing is enabled.

29 Screen Sharing's other hidden talents

Screen Sharing's toolbar contains a measly three buttons by default, but there are others – they just can't be added by customising the toolbar. Instead, they're unlocked with

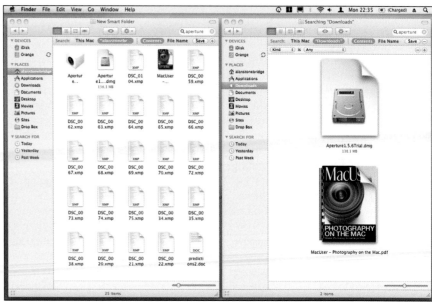

▲ On the left is a Smart Folder searching for the word aperture in the user folder, while the window on the right shows much more precise search results from within the downloads folder.

▲ The Bonjour-enabled browser window makes Screen Sharing work better as an application in its own right.

yet another Terminal command. Make sure Screen Sharing is closed, then open Terminal and type the following:

defaults write com.apple.ScreenSharing \ 'NSToolbar Configuration ControlToolbar' -dict-add 'TB Item Identifiers' \ '(Scale,Control,Share,Curtain,Capture,FullScreen,GetClipboard,SendClipboard,Quality)'

Open Screen Sharing and connect to another computer. You now have the ability to lock the display on the other Mac, so the user can't see what you're doing. Alternatively, you can observe the other Mac without your interference from your own mouse and keyboard.

A four-level slider controls quality of the display, should you prefer to rely on manual control rather than the adaptive setting, and you can then grab a screenshot of the remote desktop.

Most pleasing of all is the ability to switch into full-screen mode, in which the toolbar appears as a floating palette. While there's little clutter in Screen Sharing's window, the more self-contained feeling makes things less confusing than in windowed mode.

30 Mouse-over highlights on Stacks

Stacks work well in both fan and grid views, or at least they do until the stack grows to more than 10 or 12 items.

The downloads Stack is a good example of how busy stacks can quickly become unwieldy even when using the mouse. Icon previews and a large number of files conspire to hide the mouse cursor among the detail.

A large part of the problem is pure old-fashioned laziness, the same kind that leaves all but the most disciplined user with a cluttered desktop.

There's also a visual issue with large, grid-based stacks. When navigated using the keyboard, a highlight appears over the current selection and it can be enabled for mouse users, too. Open Terminal and type:

defaults write com.apple.dock mouse-over-hilte-stack -boolean Yes

The Dock must be restarted so enter *killall Dock* and wait a few seconds. Then simply substitute *No* for *Yes* at the end of the first command to reverse this change.

▲ Keyboard users see this highlight in grid view, but it's also helpful for mouse users, especially with large stacks.

31 Keep the downloads Stack clean

The downloads Stack is helpful but it can quickly become cluttered with both archives and their unpacked contents. Downloads can subsequently become a chore to manage if you don't trash them regularly. You can save yourself some trouble by automating how archives are handled after they've been expanded.

This is done through Archive Utility, another application that's tucked away in System/Library/CoreServices.

The second setting in the application's preferences opens up new options for managing the downloads stack. Archives can either be trashed immediately after they're expanded or moved to another folder, which is a more prudent approach if you're installing downloaded software and need to keep the archive. We would recommend creating a folder called Old Archives in your user folder and moving archives there. The end result is a tidier downloads stack that requires less frequent management.

32 Avoid icon previews on a busy desktop

If you insist upon storing documents on the Desktop, it's wise to turn off icon preview to save on resources. Otherwise you run the risk of previews slowing down your Mac, especially if it's an older one. Click on the Desktop then press Command-j to change the view options. Make sure icon preview is deselected.

33 Smarter dropping of files onto Dock icons

Dropping a file onto most applications' Dock icons will simply open them, but there's more control available when it's needed. Say you need to FTP files to a regular upload location. Drag the selection from the Finder over your FTP application's Dock icon but don't immediately drop them. Instead, press the spacebar and the application will launch, allowing you to drop them exactly where they need to be.

34 The Finder's Path Bar

Spotlight users will be instantly familiar with the path bar that runs beneath search results. It shows the location of the currently selected file. The same feature can be enabled in Leopard's Finder by selecting Show Path Bar on the View menu.

It also shares some functionality with Spotlight. For instance, Ctrl-clicking any folder in the path gives options to open it or get information about it.

There's also a new feature that lets you drag files to folders in the path to move or copy them or create aliases.

▲ No need to worry about getting out of full-screen mode as the extended toolbar floats above the remote desktop.

20 cool tools

If you're a recent convert to the Mac from a Windows PC, you may be unaware of the variety of applications that are available for the platform. We take a look at 20 applications that should find their way into your Dock.

▲ Bento presents fundamental features in an extremely accessible way – it also syncs with the iPhone.

Cool tools come and go. Today's bright idea can quickly look jaded, while those with proven staying power may become incorporated into Mac OS X or otherwise institutionalised. Here, we detail 20 tools that are worth checking out, an eclectic selection to enrich your toolset over the year.

We've omitted brand-new tools that will emerge over the coming months. Expect to find add-ons for Time Machine that trace versions of a document through its backups to function as version-control software, and a client networking configuration utility to step into the gap left by the loss of NetInfo in Leopard. Virtualisation will continue to make big strides in Mac use at several levels: not only will the battle between Parallels Desktop and VMWare be waged on our mundane Macs, but it will also come to Mac OS X Server.

Virtualisation of server operating systems is the next big thing, allowing admins to run several different images of server-operating systems at once, improving robustness and versatility. On the Internet, one obvious growth area is social networking for older users, filling the gap between the likes of Facebook and Second Life, as well as the various Reunited services.

01 Bento
URL *filemaker.com*
Price £29 (£24.68 ex VAT)

Friendly though FileMaker is, with its Server editions and an army of developers and consultants, it has become just another database. Bento promises to be the lightweight data management tool that almost every Mac user can turn to their advantage, harnessing contact details from your Address Book, appointments from iCal, imported spreadsheets and more. By concentrating on the fundamental features of a database then presenting them in an extremely accessible way, Bento should have universal appeal. Its ability to sync with the iPhone will be particularly helpful for the lightweight road warriors among us and it should sit comfortably in the company of existing iLife and iWork suites.

By focusing on the assembly of fields into attractive forms rather than constructing ingenious scripts, Bento provides clean support for the key database functions of entry and retrieval. It is no rival to MySQL or even FileMaker itself but is an excellent intermediate between the relative inflexibility of applications such as Address Book and the complexity of a full relational database.

02 BetterZip
URL *macitbetter.com*
Price $19.95 (about £10)

The venerable StuffIt started life as one of the coolest shareware applications around when there were no other good compression tools for Macs and even Zip was still in nappies. But the time has come for it to retire gracefully now that it has succumbed to bloat and some pretty hideous warts. BetterZip is everything that StuffIt used to be and more: it supports most old compression formats as well as many popular and whizzy new methods. It is also simple, no-nonsense and clean. It compresses to the widely-

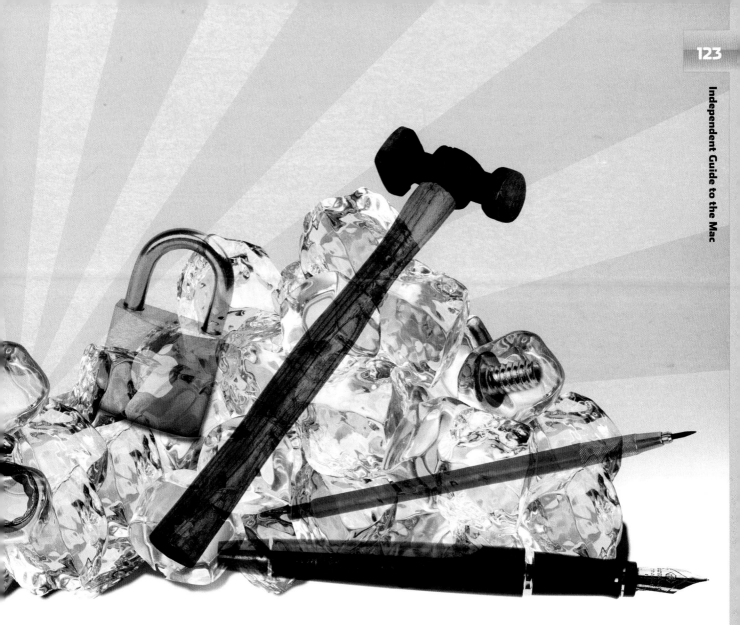

accepted Zip, GZip, BZip2 and 7-Zip formats, with or without encryption, and a Rar plugin is available separately.

A big attraction is that it can open and decompress 25 different formats from ARJ to Comicbook Zip, the only significant omission being StuffIt's newer .sitx archives, for which you will still need StuffIt Expander. Its preferences allow you to make BetterZip the default application to handle each of these formats should you wish. This is a nice touch that makes it a strong candidate to be your primary compression utility. For good measure Windows-using friends will thank you for moving away from proprietary .sit and .sitx formats.

▲ BetterZip can compress to Zip, GZip, BZip2 and 7-Zip, making it suitable as your primary compression tool.

03 Buzzword
URL *virtub.com*
Price TBA

For many developers, the future lies in Office over Internet (OoI) services, although current market expectations are almost certainly overinflated. Mobile users are most likely to be core customers who should end the year settled with the OoI service of their choice; the rest of us may dabble for a while then return to traditional local application suites.

Buzzword, from Virtual Ubiquity, has caught Adobe's eye sufficiently to be snapped up before a single product was shipped, and looks well positioned to deliver one of the better OoI experiences. For a start it makes few compromises in features despite running in a browser. Documents are fully styled, typographically respectable as you might expect from Adobe, and flow around embedded graphics, tables and other rich content.

Buzzword aims to match the versatility of powerful word processors. Imagine Pages running through your browser, and you can see how attractive this could be, while a matching spreadsheet tool could be a killer app.

▲ Buzzword allows text to be fully styled and flow around embedded graphics to create stylish documents.

04 F-Script
URL *fscript.org*
Price free

Although AppleScript and Automator remain powerful tools for integrating applications, AppleScript Studio (part of the high-end Xcode development system) has not armed the scripter with easy access to Mac OS X's Cocoa interface. F-Script is an open source development environment that provides a lightweight scripting interface to Cocoa. With it you can write your own applications as well as interface with those that support F-Script scripting, such as Colloquy (chat client), Daylite (business productivity suite), and Event Horizon (3D first-person game).

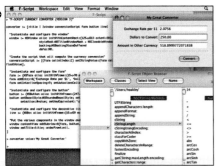

▲ F-Script provides a lightweight scripting interface to Cocoa and enables you to write your own applications.

▲ Google's sophisticated Web Toolkit is one of the best ways to build Ajax applications for interactive pages.

▲ Thanks to Hostal you can block advertisements, pop-ups and porn sites very conveniently.

Uniquely you can inject F-Script code into existing Cocoa applications – such as most modern Mac software – to explore and extend them as you wish. F-Script is also an excellent interface to Cocoa for those using other scripting languages such as Python. For the ultimate in Python, try the free add-on PyInjector tool – this injects F-Script and a complete Python interpreter into a running Cocoa application. With its Smalltalk-like syntax and powerful object browser, F-Script is everything a Mac geek needs.

05 Fluid
URL *fluidapp.com*
Price free

As web applications become increasingly popular, it can get messy having to open new windows or tabs in your browser, then rummage through them to catch up with your friends on Facebook. Mozilla Labs' Prism project aims to allow users to encapsulate a browser tied to a specific website into a discrete application.

Fluid is a Mac equivalent. Arm it with the URL of the site that you want it to take you to, an application name, destination and icon (which can be based on the site's favicon), and it will create a 1.3MB browser application dedicated to that site. You can then have your Facebook, *MacUser*, Gmail, Buzzword and other applications running at the same time, switched through the Dock or even spread over different Spaces under Leopard. It also helps you switch contexts cleanly and avoid confusion.

▲ Fluid quickly creates a 1.3MB browser application dedicated to the site that you want to work on.

06 Google Web Toolkit
URL *code.google.com/webtoolkit*
Price free

Unless you're a professional web developer your personal website will probably consist of static pages generated using an application like iWeb or Freeway and pulling no punches. If you want to stay in the vanguard, you need to make your pages interactive rather than flat, preferably with asynchronous JavaScript and XML – Ajax.

This makes them quicker to load and update, more attractive to the visitor and opens many new capabilities for you to harness their interaction. Few are geeky enough to be able to hand-roll the requisite XHTML, CSS, JavaScript, XML and content, so you need a toolkit and development platform to smooth your transition. One of the best ways of building Ajax applications is Google's sophisticated Web Toolkit, which has extensive help, documentation and examples embedded in it. You will still need to test your site out, using a range of different browsers and platforms, but this toolkit should prove an excellent aid for authoring stunning sites.

07 Hostal
URL *northernsoftworks.com*
Price $8.99 (about £4.50)

In the early days of networking and the Internet, mapping domain names to IP addresses and vice versa depended on the hosts file on each system. It is poetic justice perhaps that now we want to block advertisements, pop-ups and sites with inappropriate content such as porn, one of the best ways of doing so is through the same good-old fashioned hosts file.

Hostal provides a very convenient and helpful way of maintaining your local hosts file, so that adverts and adult sites are blocked. If you are getting fed up with persistent pop-ups enticing you to view pornographic matter and the other irritating dross that has become so obtrusive on the Internet, give Hostal's old hosts trick a try. Its single window is split into three tabs.

The first offers fairly traditional access to host definitions, which you can use to ease connections with local computers for instance. The second tab comprises a long list of blocked hosts offering adult content, while the third consists of a huge listing of all the major advertising addresses that you can block as you wish.

08 HoudahGeo
URL *houdah.com/houdahGeo*
Price £23.11 (£19.67 ex VAT)

As long as the clock in your camera is correctly set, every digital photo that you take will be perfectly orientated in time. But just where did you take all those pictures? Some will be at recognisable locations, while others may remain a mystery even when you have tried to work out where you were at that time on the given day.

HoudahGeo helps you keep your images orientated in space, either from GPS data recorded when you took the photos, or by finding each location in Google Maps. Import a block of images that you want to work on, then add positional info (latitude, longitude and altitude). Even if you don't have these from contemporary GPS records, you can zoom in and out of a Google Map window to place a cross where the photo was taken; HoudahGeo will then calculate the latitude and longitude for you. Finally you can export the geocoding data as Exif metadata to each image, export to Google Earth or publish the whole show in Flickr.

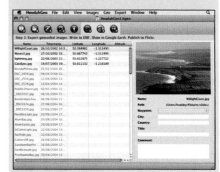

▲ With HoudahGeo, you'll always know the exact locations of the photographs you've taken.

09 Loop Editor
URL audiofile-engineering.com
Price free

GarageBand and Final Cut Studio's more technical Soundtrack Pro thrive on large libraries of audio loops. Although you can edit the content of loops in editors such as Amadeus Pro, looping aspects normally require a special tool. Apple Loop Utility is free and better than nothing for editing your own loops but is limited in features.

Enter Loop Editor, available in free unlicensed form or enhanced to its Plus version for $50 (£25): you can now work with any sample rate, bit depth or number of audio channels, edit during playback, and edit loop points with nudge and zero-cross controls. Additional features of the Plus version include detailed property editing, detailed visual slice editing and automatic slice creation.

Loop Editor also has powerful controls for customising keyboard shortcuts, which will be especially appreciated by those working on their next DVD-full of commercial loops. If you use GarageBand or Soundtrack, Loop Editor is an essential companion.

▲ Loop Editor enables you to perform just about everything when it comes to editing audio loops.

10 MobileLocate
URL mobilelocate.co.uk
Price from £1.47 monthly per phone

We are going through a revolution in the availability and use of geographical information. GPS devices have become popular in sports such as running and cycling, and can be accessed by tools such as HoudahGeo to geocode your digital photographs (see page 124).

Mobile phones can also be used to work out where someone is as long as their phone is switched on. Whether based on a GPS device connected via a phone or iPhone, or on phone location alone, tracking services can be used for a wide range of purposes from the tagging of children or partners to ensure that they do not stray, to the mundane commercial.

MobileLocate is one such service now available – expect others of even greater sophistication and lower cost in the coming year or two. Instead of your associate or partner having to send you garbled texts as they wend their way through our congested transport system, you will be able to monitor their progress on maps on your Mac or iPhone. Thankfully this should not be so precise as to distinguish whether they were stuck in a tailback or a tavern…

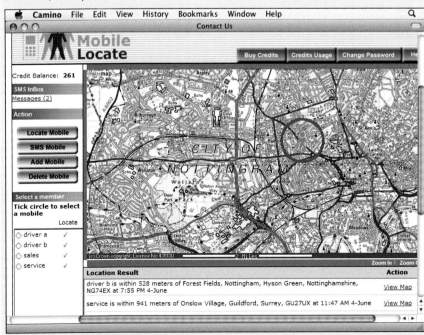

▲ MobileLocate pinpoints the exact location of a partner or colleague. But is he or she stuck in traffic – or a bar?

11 Movable Type 4
URL movabletype.org
Price free

You don't actually need much in the way of tools to maintain your own blog, but using a full-featured professional blog-authoring system can certainly help yours rise in the ratings. When Six Apart released Movable Type as a free product in December 2007, it ensured that every blogger could afford the best and most sophisticated tool in town.

Hewn in Perl and needing MySQL or a similar database to store content and data, it can maintain an unlimited number of blogs for those who are unrepentantly garrulous. Page generation can be static, in which you have to upload each updated page – or dynamic, in which the server assembles blog content from the dynamic content in its supporting database or any combination of the two.

For those with corporate interests, features, such as LDap management, can be particularly attractive. It was the first authoring system to include TrackBack that, along with its other innovative features, has been adopted by competitors. At last you can use the real thing for free.

▲ Movable Type 4 comes in very handy when maintaining an unlimited number of blogs.

12 Picnic
URL objectpark.net/picnic
Price $29.95 (about £15) per user

All the permissions and security trappings of Mac OS X made one thing harder than in Mac OS 9: distributed filesharing. Unless you run Mac OS X Server there is always something to get in its way – this despite advances such as Bonjour, which enables you to identify locally networked Macs without the awkwardness of raw IP numbers.

Picnic builds on Bonjour to automatically synchronise designated folders on each Mac in your network. Gather together your collection of reference documents, project information or finished work, then keep each system up-to-date with the latest changes and additions. It deals intelligently with laptops and other Macs that may be removed from the network, syncing back any changes made once the portable system is reconnected.

Its only real limitation is that you should not try syncing iTunes or iPhoto libraries, mailboxes or similar because of their

▲ Picnic automatically syncs designated folders on each Mac in your network.

complex structures. The trouble is that this makes it unsuitable for keeping whole home folders synchronised, a task that is still best accomplished, using a real server.

13 Purify
URL *hendricom.com*
Price $29.95 (about £15)

Spam is one of the certainties of online life, afflicting everyone with an email account. Unless you run your own mail server or trust your ISP to block junk email before it even reaches you (not the brightest of ideas), you need a spam filter that is as adaptable and versatile as those who perpetrate the stuff.

The tools from *audiofile-engineering.com* are all very well when carefully trained but spammers are constantly looking for ways to outwit the popular filters. Purify provides belt, braces and loads more tricks to trap spam, using several different techniques. Among these are a trainable, statistical Bayesian system, filter by country of origin and user-defined phrases in content, friends lists, images and addressing errors.

Fully scriptable, it works with all mail protocols such as Pop and Imap, as well as most mail clients including Mail. Although of more questionable value, Purify provides single-click abuse reporting to ISPs. The latest versions offer forwarding of filtered mail to iPhone accounts, or to any accessible SMTP server. While it may not succeed in making Spam go away completely it should give you the wherewithal to keep the unwelcome pest at bay.

▲ Purify may not trap and block all the spam out there, but it will prevent a great deal of it from getting through.

▲ Remote Presenter... tantalising glimpse of future business presentations to clients without leaving your desk.

14 Remote Presenter
URL *soundscreen.com/presenter*
Price TBA

As roads and public transport become more congested, and we grow more conscious of the carbon footprint of business travel, it is far better to stay put and instead project your presence to anywhere that the Internet can reach. There's always videoconferencing of course, except that the system remains kludgy and hardly conducive to compelling pitches or presentations.

So cue Remote Presenter, which, though still a concept, is surely the future.

15 Skim
URL *skim-app.sourceforge.net*
Price free

Acrobat PDF documents are an ideal platform for comments and annotation. Unlike printed books and papers, which are irrevocably altered when you write notes in the margins, PDFs store added comments and markings separately from their main content. Skim is a PDF annotation and reader tool designed primarily for those who referee and study academic papers and other publications.

It mirrors Adobe's Acrobat Professional but is lighter in weight – and free. In addition its display options include a full-screen mode to make study easier. It can be used for presentations, includes bookmarks and searching, and can convert PostScript print to file output into PDF. It can also capture a document in a given state to a snapshot. Skim is an excellent replacement for Preview irrespective of the content of your PDFs.

Crafted in QuickTime with XML, using LiveStage Professional for authoring, it can combine live audio and video with pre-recorded media, slides and more.

An alternative approach available today would be to control Keynote remotely, using AppleEvents (AppleScript), and add live sound via VoIP. The trouble is that this would require punching a hole through the remote Mac's firewall – and that could be exploited by an intruder. It lacks Windows support too. So watch for products that work over VPN to spare you hours of travel for that brief presentation, coupled with iChat or Skype for live audio linkage.

16 The Issue
URL *theissue.com*
Price free

If you know where to look you are bound to find the right information or opinion in a blog. But gaining any sort of coherent view over the blogosphere can take a lot of time and browsing. As with any other content the only solution for busy people is to find someone to collate and edit the disparate material into

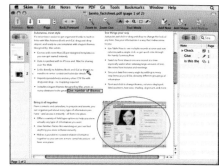
▲ The beauty of Skim is that it's lighter in weight than Adobe's Acrobat Professional – and it's free.

▲ The Issue breaks new ground by drawing together material from more than 50 blogs. It's a good read too.

▲ The multi-functional TinkerTool System still occupies the leading edge now that Apple has released Leopard.

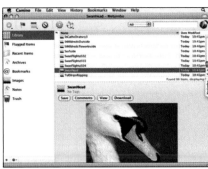
▲ In addition to storing text, images and passwords, Webjimbo gives Internet access to your Yojimbo library.

a coherent whole. This is exactly what The Issue aims to do.

As one of the first attempts to draw together material from more than 50 different blogs, it is treading new ground that others will undoubtedly follow. Perhaps inevitably it reflects a US-centric view, but it does have some excellent coverage from world-wide correspondents. Book reviews are very strong, while a WEHT (What Ever Happened To…?) feature looks back at a topic that has been heavily featured in the media in the past but which has recently faded from view. Contributors are volunteers, and finances seem dependent on Google advertisements and private donations, which perhaps cast doubt on it surviving the year.

17 TinkerTool System
URL *bresink.com/osx/TinkerToolSys*
Price €8.33 (about £4.20)

Multi-function utilities like the excellent shareware Cocktail have proved both popular and numerous – and there is every sign that they will continue to find a place on most Macs. However, one in particular has consistently supported more and better features than any other – Marcel Bresink's TinkerTool System.

Not to be confused with TinkerTool, Bresink's free utility for tweaking hidden options, this shareware tool offered the first graphical interface to Access Control Lists (ACLs) as well as extended permissions introduced with Tiger. Moreover it continues to occupy the leading edge following the release of Leopard. At the last count, it can comfortably replace System Profiler, Console, cache cleaners, file and folder cleaners, attribute and permissions editors, most panes in System Preferences, uninstallers and a fair bit of Disk Utility.

For good measure it gives ready access to dozens of features that are otherwise quite tricky or obscure when it comes to finding them. If someone suggests that you should fix a problem by repairing the help viewer or verifying your login items, then this is one of the few tools that can do the lot.

18 WaterRoof
URL *hanynet.com*
Price free

One of the persistent disappointments in Mac OS X has been its software firewall, ipfw. There is nothing wrong with the firewall itself but, despite public criticism of its facile if not misleading GUI controls, Apple has not seen fit to provide a decent control interface even in Leopard.

WaterRoof is one of several tools that write script configuration files for ipfw. It is free, open source, full-featured and accessible. Its many configuration windows give superb insight into the sophistication of ipfw: here you can add static and dynamic rules to filter network packets, manage bandwidth permitted for given types of network traffic, control the Nat daemon to map external IP addresses to internal ones, watch and block active network connections, and use some basic network tools. A configuration wizard can walk you through the basics of setting up ipfw in a few minutes. Or you can try the more basic NoobProof from the same author, Hany El Imam.

19 Webjimbo
URL *webjimbo.com*
Price $29.95 (about £15)

Yojimbo (see page 131) is a personal information organiser from Bare Bones Software that has attracted quite a following. Although perhaps not quite as slick as the hypertext-based Voodoo it can store a wide variety of different classes of information, including text, images, passwords and serial numbers, PDFs and web page archives. Add Webjimbo and you have easy Internet access to the contents of your Yojimbo library.

Away from your desktop you simply connect your laptop or iPhone via Safari. Inevitably you will need to punch a hole through your firewall to allow the incoming connection but Webjimbo endeavours to make this as secure as possible. It can get a bit messy to work with the firewall and other features of AirPort Extreme base stations, but once your configuration is working you won't need to repeat the setup wizard again. Webjimbo makes the already attractive Yojimbo completely compelling.

20 Zfs
URL *sun.com*
Price free with Leopard

For far too long we have lived with the association of logical volumes with physical hard disks: each disk can contain one or more volumes but a volume can't span two or more disks. Sun's Zfs has made its first appearance on the Mac in Leopard and, once up to production quality, will be eagerly adopted by those with loads of servers and physical drives.

But it is also the perfect answer for those with a collection of commodity drives, wishing to use Time Machine to its best. Over the next year, Zfs should help many to do away with the narrow tyranny of physical volumes. All it needs now are tools to support accessible administration.

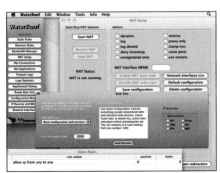
▲ WaterRoof's many configuration windows give a superb insight into the sophistication of ipfw.

▲ Once up to production quality, Zfs will be a boon to those with numerous servers and physical drives.

20 TOP BUSINESS TOOLS

Macs have seen a big growth in use in the business world, and now there is an abundance of dedicated applications from which you can choose. To help you with your dilemma, we've selected 20 of the best.

Macs are for graphics, while PCs are for business. It's a statement that has gained credibility through repetition. But however convenient a generalisation, if it was ever valid, it's only half true now.

Macs have come a long way in the past five years. They haven't yet been ushered into many of the UK's corporate boardrooms, but for small businesses or freelancers who need a tool to manage their work life, Macs are often a better choice than Windows PCs.

There are two reasons for this. First, the growing appeal of Mac OS X has encouraged a new breed of business programs and a new audience outside the Mac's traditional core market. Second, the growth in the number of platform-agnostic online applications has been of greater relative benefit to the Mac than the PC, which already had a wide choice of business software.

The result is that there are some great Mac-compatible applications on which to build your business, and here we're listing the best. We've excluded favourites that you will be familiar with, such as Microsoft Office, MYOB Accounting and FileMaker. What we're left with are the lesser-known gems: the online and desktop-based applications that make your Mac a first-class business tool.

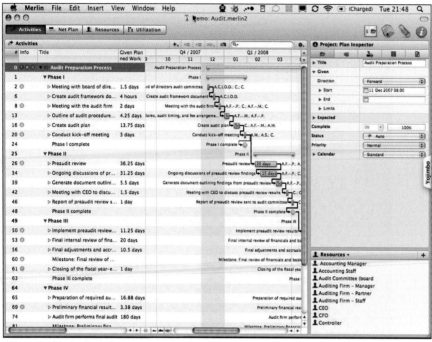

▲ The comprehensive Gantt chart in project manager Merlin 2 gives you a complete overview of your activities.

01 Merlin 2
URL *merlin2.net*
Price €145 (about £105)

Aside from Microsoft's limited Project Center, Macs were for a long time considered a poor second to Windows when it came to project management software. Well, that's no longer the case. As well as Omni Group's upcoming OmniPlan (*omnigroup.com*), Project Wizard's Merlin comfortably beats its nearest Windows counterpart, Microsoft Project, in both usability and functionality.

It's easy to set up a project – just enter its basic details and an available budget, or choose from an existing template. You then enter milestones and deadlines, and view a project's critical path and dependencies in the Gantt chart view in Merlin's Activities view, while the Netplan view more clearly displays the relationship between project components. You can also see just how effectively resources are being used in the Utilization view.

Refugees from Microsoft Project will be delighted by how seamlessly it imports native Project files, and Merlin also integrates with iCal and Address Book. Although collaborative networking isn't yet available, it's planned for an upcoming version of the software.

02 LogMeIn
URL *logmein.com*
Price free

You're on the road and you need to check some information on your office Mac. All would be well if you could contact it using Mac OS X Leopard's Back to My Mac feature – but it's only designed for .Mac subscribers. That's where LogMeIn Free comes in. Install the 8MB file on your home Mac, leave it running and you can access your home machine through the LogMeIn website from any Mac or PC. This will come as a pleasant surprise to anyone – including Back to My Mac users – who has tried to punch holes in office firewalls to use remote access software.

When you connect, you can see and control your remote Mac Desktop in your browser. Usefully, you can trigger keyboard shortcuts to launch remote applications such as Spotlight. Even better, performance is decent over modest broadband connections.

LogMeIn doesn't charge for connecting to a single computer, but to transfer files between computers, print remote files locally, or control more than one machine, you'll need to upgrade to the Pro version, priced at about £35 a year.

03 Blinksale
URL *blinksale.com*
Price $12 (about £6) per month for up to 50 invoices

Is Word a good enough invoicing tool? Not when Blinksale is the alternative. At its most basic, this program's editing window lets you create multiline invoices that you can then email directly to clients. Neatly, if your client is another Blinksale subscriber, your invoices can be automatically added to their Blinksale account. But what's really impressive about this is the way it manages your invoices. When you've been paid, you can mark a stored invoice accordingly and Blinksale tracks what's due. Its Dashboard view shows draft, open and closed invoices, as well as those that are past due, alongside their outstanding balances.

Invoices can be tagged with keywords for ease of organisation and when you select the program's Invoices tab, you can set which information you want displayed – invoices sent for the current financial year, for example. The amount that you've been paid and the invoice total are displayed below the list, so you can keep track of your earnings and any outstanding invoices.

If you're still not convinced, you can create three invoices each month for free.

04 Business Card Composer
URL *belightsoft.com*
Price $34.95 (about £18)

Because first impressions are important, business cards remain an essential business tool. If you don't have an ounce of design skill, then Belight Software's Business Card Composer is an outstanding way to quickly create the sort of cards that will impress potential clients.

Creating a card is a three-step process. First off is the design of the card. You can either select a basic design from more than 100 templates, corralled into a couple of dozen theme and subject categories, or create your own card from scratch. Business Card Composer includes a workable design whiteboard onto which you can add text, freehand design, images or a huge choice of bundled clip art.

▲ With LogMeIn, you can access and control your home machine from any Mac, or PC, from anywhere.

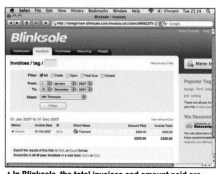

▲ In Blinksale, the total invoices and amount paid are totalled at the bottom of the list.

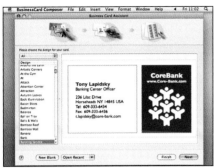
▲ With Business Card Composer, you can create business cards quickly that will impress your clients.

The second stage is to either manually enter data for the card or import information from your Mac's Address Book. This will replace the template's boilerplate text. The final step is to choose a print design. You can print onto a wide selection card stock from manufacturers such as Avery and Decadry, or even order your cards online – although as these come from the US, delivery could prove expensive.

05 Yojimbo 1.5
URL *barebones.com*
Price $39 (about £20)

Yojimbo could probably claim some of the credit for the Mac's growing popularity in the small business market. After all, there's no clear Windows alternative to this application, which stores and manages the disparate information you pick up during a business day – from text-based notes and useful web bookmarks to PDFs and images.

You can add items to the program by dragging them over the Yojimbo window or the tiny drop-dock palette that floats on the side of the screen. You can even do it through the clipboard – just press the F8 key and the current contents of the clipboard will be added to one of its collections.

Click on a collection and its contents are displayed. Yojimbo makes an impressive attempt at guessing the type of information that you've added and organising it accordingly – for example, drag a .Zip

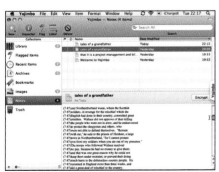
▲ Yojimbo stores and manages all the information you pick up during the day and organises it for you.

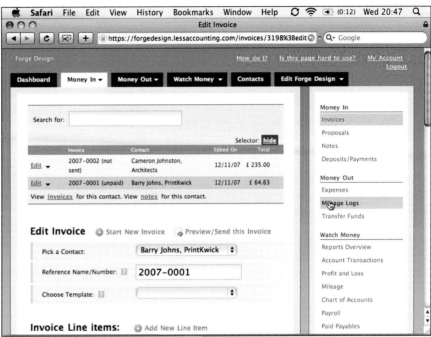
▲ Keep track of your income and expenses with the easy-to-use Web-based application, LessAccounting.

archive over Yojimbo and it will be added to the Archives collection. This program soon becomes essential to anyone who's used it.

06 LessAccounting
URL *lessaccounting.com*
Price $19.95 per month (about £10 per month)

The problem with many accounting applications is that considering the simplicity of what they do – track income and expenses and tell you if you're making money – they are surprisingly complicated to use. The result? You stick with the back of an envelope.

Web-based LessAccounting could change all this. Like Blinksale, it lets you create invoices through a web interface, but you can also create proposals to send to customers, which can be converted to invoices when accepted.

LessAccounting also stores contacts – as you add them they are accessible from a menu on the invoice creation page. This online application does much more than just creating invoices, though. It tracks suppliers and expenses, such as mileage, and from that information you can create reports, from outstanding creditors and debtors to a full profit and loss account. Any online accounting application means you don't have full control of your data, but at least reports can be exported to Excel-readable CSV format.

LessAccounting is pricey, but very flexible, although a free version lets you create five invoices, proposals or other data per month.

07 Writeboard
URL *writeboard.com*
Price free

Most business users will be aware of online alternatives to Microsoft Office such as Google Docs (*docs.google.com*) and Zoho (*zoho.com*). But if you're on the road and need quick access to a text editor, Writeboard is arguably the best option, because you don't need to login to use it. Just visit the site, enter a name for the document, a password and your email address, and you can start writing – Writeboard sends an email with a link to the document's URL so you can access it later.

Those who can't live without Word will find Writeboard's editing options spartan – there's no spell checker, word count feature or Edit window toolbar. Instead, Writeboard uses simple text formatting techniques to add styles, such as wrapping text in an underscore character to italicise it.

Writeboard is a great cross-platform collaborative tool, too. Saved writeboards

▲ Writeboard is an online text editor that lets you share your work with other people anywhere in the world.

can be shared, and when you or one of your collaborators edits a document, changes are stored as separate versions, which can be compared on the web page.

08 Anxiety
URL *anxietyapp.com*
Price free

Keeping yourself organised is the toughest part of business. Anxiety is a lightweight, Leopard-only to-do list manager that synchronises with Apple's Mail and iCal. When installed, Anxiety starts on login and floats above all running applications, displaying current tasks from your iCal calendar – different calendars are selectable from a drop-down menu.

While Anxiety's window acts as a handy reminder for upcoming tasks – even if it doesn't show their priority – you can also enter tasks directly into Anxiety by simply pressing the Return key. When the task is entered, it's automatically added to your iCal database. Double-click on a task and it opens directly in iCal or Mail for further editing. You can even create new iCal calendars just by clicking on the tick button in the top-right corner of the list window.

Anxiety uses Leopard's Calendar Store – Mac OS X 10.5's system-wide database that contains calendars, events and to-dos, which means it can't run on Mac OS X 10.4 or earlier.

09 Remember The Milk
URL *rememberthemilk.com*
Price free

An online to-do manager, Remember The Milk is a neat but powerful task manager for both home users and small businesses. When you sign up to the service, you're allocated your own remember the milk domain, which lists tasks that are due today and tomorrow. You enter tasks, organised by default under five lists, through a simple web-based form. You can assign them a due date or a priority, tag them for easier organisation and mark them as complete

▲ Remember The Milk is a neat and powerful task manager for both home users and small businesses.

▲ Anxiety is a lightweight Leopard-only to-do list that synchronises with Apple's Mail and iCal.

by pressing a button on the site's home page. Tasks can be shared with others through email or via SMS on your mobile.

Perhaps the tool's most essential feature is the fact that it integrates with iCal on your home Mac. As long as the list you create is public, you can copy its iCalendar URL from the list details box and in iCal, subscribe to it from the Calendar menu.

There's an optimised version of the site for iPod touch and iPhone users, but this is only available for paid subscribers.

10 Basecamp
URL *basecamphq.com*
Price free

Software developer 37 Signals has a knack of producing quality, easy-to-use web-based applications. Alongside BackPack, (an organisational tool) and HighRise (a shared contact manager) is Basecamp, a web application for managing projects.

Basecamp is a great tool for business collaboration with remote employees or offices. It lets you create team members, with set access rights. Each has their own Dashboard view of active clients and the projects they are involved with. These drill down to project windows that show late and upcoming project milestones, as well as list of completed tasks. If you need to change a milestone's due date, Basecamp can adjust the date of subsequent milestones to compensate. Milestones can also be linked with to-do lists, and as items on the list are

▲ Basecamp provides simple tools to improve the communication between people working on a project.

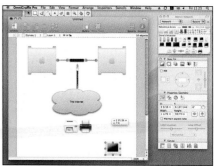
▲ OmniGraffle Pro is ideal for those who want to create an illustration but don't have an artistic bone in their body.

checked off, a record is kept of the date and the person who signed it off. Basecamp even includes the Writeboard document editing tool, so you can work on a project's documentation with others.

Basecamp works well with your desktop Mac too. Milestones can be shared with iCal and changes to a project can be highlighted through an RSS feed.

11 OmniGraffle Pro
URL *omnigroup.com*
Price $149.95 (about £75)

OmniGraffle may be used by many Mac owners as an illustration tool – a task at which it's more than adequate – but it's indispensable to business users who need to explain a process clearly, yet don't happen to have an artistic bone in their body.

It uses libraries of business-friendly object artwork to simplify the creation of common business illustrations, such as flow charts or organisational charts. But the way the program works also helps you adjust business charts with little fuss. For example, when you link objects with OmniGraffle's Link tool, they remain linked as you move the objects around the canvas. OmniGraffle also lets you quickly improve the look of an imported text-based document – it can import Microsoft Visio files, too – by applying a preset style to it as it is imported.

Another handy feature is the Outline view, which both lists the document structure hierarchically and a offers quick way to manage objects on the main canvas. Dragging them in the Outline view automatically rearranges them on the canvas.

12 Wesabe
URL *wesabe.com*
Price free

Wesabe is an online finance application with a difference. You upload your financial data in QIF or QFX format, or manually enter data and then Wesabe helps clean it up – for example, turning those lengthy transaction descriptions that no-one understands into a

SHOOT & EDIT HOME VIDEO LIKE A PROFESSIONAL

THE COMPLETE GUIDE TO
HOME VIDEO
Shoot and edit like a professional

PLUS! Camcorder buying guide inside

ONLY £7.99

PERFECT MOVIES IN 3 STEPS!

1. Shoot better video
2. Edit clips the easy way
3. Burn DVDs and Blu-ray discs

ON SALE NOW AT WHSmith amazon.co.uk

To order direct call 0844 844 0053 or visit www.magbooks.com (Free P&P on all Uk orders)

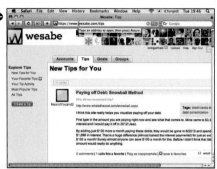

▲ Wesabe is an online finance application that makes managing your finances easy.

▲ Pulse is a simple web application that keeps an eye on the amount of money you have in your bank account.

more understandable short name. Usefully, Wesabe automatically applies this to future statements as they are imported, and a benefit of a community site such as this is that if other members have edited a transaction the same way, Wesabe automatically suggests that shortcut for all of its members.

You organise your finances by tagging individual transactions with labels such as 'groceries' or 'going out' – you can even split tags to divide a transaction between labels. You can then use the site's spending summary to graphically illustrate where your money is going. The biggest advantage of tags is that Wesabe matches money saving tips – supplied by other members – according to your tags.

While Wesabe is US-based, UK banks are supported, and you can switch the default currency to Pounds Sterling using a drop-down menu.

13 iList Data 3.6
URL *lakewoodstudios.com*
Price $69.95 (about £35)

When it comes to databases on the Mac, conventional wisdom has it that FileMaker Pro is the only choice. Bento (*filemaker.com*) could change that, but until then, Lakewood Studio's iList Data 3.6 is a cheaper option for small businesses.

iList is an unusual mix of power and simplicity. Built on a robust SQL database, its clutch of startup templates is based on popular database tasks, such as image catalogues or time-tracking. One useful business-oriented feature is the ability to create inline bar, dot or line graphs based on numerical data.

But its flexibility is its real plus point. You can use it to track any data type, including invoices, and records can be exported to Microsoft Word or Excel, while database images can be sent directly to iPhoto. You can get real value out of your data by building queries through either its Find tool or SQL commands. iList Data isn't as powerful as FileMaker Pro, but business geeks may love it.

14 Pulse
URL *pulseapp.com*
Price free

In a small business, profit and loss is a purely nominal figure. What really matters in the early years of a business is making sure that more money is coming into the company's coffers than is going out.

Pulse is a simple web application that keeps an eye on this critical area. Just enter the amount of money you have at present in your bank account, and as you receive income and spend money, you record it on the Pulse website. You can organise income and expenditure by allocating them either to user-specified categories or organise them by company or project – handily these details can be imported from 37 Signal's Basecamp application. You can also set up recurring transactions and allocate items to the future, assigning them an income potential – essentially the likelihood of you actually receiving the income – which can be handy when budgeting cash flow. Cash flow is shown as a running total for the months ahead, so you can forecast easily if money is about to get tight.

15 Cha-Ching
URL *midnightapps.com*
Price $40 (about £20)

Not that the opposition is the stiffest, but Cha-Ching might qualify as the best-looking Mac or PC finance application ever made. However, its beautiful interface doesn't come wholly at the expense of functionality.

Cha-Ching is a finance manager that lets you track multiple business or personal bank accounts – it supports QIF and QFX imports, so you can download them from an online bank. What sets Cha-Ching apart is that as you add transactions, you can tag them with keywords, such as 'Salary' or 'Entertaining'. This not only lets you build 'smart folders' to display certain groups of transactions that match chosen criteria in the transactions window, but it can also be used when budgeting – you add the tags to include in a budget comparison – you can create as many comparisons as you want – and Cha-Ching will produce a chart graphically comparing those tagged income and expenses items.

16 Stikkit
URL *stikkit.com*
Price free

Not to be confused with the less useful Mac OS X Stickies, Stikkit is a free online application that can sort out your business by intelligently organising your bookmarks, calendar events, contacts and notes.

You enter text on a stikkit, a small yellow window. As you type, Stikkit analyses this text, looking for trigger words, such as 'at', 'on' or 'buy', to interpret them and organise the results automatically. As soon as you enter a simple Stikkit, such as 'Meet Mike tomorrow at 9', it interprets 'Mike' as a proper name, creates a contact for him

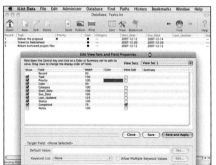

▲ Offering great flexibility when creating databases, iList is perfect for small businesses.

▲ With Cha-Ching, you can keep track of multiple business or personal bank accounts.

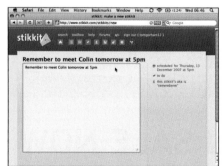

▲ Stikkit is a great way to quickly update your schedule if you're away from the Mac or even browsing the web.

and generates a new calendar event for the meeting. To prevent an item being interpreted, you just enter an exclamation mark at the start of a paragraph.

For Mac users, Stikkit is a great way to quickly update your schedule if you're away from the Mac or even browsing the web. Even better, like Remember the Milk, you can subscribe to Stikkit calendars in iCal.

17 Openomy
URL openomy.com
Price free

It's the freelancer's recurring nightmare – you're at a client's office and you realise that you don't have your most important files with you for your presentation. One way of protecting against this scenario is to store your most important files on Openomy, which is a website that lets you store your files online. These files, protected by password, are accessible from any computer with a web browser, so you can get access to them even when on-site with a Windows PC-toting client.

If you have a lot of files – up to 1GB – you can organise them on the site by assigning tags to them. And although files are private by default, you can mark them as public to give them a permanent web link and easy access from any web browser.

While Apple's .Mac web service boasts far greater capacity, it's hard to argue with Openomy's cost – it's absolutely free.

18 Contactizer Pro 3.5
URL objective-decision.com
Price €99 (about £72)

Objective Decision's Contactizer Pro 3.5 puts Mail, Address Book and iCal on steroids to organise your contact information, activities and communications.

Its Contact View shares the same underlying database as Address Book, so changes made in Contactizer are available

▲ By storing your files on Openomy, you can access them from any computer.

to other Mac OS X applications, but you can also tag contacts with colour-coded categories. You can import iCal details to use in calendar-based Event View, which shows upcoming meetings and tasks, while a Communication View is a hub for phone calls, emails, faxes and iChats, all of which can be linked to contacts. Handily, Contactizer also links to Apple Mail, so it has access to its message library database – and you can even send template-based personalised emails from Contactizer.

The newest addition to the program is a project manager that ignores fancy Gantt chart tools to list simple processes that must be followed to reach an objective. Although Contactizer manages huge amounts of information, you can manage it through smart filters, which can show today's communications at a glance or all tasks that need action.

19 Mozy
URL mozy.com
Price free for 2GB or £25 per year for the Mozy Unlimited option

Mac OS X Leopard's Time Machine may be a great backup tool, but as it doesn't backup off-site, you can't afford to trust your vital files to it. But Mozy, part small Mac backup application, part web-based recovery application, is a great tool to supplement local backups.

Mozy stores the files and folders you choose to backup online, and protects them with 448-bit encryption. It uses the same time-saving incremental backup technique as Time Machine, only copying files that have changed since the last backup. But it also supports versioning, tracking multiple iterations of changed

▲ Back up all your important files and folders online with Mozy – a great tool to supplement local on-site back-ups.

files. Mozy backups don't hog your Internet connection as you can set it to back up when your Mac has been idle for a set time.

The Mozy website shows backup details, but also lets you restore all or part of any version of your backed up data. You get 2GB of back-up free, but the unrestricted Mozy Unlimited option is a bargain for those who value peace of mind.

20 SpamSieve
URL c-command.com/spamsieve
Price $30 (about £15)

While Mac-based businesses remain resilient to almost all forms of viruses and trojans, one form of malware – spam – is still a blight on business life. While many email clients have some sort of built-in email filtering, we've never seen any application deal with email spam as effectively as SpamSieve.

SpamSieve works with Apple Mail, Entourage and a handful of other email clients. It uses highly tuned Bayesian spam filtering to learn what is spam and what isn't, alongside other tricks, such as checking your Mac OS X Address Book to ensure that messages from friends and colleagues are never marked as spam.

SpamSieve also keeps a customisable blocklist and whitelist to manage email from particular addresses. Don't expect wonders to start with: you'll need to train it with a few hundred spam and non-spam email messages. But after a while the spam that waits in your inbox every morning should start to dry up.

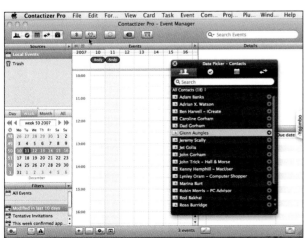
▲ Contactizer Pro 3.5 is an all-in-one solution for managing, sharing and organising your personal and business information.

▲ Using highly tuned Bayesian spam filtering, SpamSieve works with both Apple Mail and Microsoft Entourage.

Google power user

Find the information you want on the Internet in a jiffy and avoid getting sidetracked by websites that promise the earth but deliver nothing with these handy hints at making searches a breeze.

Even now, a large element of what examinations are designed to test is our ability to recall information, but in this age of having the world of digital information at our finger-tips, this seems a little anachronistic. The best illustration of this is a corrupted quote of Samuel Johnson's, usually rendered: 'The next best thing to knowing something is knowing where to find it.'

The problem is that few people truly exploit the power of searching the Internet for information. At best, we punch a search term into Google and wade through the results, but there are dozens of tips, tricks and techniques that can help you get to the information you want, fast. Some of what we'll discuss, particularly early on in this feature, will apply as readily to any search engine, but we're going to focus heavily on Google. There are a couple of reasons for this: first, it's by far the most popular search engine and is integrated into Safari's search bar, and second, the richness and power of the features it boasts makes it ideal fodder for a feature such as this.

So, there are a few very basic concepts to get out of the way before we go on. Remember at all times that you're searching for terms that appear on results pages. Another way to think about this: search for the answer, not the question. Relatively few pages will have, say, 'how do I fit a SuperDrive in my eMac' compared to the number which will contain the phrase 'fitting a SuperDrive in an eMac'. This is a coarse example – Google would still bring up relevant results with the original term – but hopefully you get the idea.

Google is case-insensitive – entering 'MacUser' is no different to 'macuser' – and it automatically assumes that you want all entered search terms to appear on the page. In the earlier days, you usually had to use + signs with multiple terms or the search engine in effect ran a standalone search for each one. Google also uses stemming, making intelligent guesses based on your search query to broaden it out and include related variations on your terms.

Most important, though, is that you realise you can combine these search techniques. Mix operators such as quote marks with prefixes such as cache: to bring up a set of super-relevant results; no longer will you wallow through multiple pages of results. We'll also highlight some of Google's market-specific tools and web-based applications that can help make your life easier. Google is running a closed beta of Google Apps for Your Domain, which lets you to run Gmail, Page Creator, Calendar and Talk on your own domain; you can apply to join the trials at *google.com/a*.

By the time we're through, you'll be searching like a pro and creating all sorts of compelling content online. Let the search begin.

SEARCH TECHNIQUES

Quote marks
This is one of the most basic tricks, but few people seem to use it. Simply enter a search term or part of a search term wrapped in double quote marks, and Google treats it as a phrase, heavily weighting results to those pages that contain the words in quotes as a group and in the order entered. The search term **"mac mini" ram 2GB** will return hits about 2GB of Ram specifically for the Mac mini more reliably than if the model was entered just as two words, and you could use the technique to search for phrases from a quotation.

info:
The info prefix is a great way to get more information about a particular website. Enter it like this – **info:www.macuser.co.uk** – and you'll get the following options:

Show Google's cache of *www.macuser.co.uk*
Find web pages that are similar to *www.macuser.co.uk*
Find web pages that link to *www.macuser.co.uk*
Find web pages from the site *www.macuser.co.uk*
Find web pages that contain the term *"www.macuser.co.uk"*

The 'similar' link is identical to using related: as a search prefix, so if that's your reason for using info: you can save yourself a click.

allintitle:
Searches for the specified terms in the title of pages. This search requires that all search terms entered be found in the page title. If you wanted to find stories about the iPhone and LG's Prada phone, you could search for **allintitle:iphone lg prada**, though this relies on the three search terms appearing in the page's title, not its content. You can also use intitle: if you don't want to force Google to include all entered search terms in the results.

URL

allinurl:
Similar to allintitle:, but here we're looking for the specified search terms in the URL – web address – of a page. The operator inurl: is also possible.

cache:
As part of its indexing process, Google takes snapshots of websites. Searching these cached copies is a great way to go back and search older versions of a page that may have been edited, and you can easily tell Google to display results from its cache rather than from the live version of the site by prefixing your search query. Entering **cache:www.macuser.co.uk** iphone for example searches for the word iPhone in Google's cache of *MacUser*'s homepage and will highlight the word iPhone on the page.

##
Put simply, a plus sign preceding a term means 'search for this', while a minus means 'omit this phrase from the results'. Let's say you wanted to search for the Virginia Tech supercomputer dubbed Big Mac. Ordinarily, the phrase 'big mac' would just return lots of pages about burgers, but entering **"big mac" -mcdonald's** means that the correct page is first in the list of results. You don't usually need to use + (see the introduction on page 136) but it's useful in some circumstances. Google, for example, usually omits common words such as 'the' and 'I' from searches, but there are occasions on which you might need to override this. **Star Wars Episode +I** for example, means that the 'I' will be heeded in the search term.

site:
This limits results to those from the specified domain. The search **iphone site:www.macuser.co.uk** will return all of *MacUser*'s online coverage of the iPhone.

Advanced search
There are some more advanced tricks you can use. From any results page you can click the search types above the search box – Web, Images, Video, News and Maps – to switch to that type of search using your entered terms. At any point you can click the Advanced Search link to the right of the search box to bring up advanced options. These can be mixed and matched at will, and the result is nothing more than a specific search URL that's a combination of the prefixes and other techniques we've explored plus the few more below.
One trick that can't (currently) be replicated with a search box prefix is Advanced Search's Creative Commons option. This allows you to tell Google to search only for content licensed with so-called copyleft licences, available for reuse without getting specific permission from the author.
A number of the options available from the Advanced Search window, though, can be replicated with a few search prefixes. As with all prefixes, this matters as it makes it easy to enter these search terms straight into the search boxes in the toolbars of browsers such as Safari or Firefox, without first going to Google and clicking on the Advanced Search link.

Personalised Search

Google's Personalised Search feature is still in beta, but the idea is to analyse the searches you perform in order to provide you with more relevant results as the system gets more used to the sorts of things you search for. Consistently clicking on links to pages about Steve Jobs rather than recruitment after doing a search for *jobs* will gradually mean that the recruitment pages will cease to appear in the results. This does mean that Google is 'listening in' to your search terms, but a robust privacy policy is in place, and you can suspend tracking of your search terms. You can't easily tie personalised search into terms entered into Safari's search toolbar module; instead go to *google.co.uk/psearch*.

date:

The basic use of date: is to restrict your searches to results from the last so many months. The term *iphone date:3* will return iPhone results from the last three months. You can also add in specific date ranges, but these have to be in Julian format, which look completely different to the Georgian dates we're used to. If you're sufficiently dedicated, once you've converted your dates to the correct format, use this syntax *daterange: startdate-enddate* but be aware that the date tagging won't be perfect.

Images

Google can also search for images, but since images are inherently more difficult to index than text, the results are rarely satisfactory. It's done from *images.google.co.uk*.

define:

Unsure of the meaning of a word? Prefix it with define: and you'll get a list of definitions drawn from all over the web. The system isn't free from error – using the Dictionary Widget if you're on Tiger can be more accurate – but it's an undeniably useful quick check.

Sets

What if you don't know exactly what you're searching for? You know it's the name of a film starring Jeff Bridges, say, but can't for the life of you remember what it was. Rather than digging through Wikipedia or IMDB, go to *labs.google.com/sets* and enter the names of a couple of films of his that you do know. Click 'large set' and you'll get a huge list of Bridges' work. It works remarkably well for many topics, and each result in the set is a clickable link taking you to a page of results using the link text as a search term.

Number range

To include a range of numbers in your search term; you use two full stops. If you wanted to know what Steve Jobs was up to when he wasn't at Apple, use *"Steve Jobs" 1985..1996*. It works for any number range including prices – such as £250..450 – but you'd be better using off product search (see page 141).

GOOGLE CALCULATOR

Put the Internet to work on more than just unearthing pages with the information you need; make it work things out for you as well. Thanks to its Calculator feature, Google can be as good at converting weights and measures as it is at finding web pages. You don't need to go to a special page as you do with the Google Images search; just phrase the query correctly to get it worked out for you. Try typing 'UK pints in a US pint' to see how much smaller an American pint is compared with an English one, or 289*0.175 to find the VAT part of a price (at 17.5%) on something offered at £289. You can do some of the same things with the OS X Calculator utility or Unit Convertor widget, but often it can be more convenient to use this feature directly from your browser.

Google's Calculator can perform basic and more complex maths, and deal with converting a broad range of units of measure and physical constants. Its scope is wider than any single person is ever likely to need, but as a worldwide service it aims to cater for just about every requirement. For example, you can convert octal (base-eight numbers) into Roman numerals, although we're not sure quite who would need to.

One particularly handy thing about using Google to perform these calculations is that if you get the phrasing of the calculation wrong Google will still attempt a regular Internet search with it. As a result, it will almost certainly show you a long list of sites that offer all the conversion information you need, even if it can't figure out how to perform the calculation. (If you'd like to try and force a calculation, try putting an equals symbol at the end. If it is mathematically resolvable in any way this should do the trick.)

The maths symbols, or operators, include plus, minus, multiply and divide, as you'd expect, and go on to cover exponent (raising a number to the power of something), modulo (giving the remainder of a division), root calculations, and, particularly usefully, a simple 'percentage of' calculation. For example, to find out what percent 12 is of 89, ask Google '12 % of 89'.

Going further, you can 'choose' (find the ways a given number of elements can be chosen from another number), find square roots, use trigonometric functions, logarithms in base e or base 10, and find the factor of a number. Use parentheses to evaluate certain parts of a mathematical expression before others, and, should you need to, use prefixes before numbers to define them as hexadecimal, octal or binary. This certainly goes much further than most people ever need, but it is all there should the occasion arise.

When it comes to units of measure, you can use both long and short names for most constants. This goes from the obvious – cm and km are synonyms for centimetre and kilometre – to the esoteric – c and g are the synonyms for 'the speed of light' and 'gravitational constant'. Others, such as 'the speed of sound', have no short name equivalent; just use the full term instead.

Examples

operator	function	example
+	add	121+157
-	subtract	212-34
*	multiply	21*6
/	divide	95/14
^	exponent (raise to the power of)	6^3
choose	number of ways a set can be chosen from another set	12 choose 3
'nth' root of	calculates the 'nth' root of a number	ninth root of 12
% of	find the percentage	20% of 128
sqrt	square root	sqrt(12)
sin, cos (etc)	trigonometric functions (degrees)	tan(45)
ln	logarithm base e	ln(12)
log	logarithm base 10	log(12)
!	factorial	6!

Note: while you can use these operators in the pure, classical sense, you can also do most of these calculations using much more sentence-like expressions. Rather than type the precise but cryptic-looking sqrt(12) you can ask for 'the square root of 12'. In this limited area, Google really does do an effective form of natural language comprehension.

DEDICATED SERVICES

Music:
The music prefix does a similar thing to movie. Enter it before an artist's name and you'll get a discography, reviews, links to official websites, image searches, news, discussions and direct deep-level links to major online music retailers such as the iTunes Store. You can also use it to look up specific albums. The level of detail is astonishing; although by no means complete, associated links to songs' cover versions and lyrics are amazing useful, and a very quick way to settle arguments. Google also maintains its own automatically-generated music charts at *google.co.uk/trends/music*. Data is gathered from opted-in Google Talk users, and all entries are hyperlinked to information pages identical to those generated with a music: prefix.

Blog searching
Google's blog search tool is a handy way of searching through what's being said on the millions of blogs that are updated every day. The dedicated service at *blogsearch.google.co.uk* offers basic searching of blogs as well as an advanced search option with some blog-specific terms. Let's say you remember reading a post on Boing Boing by Xeni Jardin around Christmas time. Simply perform an Advanced search, specify Boing Boing's url as the source, Xeni as the blog author, and the date range. Bingo. You can also use the inblogtitle: inposttitle: inpostauthor: and blogurl: prefixes but unfortunately only from *blogsearch.google.co.uk*, not from Safari's search box. Google allows you to create RSS feeds based on your search terms too. Let's say you particularly like the tips Gina Trapani puts up on Lifehacker; simply search **blogurl:www.lifehacker.com inpostauthor:gina** and you'll be provided with a dedicated link pulling her posts from the site. These search results can be added to your Google Homepage – see right – as well.

Movie:
This is a real beauty, and one that very few people know about. Simply prefix the name of a film with movie: and you'll be given local cinema listings with links to maps of their location, reviews, a link to the trailer, and a link to the film's page on IMDB. Click on the Show more movies link and you'll be taken to a page listing all locally-showing films; what's more, you have the option of sorting the list by the distance to the cinema, movie rating and popularity as well as title.

News
Google news serves as a digest of news coverage from many news outlets the world over. The main page at *news.google.co.uk* is spectacularly rich even by default, but by now you won't be surprised to learn that it's very customisable too. The page can be reordered with simple drag and drop, and you can filter the news to show only a particular channel, such as sports. The useful news visualisation tool Newsmap (*marumushi.com/apps/newsmap*) uses Google News as its data source.

Trends
Google Trends is utterly invaluable for anyone doing research. Found at *google.co.uk/trends* and technically still in beta, it's a great way to get a snapshot of the buzz around a particular thing. Enter in a search term and you'll get a graph showing Google's collated results for the buzz on the web. It's tied into Google News too, and important events connected with your search term are mapped onto the trend; it's usually easy to correlate news stories – Apple launching the iPhone, say – with spikes in interest. Better still, you can enter multiple terms, separated by commas, to compare trends. Results can be filtered by language, time and geographical location.

Books
Google Books – at *books.google.co.uk* – allows you to search through the contents of dead-tree publications. There's no denying that this is an astonishingly useful thing – imagine searching the entire works in the British Library from your laptop rather than trawling through the copies in the library itself – but there are limitations. Copyright and other intellectual property considerations – allied to a reluctance to embrace change – means that book publishers are nervous about allowing their works to be indexed. It's a search tool that will only improve, and as you'd expect, the advanced search options give you the ability to narrow the search by publication date, ISBN and publisher.

Scholar

The service at *scholar.google.com* allows researchers to track down peers' contributions. As with the blog search tool, there is a wide range of advanced options tailored specifically to academic research. You can restrict results by field and publication; Google's own advanced search help at *scholar.google.com/intl/en/scholar/refinesearch.html* goes into these options in some detail.

Finance

Google's Finance pages – at *finance.google.com* – are another example of the deceptive simplicity of Google's interfaces. Load up the home page and you're presented with a simple text and graphics reporting of various markets. A market summary at the top left shows how the main stock exchanges are faring, and you're presented with a few business headlines.

Things get interesting when you look up a particular company. Enter its ticker symbol – AAPL for Apple, for example – or just start typing the company's name and Google will start autocompleting your entry. Here you're presented with a spectacular amount of very well-handled information. The most obvious element is the graph of stock price history. As with Trends, news stories are mapped to this so you can see what effect announcements and other news stories have on the stock price. The graph's date range can be expanded or contracted and other companies can be mapped onto the same graph for comparison.

The page shows a company summary, related companies, discussions, related blog postings, board biographies and details and much more than we can justify covering here. Explore; it's astonishing.

One other tip. You can use the stocks: prefix – such as **stocks:aapl** – to get a quick glimpse of a company's trading, and this page has links to the company's profile on Google finance and other providers.

Product Search

Here at *MacUser* we regularly use price comparison engines such as Pricerunner and Kelkoo to find the lowest price that a product's available for online. These two require online stores to supply their data in a specific format, however; Google's own price comparison engine – at *google.co.uk/products* – scours the web actively looking for and indexing shops. It doesn't reply on shops tying up deals such as with Pricerunner, and so its list of results is usually much longer, and it can often find cheaper outlets.

That said, you'll often find your results contaminated with irrelevant products, and the prices quoted are often misleading, either because Product Search picks up the wrong price from the page, or because it will list VAT inclusive or exclusive prices sporadically.

Specific areas

As well as dedicated search areas such as Scholar and Books, Google also makes available four flavours of its search designed specifically for four major operating systems. You'll find search engines for Mac, BSD Unix, Linux and Microsoft (yes, we know that this last option isn't OS-specific per se, but you get the idea) at *google.co.uk/mac*, */bsd*, */linux* and */microsoft* respectively.

Alerts

Google can set up alerts to help you track particular topics of interest; at *MacUser*, for example, we might set up a news alert flagging any story containing the term "Steve Jobs".

Go to *google.co.uk/alerts* to set one up. You have the option of searching news, blogs, the Internet, user groups or all four. Content that matches your search terms will be collated into an email that's delivered daily, weekly, or as soon as the term is matched. Annoyingly, at the time of writing, only email alerts are offered; there's no way to set up custom RSS feeds from the main alerts page. You can, as mentioned previously, set up a customised blog keyword RSS feed from *blogsearch.google.co.uk*, and do the same thing from News, so Google obviously has the technologies in place. We expect to see RSS feeds offered as an option from *google.co.uk/alerts* soon.

Homepage

By now, you're only human if you're beginning to feel a little overwhelmed. Never fear: there's a way to help bring all these disparate services together, and add a whole lot more. Google's personalised homepage allows you to drag in modules and reorganise them to suit.

Google itself supplies many – modules for Gmail, Google Maps, Groups, stocks and the like – but they're so easy to code that there are many hundreds covering almost every conceivable niche. Once you have the homepage set up as you like it, you can set it as your browser's default URL. You could also use a tool such as WebDesktop (*stevenf.com/software/webdesktop*) to display your personalised homepage on your Mac's desktop, setting it to refresh every so often.

APPLICATIONS AND MORE

Analytics
Many website packages include basic web traffic statistics packages, but Google's own package, dubbed Analytics, and found at *google.co.uk/analytics*, is spectacular. The level of granular detail continues to astonish us, particularly given that it's free. If you have a website, you have nothing to lose by signing up for Analytics, and you'll almost certainly gain a much deeper understanding of how people are interacting with your site. There's also a very nice little Widget for viewing Analytics from Mac OS X's Dashboard layer; find it at *dashalytics.rovingrob.com*.

Language tools
Google also has its own translation service – it's at *google.co.uk/language_tools* – and while no translation tools will give perfect results, it's good to have an option of using them. Like the venerable Babel Fish service at *babelfish.altavista.com*, Google offers you the ability to translate entire web pages in one go.

Reader
Google also has its own online RSS reader. Unlike the pairing of the desktop NetNewsWire application with an online service such as Newsgator – which allows you to sync from desktop to online and vice versa – Google Reader at *google.co.uk/reader* is an online-only system. This doesn't mean it's underpowered, though; indeed, it's more richly featured than some desktop clients we've used, and allows you to import and export lists of feeds from any serious RSS reader. You could use Reader to link together dynamic RSS feeds that you've created with, say, blog searches from Google's blog search page, and have access to them from any Internet-connected computer in the world.

Docs and Spreadsheets
Writely, the online word processor that was one of the darlings of the early Web 2.0 movement, was acquired by Google in March 2006, and is now offered by it as part of its Docs & Spreadsheet bundle at *docs.google.com*. Though these don't have the same slick interface or user-friendliness offered by Zoho's suite, they're genuinely very powerful, and for anything up to and including middleweight uses, they compete on an equal footing with desktop applications such as those in Microsoft's Office suite. Both are collaborative, too, so you can easily invite others to contribute and publish the results. Being web-based, your documents are stored centrally – accessible from any Internet-connected computer on the planet – and you can upload documents in a range of formats, or email them directly to your Docs account.

Maps and Earth
Google Maps (*maps.google.co.uk*) have supplanted tools such as MapQuest and Streetmap for us. The service exemplifies Google's commitment to pared-down interfaces behind which immense power lies, and it's a great way to check where meetings are taking place or track down local amenities. Its API allows it to be integrated into your site with relative ease – take a look at *ononemap.com* for example – and again there's a lot of functionality tucked in behind the surface. The stand-alone application Google Earth (*earth.google.com*) performs some of the same functions, presented in a 3D environment, with emphasis on satellite imagery rather than schematic maps.

Widgets
From the page at *google.co.uk/macwidgets*, you can download Widgets for Tiger's Dashboard that give you access to posting to Blogger, Google's blogging platform, viewing your Gmail inbox, and showing your search history. You can also download a handy notifier that sits in your menu bar and alerts you to incoming Gmail email and upcoming Google Calendar events; it's at *google.co.uk/mac*.

Page Creator
Released to little fanfare a year ago, Google Page Creator (*pages.google.com*) gives you a basic set of tools with which you can build simple websites. They're hosted by Google – you get 100MB of free storage – though one criticism levelled at the system is that because the URL for your pages is based around your Gmail address, you could be opening yourself to spammers. Regardless, it's a handy way to throw up a few simple pages for a club or the like.

Groups
Google groups (*groups.google.co.uk*) both offers you the ability to search through old Usenet archives, and to create groups of your own. These give you the ability to bring together groups of people for discussions – that can take place using email or through a web-based online system – create custom pages filled with rich text and graphics, and host shared files.

Gmail and Calendar
There remains little more to be said about Google's excellent email service that hasn't already been said. You get more than 2GB of storage space, a rich online email client, plus the ability to pull email securely down to your Pop3 desktop client. And that gets three cheers from us. Over at *calendar.google.com* you can access Google's online calendaring system, which allows you to subscribe to iCal-published calendars and vice versa.

THE HOTTEST GUIDE TO APPLE'S COOLEST KIT

The Ultimate iPod Guide

Fully updated for 2009

- Latest iPod line-up revealed
- The best accessories reviewed
- Do more – 100s of tips and tricks

ONLY £8.99

To order direct please call
0844 844 0053
or visit www.magbooks.com
FREE P&P for UK orders

Also available on magazine newsstands at the following retailers:

WHSmith BORDERS

WEBSITE
IN A WEEKEND

Could you build a dynamic website, complete with blogging and e-commerce tools, in 48 hours? We test nine CMS applications that can help you do just that.

Surely anyone can build a website in a weekend? Armed with a copy of iWeb, it's possible to create presentable pages in no time. But could you go a step further and build a dynamic website with easily updateable content in 48 hours?

Building dynamic websites isn't as difficult as you might think, thanks to the availability of content management systems (CMS). These work in a similar way to blogging applications: they separate content – a website's text and images – from its appearance and management, so it's easy for more than one person to edit. As the CMS resides on a web server, updating its contents is easy no matter where you are.

Most CMSes are modular, which makes it easy to add functionality, whether it's a shopping cart or an interactive forum. But perhaps the best thing about a CMS is that you don't need to be a coding expert to create a website. CMSs ship with ready-made themes that define a website's look. In most cases changing the site's appearance can be simply a matter of selecting a different theme and uploading it to your site.

● In the past, the drawback of web-based CMSes was that they cost thousands of pounds, with hefty annual support costs. That fact alone ruled them out for many individuals and small companies. Their features were limited, too, and adding content could be an arcane process.

Since then the situation has changed. CMSes are available for a fraction of the cost – many are even free – and the number and variety of features on offer has ballooned. We've looked at some of the most popular low-cost systems on the market to find out how well they are suited to personal sites and business websites. The CMSes range from free or open-source applications with the backing of a large developer, to fully supported commercial offerings.

Their system requirements are broadly similar: most are based on PHP, a scripting language that runs on your website's server. This means you'll need to check with your ISP that your site supports PHP. CMSes are also built around a database – most frequently a variation of the popular SQL database – so your website provider will need to offer that too.

WORDPRESS
Contact wordpress.org
Price free

There can be few content management systems that are easier to manage than WordPress. Even its installation process – frequently a showstopper with such systems – is a cinch. Once you've downloaded the program folder from the WordPress website, you simply enter the MySQL database details supplied by your ISP into a configuration file, upload it with the rest of your WordPress files to your server's web space and step through the browser-based setup script. Your site should be up and running in minutes.

Although WordPress has a reputation as a blogging tool, the program's open source status has encouraged a vibrant developer community to build powerful plug-ins that take the program into the realms of low-end content managers. It's not as if boosting WordPress's power is difficult, either: you simply download the well-documented plug-ins from the WordPress site, upload them to your WordPress plug-ins directory and activate them inside WordPress.

This may satisfy business users who would otherwise find WordPress lacking some high-end options. For example, there are no built-in e-commerce functions, but you can download a free module (*instinct.co.nz/e-commerce*) that does the job very well. Similarly, those who want to display an online portfolio might be initially disappointed that there is no image gallery, but there's plenty of choice when it comes to plug-ins, including the excellent YAPB (*johannes. jarolim.com/blog/wordpress/yet-another-photoblog*).

WordPress's Dashboard administration section, an area hidden from site visitors where you manage blog content and layout, is well organised. Under the Write tab you can generate either blog-style posts or create pages for static content that's unlikely to change frequently. This provides a lot of flexibility, even allowing you to add custom fields or metadata to a post. WordPress offers good access management, so you can determine who can post or edit entries, upload images or authorise user comments. RSS support is top-notch too. WordPress not only lets you generate RSS feeds for recently changed content, but also lets users subscribe to comments made to blog posts – handy if you want to keep up to date with what's being said about your site.

The application comes with only a couple of built-in themes, but the WordPress website includes an extensive library of user-contributed themes, helpfully divided into categories. To use these themes you simply upload them to the themes directory on your website.

WordPress also makes it easy to import content from other blogs or CMS engines. Scripts are available for converting content from two dozen rival applications. Even neater is the ability to import data using the syndicated RSS feed from any website. Just save the feed locally, navigate to it in WordPress and click the Import button.

Unlike most other CMSes, updating your WordPress installation is as easy as setting it up in the first place. Simply delete your old WordPress files, keeping those you've modified, and upload the new ones.

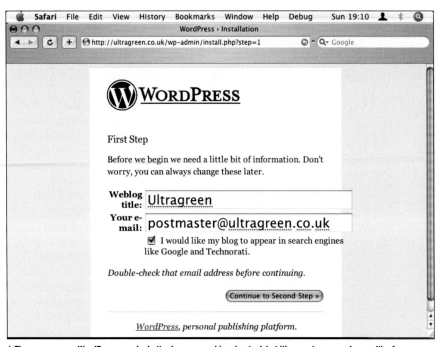

▲ The open-source WordPress may be better known as a blogging tool, but it's easy to use, and a wealth of sophisticated CMS features are available through plug-ins, thanks to its thriving community of developers.

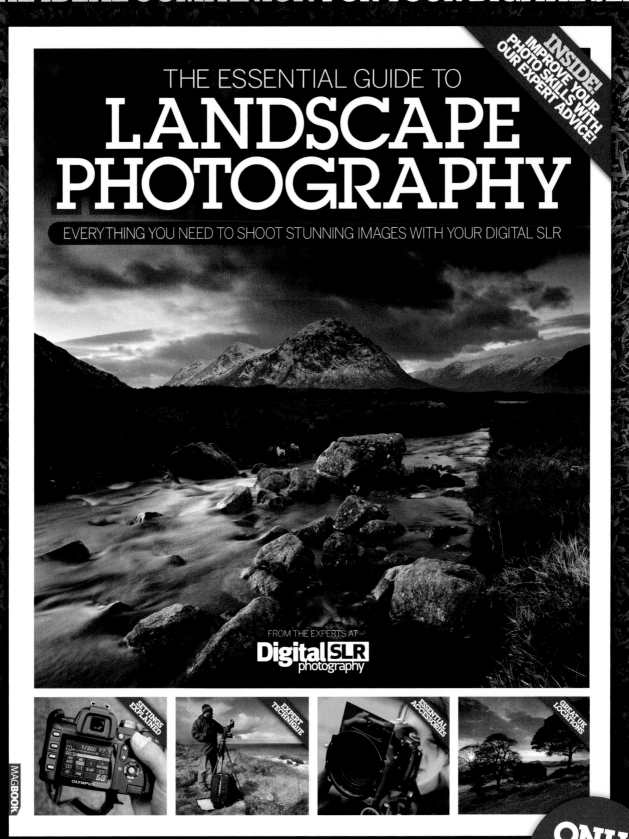

CMS MADE SIMPLE

Contact cmsmadesimple.org
Price free

As its name suggests, the open-source CMS Made Simple 1.1 is another web application that can help you build dynamic websites quickly. Installation is straightforward and – although it won't win any prizes for its looks – the Admin Panel is just as easy to understand as WordPress's. CMS Made Simple also provides excellent, well-written documentation in the form of a 'wiki'.

As with most other content management applications, CMS Made Simple separates content from style. The Admin Panel includes the JavaScript-based TinyMCE Wysiwyg text editor, which enables users who have little or no coding experience to style text and other content to make it visually appealing.

CMS Made Simple works along familiar principles. Web pages are based on templates that include variable 'tags'. These take information from the underlying database that defines how a page appears to a user. The templates can be fully customised and the library of tags, while limited compared with some alternatives, is at least easy to understand.

Cascading style sheets (CSS) define the way templates look. Each default template has five general stylesheets already applied to it and one template-specific stylesheet attached. You can edit the style sheets by opening an 'edit stylesheet' form and pasting in fresh CSS code: there are no fancy extras such as versioning available. It's certainly a bare-bones approach, but it works well.

CMS Made Easy is a promising tool for managing web content. It doesn't yet have anything like the same extensive user community that surrounds the likes of WordPress, Drupal or Joomla, which inevitably means you have less choice when it comes to add-on modules. While modules are available that extend CMS Made Simple into a full e-commerce application and enable you to host an image gallery, in general they are not up to the same polished standard as those in other CMS applications. If your needs are simple, though, or you just want to dip a toe into CMS modules, CMS Made Simple provides much of what you need.

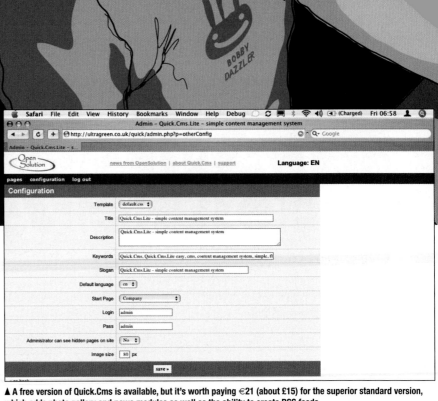

▲ A free version of Quick.Cms is available, but it's worth paying €21 (about £15) for the superior standard version, which adds photo gallery and news modules as well as the ability to create RSS feeds.

QUICK.CMS

Contact opensolution.org
Price free

The tiny Quick.Cms application is an ideal introduction to content management, as it's a doddle to set up and use. Its other principal advantage is that, unlike almost every other comparable tool, it doesn't rely on an SQL database to run. Instead, it does everything through PHP scripting – so your web server will have to be PHP compatible. The absence of a central database may not be too much of a drawback, because the small site we set up in Quick.Cms felt nippy, although we imagine data-heavy sites would struggle to cope under the strain.

As you'd expect, Quick.Cms separates content from style. By default, a single CSS file governs the site's appearance, although you can add further CSS files to the templates directory and apply them through the configuration menu.

Content creation is rudimentary. You create pages, which can be sub-pages or master pages and are categorised so that

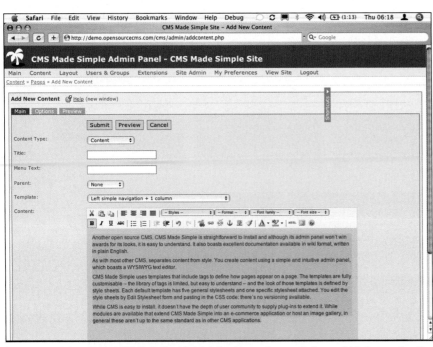

▲ It's not exactly beautiful, but CMS Made Simple's Admin Panel is easy to use and offers useful features such as the JavaScript-based TinyMCE Wysiwyg text editor, which lets users style text visually without the need for any coding.

► ExpressionEngine is one of the diminishing breed of commercial CMS applications, but it provides excellent documentation and support as well as being very flexible.

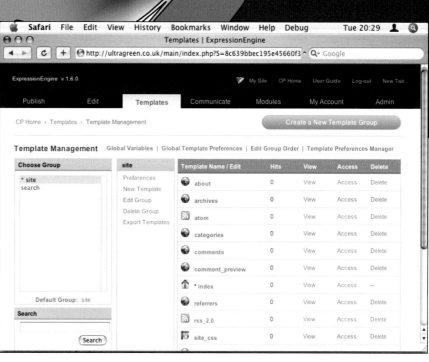

they appear under particular menus. You can then attach files and images to these, and specify the dimensions of images.

This might sound a little restrictive, and there's little doubt that while setting up simple content management is easy, taking it much further is difficult without extra work. Quick.Cms has no concept of themes, for example, so if you want to modify the templates underlying your web pages, you'll need to master HTML or PHP coding.

A free version of the program is available, but the best value lies in the €21 (about £15) standard version, which includes a snappy, if unsophisticated, photo gallery, a dedicated news module and the ability to create RSS feeds. There's also a €59 (about £40) extended version, which adds features such as site maps, contact forms and newsletters. Although they're not bundled with Quick.Cms, the developer also offers a freeware shopping cart and forum module on its website.

EXPRESSION ENGINE
Contact *expressionengine.com*
Price from £50

EllisLab's ExpressionEngine is one of an increasingly rare breed of proprietary CMS, although at about £50 for a personal licence and £125 for the full commercial version, it still qualifies as affordable for personal or business use. There is also a free version, ExpressionEngine Core, for personal or non-profit use, which lacks a couple of the full version's features.

ExpressionEngine's installation is straightforward – you simply adjust a few permissions when you upload the ExpressionEngine directory to your website – and most of the installation is scripted through a browser.

The principles used to set up a website with ExpressionEngine can take some getting used to, but the application is backed by thorough documentation and – as you would expect from a commercial program – good support. There are also excellent tutorial videos that explain the basics of the program.

An ExpressionEngine site can contain any number of 'weblogs'. These are not blogs in their traditional sense, but simple data containers that can hold information in discrete blocks on a page. Unusually, you can add custom fields easily to weblogs – anything from text to images or drop-down menus. Even more unusually, you can have as many weblogs as you want on your site.

ExpressionEngine relies on editable templates that are converted into HTML pages only when a user visits the site. This allows information to be presented dynamically through tags that pull content from the underlying database. These features give ExpressionEngine almost limitless flexibility.

Templates are edited either through ExpressionEngine's well-designed and attractive administration panel or – if you're wedded to desktop applications – through a standard FTP connection, which enables you to use third-party authoring applications such as Dreamweaver or BBEdit. Editing in the administration panel offers the advantage of 'versioning', where ExpressionEngine stores previous versions of templates enabling you to return to them at any point.

ExpressionEngine has some unique features. One that's particularly useful to designers is the built-in Image Gallery module. This isn't a half-baked plug-in: it supports image watermarking, cropping, resizing, rotation and thumbnailing. ExpressionEngine also ships with a Simple Commerce module that lets you sell items through PayPal – something that most of the systems we looked at lack, although you can easily add shopping carts to Drupal and Joomla through plug-ins.

A powerful built-in forum module shares login information with other areas of the site, which is useful. It also uses the same database as the rest of ExpressionEngine, so you don't need an additional SQL database to run it. The downside is that it costs an additional $100 (about £50) – on top of the standard commercial licence. Another add-on is the multiple site manager, which allows you to create and manage multiple websites from a single ExpressionEngine installation. This costs £100 on top of the price of the main program.

Another plus for this program is its apparent security. In the past it has suffered less from security breaches than most systems, and it provides built-in spam-blocking tools, such as Captchas, which ask users to verify that they are a person rather than a web bot by entering text hidden in an image before they can enter comments and registration forms.

ExpressionEngine's disadvantage, apart from the fact that you have to fork out money for it, is that as it is a commercial application it has a smaller user community than most other systems. That means there are fewer third-party modules on offer. It's just as well that those available are so good.

Try 3 issues for £1
Master your SLR with this trial offer!

Get the next **3 issues of Digital SLR Photography for just £1** and start taking your best-ever images. Your 3 issues will be packed with expert tips and tricks, easy to follow equipment guides, as well as inspirational images and advice from a community of DSLR users!

Digital SLR Photography is No.1 for SLR advice and technique – find out today with this **fantastic introductory offer**.

YOUR GREAT DEAL

- ✓ **3 issues for £1** to start your subscription
- ✓ **FREE delivery** of every issue
- ✓ **SAVE 18%** on the shop price
- ✓ News, reviews and advice, hot-off-the-press

Get your 3 issues for £1 today

☎ **PHONE: 0844 249 0482** Please quote offer code below

🖥 **ORDER ONLINE: www.dennismags.co.uk/dslr**
Entering the offer code below

Offer Code: G0906MC2

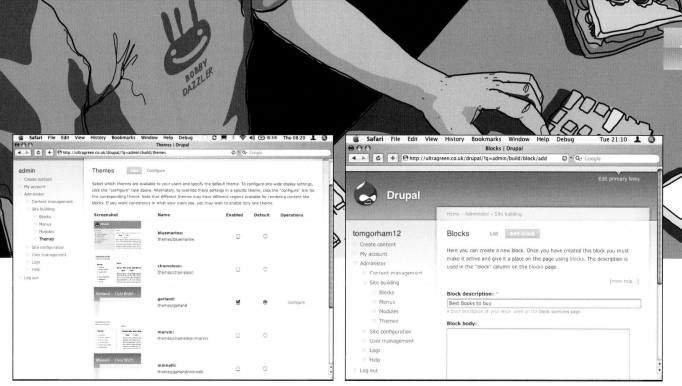

▲ Despite a fearsome reputation, Drupal offers a powerful modular approach to dynamic website creation for those willing to put the effort into learning how it works.

DRUPAL
Contact drupal.org
Price free

The open-source Drupal has a reputation for being one of the most powerful modular tools for managing content. Despite this, it's a fairly small application. The core version takes up only a couple of megabytes of space on a web server.

Drupal is also known for being difficult to use. That was certainly true of earlier versions, where even the installation routine could put off prospective users. Version 5 comes with an install script, which makes installation much simpler.

That said, Drupal and its terminology still demand a lot of the newcomer. For a start, its content is housed in individual 'nodes', which can comprise anything from stories – generally news-type entries that have an expiry date – or blog entries to pages or even part of a forum. This can be a difficult concept to grasp.

Drupal uses a simple HTML-like template language, and templates are modified through the admin panel, where you can also create menus and sidebars as well as add blocks of HTML for site navigation.

Once you understand how Drupal works, you'll have little doubt as to its power. A single installation can host several Drupal-powered sites in a single directory, each with its own configuration settings. You can add modules or themes to individual sites by creating new modules or themes folders in that site's subfolder.

▶ Joomla is a fairly large download, but it's packed with useful features, such as installation scripts, that make life easier.

Drupal offers excellent RSS support. By default you can create an RSS feed of your site's frontpage items, and there's an RSS feed aggregator that can import RSS feeds and present them as a set of HTML pages.

Another impressive feature is the Book, which groups sets of pages together. This makes Drupal good for teaching or collaborative work. A basic forum module is included, and you can turn it on simply by activating a checkbox.

Tweaking sites in Drupal isn't as easy as it could be, but there are six themes that you can switch between easily. These can also be configured quickly through a checkbox list to show important page elements, such as logos and site names.

Adding modules to the program isn't difficult – usually it's enough just to copy the module into the Drupal modules folder.

JOOMLA
Contact joomla.org
Price free

Joomla is a relatively recent arrival but, like Drupal, it's an open-source CMS

application that runs on the combination of PHP and MySQL, and can trace its heritage back to the highly popular Mambo CMS from which it developed.

Joomla runs on a MySQL database. A hefty 11MB installation, it isn't exactly svelte, but the extra time it takes to download pays immediate dividends. Most other CMSes require you to adjust file permissions manually to make sure that the correct folders and files are writable. That almost inevitably means a trip to an FTP application. But Joomla offers helpful installation scripts that flag potential permissions problems before the installation takes place, letting you know which you can safely ignore.

Joomla's Control Panel could lay claim to being the best-looking on the market, and offers management tools that allow you to limit authoring, editing or admin access. You can enter text content through a Wysiwyg editor.

As with other content management systems, Joomla uses templates to control the appearance of your website, and these are maintained separately from website content. Modules, such as menus or polls, add functionality to the templates.

Joomla also has an extensive pool of additional, user-created modules. Although the application doesn't come with a built-in forum module, for example, an integrated and sophisticated forum, Fireboard, can be installed in a few clicks.

Joomla doesn't offer the same multiple site management features as Drupal, but few users will stretch its capabilities.

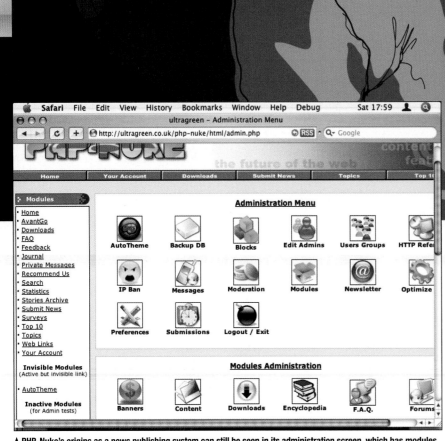

▲ PHP-Nuke's origins as a news publishing system can still be seen in its administration screen, which has modules for news and advertising. This CMS is one of the oldest and has 175,000 registered users, but its popularity is falling.

E107

Contact e107.org
Price free

Like most other CMSs, e107 uses the standard MySQL/PHP combination. Tailored as a general CMS, it's suitable for the beginner who's starting their first dynamic website. While it lacks thorough documentation, its well-written wiki compensates and it features useful 'how to' guides that cover topics such as how to add JavaScript to your site, or speed up page loading.

The administration panel lacks the sort of polish found in some other CMSes, but while e107 has far fewer plug-in modules available than WordPress or Drupal, there are powerful modules available, particularly for handling community forums. There are even bridges to popular forums such as phpBB, that can share user registration information with the main site.

If you're thinking of professional uses for your site, e107 offers a basic e-commerce module and comes with built-in features including banner management. Configuring your own standalone pages can be tricky though – and a fair understanding of PHP code is recommended.

▶ e107's interface lacks polish, but it offers basic e-commerce tools and includes 'how to' guides for beginners.

PHP-NUKE

Contact phpnuke.org
Price $12 (about £6)

Released nearly a decade ago, PHP-Nuke is one of the oldest content management systems, with 175,000 registered users. It was originally free software, but downloading the latest version costs $12.

PHP-Nuke works with SQL databases and requires PHP to be installed on the web server. It started life as a news publishing system, and although it has broadened its horizons into full-scale content management since then, it's much better at building news-led websites than online communities.

This bias is evident from the modules in the cluttered administration screen. The News module is for uploading news, while an Advertising module helps you set up banner ads and a download module is available for website visitors. PHP-Nuke's strong points include an easy-to-use newsletter generator, a poll module that lets you host surveys and a 'top 10' module that automates the creation of links to your most popular pages. There are also a few elements missing, most notably image gallery and shopping cart modules, and while the existing modules are useful, tweaking them is awkward.

Other drawbacks include the lack of a true built-in Wysiwyg editor, and the most difficult-to-read documentation we've ever seen in a CMS module.

More seriously, the program has been criticised in the past for its security leaks, and recent versions don't appear to have addressed this. Perhaps as a result of this – and because it's difficult to download a recent version – it has lost popularity to rivals, although it still offers a wide range of user-contributed modules.

MOVABLE TYPE

Contact movabletype.org
Price personal version free

Movable Type is certainly one of the most flexible CMSes around in terms of the range of databases that it can communicate with. As well as the popular MySQL, Movable Type works with several other database flavours; the Enterprise version of the software can be installed on Oracle databases, which makes it ideal for some corporate environments.

Movable Type is a hefty 4MB download, and despite a fresh installation wizard in the new version, it's still not quite as easy to get up and running as WordPress. But its administration panel is impeccably user friendly,

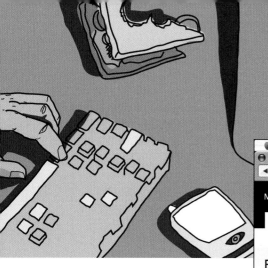

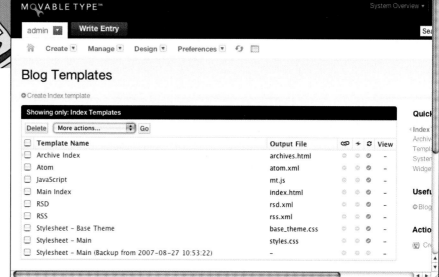

▲ MovableType 4 comes in a range of versions, from the free personal version to a five-user one. The Enterprise version supports Oracle as well as PHP, which makes it suitable for corporate websites.

dividing functions logically into Create, Manage, Design and Preferences sections.

However, while WordPress is written in PHP and is easy for anyone with basic web skills to implement and tweak, Movable Type is written in Perl. This is arguably more powerful and opens up new channels onto the server, which means it must sometimes be installed in a specific directory where its permissions can be controlled. As such, novices may do better using its hosted *typepad.com* service.

When editing entries, you have access to a full Wysiwyg editor, and you can assign publication dates and choose whether each entry is trackable – this feature lets you see which other websites are linking to your post – or accept comments from browsers to your site.

Movable Type's most obvious highlights are its support for unlimited blogs and a neat asset and file manager. This allows the system to track every image or other asset uploaded to your blogs, which makes them easy to re-use.

The application is also highly customisable. Like other CMSes, it uses a number of user-definable templates to generate pages, while variable content is added through Movable Type's own HTML-like template tags. It doesn't offer the same powerful custom fields as some systems, but plug-ins that add this functionality are available from the Movable Type website, and are clearly documented. One caveat is that the recent upgrade to version 4 may have broken some modules, but upgrades are arriving quickly.

Although CMSes are ideal for creating dynamic websites, with content fed from an SQL database when it is needed, Movable Type 4 makes it easy to create static web pages too. There is logic behind this dual approach. In general, static web pages load much faster than dynamic ones, so if your site has a lot of content that doesn't change, such a feature could be an advantage.

Movable Type was the first popular blogging tool to introduce support for trackbacks, but its RSS support isn't quite as powerful as that offered by WordPress – it would be handy, for example, if you could subscribe to comments made to blog posts.

Fortunately, Movable Type 4 has a few tricks of its own. It includes OpenID support for people who comment on Movable Type posts. Any user can sign in to a Movable Type site using their OpenID details and comment without having to supply a site-specific login or password.

Like ExpressionEngine, Movable Type lets you create your own fields in individual blogs, although only as a plug-in module.

CONCLUSION

It's impossible to measure the merits of CMSes precisely against each other. Many are built for different purposes – PHP-Nuke, for example, was built as an engine for a news-driven site, while WordPress has its origins in the blogging arena.

Even taking that into account, if one content management application lacks a feature compared with a rival, there will probably be a plug-in somewhere that fills the gap. And as most CMSes are based on the PHP scripting language, it's possible – if you're prepared to get your hands dirty with code – to tweak whatever CMS you choose to suit your particular needs.

That said, if you want a CMS up and running over a weekend for personal use, it's hard to see beyond WordPress. We don't know a CMS that is easier to set up. What really stands out in its favour is the breadth of its development community. Rival applications such as Movable Type may look more polished and have more built-in functionality, but many of its features can be replicated in WordPress through user-contributed plug-ins.

The choice is even more difficult when it comes to recommending a CMS for commercial purposes. PHP-Nuke may be fine for a news-driven site, but it's not suited to more general sites, and its lack of documentation and security concerns stand against it. CMS Made Easy is simple to use, but isn't as extensible as others.

Out of the box, Drupal is the most powerful CMS we looked at, with the most extensible architecture, as well as a massive user community that regularly submits additional modules. But it is also arguably the most complicated to use, and would take a fair amount of learning to begin to get the most out of it. Joomla, while not as feature-laden, is easier to use. That's important in a commercial environment where the tasks of updating and editing the website may be shared between a number of people.

However, if we were to pick the ideal CMS application for commercial use, we'd have to plump for EllisLab's ExpressionEngine. It's not open source like Drupal or Joomla, but it has two critical advantages. First, it has excellent support, and second, its approach is so flexible that we could see it being equally at home handling a single designer's website or a corporate site with huge traffic.

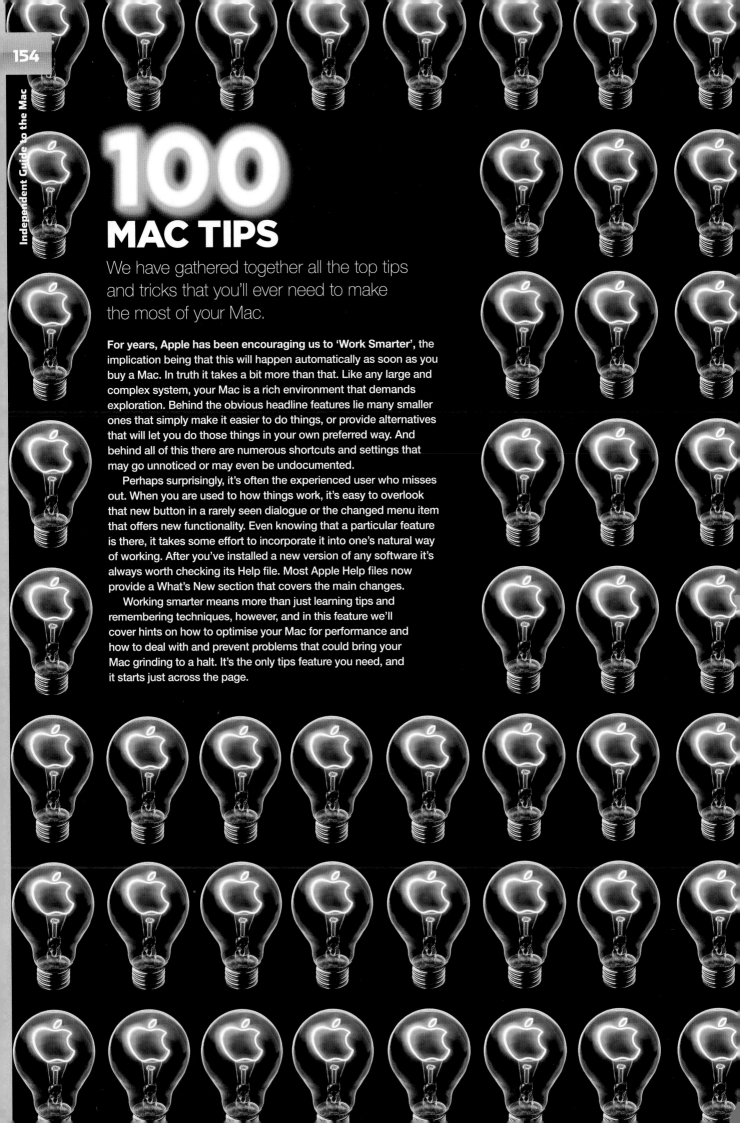

100 MAC TIPS

We have gathered together all the top tips and tricks that you'll ever need to make the most of your Mac.

For years, Apple has been encouraging us to 'Work Smarter', the implication being that this will happen automatically as soon as you buy a Mac. In truth it takes a bit more than that. Like any large and complex system, your Mac is a rich environment that demands exploration. Behind the obvious headline features lie many smaller ones that simply make it easier to do things, or provide alternatives that will let you do those things in your own preferred way. And behind all of this there are numerous shortcuts and settings that may go unnoticed or may even be undocumented.

Perhaps surprisingly, it's often the experienced user who misses out. When you are used to how things work, it's easy to overlook that new button in a rarely seen dialogue or the changed menu item that offers new functionality. Even knowing that a particular feature is there, it takes some effort to incorporate it into one's natural way of working. After you've installed a new version of any software it's always worth checking its Help file. Most Apple Help files now provide a What's New section that covers the main changes.

Working smarter means more than just learning tips and remembering techniques, however, and in this feature we'll cover hints on how to optimise your Mac for performance and how to deal with and prevent problems that could bring your Mac grinding to a halt. It's the only tips feature you need, and it starts just across the page.

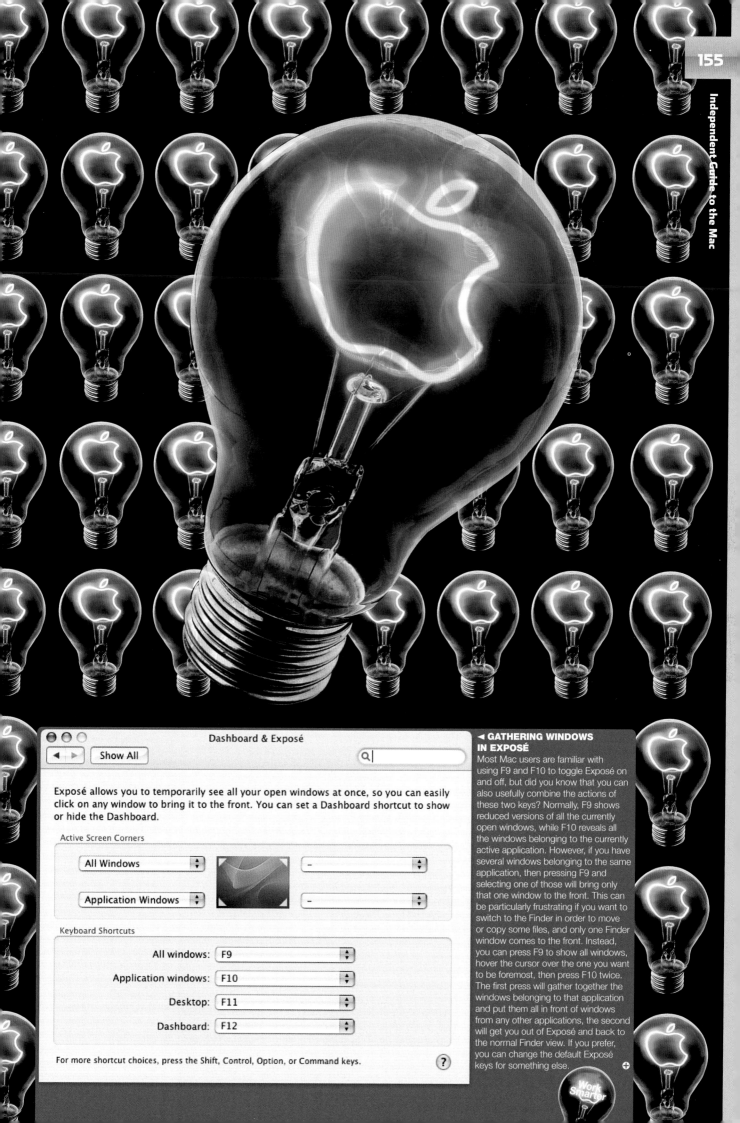

◀ GATHERING WINDOWS IN EXPOSÉ

Most Mac users are familiar with using F9 and F10 to toggle Exposé on and off, but did you know that you can also usefully combine the actions of these two keys? Normally, F9 shows reduced versions of all the currently open windows, while F10 reveals all the windows belonging to the currently active application. However, if you have several windows belonging to the same application, then pressing F9 and selecting one of those will bring only that one window to the front. This can be particularly frustrating if you want to switch to the Finder in order to move or copy some files, and only one Finder window comes to the front. Instead, you can press F9 to show all windows, hover the cursor over the one you want to be foremost, then press F10 twice. The first press will gather together the windows belonging to that application and put them all in front of windows from any other applications, the second will get you out of Exposé and back to the normal Finder view. If you prefer, you can change the default Exposé keys for something else.

Work Smarter

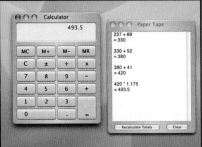

▲ USING THE CALCULATOR
Macs have provided a Calculator application right from the beginning. Over that time, its capabilities have been steadily increasing, but with little fanfare, so you may not have noticed some of the many things that Calculator now offers. For example, use the Paper Tape option (View > Show Paper Tape) to create a printable tape that records a whole sequence of calculations step-by-step. If you prefer, you can type your calculation directly onto the tape and click Recalculate Totals to show the result. The Convert functions are also very handy, allowing you to convert between all sorts of everyday measurements as well as various technical and scientific units. Particularly useful is the currency conversion option, which covers most major currencies and lets you download the latest exchange rates for an up-to-date result. Finally, you can also swap the default simple calculator for a Scientific model with various mathematical functions or a Programmer's calculator which can handle geek arithmetic in hexadecimal, octal and binary. For an added display of calculating prowess, there's also an option to use Reverse Polish Notation (RPN) for your calculations (if you don't know what this is, you don't need it).

OPEN DOCUMENTS IN ANOTHER APPLICATION
It's very convenient that double-clicking a document will automatically launch its application if necessary. However, you don't always want to use the default application. To open a document in another application, but without changing the default, right-click the document and choose Open With from the contextual menu that pops up. This will display a list of applications that can open that type of file as well as an option to pick some other, non-standard application if need be.

▼ CLIPPINGS
A quick way to save a copy of just about any picture that appears in a document is to drag it to the desktop. Your Mac will automatically save it as a Picture Clipping, retaining the original file format. Do the same with text, and you'll create a Text Clipping, but the process doesn't always work as smoothly. Some applications let you drag and drop the clipping with no problem, others assume that moving the cursor is a sign that you plan to alter the selection. In this case, it often works to press the mouse button and hold it for a second or two before you begin to drag. This gives the application time to work out your intentions, and a text clipping will be created on the desktop. Cluttering your screen desktop with file icons is generally not a good idea, but as a temporary measure it's an easy way to collect images and text snippets from all over before you file them away to somewhere more appropriate or drag them into another document or application.

▲ MULTIPLE RSS FEEDS IN SAFARI
Rather than show just one RSS feed at a time, Safari can aggregate feeds from multiple sites into a single window and display them all together. Start by creating a new Bookmarks folder (Bookmarks > Add Bookmark Folder), then place a bookmark in it for each feed that you want to include. To display the articles, click the Show All Bookmarks icon and then control-click the relevant folder. This will bring up a small contextual menu where you need to select the first item: View All RSS Articles. Alternatively, you could place the folder in your Bookmarks Bar, click on it to reveal its drop-down list and select View All RSS Articles from there. The articles from all the chosen feeds will now appear interleaved in time order with the source feed listed alongside each title. Look at the sidebar on the right of the window and you'll see that under the heading RSS Feeds you now have a list of all the sources as well as All. Clicking here lets you narrow down the view to any one feed or go back to showing them all. Additionally, if you change any of these parameters, the URL in the address bar changes too, allowing your filtered search to be itself bookmarked.

◄ SEARCHING SAFARI HISTORY
So you've seen a useful web page earlier, but forgot to bookmark it, and now you need to find it. Rather than scroll through the thousands of items in your History folders, you can use Safari to search through the History entries. Click on Show All Bookmarks (the open book icon at the left of your Safari Bookmarks Bar), select History from the list of Collections in the left-hand sidebar. Go to the search field at the foot of the window, select In History from its pop-up and enter a search term into the field. Safari will search the URL and the page title, so it should be possible to find what you want or at least narrow the field.

◄ EXTRA DOCK OPTIONS
As well as providing quick application switching, the Dock also gives you access to other controls. Rather than just click on an icon, press and hold the mouse button over it – after about a second, a pop-up menu will appear with various options. Some of these, such as Quit, Hide and Show in Finder, appear on all applications, but others are application-specific, which, for example, allows you to Get New Mail in Apple Mail or to change the Repeat and Shuffle settings in iTunes. When an application has more than one window open, its Dock pop-up lets you switch between them. You can access the pop-ups instantly by right-clicking any icon in the dock.

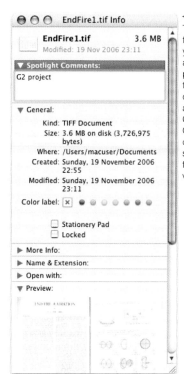

◀ SPOTLIGHT COMMENTS
There are so many items of metadata that can be attached to any file it's sometimes hard to know which ones to use. For example, you could group files that relate to the same project by placing them all in a common folder, by giving them a name that includes the project, by giving them a coloured label (select the file or files, click the action button in the Finder window's toolbar, and pick a colour), or by using Spotlight Comments (select the file, press Command-i and enter keywords or the project name into the Spotlight Comments field). Use whichever one of these feels right – but Comments are less immediately accessible, so they are good for data that won't change, while Label Colour is easy to change and to see, so it may be better suited to temporary use such as marking up files that need urgent attention. Of course, with media files, there is a vast list of additional metadata fields that can be employed.

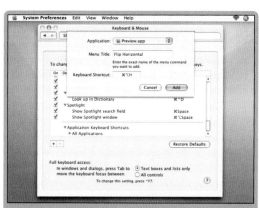

▲ CREATING CUSTOM KEYBOARD SHORTCUTS
For anyone working in a primarily text-based environment, keyboard shortcuts are a great time-saver, allowing you to access most commands without having to fiddle with the mouse. Not all software is equally good at providing shortcuts though, so it's just as well you can create your own generic or application-specific shortcuts very easily. Begin by noting down exactly what the menu item is called – it's the name of the command itself that you need, not the name of the menu it appears in. Next, open the Keyboard & Mouse pane of System Preferences and click on the Keyboard Shortcuts tab. You'll see a list of all the System keyboard shortcuts that Apple provides. Click on the '+' button that's below this list. This will open a dialogue where you can select the application and enter the name of the menu command. Finally, click on the Keyboard Shortcut field and press the actual keys that you want to assign to this shortcut. Then click Add. You can also create a generic shortcut by selecting All Applications rather any specific one.

▲ iCAL CALENDAR GROUPS
iCal's ability to store multiple calendars is great for differentiating work and home commitments, or for keeping a whole family's diaries together in one place and yet separate. In the latest version of iCal, you can take this idea even further by making use of Calendar Groups. Choose File > New Calendar Group or just press Shift-Command-n to create a new group, which will appear in the Calendars list on the left of the window. It operates much like a folder so you can drag any calendar that's on the list into the group. The benefit is that you can now hide or reveal multiple calendars with just a single mouse click. Of course, you can still control each grouped calendar individually when you need to.

THE INSPECTOR
If you select a file and press Command-i, you'll open its Get Info window. But if you need to see Get Info for several files – perhaps to add a common Spotlight Comment to each one – then opening and closing Get Info every time will soon become very tedious. This is when you need to use The Inspector. Press Alt-Command-i and you'll open exactly the same Get Info window as before, the difference is that this window will remain open and display the data of any file you select in the Finder window. When you've finished, close the Inspector window.

SWITCH FINDER WINDOW VIEWS
To switch quickly between the different views available in a Finder window, you can press Command-1 for Icon view, Command-2 for List view and Command-3 for the Columns view.

MOVE UP THE HIERARCHY
One useful Windows feature that the Mac lacks is a button to take you up one level in the folder hierarchy to the folder or volume that contains the currently displayed level. However, you can achieve this easily by pressing Command-up arrow.

MIGHTY MOUSE BUTTONS
If you're using Apple's Mighty Mouse, make sure you're getting the full benefit of its four buttons. Most people won't want to change the behaviour of the main left-click and right-click buttons, but the scrollball and side buttons are up for grabs and they can usefully be programmed to do various tasks or to open any application. Choose Apple Menu > System Preferences > Keyboard & Mouse and click on the Mouse tab to change your mouse button settings.

SHIFT TO REVERSE
The Shift key is often used as a modifier to reverse the direction of a default action. For example in the Application Switcher, pressing Command-Tab moves you to the next application on the right, while Shift-Command-Tab moves you one application to the left. Similarly, in Safari, pressing the space bar scrolls a web page down by one screen, and pressing Shift-Space bar scrolls up by one screen.

OPENING DOCUMENTS FROM GET INFO
If you've opened a document's Get Info window to check details of the file or to see a preview of its contents, you can open the document directly without having to close Get Info and go back to the Finder window. Just double-click the preview panel.

▼ SPOTLIGHT SYSTEM PREFERENCES
System Preferences are generally quite logical, but some topics inevitably span several panes. Mouse settings, for example, appear in Universal Access and Dashboard & Exposé, as well as the obvious Keyboard & Mouse. You can find all the panes that relate to a particular topic by typing it into the Spotlight field at the top of the System preferences window. A drop-down list of settings will appear and the appropriate Preferences pane for each one will be spot lit.

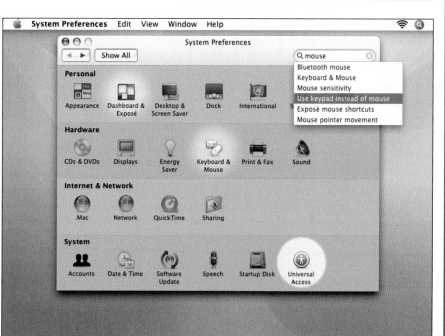

▶ PRINTING ENVELOPES IN ADDRESS BOOK

The Address Book in Mac OS X Tiger onwards allows you to print envelopes directly from the application without having to copy the address label and paste it into a word processor. However, the technique is rather quirky. If you have a simple card for an individual or a business, there's no problem. Choose File > Print to open the Print dialogue and select Envelopes from the Styles field. Next, click on the Layout tab to choose an envelope size. By default, Address Book puts your return address in the top-left corner of the envelope, if you don't want to include it you'll need to click the Labels tab and de-select it. The process gets more complicated if you've entered a name into any of the family member fields, such as Spouse, Parent, Child and so on. Inexplicably, Address Book will include them all on the envelope. Thankfully, Apple hasn't extended this to include fields such as Friend or Manager, but it needs to be sorted out. Until then, you may want to put details of family members into the Notes field. Of course, there will be times when you want to write jointly to a couple, in which case you could create a duplicate card with the Spouse field filled in, but make sure you include both the first name and surname in the Spouse field.

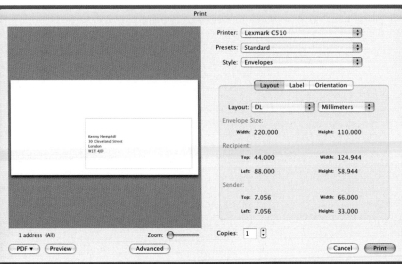

◀ SERVICES

Most applications include an item called Services in their application menu. This provides access to a strange ragbag of functions ranging from the obviously useful to the bizarrely esoteric. For example, how often do you need to calculate an Image Checksum or convert between Simplified and Traditional Chinese text? Making sense of Services isn't made easier by the fact that different items appear in the Services sub-menu according to which application you're in and, just because a command is there, doesn't always mean that it will work. Even so, it's worth looking at Services especially if you use a few applications regularly and so can become familiar with the particular facilities they offer. In many cases, you need to select something – often a piece of text – before you can apply a Services command to it. For example, one useful command creates an email with the currently selected text in the body of the message. Many applications will let you send the current document as an email attachment, but if you just want to send an extract, this is the easier option. Other useful commands will run a Google search on the selected text, create a Sticky Note from it or do a Spotlight search on it. In each case saving you from having to copy, switch application and then paste.

BE ORGANISED

According to the hype, you need never worry about where to save documents – just put them anywhere and let Spotlight find them when they're needed. It's true that Spotlight can track down anything anywhere, but that doesn't make reliance on Spotlight a smart strategy. Creating at least some basic folder structure gives you a better overview of what files you have relating to a particular subject, and is especially useful if you're working on a collaborative project. Also remember that when Spotlight returns a long list of matches, your ability to find the file you need often depends on knowing what it's called. A cryptically named file will be easier to find if it's in a sensible place than if it's floating in a free-form soup of files.

UNSAVED CHANGES

A quick visual check to show whether your document contains unsaved changes is to look at the Close button in the top-left corner of the window. If there are unsaved changes, this button will have a dark dot in the centre. Otherwise, its centre will be clear

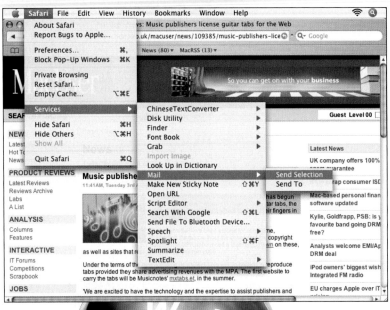

◀ TAB TO FIELDS OR TO ALL CONTROLS

Within any window or dialog box, pressing Tab will normally move focus to the next field or list, but you can extend this idea to allow buttons and other controls to be included in the tabbed sequence. To toggle between these two settings, just press Crtl-F7. Alternatively, you can make either behaviour the default. Just click Keyboard & Mouse in System Preferences and you'll find buttons to select the desired behaviour under the Keyboard Shortcuts tab. If you choose to allow tabbing to all controls, you'll be able to operate them from the keyboard, but you'll need to work out what keys to use. It's mostly fairly obvious – for example, in a vertical group of radio buttons you'd use the Up and Down Arrows to switch between them. In a pop-up list, those same keys will move through the list and Enter will confirm your choice. However, if you know what the list items are, you can often select one directly just by typing its initial letter. The situation with single buttons is less obvious, you'll need to press the space bar in order to toggle the button on or off. In an unfamiliar window all this can be confusing, but it's handy if you use an application regularly and know your way around it.

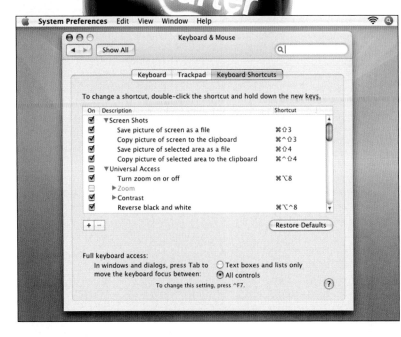

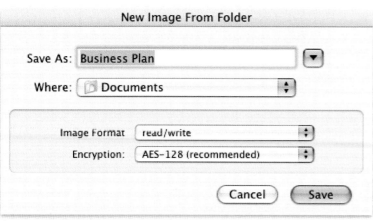

▲ SECURE YOUR FILES
Mac OS X doesn't allow individual folders or documents to be encrypted in situ, but it will let you create encrypted disk images that can contain any mix of applications, folders and documents. These encrypted images are protected by the AES-128 algorithm, which has never been broken and is approved by the US National Security Agency for secret documents. The slow way to create an encrypted disk image is to open the Disk Utility application and work through the process. A faster way is simply to drag the folder that you want to encrypt onto the Disk Image icon. This will launch Disk Utility and open a dialog box called New Image From Folder where you can name the disk image and specify a location where it will be saved. Unless this image is just for archiving, select Read/Write from the Image Format pop-up so that you can add, modify and delete the contents in future. Make sure you also select the encryption option (it's off by default), and then click Save. You'll be asked to enter and re-enter a password which can optionally be saved to your keychain. If you decide not to add it to your keychain, don't forget your password, as you won't be able to open the image again without it.

When the image has been created, you must delete the original folder and, preferably, use Finder > Secure Empty Trash to make sure that no easily recoverable traces remain of it. To access the contents of your secure disk image, just double-click it. Once you've supplied your password, this will mount the image which you can then open to show the contents. Provided you selected the Read/Write option, you'll be able to work with the files that are in the image and add new ones in the usual way. When you close and un-mount the image, everything inside it will once again be fully encrypted against the most prying of eyes.

▼ USING THE GRAPHER
Apple's free Grapher application, which lives in the Utilities folder inside your Applications folder, can do more useful things than might at first be obvious. Its main role is to plot 2D or 3D graphs of mathematical equations. You pick the style of plot you want (linear, logarithmic, polar, and the like), type in the equation and the graph appears. Rather less obviously, Grapher is an excellent way to produce your own blank graph paper. If you print the graph without first entering an equation, you'll get a blank sheet of graph paper that can be filled in by hand, which is useful if you just need an occasional sheet, and it could be handy in education too. Obviously, this works best on a laser printer rather than an inkjet. Another way to use Grapher is as an equation editor. Some applications, such as Microsoft Word, come with their own equation editor. Others, such as Apple Pages, don't. If you type the equation in Grapher, using its Symbol Palette for any special characters, it will be laid out in correct mathematical form. You can then copy this and paste it into another application.

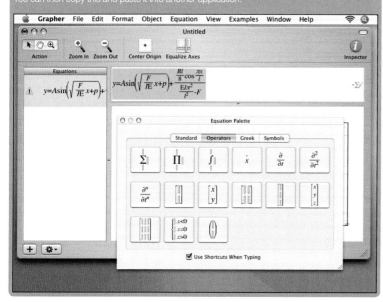

▲ FINDER TOOLBAR AND SIDEBAR
The Dock isn't the only place where you can put commonly used files. Any application, folder or document can be dragged into the Finder sidebar and will then appear there in all Finder windows. You can also do this by selecting the item you want to put in the sidebar and pressing Command-t. Another even more prominent place for regularly used items is the toolbar that appears at the top of each Finder window. To move something into the toolbar, drag its icon there and hold it until a green '+' appears at the cursor. When you release the mouse button, the icon will be added to the toolbar in all Finder windows. To remove an icon from either place, right-click it and choose Remove From Sidebar or Remove Item.

▲ SAVED SEARCHES
There are lots of ways to make use of Saved Searches and it's worth doing so because they can really boost your efficiency whenever you need to perform a similar search more or less regularly. A Saved Search could be as simple as finding every Excel document on your hard disk or as complex as you want it to be. With metadata becoming more common and detailed in media files, the options for searching are expanding rapidly. To create a Saved Search you need to begin with the Finder's Find command and not with Spotlight. Choose File > Find or press Command-f to open the Find window. Using the pop-ups, select the attribute you want to match and what value it should have. You can add or delete criteria by clicking the '+' or '-' buttons at the end of each line. The button bar above lets you confine the search to a specific folder, disk or server. To see the full range of attributes or values that can be searched, choose Other from any of the pop-ups and you'll get a long list of possible options including such detailed attributes as the focal length of lens used to take a photo or the language of a text-based file. In order to save the search, click on the Save button and specify a name and location. Because you're saving the search criteria rather than just the result of the search, you'll get up to date hits every time you run it.

SCROLLBALL ZOOM
Pressing the Ctrl key while rolling the scrollball on a mouse that has one lets you zoom-in to an enlarged image of everything that is on screen. This is an OS-level action that works in all applications and the Finder, but some applications also support useful actions when you Alt-scroll. For example, in Adobe Reader this will zoom the PDF within the window without altering the overall screen display. In iCal, Alt-scroll lets you increase or decrease the hours visible in either Day or Week view.

optimise

DROP ICONS – AND WINDOWS
Mac OS X uses a small amount of its memory to display every icon on your desktop. That means a performance hit for those with cluttered desktops.

And while the arrival of Exposé has meant its much easier to manage multiple open windows, your Mac is still using processor cycles to redraw each one. Try to only keep those windows that you need open.

RUN MAINTENANCE SCRIPTS
Mac OS X runs regular maintenance scripts to clear system logs and temporary files. Under Mac OS X versions prior to 10.4, these were scheduled to run in the small hours of the morning. If your Mac was turned off or asleep, the scripts didn't run. If you use pre-Tiger operating systems run a utility such as Cocktail (*macosxcocktail.com*), which runs these tasks at the click of a button.

Apple has changed the way maintenance scripts are run under Mac OS X 10.4 Tiger, so scripts should now run even if your Mac is switched off overnight. Reports suggest, however, that the new system is buggy so manual maintenance is still worthwhile.

MAKE FREE SPACE
There may be no better way of improving your Mac's performance than by increasing its Ram or investing in a faster hard drive. But you can still accelerate it without investing in hardware.

Removing unwanted files and folders is one of most effective – and, strangely, the most therapeutic – ways of keeping your Mac fast and trouble free.

The fewer files on your Mac, the quicker you can search it and the faster backups can be.

But free space is most critical in terms of raw performance. You should aim to keep at least 15 per cent – but preferably more – of your hard disk free to allow sufficient room for Mac OS X's virtual memory. Any less and Ram-hungry applications can slow to a crawl.

TRASH
The quickest way to grab disk space is to empty the Trash, but don't forget the Finder isn't the only place to delete files. Many applications have their own Trash, including iPhoto, iDVD and iMovie. You need to delete their trash from within the application.

DELETE APPLICATIONS
All those applications you're never likely to use can take up surprising amounts of disk space. Dragging the applications themselves to the Trash may be the quickest way to get rid of them, but it's often their associated files that annex most space. Between them, the Garageband and iDVD support files in the Library/Application Support/directory on your Mac's hard disk use about 4GB. To delete files, it's best to use the applications original installer – it often has an uninstall option – or use the free AppDelete (*reggie.ashworth.googlepages.com/appdelete*).

DELETE UNWANTED PREFERENCES
Check your User's Library/Preferences folder for old, orphaned preferences files. They may not take up much space, but a corrupt preferences files can affect performance.

REMOVE CLASSIC
When was the last time you used Mac OS X's Classic Environment? To delete it – and save disk space – open the Mac OS 9 System Folder on your hard disk, drag its contents to the trash and empty it. Now log out and back in again and drag the folder itself to the trash and delete the Mac OS 9 applications folder.

LIMIT YOUR APPS
Mac OS X's excellent multitasking abilities have spoilt Mac users in recent years, allowing us to keep plenty of applications open at once. But it's common sense that you should run only the applications you need. The more applications you have running, the less Ram they can grab for themselves.

TAME SPOTLIGHT
Spotlight's content indexing marginally detracts from performance while it's taking place, so it's a good idea to prevent it indexing unnecessarily. Add volumes such as a scratch disks or backup volumes to Spotlight's privacy list in the Spotlight System Preferences pane. This ensures that only those volumes and folders you need indexed are included.

USE A SECOND DRIVE
To optimise the performance of demanding applications, such as audio and video programs or Photoshop, use a speedy second hard disk as a project or scratch disk and make sure it has plenty of free space. Don't allow Spotlight to index it.

CLEAN CACHES
Application caches hold frequently-used data to allow quicker access time. Ironically, some application caches can become bloated over time and detract from performance. Commonly affected applications include Dashboard widgets (delete the Dashboard cache from the DashboardClient folder in your user's Library/Caches directory) and Safari. You can delete Safari's cache from inside the application: just select Safari > Empty cache.

SLICK SAFARI
Other drags on Safari's performance include a bloated history list (to correct this, select History > Clear History). If you really want to start from scratch you can reset Safari (Safari > Reset Safari). Not only does it delete your cache and scrub your History list, but it also clears the Downloads window, removes cookies, saved AutoFill data and Google search entries.

LOG OUT OTHERS
Mac OS X's Fast User switching looks so impressive because it maintains other users' system resources while you're logged in. To get the most speed out of your Mac, though, make sure you're the only user connected.

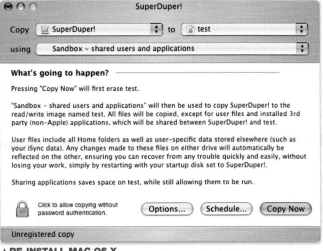

▲ RE-INSTALL MAC OS X
The most drastic, but effective, way to optimise your Mac's performance is to re-install it over a clean disk. Mac OS X 10.4 users can do this without losing any of your important data if you first copy your existing Mac OS X installation to an external FireWire drive using a utility such as SuperDuper! (*shirt-pocket.com*).

Now reinstall Mac OS X from the install CD using the Erase and Install option. When you perform the installation, make sure you perform a Custom Install, so you can elect not to install printer drivers or languages that you don't need.

You can then use Apple's Migration Assistant tool to copy your most important settings from your backed-up system.

▼ CHECK ACTIVITY MONITOR
Regularly keep a eye on what's taxing your processor with Activity Monitor, a utility in your Applications/Utilities folder. Select All processes from Activity Monitor's toolbar drop-down menu, and click the %CPU heading to sort the processes by descending order of CPU usage. You don't even need to open the Activity monitor window to check processor and memory usage, or disk or network activity – just right-click on Activity Monitor's Dock icon to view those details from the Dock.

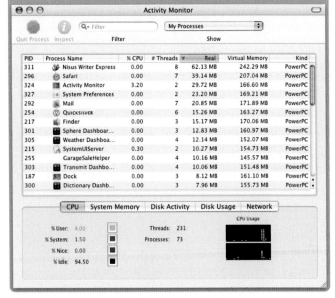

◀ FIND FREE SPACE
How do you find those applications and files that are eating up your free disk space? In the Finder choose File, Find and in New Search window, select Size and choose greater than 100MB – or whatever.

To find invisible files, under the Kind pull-down menu, select Other and choose Visibility from the list. Choose Visible or Invisible items.

▲ OPTIMISED EMAIL
Improve email performance by archiving old messages to a backup disk and starting afresh. It's easy to do: copy your Library/Mail folder to an external drive – if you want to do this with an Imap mail server's contents, temporarily choose 'Keep copies of messages for offline viewing' in Mail's Preferences Accounts pane, under the Advanced tab. You don't have to remove your entire message base. In Mail, create a new folder and drag older emails to it. Drag this to the desktop and archive to a CD or DVD. You can now move your originals to the Trash. The simplest way to boost your speed is to rebuild Mail's database index, shrinking it and in most cases making it much faster. Quit Mail, drag the Envelope Index out of your user's Library/Mail folder, and relaunch the program. Mail automatically re-imports messages.

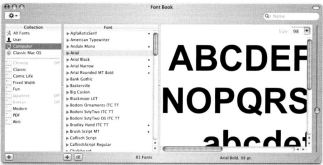

▲ LIMIT YOUR FONTS
Application launch times and font menu performance can both be affected by too many fonts – especially if there's a corrupt font. Just about every Mac user has dozen or more fonts they're never likely to use. Remove unwanted ones using Apple's Font Book application, but first make sure that Apple's core list of necessary fonts isn't affected – check Apple's list at *docs.info.apple.com/article. html?artnum=25710*. It's wise – as with any optimisation tip – to make a backup before deleting anything. Font Book also instantly shows you duplicate fonts – a bullet (•) appears before the names of duplicates in the Font list. These can be safely removed. You can check individual fonts for corruption using File > Validate fonts.

▲ NO WIDGETS
Active widgets eat an extraordinary amount of Ram – sometimes up to 10MB each – considering the simple tasks they perform. While you can't turn off the Dashboard entirely, the golden rule with widgets is to treat them like applications, only opening them when you need them. To close a widget with Dashboard active, hold the alt key down and click the close button at the top left of the widget.

◄ DON'T SAVE ENERGY
Allowing your hard drive to be put to sleep is a great way to save battery life on laptops, but for the best performance, make sure the Energy Saver settings in your System Preferences Energy Saver pane are speed optimised. Deselect the option to have your hard disk to sleep when possible to prevent slowdowns caused by your hard disk spinning back up from sleep.

► DELOCALISE
Another way to save space is by removing unwanted language localisations, which will have been installed if you chose the Easy Install option when you installed Mac OS X. While you can remove extra languages manually, the freeware Monolingual (*monolingual.sourceforge.net*) makes the process simple.

◄ UPDATE YOUR SOFTWARE
Most software can check for updated versions of itself. Turn this option on wherever possible as the performance and reliability improvements offered by upgrades can be significant, and it's far easier to have the application check these things for you than have to do the checking yourself. Updating software is particularly important if you're running an Intel Mac. Now that CS3 is here, just about every major application has a Universal Binary version, so make sure the latest version of your favourite software takes advantage of the speed boost that native Intel support brings.

► CLEAN OUT LOGIN ITEMS
Every program or process that automatically launches when you login to your Mac increases login time and increases Ram demands. Keep an eye on them in the Accounts System Preferences pane under the Login Items tab – it's odds on that you'll find a couple in there you never knew you had installed.

◄ REDUCE EYE CANDY
In the Dock preferences pane of System Preferences, select Scale Effect in the Minimize Using field and uncheck the Animate opening applications option. This saves a few processor cycles.

► TURN OFF FILE SHARING
Improve performance by turning off unwanted networking options. For example, if you don't need to share files on your Mac, Mac OS X's file sharing feature is a clear waste of processor cycles. Turn it off in the Sharing pane of System Preferences. You can also disable Bluetooth in the Bluetooth pane if you don't need it.

Troubleshooting

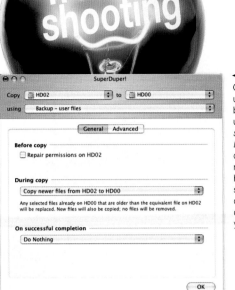

- Take kernel panics seriously, if your Mac suffers from them. Their most common cause is a problem with hardware, particularly failed or failing memory modules. If you suffer a kernel panic, check all your installed memory using Rember (free from *kelleycomputing.net*), running a long test that is more thorough than quick tests provided by other tools. Also remove all non-essential peripherals, whether connected via USB or FireWire, suspect PCI cards, and so on. Prevent memory problems by purchasing Ram specified for your particular model. When buying for a Mac Pro, watch for the adequacy of the heat sink; if in doubt, buy from Apple.

◄ **MAKE A BOOTABLE COPY**
Once you are happy that a system update is problem-free, make a bootable mirror copy, for example using SuperDuper! ($27.95 from *shirt-pocket.com/SuperDuper/SuperDuper Description.html*) on an external FireWire or USB hard disk, and keep that as a recovery and emergency disk. If you have time when doing this, clone your startup disk to the external drive, then clone it back to your startup disk, to completely defragment and clean up your startup drive.

▼ **CHECK YOUR LOGS**
If your Mac is sluggish, is rattling away accessing a hard disk for no apparent reason, suffers from crashes (not kernel panics), or has missing services or strange errors, check your logs using Console, or similar. You may see Spotlight's indexing engine, listed as mdutil in Activity Monitor, choking over one file, for instance. If so, remove the troublesome file, or rename the folder containing it with the .noindex suffix to exclude indexing. Indexing should then complete normally and performance will be restored. If another service seems to be cyclically crashing and restarting, find out why, and deal with that issue.

◄ **DO NOT DISTURB**
Keep your core operating system and applications intact and undisturbed to avoid update issues. Try and do manual installations of system updates. Back up at least your key files before updating. If you have slimmed applications down by stripping foreign language localisations, restore the original version. If you have relocated Apple applications, put them back into their correct places and install the update. If your Mac suffers blue screen or other problems when restarting, wait: don't rush to do anything. If it's definitely frozen, force your Mac to shut down by pressing and holding the power button, start it up with your latest install CD/DVD or in single-user mode and repair the disk, and restart again.

▲ **RESCUE DVD**
Startup or restart problems strike when you are least prepared. Make yourself a rescue DVD and keep it to hand for those dreaded occasions. One way of doing this is to create a new 4.7GB DVD disk image in Disk Utility, install Mac OS X into that from your most recent system DVD, then apply the latest Combo updater. You should be able to burn this disk image to DVD using Disk Utility. Keep the disk image updated with the latest release of Mac OS X and its tools. To ensure you can cope with most emergencies, include Disk Utility, Network Utility, your backup and restore tools, and third party essentials such as Disk Warrior and TechTool Pro.

▲ **SPARE ACCOUNTS**
If you are trying to solve a setting or related problem, have a spare 'clean' admin user account available, and try logging into that. Preference and other setting files can become blocked, but should remain clear for this 'clean' user, so you can use the account to locate the problem. Ensure that it has a strong password, or it could prove vulnerable, for instance if you have SSH remote access enabled. For an ultra-clean environment, restart into that clean account with the Shift key held down to disable third party extensions. If you think that a preference file is causing a problem but are not sure exactly which one, set a Finder window to list the contents of the suspect Library/Preferences folder by Date Modified. Open the pane or application and change its preference settings. The file containing those settings should then be updated and appear at the top of the list, with the current modification time.

WRITE IT DOWN
Keep a written record, supported by screenshots, of all your key settings, especially those for your network and broadband modem-router. With it, record all key usernames and passwords. Lock this record away if necessary, but keep it accessible in case you need to check or reset any of those key items.

Let your Mac store usernames and passwords in its keychain. If you then want to access one of those protected services, but cannot recall the username or password correctly, use your Keychain Access utility to look up the stored username and password.

Troubleshooting

◀ **RESTORING TRASHED OR MISSING COMPONENTS**
Restore trashed or missing components from Mac OS X and its updates using Pacifist ($20 from *charlessoft.com*). Open the latest Combo or other updater first and look for the items you need. You can also use this to revert individual components such as system libraries if a Mac OS X update breaks hardware or software you need to use, although using older software components can cause severe system instability.

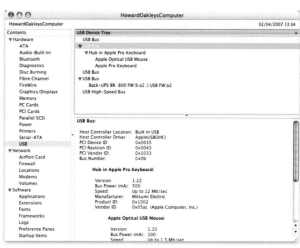

▲ **PESKY PERIPHERALS**
When peripherals are playing up, shut everything down and check cables and connections. Swap components around to try to isolate the defect. With a monitor or graphics card problem, test your monitor on a different Mac, use a different cable, and so on, applying logic to deduce which of the host Mac, graphics card, cable, and monitor elements is at fault.

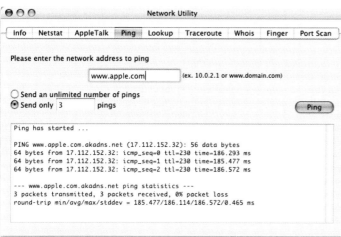

▼ **BE WARY OF UPDATES WITH USB MODEMS**
If your broadband connection relies on a USB modem, be wary of Mac OS X system updates. Check before installing an update that it will be compatible with the modem's driver. Otherwise you may lose your Internet connection if the driver is broken by the system update, and you might find it very messy to restore. When you can, switch to a networked modem-router that does not suffer this problem.

▲ **TESTING, TESTING...**
With network or Internet problems, use Network Utility first to 'ping' a known IP address, either on your network or a remote site such as Apple's (17.112.152.32). If that works well, try a domain name such as *www.apple.com*, which tests name resolution (DNS). If pinging IP addresses fails, you are no longer connected to that network. If your broadband connection is down, try restarting your modem via its web interface.

DON'T JUST REINSTALL
If you are trying to fix a problem, don't keep re-installing applications or Mac OS X itself: this is not Windows or Mac OS 9, where re-installing can be a panacea. Archiving and re-installing can recover Macs after they have suffered damage to their system files, though. This might be a valuable last-ditch measure if you have inadvertently been using your Mac when it 'optimised' your system during a Mac OS X update, and has led to file loss, but it often just creates a lot of work and adds to confusion. Instead of using sledgehammer solutions, try to identify where the problem lies and tackle the problem methodically.

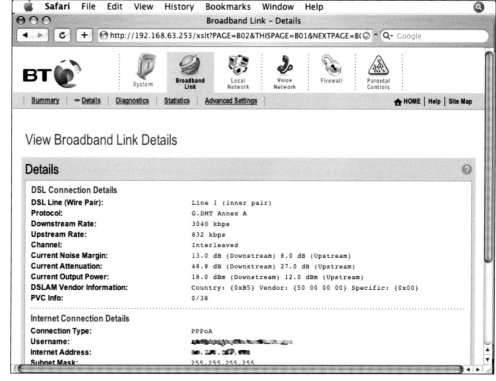

Troubleshooting

◀ BE WARY OF SLEEP
Some Macs don't like waking up from sleep and may freeze, requiring a forced restart. This can be the result of third party software or hardware, and is less likely when using the latest release of Mac OS X and any third-party software. Although important for laptops to conserve battery power, sleeping is of little benefit to desktop systems, and you should consider just sleeping the display, set in the Energy Saver pane. Putting hard disks to sleep can shorten their lives unless they are designed to withstand it, as those in laptops are. Routine housekeeping will only occur normally if your display is sleeping, but it won't take place if your whole Mac is asleep.

KEEP A WIRED SPARE
Wireless keyboards and mice are a boon, but you should always keep an emergency wired keyboard and mouse to hand. If the wireless ones fail, or you have to start your Mac up without Bluetooth software support, you can then connect the wired devices and work normally.

UPDATING THE UPDATES
Software Update will normally keep offering you an update that you think you have already installed, if that update has not been applied fully. For example, an update that replaces iChat will not take if you have tampered with your old iChat application, and you will continue to be offered that same update. If this happens, identify the file(s) that have not been updated, and use Pacifist or something similar to update them by hand, if necessary, then re-apply the update. Software Update should recognise that the update is complete, and leave you alone.

KEEP RECEIPTS
Disk Utility complains about losing communication when you try to check or repair permissions with a damaged bundle in your /Library/Receipts folder. If affected, remove those receipts one by one to identify which is to blame, and you will eventually be able to repair permissions again. Never trash those receipts, as that will stop Disk Utility from working properly until you have restored the receipts from backup.

ALWAYS DOUBLE CHECK
Test your backups and archives periodically. The best time to perform a test of full restoration is just before a major Mac OS update, such as installing Leopard, but you must have an additional reliable clone of the disk to be restored as well, in case restoration fails. In addition, every so often identify a document or application that should be stored in your backup set or archive, find it in the set, and restore it to a test folder.

KNOW YOUR BATTERIES
Know what PRam backup battery your Mac uses, and keep a spare to hand so that you can replace it as soon as required. Recent models either take the traditional half-AA 3.6 V lithium unit, or CR-2032 'coin' cells. iMacs that do not take the former seem to use CR-2032, although you can pay much more for branded replacements.

DOUBLE MAC SOLUTION
If you have more than one Mac, FireWire Target Disk mode can be an excellent way of dealing with serious glitches such as freezing during startup. Connect the problem Mac to your host Mac using a FireWire cable, and start up the problem Mac with the T key held down until the FireWire icon appears on its screen. You should then be able to access its startup disk as an external FireWire drive connected to the host. Also use this to recover key documents from a Mac that has suffered hardware failure, and to back up your disk before sending a broken Mac away for repair. Desktop systems with two ATA drives as Master and Slave will not mount both drives as FireWire targets: to access the second (Slave), shut down and swap Master and Slave settings, normally using jumpers on the hard disks. When you have finished accessing a drive in Target mode, remember to eject it from the host Mac before shutting the problem Mac down by pressing and holding its power button.

▶ CHECK YOUR BACKUP
Having made a recent full backup, test your UPS automatic shutdown software. Close all applications, and turn the mains power supply off at the wall socket. Time how long it takes your Mac to shut down, and when you have restored the mains and started up again, adjust or fix the UPS settings in your Energy Saver pane (or third-party tool such as PowerChute) so that it works properly. Also keep an eye on the battery in your UPS recharging, using that pane.

▶ KEEP IT SLIM
The commonest cause of bizarre behaviour in a mail client, such as missing emails, is letting its mailbox(es) grow too large. Although most recent releases of Mail, Microsoft Entourage and others can cope with mailboxes over 1GB, keep yours down to 100MB or less to ensure best performance. Periodically archive out messages that you need to keep but do not need to refer to daily, to keep your main mailbox or database down in size.

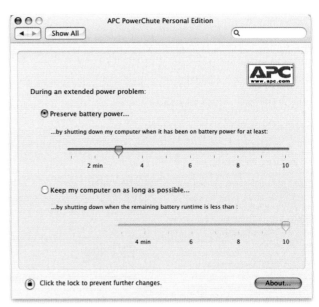

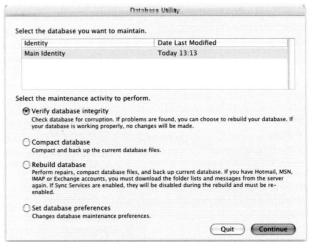

ON BOOT

alt	Allows you to chose which volume to boot from on modern Macs
shift	Starts up in Safe Boot mode
command-alt-P-R	Zap PRam; keep keys held down at least until second chime
command-alt-O-F	Boot into Open Firmware (PowerPC Macs only)
command-V	Boot in verbose mode
command-S	Boot into single user mode
C	Boot from CD
T	Put FireWire machine into FireWire Target Disk mode
X	If Mac OS X and Mac OS 9 are on the same boot partition, this will force the Mac to start up from OS X
left mouse button	Eject removable media

AS FINDER STARTS

shift	Disables the launch of login items specified in the Accounts preference pane

IN FINDER

tab	Select next icon alphabetically
shift-tab	Select previous item alphabetically
command-delete	Move selected item to Trash
space	When using Spring-loaded folders, immediately opens a folder you're hovering over
command-1	Switch to icon view
command-2	Switch to list view
command-3	Switch to column view
command-alt-W	Close all open Finder windows (except popup windows)
command-shift-alt-W	Close all open Finder windows (including pop-up windows)
command-right arrow	Open folder in list view
command-alt-right arrow	Recursively open folder and nested folders in list view
command-left arrow	Close folder in list view
command-alt-left arrow	Recursively close folder and nested folders in list view
command-up arrow	Open parent folder; opens user's home folder in OS X if no other windows are open
command-alt-up arrow	Open parent folder, closing current folder
command-down arrow	Open selected item; opens user's home folder in OS X if no other windows are open
command-alt-down arrow	Open selected item, closing current folder

APPLICATION SWITCHER

command-tab	Bring up application switcher, then…
tab	Move to the next application in the switcher
shift-tab or `	Move to the previous application in the switcher
q	Quit the highlighted application
h	Hide the highlighted application

CLICKS

alt-click in second application	Switch to second application and hide the first application
command-drag (window)	Drag window without bringing it to front
command-click (window title)	Displays pop-up menu showing path to current document or folder

ITEMS IN DOCK

command-click	Reveal Dock item in Finder
command-alt-click	Activate application and hide other applications
command-drag into Dock	Freezes Dock items so you can drop dragged item into folders
command-alt-drag into Dock	Force the target application to attempt to open item

POWER MANAGEMENT

On Macs with a power key

power	Bring up dialog for shutdown, sleep or restart
command-control-power	Unconditionally reboot; use as a last resort
control-command-alt-power	Fast shutdown

On Macs without power key

control-eject	Bring up dialog for shutdown, sleep or restart
command-control-eject	Unconditionally reboot; use as a last resort
control-command-alt-eject	Fast shutdown

IN POWER DIALOGUE

S	Sleep
R	Restart
esc	Cancel
return or enter	Shut down

Make RSS work for you

From getting a job to following a news story to making sure your MP is earning their keep, RSS is the way to go. Here, we dish up 10 ways to get the most from feeds.

It's no wonder that RSS is still really only used by alpha geeks; it's just another TLA (three-letter acronym) for folks to get their heads around. And that's a real shame, as RSS – 'feeds', 'live bookmarks' or whatever else you call them – can be spectacularly powerful.

Here, we're going to show you 10 innovative ways you can put RSS to work. What we're not going to do is plod through the basics of subscribing to normal RSS feeds. We're going to assume you might already have added, say, a magazine like *MacUser* to an RSS reader such as Safari, NetNewsWire or NewsFire. We're looking at novel ways of leveraging the power of RSS to help you find a job, track down the perfect item on eBay, create a personalised podcast, and much more.

We'll also be highlighting some of the features of Safari's RSS reading capabilities that few people still know about, showing you how to create your own RSS screensaver, convert RSS feeds to speech to allow you to listen to news and more on your morning commute through your iPod, and much more.

And it's important that you bear in mind that we're only scraping the surface. Even within the examples that we quote, there are many options to explore to get the right results for you. The easy way to learn new ways of expanding the abilities of RSS is to watch out for your browser alerting you to RSS feeds for the pages you're on. One of the uses we'll demonstrate, for example, involves targeted feeds created from news search engines such as Yahoo! or Google, and we only noticed that such a thing was possible because the telltale blue RSS icon appeared in Safari's address bar once we'd landed on a page of results; other browsers have their equivalents, and keeping an eye out for feed alerts, particularly when you've done something such as search by tags to drill down into the results, can result in a leaner, cleaner and more personalised browsing experience.

RSS SCREENSAVER

You probably know you can set any RSS feed as a screensaver in Mac OS X, but you may not know that you can create your own customised RSS feeds using Quartz Composer. This tool is part of the developer tools that can be found on and installed from your original system discs, which came with your Mac, and allows you to conjure up personalised RSS feed screensavers.

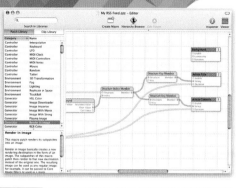

DISCOVER RELEVANT PHOTOS

As well as generating RSS feeds for users and groups, Flickr does the same for any tag on the system. Just click on a tag (or navigate to *http://flickr.com/photos/tags/yourtag*, replacing yourtag with the relevant tag) and you'll get an RSS feed of images for that tag. Try it with tags for your place of birth, current home, interests and the like, and you can get nice little sporadic surprises in your reader.

GET A JOB

Think the grass might be greener on the other side of the fence? Use *The Guardian*'s job search pages to find something better. Best of all, because we'll generate a tailored RSS feed, you'll only be alerted to jobs you want, and seeing new listings quietly populate your feed reader is a great way to get in early with job applications. Go to *guardian.co.uk/jobs* and use the filters to narrow down your field of expertise, location and salary. Subscribe to the RSS feed generated at the results page.

READ EVERYTHING BY A PARTICULAR WRITER

Point your browser at *news.yahoo.com* and click Advanced next to the Search field. Here, we're going to create a news feed that picks up everything Polly Toynbee writes in *The Guardian,* so enter her name in the 'the exact phrase' field, and 'Guardian' in the Source field. On the results page, you'll get an RSS feed to which you can subscribe. This particular example isn't perfect – you'll get stories that mention Polly Toynbee as well as those written by her – but there are tricks you could use to refine your search. Consider, for example, searching not for a writer but for the name of his or her column, or looking to see if bylines are prefixed by, say, 'author' or 'by'. Many news outlets already offer writer-specific feeds, so poke around the site first.

FIND WHAT YOU ALWAYS WANTED ON EBAY

Go to *ebay.co.uk* and click on Advanced Search in the upper-right corner. Enter your search terms, then click Search. You might need to go back and further refine it – say, by specifying a minimum price of £200 on MacBooks to weed out cases and Ram – but once you're happy that the results are appropriate, subscribe to the RSS feed that you get on the results page. You'll now be alerted whenever new items are listed; great for tracking rare items or bargains.

KEEP TABS ON A PARTICULAR STORY

You can track a particular news story through your RSS reader by using a service such as Google News. The most efficient way to do this is to take advantage of Google's own news grouping technology to track a current story. Go to *news.google.co.uk* and you'll get a list of headlines. Under each is a link that reads 'all 3462 news articles' or similar. Click this to show all coverage of that story, and subscribe to the RSS feed on this page. Any new coverage will pop into your reader.

SAFARI RSS

Safari has RSS abilities that put many third-party options to shame. Chief among these is the ability to create metafeeds based on individual feeds. Let's say you were only interested in news of the latest version of Mac OS X – Leopard. Create a folder full of links (anywhere in your Bookmarks menu) to Mac news sites' RSS feeds, and then select View All RSS Articles for that folder. In the search field – not the Google search field in Safari's title bar – type 'leopard' and, if you like, further define how you'd like to have the news presented by using the settings and sliders. Making any change to these alters the URL in the address bar, which can then be bookmarked. Drop it into your bookmarks bar and set Safari's preferences to auto-refresh RSS feeds, and whenever there are new stories about Leopard from the news sites you defined, you'll be alerted by a number appearing next to your bookmark.

OPML

Remember that most feed readers allow you to import and export feeds, so don't feel tied to any one piece of software. Most export feeds as an OPML file, although Safari is a notable exception. If you feel like getting your hands dirty, visit *tinyurl.com/ynwu9d* for a shell script and Automator action to make it easier to get feeds out of Safari.

bookmarked RSS feeds to that folder. Now all you have to do is click that folder in the bookmarks bar and pick View All RSS Articles.

To make the process even faster, check the Auto-Click box next to this folder from the bookmarks view. This means you can simply click the folder rather than clicking, holding, and picking View All RSS Articles. Most RSS reader software has an equivalent, so check your manual. If you find it doesn't, you could use Feedshake from *feedshake.com* to combine multiple feeds into one single feed.

TRACK A TOPIC
Similarly, you can perform searches from *news.google.co.uk* for topics, and subscribe to an RSS feed for that search term. In this way, you can keep track of, say, iPhone news without having to comb the web manually.

PERSONALISED PODCASTS
Del.icio.us is a social bookmarking site where, as far as anyone browsing the web is concerned, group wisdom narrows down the billions of web pages to a few good ones. At least, that's the theory. Visit *del.icio.us/tag* and you can click on tags in the cloud to generate RSS feeds for those tags. You can also enter your own tag text – such as 'steve jobs' – in the field at the top of the screen. Where it gets interesting, though, is that del.icio.us can track media types. Enter 'tutorial+system:media: audio' into the tags field and the system will create a page listing all audio files tagged with 'tutorial'; MP3s can be previewed inline. An RSS is also generated, so you've just rolled yourself your own podcast of tutorials from del.icio.us. Visit *del.icio.us/help/mediafiletypes* for details of tags for other filetypes.

CREATE A COMBINED FEED
Part of the joy of RSS is that you don't have to trawl through dozens of sites by hand, so it makes sense that instead of clicking through dozens of feeds, you combine them into one single megafeed.

There are a couple of ways to do this depending on what reader software you use. In Safari, you simply create a folder (Alt-Command-b to show bookmarks, and then Shift-Command-n to create a new folder) and add your

RSS TO iPOD
iSpeak It, $19.95 (about £10) from *zapptek.com*, uses your Mac's built-in text-to-speech capabilities to transcribe RSS feeds to audio tracks that can be synced to your iPod. Although the results aren't perfect, it is a good way to keep up-to-date with news stories, when paired, say, with our trick of creating a personalised Google news feed. You can correct the system's mispronunciation of words by applying manual overrides.

TRACK CHANGES TO DOCUMENTS
Many online services, especially those that encourage collaboration, offer the ability to publish an RSS feed of revisions. Click on any Wikipedia page's History tab, for example, and you'll get a rich summary of each change in RSS format. It's great way to track what's being said about a particular topic, and is particularly useful if you're in any sort of role that puts you in charge of the project being written about. Google Docs and Spreadsheets does a similar thing, as does the excellent collaborative notepad service, Writeboard.

STALK YOUR MP (LEGALLY)
Democracy really only works if you're aware of being what's being done in your name. While it's easy to see what's happening at a national scale, keeping tabs of what's happening locally can be a much more problematic. There's an easy way to track what your MP is up to, though, and, yes, it's all thanks to RSS. Visit *theyworkforyou.com*, punch in your postcode, and subscribe to the RSS feed on the next page. You'll be told how your MP contributed to Commons debates and what written answers they gave.

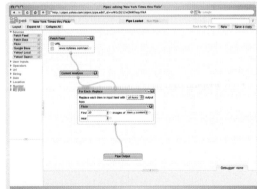

PIPES
If you're really, really into RSS, you could use Yahoo Pipes. The technology at play at *pipes.yahoo.com* is undeniably powerful, and allows you to remix and reuse information from feeds in ways that few people could have imagined. Although it's touted as an accessible system, we still recommend patience, creativity and a mind that works in gigahertz if you plan to create a pipe.

Want to find out what's really going on in the Mac community?

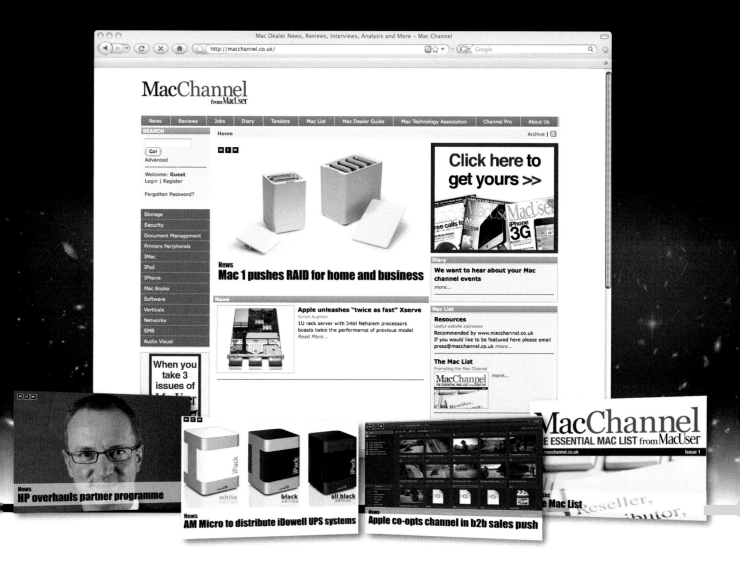

Keep up at Mac Channel
The essential bookmark for the UK Mac Channel

- The inside track on the latest industry news
- The MacList: **the** guide to the main players and companies in the channel
- The home of the Mac community online

Visit www.macchannel.co.uk

Profit from Social Networking

Social networking isn't just about MySpace and having bands as 'friends'. With big players like BT getting in on the act, it's an important tool for businesses, too. Here's how you can use social network sites to build contacts and generate leads.

If you haven't heard someone in the past six months refer to 'my MySpace page', then you have probably been living under a rock. Social networks – websites designed to let you link together your friends and acquaintances in groups – have become the biggest thing to invade the Internet since, well, the last biggest thing to invade the Internet.

But can social networks be more than just fun? Can they also be serious tools for doing business? After all, business is all about making, tracking and keeping contacts, as reflected in the old saying that it's not what you know, it's who you know.

In this feature, we'll be looking at social networks from this perspective to see if you can use them as more than just fun pastimes. If you want to make new business contacts, which are the best social networks to join, and what kinds of things should you be putting in your profile if you want to be found by the right kind of business partners? We'll also look at some of the common mistakes people make when creating their profiles; things that do more to damage your professional image than add to it.

HOW SOCIAL NETWORKS WORK

The basic template for social networks was set back in 1997, with the launch of a site that proved to be well ahead of its time, Six Degrees.com. Six Degrees followed a simple model generally called the 'web of contacts'. In this kind of social networking, you list your friends and have some kind of access to friends of friends – for example, sending messages to anyone within a few circles of you, as well as seeing if there was any kind of relationship between you and any other user on the site via friends, friends of friends, and so on.

Despite becoming the hippest site around for a short period of time, Six Degrees wasn't a success, and it was bought out in 2000 for $125 million, with the site itself effectively closing in 2001. However, the core idea of listing friends and using them as a method to connect to other people was picked up by several other sites, with varying degrees of success.

Social networks really began to take hold of the public imagination with the inexorable rise of MySpace, which, in the four years of its existence, has risen from nowhere to a £330m takeover by News Corporation, and hundreds of millions of users. MySpace took the basic 'friends and friends of friends' approach of Six Degrees and added to it the ability to highly customise the information you display on your page, effectively adding features that had been common in simple web creation sites such as Geocities.

Importantly, MySpace was targeted not at hip first-generation web users, but at the true 'net natives' – teenagers and young adults who'd grown up with the existence of the web, and who were hungry for a kind of site that allowed them to express themselves and link to their friends. With a huge audience of young people, it made sense for anyone wanting to communicate with young adults to start doing so via MySpace. For example, bands set up their own MySpace pages in order to directly reach their fans. Because MySpace lets you easily embed streamed songs, it makes it easy for bands to do this, and, because people tend to listen to things that their friends also like, the 'web of friends' approach makes it an ideal way to get new listeners directly, without having to rely on traditional promotional tools such as radio.

This combination of the web-of-friends approach and customisation was the killer feature for social networking websites, and a variety of others have popped up in the wake of MySpace, either with the aim of targeting specific communities, or with added features.

▲ MySpace is great for sharing your new tunes, which means you can reach a large audience very quickly.

MYSPACE
URL *myspace.com*

MySpace was by no means the first social networking site, but it was the first one to gain serious traction and publicity – so much so that News Corporation was prepared to pay around £330m to buy it in July 2005. The site still dominates the social networking market, with more than 100 million members.

MySpace follows the standard template for social network sites, enabling you to add friends, post pictures and customise your page to a reasonable degree. The customisation is a good thing, as the default templates for a MySpace page are pretty ugly. You can, of course, leave messages for friends, either public on their page or private, and there's a small, simple blogging engine if you're interested in posting regular updates.

The key advantage MySpace has over its rival is numbers, rather than technology or design. With so many members, if you're hoping to use your MySpace page as a public billboard, then you're going to have the maximum possible audience. This extends to groups, too: there are more than 21,000 groups devoted to different types of business, which means there's almost certainly a specific group for whatever you're interested in, whether that's email marketing or market gardening.

The problem, though, is with the interface: unless you're finding groups and so on through your contacts, it can be quite tough to sort the wheat from the chaff. Try doing a search on 'Marketing', for example, and you'll be given all 158,000 MySpace pages that mention the subject, in no coherent order. It makes MySpace daunting to get into, and a lot more difficult to use than it should be.

Overall, MySpace's main advantage is it's sheer size, but this is also its main disadvantage. No matter what your business, you probably ought to have a MySpace page, but making it the main centre of attention might not be the best use of your resources.

◄ Social networks such as MySpace are the ideal way to contact friends of friends of friends…

FACEBOOK
URL *facebook.com*

MySpace's main competitor, Facebook, was restricted to students until a few years ago. Since opening up to everyone, the site has started to gradually grow in popularity, and since the beginning of the year, its growth rate has surpassed that of virtually every other social networking site.

Like MySpace, Facebook uses the 'web of friends' approach, coupled with a highly customisable profile page that lets you list your contact details and add new content. The site's design is cleaner and more 'grown up' than MySpace, and includes modules for comments, photos, status updates and much more besides.

Recently, Facebook added more customisation options by announcing what it called 'Facebook/F8', a method of creating small web applications that can be displayed on profile pages. Although this approach is nothing new – MySpace has offered this level of customisation for some time – Facebook/F8 has seen a massive increase in interest as a platform for social networking.

What's more, Facebook has one crucial advantage over MySpace: it allows you to place adverts and sell services from your profile without it taking any kind of fee. In fact, the service already includes a method of selling goods and services with its Marketplace application, which allows you to list items for sale in specific areas.

▲ Facebook allows you to place adverts and sell services from your profile, and it doesn't take any fee.

This makes Facebook arguably a better option for businesses looking to do more than just promote themselves; in fact, some businesses are already using Marketplace to advertise their services.

Overall, of the general social networking services, Facebook looks a better option than MySpace if you're seeking to advertise and directly sell products or services.

▲ You can upload galleries, which is a great way to show off your work or products.

However, bear in mind that it also has fewer visitors at present than MySpace. As such, it might be worth making a profile on both simply to ensure that you have all the bases covered.

LINKEDIN
URL *linkedin.com*

Unlike both Facebook and MySpace, LinkedIn is focused firmly on social networking for business – in particular, on making and cultivating individual contacts in your business life. The principle is simple and similar to the original template created by Six Degrees: you connect to people using their email addresses, and through them you can connect to others. Profile information is firmly oriented around business, and you won't find any favourite music options or the ability to embed songs.

LinkedIn includes a section for hiring, so you can post job adverts for a small fee and reply to them for free. For any job advert, you can see if you're connected via your web of friends to the person posting the job or replying to your advert, which makes it simple to recruit friends of friends if you want to. You can also find people providing services according to how many people have recommended them, narrowing it down to people recommended by your first-degree contacts if required.

◀ LinkedIn is focused solely on networking for business, rather than for making new friends.

Most services on LinkedIn are free, although some are limited. For example, you're only allowed to request five introductions to people not in your immediate circle of contacts before you run out and have to wait to get more. However, you can optionally upgrade to a Business Plus account, which gives you additional features such as the ability to directly contact friends of friends without going through the friend and getting an introduction first. You also get expanded search abilities, which let you find business contacts more easily.

Overall, LinkedIn combines a lot of very smart features for business networking, making it something worthwhile for any individual to sign up to. What it lacks on the business side is any company-level tools, which means it's much more suitable as a promotional tool for sole traders than small companies. Whether it's worth upgrading your account depends on how much use you're getting out of it, but it's certainly worth getting yourself a free account and making some new contacts.

XING

URL *xing.com*

Xing, which until last year was known as Open Business Club or OpenBC, is another service dedicated to business rather than appealing to the general public. The product is unique in that the majority of users are in Europe, rather than spread out around the world, with a large core of users in Germany and many languages supported.

The site offers the full plethora of social networking features, allowing you to link to users as trusted contacts, and offers event co-ordination and so on. Most services are free, but some – including detailed searches and messaging to people with whom you're not directly connected – are for premium members only.

Premium membership costs £4.11 a month, but includes a variety of benefits above and beyond the site itself, such as a 5% discount on Avis car rental and additional benefits with some hotel chains.

Like Facebook, Xing offers a marketplace that allows you to post offers for jobs and the like, and it's easy to search and find services – many of them in the high professional end of the market. The most popular offers have had thousands of views. When you consider the business focus of Xing users, this is impressive and potentially extremely useful.

The main drawback with Xing at present is also its main strength: its European focus. This means it lacks a large number of contacts from the US. Of course, if you can get your contacts to sign up when you do, this makes no difference – but it's worth bearing in mind if you're looking to sign up to just a single social networking site. However, the flip side is that if you're looking for a social networking service that has a large core of users in Europe, particularly in Germany, then Xing should be your first port of call.

▶ Just like LinkedIn, Xing is dedicated specifically to business and not to the general public.

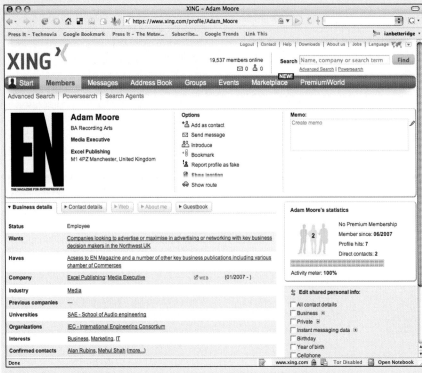

▲ Xing is largely European focused, which means you may miss out on US contacts.

BT TRADESPACE

URL *bttradespace.com*

BT might not be the most obvious company to introduce a social network, but its recently launched Tradespace site shows some promise. Like LinkedIn, Tradespace is directed firmly towards business, but it differs in its approach: rather than target individuals, it aims for small businesses, allowing them to create a simple web presence, belong to interest groups, and recommend other businesses that are also on Tradespace.

Like a clearer, more business-focused version of MySpace, Tradespace allows your business to have a small blog, promote events, and upload podcasts and images. You can put up a downloadable business card, and optionally include a 'Call Free' button, which will place a call directly between your listed phone number and a customer.

Unlike other social networking services, Tradespace also gives you a range of statistical reports – for example, enabling you to track the number of requests for your business card and downloads of any podcasts you've put up.

The worst thing about Tradespace is that it can be difficult to navigate at times:

WHAT NOT TO DO

Let's face it – if you've used a general social networking service such as MySpace or Facebook, then you've probably created some kind of profile for yourself. And, if it's like millions of other profiles out there, what you've posted may not be the most professional thing you've ever written. There may even be pictures of you attached that might not paint the most flattering portrait of your social life.

But why would this matter? After all, social networking services are just a bit of fun, aren't they? Unfortunately, they can also be a prime source of information about you for potential employers and business partners, which means that a MySpace profile that includes jokey references to skiving off work might not be the best thing if you want to attract employers. For example, one senior BBC executive suffered some minor embarrassment when he posted photos taken of him at a friend's stag night to social photo site Flickr and forgot to make them available to friends only. While it might not have done any long-term damage to his career, it's clear that there are potential problems here.

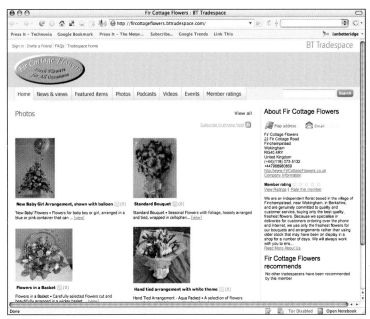

◀ Tradespace is aimed directly at small business users who want a web presence.

BEST SITE

Picking a single social networking site that's best for business is a tricky job, as all of the sites have different strengths and weaknesses. MySpace has the largest pool of users, and if you're looking to appeal to a youthful audience, it's certainly worth establishing a presence there. Facebook has the fastest growth and is clearly the place to be at the moment. LinkedIn is great for individuals looking to manage business contacts, while Xing offers a solid European base and simple features. BT Tradespace is the only product to focus on small businesses, rather than individuals, and shows a lot of promise, but costs money if you're to get the most out of it.

Overall, though, if we had to choose a single service, LinkedIn would be the one to go for. It's easy to use, focuses on a single area – managing business contacts – and expands on this well without trying to do too much. It's simple to use, too. However, the nice thing about these kinds of services is there's nothing to stop you trying them to find out which one suits your type of business. The best thing to do, then, is register, play, and see what fits.

irritatingly, the front page doesn't allow you to log in, and you need to go to your own home page and sign in there in order to access your account details and change your page.

Overall, Tradespace is interesting, but feels a little '1.0' in nature at the moment. While almost everything on Tradespace is free, some features – most notably Call Free – are only available to subscribers who pay an optional fee of £15 a month, or £135 a year. However, if you simply opt for the free version, there's plenty you can do and it's certainly a service that's worth trying out. It will be interesting to follow the development of the service over the coming months.

And employers aren't stupid. They know that people use social networking sites, and that they're likely to reveal more about their personality, likes and dislikes there than in the 'personal' section of a CV. A few quick searches on Google, MySpace and Facebook might tell them more about a potential employee than an interview. And, importantly, it'll also tell them who their friends are, and if they have any contacts in common – a very important factor in business.

So bear in mind the prospect that an employer or business partner might be reading your profile. However, this doesn't have to mean stifling your personality and producing something bland and boring. Be yourself, but don't write anything that you wouldn't want a potential employer to read. Be open about who your friends are, but don't try to link to people as friends unless you really know them – if you're linked to someone that a potential employer knows, and it turns out that you're not really friends at all, then it won't do you any good and may even make you look silly.

However, don't be afraid to post things that reflect your real personality. Employers aren't stupid enough to think that people have no social lives, and the fact that you're

▲ Try to avoid using drunken or embarrassing photos of yourself, you never know who is searching the web – some things just don't need to be shared.

a sociable person is unlikely to do you much harm in all but the most prurient of businesses. That said, the higher the position you're looking for, the more cautious you should be. While pictures of you on a stag night might not be an issue if you're not managing people, it will be if you're a head of department – as our BBC executive found out.

Most important of all, monitor your web presence by doing some light 'ego surfing' – typing your own name into Google and checking to see where you turn up. It's great for your profile if you're on the first page of Google results, unless, of course, it's pointing to a MySpace page with photos of you passed out drunk on holiday.

Masterclass

Welcome to *The Independent Guide to the Mac*'s comprehensive masterclasses. These easy-to-follow workshops will guide you through more than 20 key tasks, step-by-step, so that by the time you get to the end you'll know how to perform vital jobs using a wide range of applications.

We'll also show you how you can use your iPod as a tour guide, set up your printer, connect your camera to your Mac and get online. For anyone living in a home where other family members use Windows, or who is switching from a PC to a Mac, we'll also show you how to use Macs and PCs side by side. Finally, we'll reveal the remarkable history of the Mac and an extensive glossary to help you decode any Mac terminology that you might come across online, in print, or in discussions with your friends and colleagues.

Getting online	178
Setting up a printer	182
Working with your camera	184
Using Macs and PCs together	186
Using your iPod as an interactive tour guide	190
Graphics in Word 2004	193
Tables of Contents in Word	196
Text styles in Pages	199
Handling photos in Pages	202
Advanced charting in Excel	205
Filtering mail in Entourage	208
Using signatures in Entourage	211
PowerPoint's drawing tools	214
Advanced animation in PowerPoint	217
Creating a navigation bar in PowerPoint	220
Using Hyperlinks in Keynote	223
Unscrambling a file that won't open	226
Protect your portable USB drive from prying eyes	229
Creating cool photo cubes	232
Automatically resize images	234
15 steps to better photos	236
Personalising Front Row	243
Make your own RSS screen saver	245

MASTERCLASS
Getting online

Apple has built its range of Macs with a strong focus on the Internet, so getting online is a relatively simple task and going wireless altogether isn't much harder. Here's how.

Kit required Broadband connection + Wireless router
Time 15 to 30 minutes
Goal To get your Mac connected to the Internet and access your email accounts
Skill level Beginner

Getting online these days usually means signing up for a broadband account. Broadband prices have now dropped to the point where dial-up makes little sense economically, even for occasional Internet surfers. The exception, of course, is in those parts of the country that don't have access to a broadband connection. Those areas are few and far between, however, so we'll concentrate here on using a broadband connection to get online. We'll also cover setting up a wireless network so two or more Macs can share the same broadband connection wirelessly.

There are two types of broadband connection, cable and ADSL. From our perspective they offer exactly the same although technologically they are different. The only cable broadband supplier in the UK is Virgin Media and whether or not you can access its services will depend on the area in which you live. Check its website at *virginmedia.com* for more information. By contrast, there are dozens of ADSL broadband providers. We can't tell you which one to choose, so spend some time researching tariffs to find one that meets your needs.

If you opt for cable, you'll be supplied with a cable modem. You can connect this to your Mac or, if you want a wireless network, to a wireless router. Depending on your choice of ADSL supplier, you may be provided with a modem or an ADSL modem/router with a built-in wireless access point.

ROUTER SET-UP

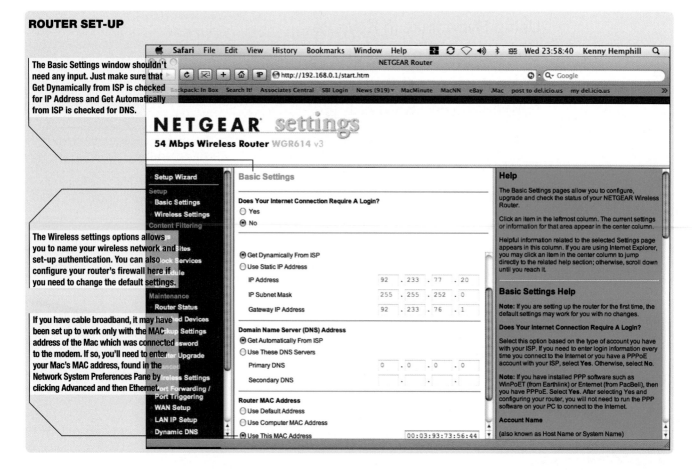

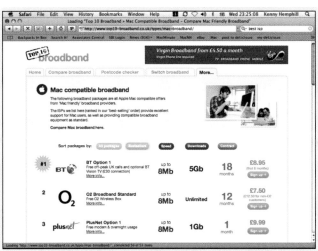

▲ **STEP 01 DECIDE WHAT YOU WANT FROM AN ISP** Before you can choose an ISP you need to decide exactly what you want. Is maximising connection speed important? For most of us 2-8Mbit/sec is fine. Will you be comfortable with a monthly bandwidth limit, or do you need unlimited downloads?

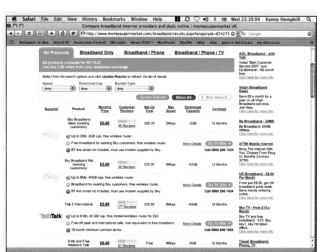

▲ **STEP 02 RESEARCH** Do a cost and feature comparison, using a site such as *moneysupermarket.com*, comparing providers and the services they offer, being careful to note limitations. If you want wifi, look for a provider that includes a wireless router. Are you cabled? If so, Virgin Media's cable service may suit better than ADSL.

▲ **STEP 03 LOOK OUT FOR SPECIAL OFFERS** Check sites like *moneysavingexpert.com* to see if your chosen provider is running any special offers. If so, read the terms and conditions carefully, particularly with regard to any minimum contract period. And before you place your order, check what their Mac support is like.

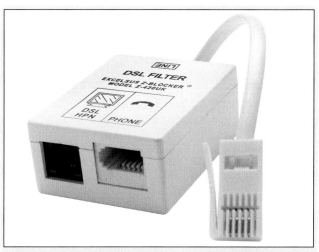

▲ **STEP 04 GET HOOKED** To enable you to use a telephone and modem on the same line, you need an ADSL filter. If one wasn't supplied with your modem or router, you'll need to buy one separately. Connect it to your telephone socket and plug your modem into the larger connector and telephone into the smaller one. You don't need a filter for cable.

▲ **STEP 05 CONNECT YOUR MAC** If you're connecting your Mac directly to an ADSL modem, all you need to do is power it up, plug it into your Mac's Ethernet port and open System Preferences. Click on the Ethernet heading in the sidebar of the Network pane, and configure using your ISPs instructions.

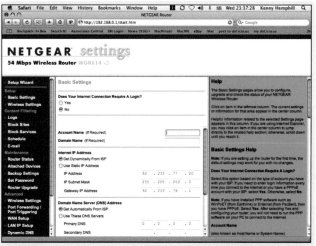

▲ **STEP 06 USING A WIRELESS ROUTER** The only difference here is that you enter the information from your ISP in the router's configuration web page, instead of System Preferences. The IP address of the configuration page is in your router's manual, along with instructions on how to set it up.

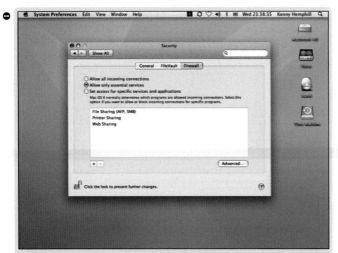

▲ **STEP 07 SWITCH ON YOUR MAC'S FIREWALL** Now that your Mac is permanently connected to the Internet, it's at risk of being infected by a virus or other malicious software. To protect it, you should use the firewall built into Mac OS X. Open System Preferences then Security and click the Firewall tab.

▲ **STEP 08 CONFIGURE FIREWALL** Click on the Advanced button and enable Stealth mode by checking the box. This prevents other computers on the Internet 'pinging' your Mac, a technique for checking whether your Mac is there before launching an attack. Click on OK and quit System Preferences.

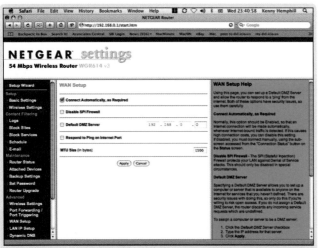

▲ **STEP 09 CONFIGURE YOU ROUTER'S FIREWALL** If you have a wireless router connected to your Mac, it too will have a firewall. Check the manual that came with it to find out how to configure it. Usually the default settings, as in the grab here, offer the most protection. Be very careful before making any changes.

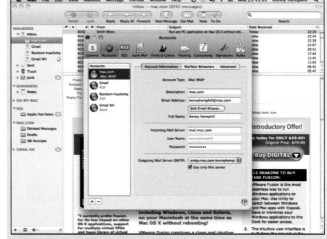

▲ **STEP 10 SETTING UP YOUR EMAIL CLIENT** If you want to send and receive email, you'll need an email application, such as Apple Mail, which is bundled with Mac OS X. To set it up, go to Applications and double-click Mail. Go to the Mail menu and select Preferences. Click on the Accounts tab in the toolbar.

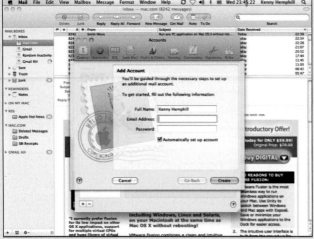

▲ **STEP 11 CREATING AN ACCOUNT** Click the '+' button on the bottom of the left-hand sidebar. Fill in your name, email address and password. The email address and password should have been provided for you when you opened your account with your ISP. Uncheck Automatically set up account, and click Create.

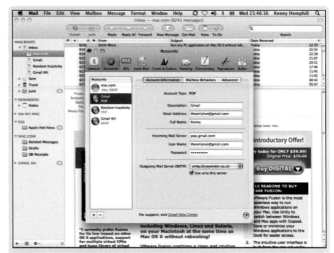

▲ **STEP 12 ENTER YOUR ISP'S SETTINGS** Your ISP should have given you details of its servers in order that you can send and receive email. Your account will almost certainly be Pop 3, so choose that and fill in details of the Pop 3 server. On the next screen fill in details of your ISP's SMTP server.

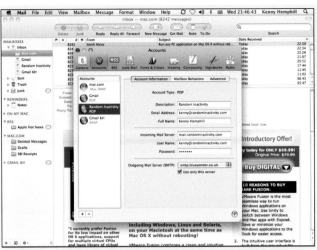

▲ STEP 13 **SETTING UP ANOTHER EMAIL ACCOUNT** If you have your own domain and an email address that goes with it, you should enter the details for that domain's email server in the incoming mail section. But in the outgoing mail page, you must still enter your ISP's details.

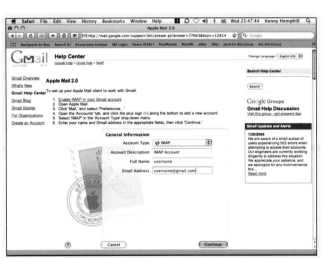

▲ STEP 14 **IMAP MAIL** If you use .Mac mail, you should follow step 11, but check the Create account automatically box. If you have a Gmail account and want to use it with your iPhone, or another computer, follow Google's instructions for setting up an Imap account. You can find these by logging into your Gmail account in a web browser.

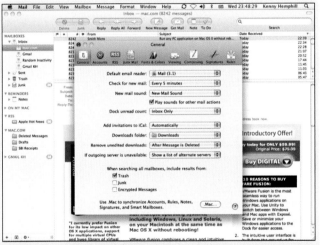

▲ STEP 15 **SET YOUR PREFERENCES** Take some time to trawl through Mail's General preferences and set it up the way you want it to work. If you get lots of Mail, you may want it to automatically check every five or ten minutes, for example. Visit the Composing and Viewing tabs too, and configure those to suit your needs.

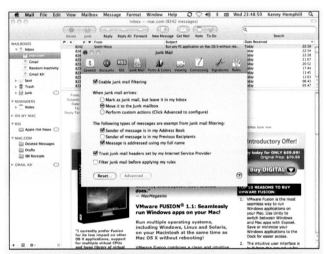

▲ STEP 16 **JUNK MAIL FILTERING** Dealing with junk mail is a necessary evil, but luckily Mail has a decent junk mail filter. In Mail's Preferences, click on the Junk Mail tab. Tick the checkbox marked Enable junk mail filtering, and select the second of the next set of three options, Move it to the Junk mailbox.

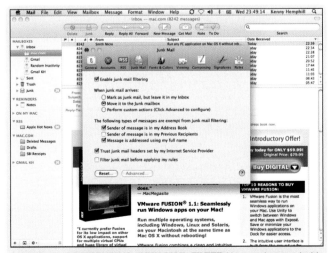

▲ STEP 17 **CONFIGURING JUNK MAIL FILTER** Now you have to decide which mail to 'whitelist'. As a minimum you should select Sender of message is in my Address Book. Check your Junk Mail folder regularly to make sure it's not catching legitimate messages. If it does, select Not Junk at the top of the message, to train Mail's junk filter.

▲ STEP 18 **SETTING UP RSS** If you want to subscribe to RSS feeds but don't have a specialist reader, you can subscribe to and read feeds in Mail. In Mail's Preferences, click on the RSS tab and set your default RSS reader as Mail. Now whenever you click on one of those little orange icons, the feed will be added to Mail.

MASTERCLASS
Setting up a printer

Whether you use your Mac for work or for leisure, at some point you will probably want to print something. Here's how you can take the frustration out of setting up a printer.

Kit required Printer
Time 10 minutes
Goal Setting up a printer
Skill level Beginner

Printing is one of the most common tasks that any computer is asked to perform, yet setting up a printer and getting it to work flawlessly every time is still a frustrating business.

The easiest way to connect a printer and print to it with the minimum of fuss is to connect it to a USB port on your Mac. However, if you want to share the printer with other Macs or PCs on a network, it's not the best option. You can share a printer directly connected to a Mac with other machines, but it means that the host Mac has to be running and will consume processing resources on that Mac.

The best solution if you want to share a printer is to connect it to your network directly. You can either do this with an Ethernet cable, or wirelessly on a wifi network. You'll need to consider whether you want to connect the printer to a network before you buy it because this will govern the kind of printer you buy.

Something else you'll have to consider is the type of material you'll be printing. For example, if you're going to be churning out text documents in high quantities, a laser printer is the best option. If you want a printer to render your digital photos on high-quality paper, you should choose an inkjet. And if you want a device capable of scanning, copying and faxing as well as printing, you'll need to buy a multi-function device.

You should also consider consumables such as ink and paper. Ink, in particular, is very expensive when you measure the cost per millilitre and it's tempting to consider buying generic ink cartridges rather than the manufacturer's own brand, or to have your existing cartridges refilled.

Although many generic inks are very good these days and produce decent prints, printers are complex beasts and the communication between printer and ink cartridge is essential to the smooth running of the printer. For this reason, ink cartridges on inkjet printers have a microchip fitted to them. Buying generic ink means swapping the chip on each tank, which is a fiddly and messy business. Remember too, when buying a laser printer to take into account the average cost per print and the lifespan of the drum. There is a surprising variation in both between manufacturers.

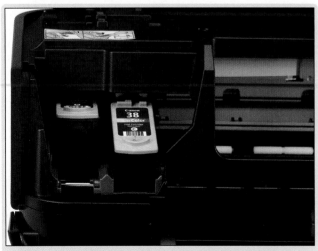

▲ **STEP 01 USB PRINTER: INSTALL THE INK CARTRIDGES** This process will vary depending on the printer you have, so be careful to read the Quick Start Guide. Plug the printer into the mains before you start so that the print head can be moved to the correct position. In most cases, the slots for the cartridges will be colour-coded, making it easy to see where each one goes.

▲ **STEP 02 USB PRINTER: CONNECT THE USB CABLE** With the printer switched off, connect one end of the USB cable (which you may have to buy yourself) to the printer and the other end to your Mac. Now switch the printer on and wait for it to run through its set-up routine. Once it's done, check whether Mac OS X already has drivers for it installed by opening System Preferences.

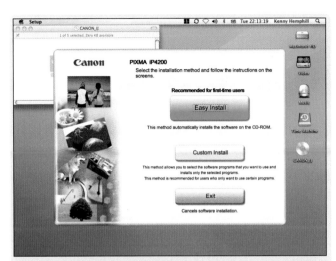

▲ **STEP 03 INSTALLING DRIVERS** In System Preferences, click on Print and Fax. If your printer shows up in the list on the left of the window, you need do nothing more. If not, and it's a USB printer, you need to install the drivers. Quit System Preferences and insert the printer's CD into your Mac. Choose to do a Custom Install and deselect the applications you don't want.

▲ **STEP 04 CONFIGURE USB PRINTER** Now go back to Print and Fax in System Preferences. You should now see your printer listed. As it's the only printer connected to your Mac, it will automatically be the default printer. Select the default paper size, this is the paper that will be printed to if you hit Print from an application and don't change any options.

▲ **STEP 05 ADDING A NETWORK PRINTER** Network laser printer drivers tend to be more generic than USB printers so there's more chance that your Mac will have the right one installed. Connect the printer to your network router and go to System Preferences/Print and Fax again. Press the '+' button and wait for your Mac to discover the printer. When it does, select it and press Return.

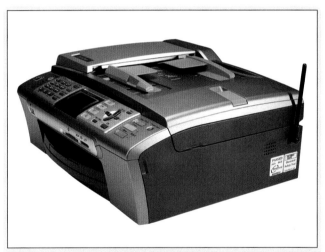

▲ **STEP 06 ADDING A WIRELESS PRINTER** Printing over a wifi network is still in its infancy and so manufacturers use different methods to install and set-up printers. Getting a wireless printer up and running can be a frustrating business, even for experienced users, so consider before you buy whether you really need wireless. And read the manual that came with your printer carefully.

▲ **STEP 07 SHARING A PRINTER** To share a printer connected to a single Mac, go to System Preferences and click on the Sharing pane. Tick the box next to Printer Sharing and in the main window, tick the printer you want to share. To print from another Mac, add the printer by going to the Print and Fax pane and clicking on the '+' sign: the shared printer will be clearly identified.

▲ **STEP 08 PAGE SETUP** Ensuring the printer is configured correctly before printing is essential. In any application, go to File then Page Setup… Choose your printer from the Format for menu and the paper to which you're printing from Paper Size. Now choose Landscape or Portrait from Orientation, and if you want to change the Scale do that too.

MASTERCLASS
Working with your camera

If you have a digital camera, the iPhoto application, which came already installed on your the Mac, is the ideal tool to store and organise your photos.

Kit required iPhoto
Time 30 minutes
Goal Connect your digital camera to your Mac, download your photos and organise your collection in iPhoto
Skill level Beginner

Whether you only ever take snaps with your mobile phone, carry a compact digital camera wherever you go, or have spent serious money on a digital SLR and extra lenses, there's no better platform than the Mac for making the most of them.

And the good news is that one of the best applications there is for organising and sharing your pictures, iPhoto, came pre-installed on your new Mac. Just plug in your camera to a USB port on your Mac, or slot its memory card into a reader, if you have one, and iPhoto will do the rest.

iPhoto imports your photos and organises them into rolls. It's smart enough to read the date each photo was taken and split them up into what it calls Events. So, for example, if you went to a wedding on Saturday and a 40th birthday party the following Friday, iPhoto will split the photos from each into separate Events.

Although iPhoto's editing features are fairly basic, it's fine for most needs, including removing red-eye, straightening, cropping and boosting contrast. And you can always export pictures to another application, such as Photoshop Elements, for more refined editing. iPhoto's real strength however, is the way it allows you to share photos, either by publishing them on a website, emailing them, or printing them in a book. We covered that in the iLife section on page 48.

Here we'll take you on a whistlestop tour of iPhoto and show you how to use it to get the most from your pictures. We'll also explain how to export photos from iPhoto to your preferred image editor.

Keys to using iPhoto is to let it take the strain of organising your photos and make any adjustments to albums and events within the application.

Although it is possible to locate individual pictures in the Finder and manually move them around, copy them, or open them in other applications, you should avoid this at all costs. This is because iPhoto stores multiple copies of each image and maintains links between them.

Manually moving photos around will break those links and will cause untold mayhem within iPhoto. Much better to import, edit, organise, and export from within iPhoto. That way you don't have to worry about the directory structure at all.

▲ **STEP 01 CONNECT YOUR CAMERA** Either use the cable that came with your camera to plug it into a spare USB port on your Mac, or slot its memory card into a card reader. iPhoto will launch automatically and ask you if you want to download all or a selection of photos from the card. To import a selection, click on the first one, hold the Shift key and click on those that you want.

▲ **STEP 02 MANAGE EVENTS** Click on Events underneath the Library heading to see how iPhoto has split your photos. Events are created by date, but this doesn't always make sense, as events can last several days or fill only part of a day. From the Events menu, you can Auto Split Events, which separates them into morning and afternoon, merge Events or even create new Events.

▲ **STEP 03 REVIEW IMAGES IN EVENT** Place your mouse pointer over an Event and drag it from side to side. Its photos will be displayed sequentially. The speed at which you drag the mouse dictates how quickly you scroll through the pictures. When you find one you like, stop scrolling and either click the right mouse button or hold down the Control key and click to reveal a contextual menu.

▲ **STEP 04 SET THE DISPLAY IMAGE** With the mouse button held down, move the pointer down to Make Key Photo, to use the current photo as the display picture for the Event. To view all the photos in an event right-click or Control-click on the Event again and choose Open Event in a Separate Window. In this window you can control the size of the images using the slider.

▲ **STEP 05 EDIT IMAGES** You can't edit pictures in this window. So, click on Photos in the Library and scroll down to the picture you want to edit. You can click the Edit button in the toolbar to edit the picture, but the full-screen display is much more satisfying. Right-click on the image and select Edit using Full screen. Drag your mouse to the bottom of the screen to access the controls.

▲ **STEP 06 ADD EFFECTS** iPhoto's editing controls are pretty sophisticated. You can use automatic tools such as Red-eye removal and Enhance to get instant results or play around with the other controls to see how they affect your photo. This is also the place to crop or straighten your picture and, using the Effects button, to convert it to black and white or sepia.

▲ **STEP 07 MAKE ADJUSTMENTS** To gain more control over adjustments, click on Adjust. Here you can alter the contrast, change the exposure, sharpen, and add a tint to your picture. Pay attention to the histogram and avoid clipping the edges of the graph, but don't be afraid to experiment. Hitting reset is all it takes to get back to where you started. When you're finished, click the cross.

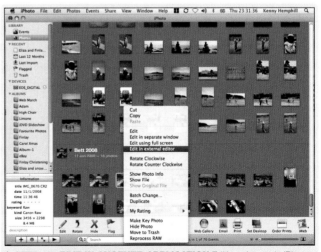

▲ **STEP 08 EDIT IN ANOTHER APPLICATION** Editing pictures in iPhoto is fine for most purposes, but if you want to get really creative with your photos, you'll need a dedicated image editing application. Photoshop Elements is ideal, if you have it. Right-click on the image you want to edit and this time select Edit in External Editor. Choose the application you want to use.

MASTERCLASS
Using Macs and PCs together

Macs and PCs needn't be strangers and connecting them to share files has never been easier. You can even run Windows applications on your Mac.

Kit required Mac OS X 10.5 + PC with Windows XP or Vista
Time 15 to 30 minutes
Goal To connect your Mac to a PC; run Windows applications on your Mac
Skill level Beginner/intermediate

Using Macs and PCs together has never been easier, which is partly the reason for the rise in popularity of the Mac in homes and offices around the world. Apple realised several years ago that if the Mac was going to break out of its tiny niche it had to be able to communicate easily with Windows PCs.

So, now when you connect a Mac running Mac OS X Leopard to a network containing Windows PCs and workgroups, they automatically show up in the Finder's sidebar. Connecting to one of them and sharing files is no more complicated than double-clicking on it and entering a username and password.

You don't, however, need separate computers to use a Mac and a PC together. In Leopard there are two ways of running Mac OS X and Windows on the same Mac and sharing files, Internet access, and peripherals. One method is Boot Camp, which comes with Mac OS X Leopard and allows you to install Windows XP or Vista on a partition on your hard drive and boot into Windows instead of Mac OS X when you start up your Mac.

The other method is known as virtualisation and allows you to run Windows applications alongside Mac applications without having to restart your Mac, or even work with Windows Explorer, you just use the applications you need. Two companies, VMWare and Parallels Inc currently produce virtualisation applications for the Mac.

INTERFACE

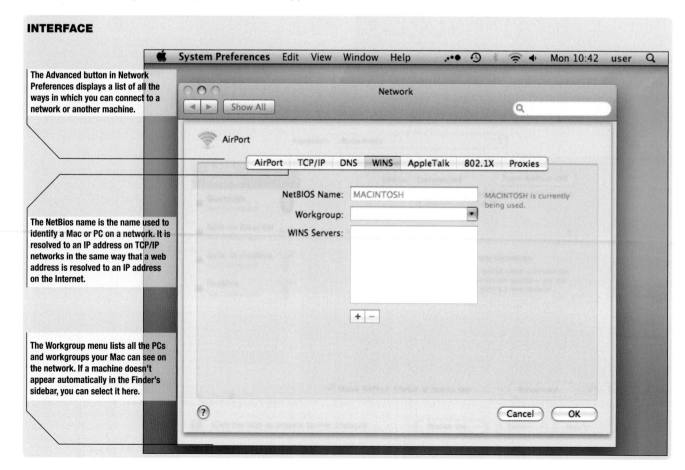

The Advanced button in Network Preferences displays a list of all the ways in which you can connect to a network or another machine.

The NetBios name is the name used to identify a Mac or PC on a network. It is resolved to an IP address on TCP/IP networks in the same way that a web address is resolved to an IP address on the Internet.

The Workgroup menu lists all the PCs and workgroups your Mac can see on the network. If a machine doesn't appear automatically in the Finder's sidebar, you can select it here.

▲ STEP 01 **CONNECT TO A PC** To connect to a PC and share files in Leopard, double-click on it's name in the Finder's sidebar (you might have to click on More at the bottom of the list, and enter a username and password to authenticate yourself. You will then have access to the files and folders enabled by the administrator.

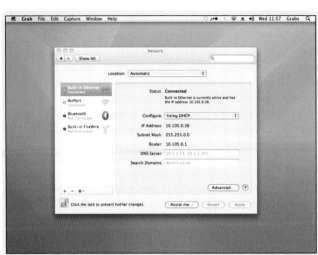

▲ STEP 02 **IF THAT DOESN'T WORK** If the PC to which you want to connect doesn't appear in the Finder's sidebar, go to System Preferences and click on the Network tab. Click on the method you used to join the network and click on Advanced. Now click on WINS, which stands for Windows Internet Name Server.

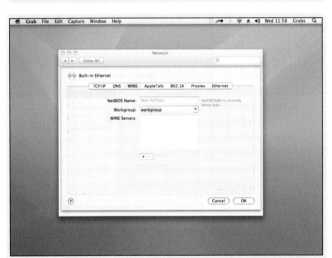

▲ STEP 03 **SELECT THE PC YOU WANT TO CONNECT TO** The window that opens displays the NetBios name of your Mac and has a drop-down menu which displays the names of the other workgroups on the network. From this menu, select the group or PC to which you want to connect and click on OK. Now click on Apply in the Network pane.

▲ STEP 04 **SHARE FILES AND FOLDERS** To access your Mac from a PC, or another Mac, open System Preferences and click on Sharing. Tick the File Sharing checkbox. By default the Public folders for each user account are shared. You can add other folders by clicking on the '+' button.

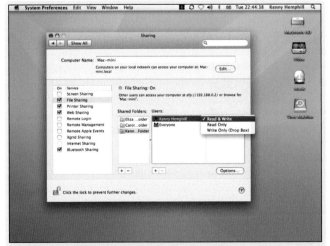

▲ STEP 05 **SET PRIVILEGES** The box labelled Users lists groups of users that are able to access each shared folder and their access privileges. To change this or modify other users' privileges, click on the drop-down menu and select Read Only, Write Only or Read & Write.

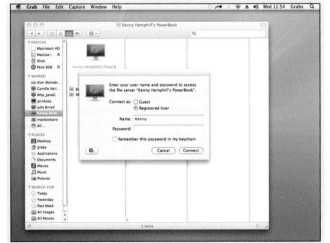

▲ STEP 06 **CHECK IT WORKS** From another Mac on the network, open a Finder window. You should see the Mac you want to connect to in the sidebar under Shared. Double-click on it and when prompted, enter a username and password. You should now have full access to the folders for which you set appropriate privileges in Step 5.

▲ **STEP 07 CHECK OTHER ACCOUNTS** Disconnect from the shared Mac and repeat Step 6, but this time log in as a regular user and then as a guest. Check that you have only the privileges set in System Preferences on the shared Mac. So if you set guest access as being able to read but not write, for example, that's what you should be able to do.

▲ **STEP 08 ENABLE SMB SHARING** Next click on Options in the File Sharing section of the Sharing pane in System Preferences and check the box labelled Share files using SMB and check the names of the users whose files you want to share. You'll have to enter the password for each account you want to share. Now click on Done.

▲ **STEP 09 SET-UP YOUR MAC FOR PC NETWORKING** If you want to change the Computer Name of your Mac, do it here. Now, make a note of the name or IP address of your Mac, shown in the middle line of the Sharing window after afp://. You can connect to this Mac using either it's name or IP address.

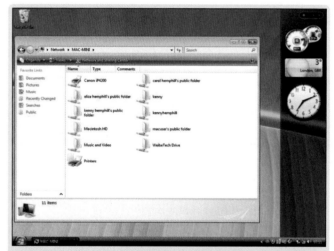

▲ **STEP 10 CONNECT TO YOUR MAC FROM A PC** In Windows XP open My Network Places, or in Windows Vista select Network from the Start menu. Double-click on the name of your Mac and in the username box enter the name or IP address you noted in Step 9, then backslash, then an account username. In the box below, enter the appropriate password and click OK.

▲ **STEP 11 GET READY FOR BOOTCAMP** The easiest way to run Windows on your Mac is to use the Bootcamp feature of Mac OS X Leopard. This creates a partition on your hard drive onto which you can install Windows and start-up your Mac as a Windows PC, then restart in Mac OS X when you want to go back to working in Mac OS X.

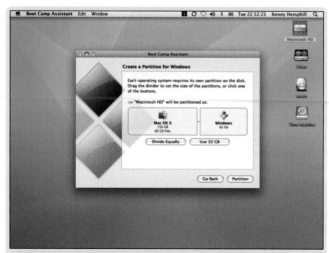

▲ **STEP 12 PARTITION HARD DRIVE FOR BOOTCAMP** Go to Applications/Utilities and launch the Boot Camp Set-Up Assistant. This guides you through the process of installing Boot Camp and a copy of Windows on your Mac. The first stage is to specify the Boot Camp partition size. Select either Divide Equally, Use 32GB, or use the slider to specify a partition size.

▲ STEP 13 **CONFIGURE STARTUP DISK** With Boot Camp and a copy of Windows successfully installed, you can now boot your Mac into either Mac OS X or Windows. You can specify which to use in System Preferences/Startup Disk or by holding down the Alt key when you start your Mac and choosing when prompted.

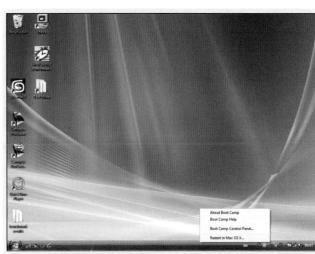

▲ STEP 14 **CHANGING BACK AGAIN** If you decided to startup in Mac OS X and want to change to Windows, you just repeat Step 13. But going the other way round is different. In Windows, open the Boot Camp control panel by clicking on its icon in the System Tray on the bottom right of the Windows desktop. Now select Mac OS X as the startup disk.

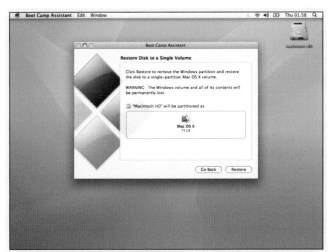

▲ STEP 15 **REMOVING WINDOWS** If you no longer need Windows, you can remove it easily. Copy any files you need to a separate disk, and with your Mac started in OS X, no applications running, and you the only user logged in, go to Applications, then Utilities. Open the Boot Camp Assistant and click Restore the startup disk to a single volume then Continue.

▲ STEP 16 **INSTALL A VIRTUAL MACHINE** As an alternative to running Boot Camp in order to run Windows on your Mac, you can install a virtual machine. This allows you to run a PC or multiple PCs on your Mac and access the applications on them without having to reboot, or even work in the Windows environment.

▲ STEP 17 **PARALLELS OR FUSION?** There are two options if you decide that you want to install Windows as a virtual machine on your Mac, Parallels desktop and VMWare. They both do exactly the same thing, but in different ways. A less-polished, but free option for running Windows in a Virtual Machine is the Open Source Virtual Box (*virtualbox.org*)

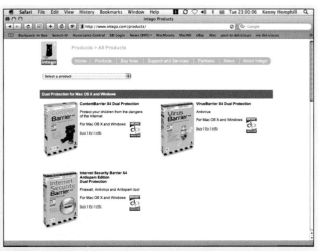

▲ STEP 18 **SECURITY** If you plan on running a PC on your Mac, either through Boot Camp or a virtual machine, you should take specific precautions to protect you Mac from malicious attacks. Running Windows makes you more vulnerable, and you're not protected by Mac OS X's firewall. Install security software such as Intego's Dual Protection range. See *intego.com* for details.

MASTERCLASS
Using your iPod as an interactive tour guide

If you need to create a compelling tour guide or interactive learning aid, you can use your iPod's Notes capability for surprisingly effective results.

Kit required An iPod with Dock Connector
Time Depends on complexity of the presentation
Goal To create an interactive guide for use on an iPod
Skill level Intermediate

The iPod is primarily a portable music device, but this doesn't mean you should confine its use to such a one-dimensional pursuit. The increased size and quality of the iPod screen has enabled a number of new and interesting ways to use the device.

The Notes capability of the iPod has been available for a long time now, but it's hardly a feature that will get regular use. With a little work, however, the Notes option can put an iPod to work in a very effective way. If you've ever been to an historic monument or museum, it's likely that you'll have been offered an audio guide to help you navigate your way around. You can use an iPod to create a similar but much more interactive presentation that would really impress. You don't have to limit yourself to interactive audio guides, either: the Notes section can also help make lessons more interesting and, best of all, it doesn't require all that much work.

All you need is an iPod with a Dock Connector, but you'll get more use and interactivity from more recent iPods with colour screens and video capabilities. If you want to create truly professional interactive documents, you can use applications such as GarageBand to create podcasts or vodcasts to extend the Notes feature's usability. Pictures, text, music and video can all be put to good use with an iPod guide – and, best of all, it's really simple to do.

INTERFACE

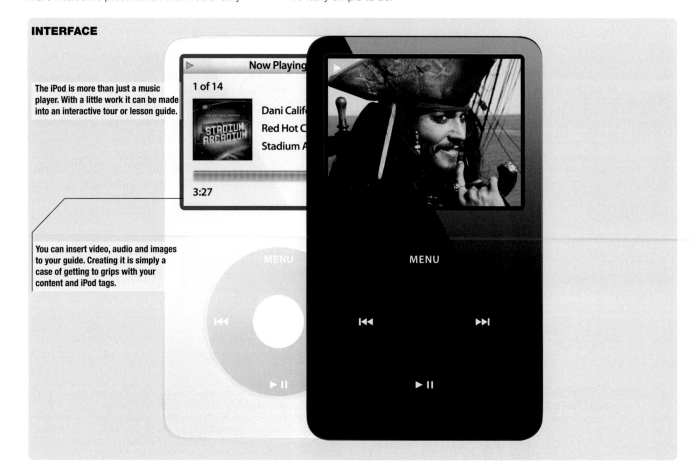

The iPod is more than just a music player. With a little work it can be made into an interactive tour or lesson guide.

You can insert video, audio and images to your guide. Creating it is simply a case of getting to grips with your content and iPod tags.

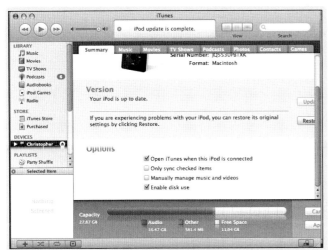

▲ STEP 01 **GETTING STARTED WITH NOTES** In order to use Notes, your iPod has to be set up for use as a storage disk as well as a music player. Connect your iPod to your Mac, and click on the devices and then on the Summary tab. Go to the Options area and click the Enable disk use checkbox.

▲ STEP 02 **DISPLAY ONLY NOTES** It's a simple process to lock the iPod so users can't navigate away and use the other features. Create a new file in TextEdit, make sure it's a plain text document and then save it as Preferences. Type *<meta name="NotesOnly" content="true">* in the body of this document. Copy this document to the Notes folder on the iPod.

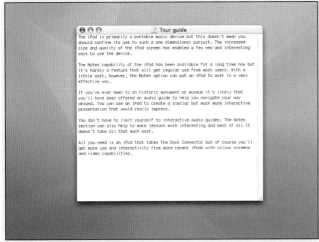

▲ STEP 03 **RESTRICTIONS** It's obvious that too much text on an iPod screen will be a bit overwhelming for most users, so it's best to keep your text down to shortish chunks. Another reason to limit text is that text files are limited to 4KB. This equates to about 1000 words. As we'll show later, you can link together a number of text files to create longer presentations.

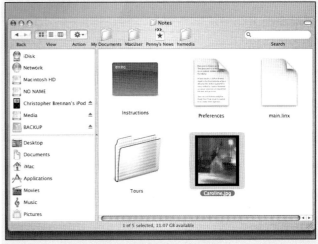

▲ STEP 04 **ORGANISING THE NOTES FOLDER** To keep things in order, it's best to think about how your notes will be organised. Give your tour an appropriate folder name and store all your notes there. If you have multiple languages or versions, store them appropriately, too.

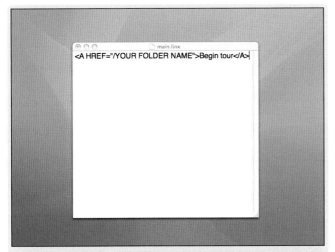

▲ STEP 05 **CONTROLLING THE NOTES INTERFACE** The Notes folder will contain any images you need as well as the main folders. To hide these and provide only a link to your tour folder, you need to create a .linx file. Open a new Text Edit document , type *<A HREF="/YOUR FOLDER NAME">Begin tour</A>* save this as *main.linx* and put it in the Notes folder.

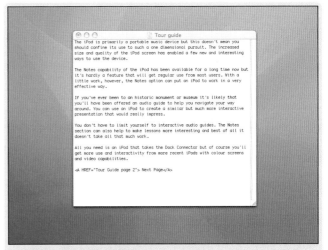

▲ STEP 06 **LINK TO NOTES** If you've created a long document, you'll need to split it into smaller documents so it doesn't go above the 4KB limit. You link these together by placing the following text at the bottom of each document: *<A HREF="NAME OF NOTE TO LINK TO"> Next Page </A>* Now when the user reaches the end of the text file, they simply click on the link to move on.

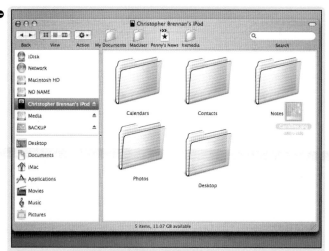

▲ STEP 07 **LINK TO PICTURES** Each text note can link to any Jpeg image. This is great if you want to put an image of what you're describing at the foot of the note and not affect the 4KB limit. You need to copy the images you want to use to the top level of the notes folder. Next, type *<A HREF="/image name">Link title</A>* into the note from which you want the image to link.

▲ STEP 08 **LINK TO AUDIO** One of the most compelling features here is the ability to link to audio stored on the iPod. This time, you don't have to copy the audio to the Notes folder. Type *<A HREF="song=TRACK NAME">LinktoTRACK NAME</A>* into your note. Make sure the TRACK NAME is replaced with the name as it appears in iTunes.

▲ STEP 09 **LINK TO VIDEO** If you want to go one better than plain old audio and text, you can link to videos stored in iTunes. Again, it's simply a case of putting a link in the note where you want it to appear: *<A HREF= "video=VIDEO TITLE"> Link to VIDEO TITLE Music Video</A>* When the video finishes, you'll be returned to the note.

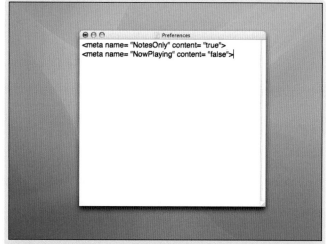

▲ STEP 10 **CONTINUE SHOWING NOTE** If you've included a link to an audio file, it will play in the normal manner, showing the album art and title. If you'd rather it continue to show the note, you need to add a new meta tag to the Preferences file from step 2. Type *<meta name="NowPlaying" content="false">* and save the file. Now audio will play without displaying album artwork.

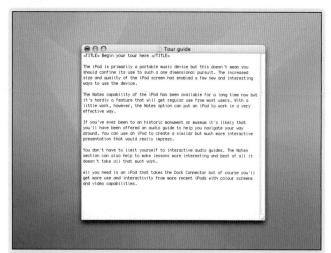

▲ STEP 11 **NOTE TITLE** By default, the iPod will display the filename of each text document. If you wish to give a note a different display name than the document title, all you have to do is type a title tag into the note. For example, type *<TITLE>NEW NAME</TITLE>*, save it and the iPod will display this name rather than the document's actual title.

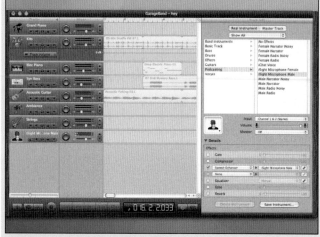

▲ STEP 12 **PODCAST ALTERNATIVE** If the idea of typing guides and linking them all together is a bit much for you, you can use GarageBand to offer an audio alternative. All you have to do then is create an audio link as described in step 8.

MASTERCLASS
Graphics in Word 2004

It's easy to add graphics to your Word documents, but there are multiple ways to manage them when they're on the page. Here we show you how to get the most out of each.

Kit required Microsoft Office 2004
Time 30 minutes
Goal Positioning graphics in Word
Skill level Intermediate

Take a Word 2004 file to a print bureau and they'll either slam the door in your face, laugh up their sleeves and charge you double, or try to persuade you to do it in InDesign instead. Word itself isn't a problem, it's Word documents with graphics that cause the trouble. Pictures appear to reflow from one page to the next without reason or warning, move around of their own volition even when they're 'floating' (that is not inline graphics), and even if you 'disconnect' them from the text, using the Advanced Layout dialog, they carry on doing it anyway.

Things improved markedly in Word 2008, but if you have yet to upgrade then you may need to apply a few workarounds.

A document that's fine on one machine can come out differently on another, depending on the margins, the font metrics, the wrap preferences – who knows? Word appears to have all the capabilities of a conventional DTP program, but it's an illusion. DTP programs let you assign fixed, immovable positions to objects on the page, but Word will never quite let go of the idea that pictures 'belong' to bits of text.

You can't stop it doing this either. But once you understand what Word is doing it is possible to work around it. This will make it easier to add and control graphics in your own documents. For good measure, it will also help you troubleshoot documents that you've been sent by other people.

INTERFACE

Inline graphics act like text characters, flowing with the text automatically. This one's been set up as a drop cap.

Floating graphics can be given regular or irregular text wraps, and they can be anchored to move with the text they're associated with.

It's possible to fix the position of graphics on the page, but (annoyingly) they may still change position if the text moves.

▲ **STEP 01 SWITCH TO PAGE LAYOUT MODE** Whenever you're working with graphics in Word it's important to switch to Page Layout mode. There are two reasons for this. The first is that in other modes (Outline mode, specifically) not all graphics formatting options are available. The second is that you need to see exactly how the text and graphics will flow on the page.

▲ **STEP 02 INSERTING INLINE GRAPHICS** We'll start by inserting a piece of clip-art, though this works just the same if you select an external file. First, place the insertion point where you want the picture to go, then insert it. It's added as an inline graphic embedded in the text at the insertion point. If the text reflows, the graphic goes with it.

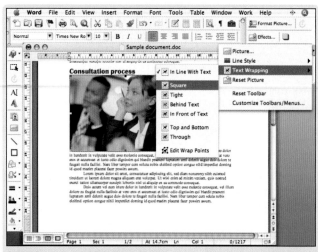

▲ **STEP 03 INLINE GRAPHIC PROPERTIES** To resize an inline graphic, just drag a corner handle. When you click on a graphic, the Picture toolbar appears. You can click the right-facing arrow at the side to show the wrap properties. As you can see, ours is an inline graphic. You can turn these into floating graphics just by choosing one of the other wrap options.

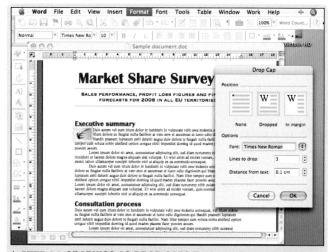

▲ **STEP 04 GRAPHICS AS DROP CAPS** That's not what we're going to do here, though. Instead, we'll demonstrate a neat little Word trick for insetting the graphic in the paragraph. To do this, use the Format > Drop Cap command and choose the number of lines for the drop. Then just add a small Distance value so that the text doesn't go right up to the edge of the graphic.

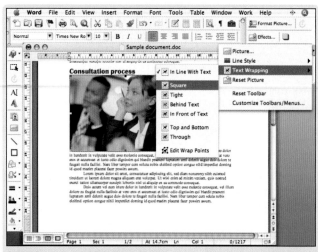

▲ **STEP 05 FLOATING GRAPHICS** Now we're adding another graphic – and again we have to choose an insertion point (all graphics are imported as inline). To float the image, select it and then choose one of the wrap options, using the Picture toolbar. Go for Square or Tight – Behind or In Front puts the image on a separate layer and the text no longer wraps around it.

▲ **STEP 06 RESIZING AND REPOSITIONING** Now that the graphic is floating it's easy to move it to a new position by dragging it from the centre, and to resize it by dragging the corner handles. But although the picture now appears to be independent of the text, its position will change if the text reflows after any editing changes.

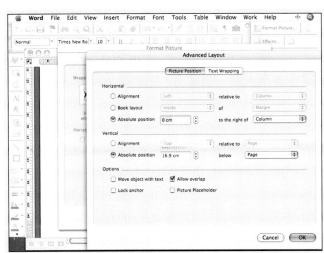

▲ **STEP 07 STOPPING GRAPHICS MOVING** This is the Word behaviour that causes all the problems. Its designers obviously felt that everyone would want pictures to stay alongside specific text. First, use the Format > Picture command and select the Layout tab. Now click on the Advanced button and the Picture Position tab, and deselect the Move object with text checkbox.

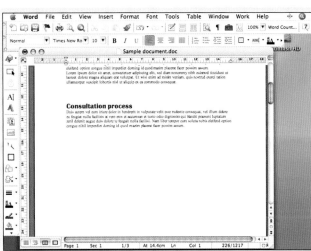

▲ **STEP 08 PAGE REFLOW PROBLEMS** But Word's not done yet. If we test these settings by typing in a few blank carriage returns above our 'Consultation process' heading, sure enough the picture stays where we put it. But if we type a few more, the picture disappears off the page. What's going on? This is not a bug. Word is doing exactly what its designers intended...

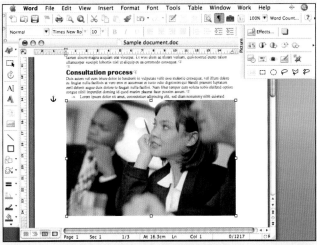

▲ **STEP 09 SHOW NON-PRINTING CHARACTERS...** To see what's happening you need to use the Show/Hide button on the toolbar to display non-printing characters. If you now click on a graphic, you'll see an anchor symbol located next to a nearby piece of text. The graphic is still anchored to a specific piece of text.

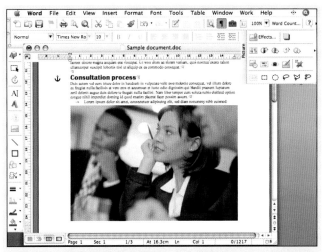

▲ **STEP 10 MOVING ANCHORS** The graphic will indeed stay where you put it unless the text it's anchored to gets shunted to a different page. Word will not tolerate this – it will move the graphic to the new page too. The only way to fix this is to reposition the graphic's anchor – here, you can see it's been moved from the second paragraph under the heading to the heading itself.

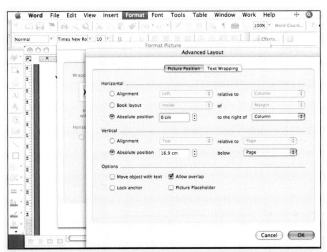

▲ **STEP 11 NOT QUITE ABSOLUTE?** Even the Absolute positioning in Word's Advanced Layout dialog isn't absolute. Look at the positioning pop-ups to the right of the Horizontal and Vertical settings. The picture's absolute position will in fact be relative to a number of choices, including the page, current page margins, current column and specific lines or characters.

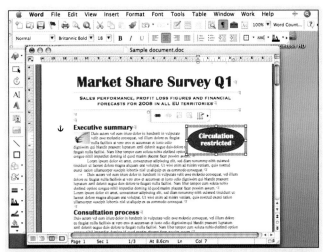

▲ **STEP 12 IRREGULAR WRAPS** When you understand Word's graphic anchors, everything starts to make sense. It's then easier to add other graphic items such as this red 'Circulation restricted' bullet and have it behave in a predictable manner. It's been set up as a floating object with an irregular text wrap, but the anchor symbol shows it's locked to the 'Executive summary'.

MASTERCLASS
Tables of Contents in Word

The longer your documents, the more your readers will demand some kind of breakdown of what's in them, and where to find it…

Kit required Microsoft Office
Time 30 minutes
Goal Create a Table of Contents in Word
Skill level Intermediate

You could write a book about Word if you were so inclined, but you could also write a book in it. Long text-based documents require some kind of navigational help so that readers can steer straight to the bits they need. That's where you need a Table of Contents (TOC).

In its simplest form, a TOC tells you what the chapters are and what page they start on. But they can be a lot more complicated than that, adding extra 'levels' for headings and sub-headings within these chapters. What you don't want to do, of course, is plod through the whole document jotting down headings and page numbers and then typing them in manually yourself. But with some forward planning and some consistent text styling, you don't have to. Word generates its TOCs by finding every instance of specific text styles and putting them in a list – simple as that.

Word's TOCs can accommodate up to nine heading levels, but you need a bit of common sense, or the TOC will end up longer than the publication it describes. What Word generates is a 'field' object. If you click on a TOC it's highlighted in grey to show this. You don't edit the text within a TOC directly; instead you simply edit the TOC's overall properties (including its text styles). Our 'Digital imaging dictionary' example demonstrates how TOCs are defined, styled and formatted. Follow this simple guide to make your documents easier to navigate.

INTERFACE

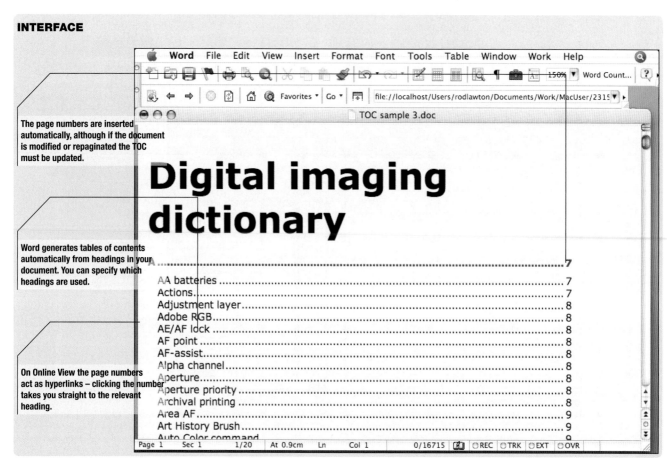

The page numbers are inserted automatically, although if the document is modified or repaginated the TOC must be updated.

Word generates tables of contents automatically from headings in your document. You can specify which headings are used.

On Online View the page numbers act as hyperlinks – clicking the number takes you straight to the relevant heading.

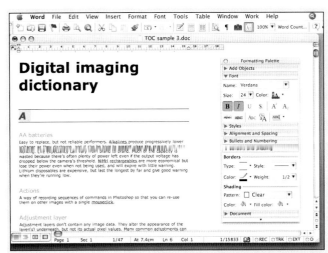

▲ **STEP 01 DEFINING TEXT STYLES 1** You can use Word's default text styles for the headings in your document, but it may prove less confusing to define your own because these will be easier to identify later. The first step is to choose the text properties – here we're using 24pt Verdana bold italic with upper and lower borders (see the settings in the Formatting Palette).

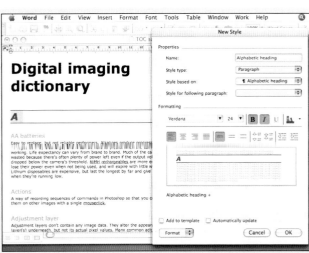

▲ **STEP 02 DEFINE TEXT STYLES 2** Once text has been styled up manually, it can easily be turned into a Style. With the modified text still selected, extend the Styles section of the Formatting Palette and then click the New Style button. The New Style dialog will display the text formatting you've just applied, so all you have to do is type in a Name that you'll remember later.

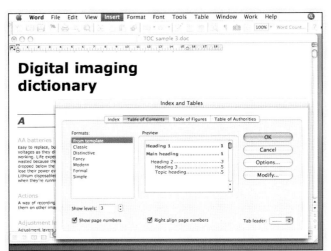

▲ **STEP 03 TABLE OF CONTENTS DIALOG** We've set up one more text style for the topic headings in our document, and now we can create a TOC using the Insert > Index and Tables command. Now click the Table of Contents tab. The Preview panel, centre, shows what the TOC will look like with the current settings, and you'll almost certainly need to change the defaults.

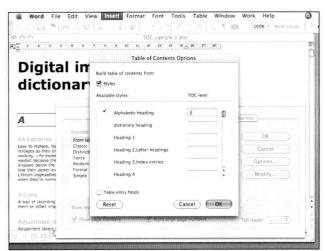

▲ **STEP 04 ALLOCATING STYLES TO TOC HEADINGS** The Options dialog lists all the Styles in use in your document. To the right of each is a TOC level box. If you don't want a Style to appear in the TOC, leave the box empty. Find the Style which represents your primary TOC heading and type a '1' in the box. Lower down in the list we've typed '2' next to the 'Topic heading' style.

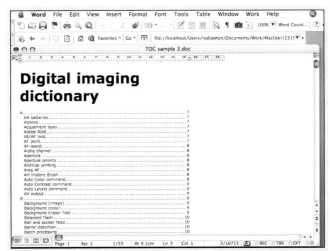

▲ **STEP 05 THE TOC INSERTED** Now we can go ahead and insert the TOC. These are placed at the insertion point. We've put ours directly below the document's main title. We can see now that all the instances of our 'Alphabetic heading' style are the main TOC headings (Level 1), and the 'Topic heading' items are secondary (Level 2) items. That was easy, wasn't it?

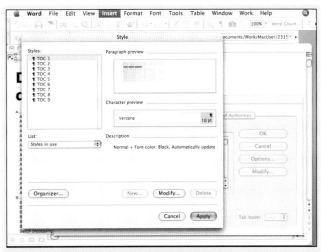

▲ **STEP 06 MODIFYING THE TOC STYLES 1** The text formatting in our TOC looks a little bland. To change this you use the Insert > Index and Tables command again – there's no way of directly modifying existing tables. This time, click the Modify button. This displays the TOC styles. These go all the way down to a Level 9, although we've only used two levels in our example.

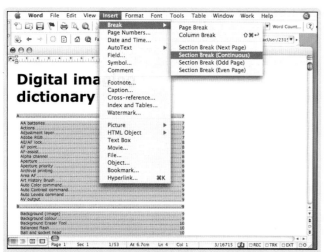

▲ **STEP 07 MODIFYING THE TOC STYLES 2** We want to change the Level 1 style so that it stands out a bit more. To do this, we select it in the list and then press the Modify button to get the Modify Style dialog. We've set the text to bold, chosen the same brown colour used for the alphabetical headings in the document and increased the paragraph spacing.

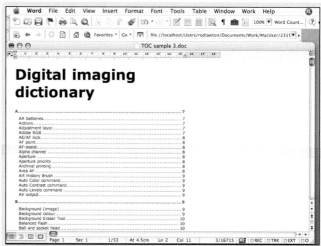

▲ **STEP 08 FINISHED TOC** Now when you've finished with the modifications you'll be asked whether you want to replace the existing TOC or not. The Level 1 TOC headings now stand out much better. They do take up quite a bit of space in the document, although there is a way of reducing this space without reducing the size of the text and making it hard to read.

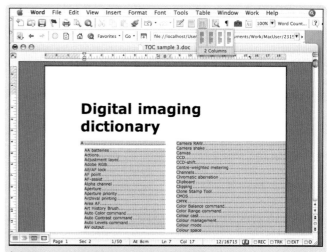

▲ **STEP 09 INSERTING SECTION BREAKS** Instead of using a single column for the TOC we can run it across two columns. And we don't have to commit to a two-column layout for the whole document, either, because we can split it up into Sections. First, we need to put the insertion point directly before the TOC and choose Insert > Break > Section Break (Continuous).

▲ **STEP 10 SWAPPING TO TWO COLUMNS** We also inserted another continuous section break after the TOC, effectively enclosing the TOC in a section all of its own. Now we click anywhere inside this section, click the Columns button on the toolbar and choose a two-column layout. However, this does affect the formatting in our example.

▲ **STEP 11 UPDATING THE TOC** This reflects the fact that TOCs don't contain 'live' data. Whenever you make a change to the documents' text or, in this case, changes to the formatting, the TOC must be updated. To do this, control-click on the TOC and choose Update Field. Update page numbers only is for minor repagination – we need the Update entire table button.

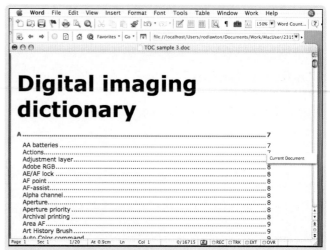

▲ **STEP 12 ONLINE VIEW** We're not quite done yet. Word's TOCs have an extra trick up their sleeve. If you switch to Online View, which is for documents designed to be read on screen rather than printed, you don't just get the chance to add a fancy background. You'll also discover that the page numbers are hyperlinked to the headings they refer to.

MASTERCLASS
Text Styles in Pages

Text Styles in Pages 08 will quickly make your documents look so much more professional – and it's well worth making the effort to master them.

Kit required iWork 08
Time 30 minutes
Goal Create quick and consistent text styling
Skill level Intermediate

There are three very good reasons for using Text Styles in Pages. The first is that they greatly speed up the job of formatting text in long documents and the second is that they bring consistency. In addition, Text Styles are an easy way to make global changes. Want to alter the body copy font or the heading style in your 60,000-word novel, for instance? It's about 15 seconds' work…

Pages has three types: Paragraph Styles, Character Styles and List Styles. Paragraph Styles are used for styling headings and larger bodies of text. You can't apply a Paragraph Style to single words, phrases or sentences unless they're on a line/paragraph of their own. For this, you need Character Styles, which override Paragraph Styles, so that you can use the latter for basic text formatting throughout the document but apply a Character Style for words or phrases you want to emphasise in a particular font, colour or style. What's clever about Pages' Character Styles is that you can choose what Paragraph Style properties they override. You can opt to simply change the text colour, for example, or its font.

Paragraph and Character Styles are found in most word processing documents but Pages has a third – List Styles. These define the bullets for simple lists or the number/letter scheme but don't include font or formatting information. They work alongside existing Styles, so you don't get any style conflicts.

INTERFACE

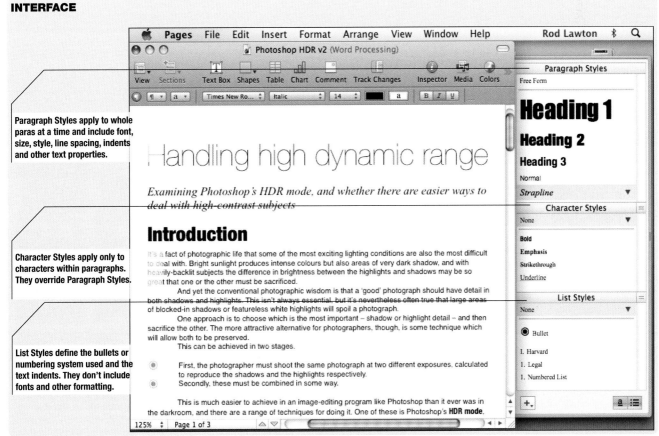

Paragraph Styles apply to whole paras at a time and include font, size, style, line spacing, indents and other text properties.

Character Styles apply only to characters within paragraphs. They override Paragraph Styles.

List Styles define the bullets or numbering system used and the text indents. They don't include fonts and other formatting.

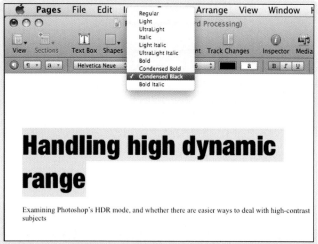

▲ **STEP 01 PARAGRAPH STYLE** To apply a paragraph style to some text, select the text and then click on a Paragraph Style in the Styles Drawer. Here, we've applied the Heading 1 style to the text. You don't have to select the whole paragraph – just placing the insertion point somewhere in the paragraph is enough as Paragraph Styles always apply to whole paragraphs at a time.

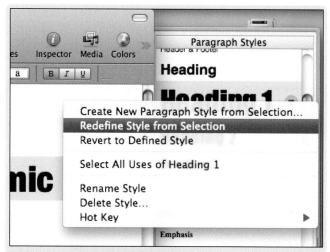

▲ **STEP 02 APPLYING A CHARACTER STYLE** Character styles are slightly different. You use these when you want to apply styles to text within a paragraph, not to the paragraph as a whole. We could just have put this HDR mode text in bold to emphasise it but using Emphasis Character Style gives us more flexibility later, including the ability to change this style globally.

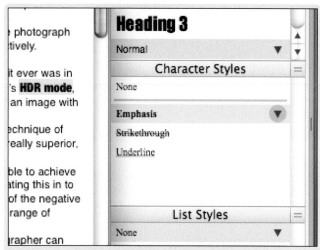

▲ **STEP 03 MODIFYING AN EXISTING PARAGRAPH STYLE** The current Heading 1 style used for our heading was inherited from the original Microsoft Word document (Pages imports Word styles automatically). What about using a different font? First, select the text, then make any changes you want with the Formatting Bar. Here, we've swapped Impact for Helvetica Neue.

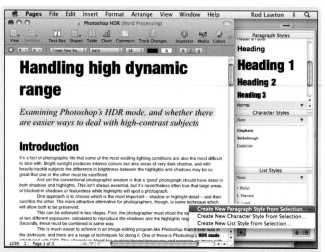

▲ **STEP 04 UPDATING THE STYLE** When you do this, you'll notice that the drop-down arrow to the right of the style name in the Styles Drawer turns from red to black. This indicates the style has been overridden by manual adjustments. Just click on the arrow to open the drop-down menu and choose Redefine Style from Selection to update the style.

▲ **STEP 05 MODIFYING A CHARACTER STYLE** The procedure is the same for Character Styles. First, select a piece of text that uses the Character Style you want to modify and make your changes manually. You will see that the arrow to the right of the Character Style turns red, as here. Again, click on the arrow to open the pop-up menu and redefine the style as before.

▲ **STEP 06 CREATING A NEW PARAGRAPH STYLE** Creating Paragraph Styles from scratch is as easy as modifying existing ones. First, style up the text manually – here we're using italicised 18pt Times Roman as a standfirst. Now, click and hold the '+' button in the bottom left-hand corner of the Styles Drawer and choose Create New Paragraph Style from Selection.

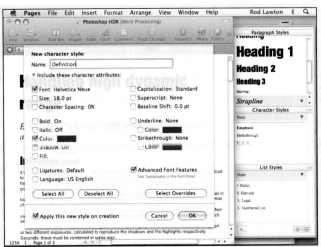

▲ STEP 07 **CREATING A NEW CHARACTER STYLE** You can create new Character Styles in the same way but there is a key difference. When you create either kind of style, a dialog prompts you for a name for the style. But the Character Style dialog has extended options. You can use these to control the degree to which the Character Style overrides the existing text attributes.

▲ STEP 08 **DELETING UNWANTED STYLES** Depending on the origins of your document there may be a large number of styles already which you're not using and just get in the way. You can delete them by clicking on the style's pop-up arrow in the Styles Draw and choosing Delete Style. If the style is in use, you'll be prompted to choose another style to apply to the affected text.

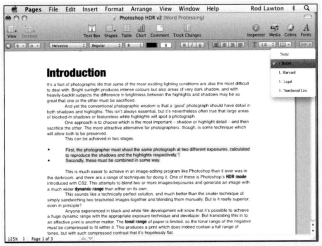

▲ STEP 09 **APPLYING A LIST STYLE** Finally, we'll take a look at List Styles. The simplest and most obvious use for these is when you have a series of bullet points in the text. You just select the text and choose the style you want from the List Styles pop-up on the Formatting Bar (you may need to increase the width of the document window for this to be visible).

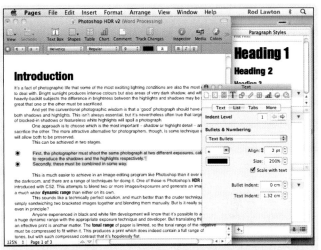

▲ STEP 10 **CHANGING THE BULLET PROPERTIES** The default bullets are on the small side but this is easily fixed. Using the Text Inspector – click on the List tab to see the options available. Here we've chosen a larger bullet style from the pop-up on the left, then fine-tuned its vertical alignment, its size and the text indent, using the controls on the right.

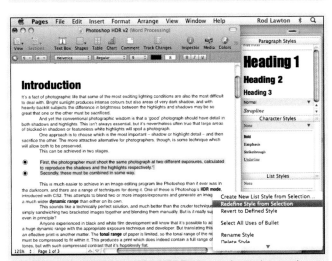

▲ STEP 11 **MODIFYING A LIST STYLE** When you've made manual changes to a List Style you can redefine that style in the same way that you update Paragraph Styles and Character Styles. Click on its arrow in the Styles Drawer and choose Redefine Style from Selection. Alternatively you can create your own List Styles from scratch.

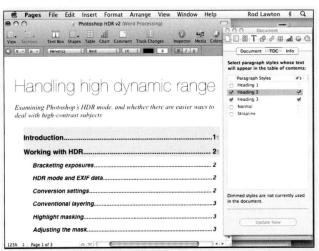

▲ STEP 12 **CREATING TOCS** Pages Styles don't just speed up your document formatting and make it more consistent. They enable you to generate Tables of Contents (TOCs) automatically from the Insert menu. This displays a dialog listing all the Paragraph Styles used in your document. Simply select those which you want to appear in the TOC.

MASTERCLASS
Handling photos in Pages

Sooner or later you'll want to illustrate a document with photos. It's a prospect you probably face with dread in Word, but in Pages it's simple.

Kit required iWork 08
Time 30 minutes
Goal Understand what you can do with photos in Pages
Skill level Intermediate

Pages is very good at handling photos. In principle it works in much the same way as Microsoft Word. In practice, it's a whole lot simpler and more predictable in the way it goes about it. Like Word, Pages offers either inline graphics or fixed graphics. Inline graphics are embedded in the text and move around with the text when you make changes. Fixed graphics stay in the same place on the page and the text flows around them. The problem with Word is that even if you think you've added a photo as a fixed graphic, it will still try to keep it with the text unless you disable this feature, which can be a real nuisance.

Pages offers some surprisingly sophisticated photo and layout tools. You can add rectangular masks to photos to crop unwanted areas, or you can make them with shapes. Masked photos can be given outlines and drop shadows, too, and you should try out the neat Reflection effect while you're at it. The text wrap options for fixed graphics are extensive and easy to use, even irregular wraps around cutouts.

Pages integrates with iPhoto and Aperture too, so that if you open the Media panel you can drag and drop photos directly from your albums. It's much faster and simpler than having to return to the Finder to retrieve media. It's even possible to make basic image adjustments within Pages using the same tools available in iPhoto. All this is explained in detail in our workthrough.

INTERFACE

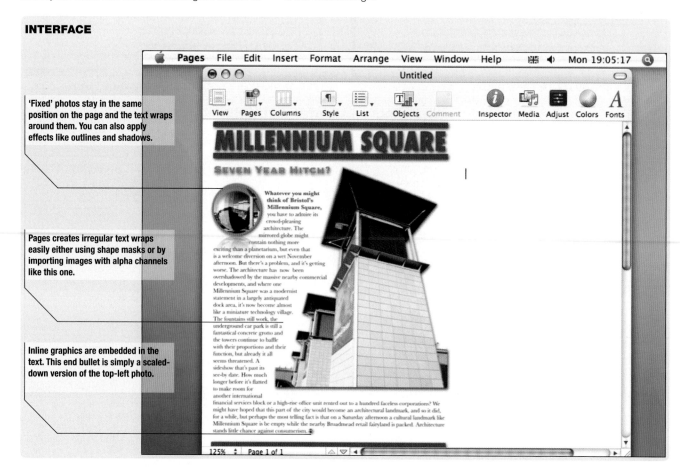

'Fixed' photos stay in the same position on the page and the text wraps around them. You can also apply effects like outlines and shadows.

Pages creates irregular text wraps easily either using shape masks or by importing images with alpha channels like this one.

Inline graphics are embedded in the text. This end bullet is simply a scaled-down version of the top-left photo.

▲ **STEP 01 PREPARING YOUR PHOTOS** You can start off by choosing the photos you want to use in your layout. Here we're creating an Album in iPhoto and adding the images we might want to use. The Media panel in Pages displays a cut-down version of the iPhoto interface, but you can still browse all your Albums and carry out text searches.

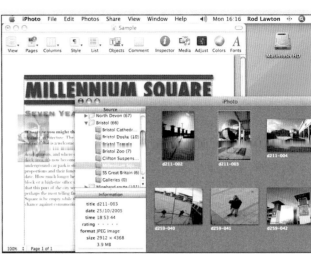

▲ **STEP 02 ADDING PHOTOS WITH DRAG AND DROP** You don't have to use the Media panel at all. You can drag and drop photos directly from iPhoto or from the Finder. Simply dragging an image across drops it on the page as a 'fixed' graphic. To add a photo as an inline graphic, hold down the Command key as you drag and move the mouse to position the insertion point.

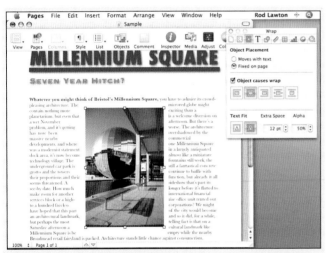

▲ **STEP 03 CHECK THE WRAP OPTIONS** If you don't hold down the Command key, new images are added as fixed graphics – check the settings in the Wrap Inspector. At the top are radio buttons for fixed versus inline positioning, below this you choose the wrap style (one side, both sides, top and bottom) and the bottom section offers regular versus irregular wrapping.

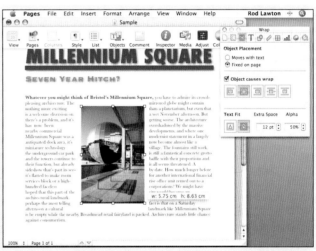

▲ **STEP 04 RESIZING AND MOVING PHOTOS** To move a fixed graphic, just drag it. The text reflows in real time as you do it. To resize the photo, drag any corner or edge handle. Note that the image proportions are constrained automatically. Inline graphics work slightly differently in that only the bottom and right-hand drag handles are available.

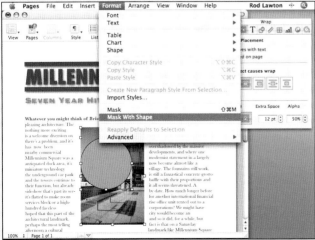

▲ **STEP 05 ADDING A SHAPE MASK** At the moment our imported photo is a regular rectangular shape, but we want to make it circular to echo the shape of the mirrored sphere. To create a shape mask, first create the shape and position it over the photo you want to mask and use the Format > Mask with Shape command. The shape's line and fill don't matter.

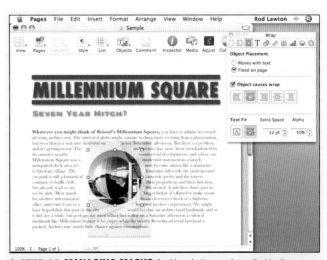

▲ **STEP 06 MANAGING MASKS** And here's the mask applied to the photo. At the moment, the mask is still visible and selected, and we can resize it and move it if we need to. Once you click away from the graphic, though, the photo is masked fully and the mask and photo move around as a single item. To edit them individually again you need to double-click.

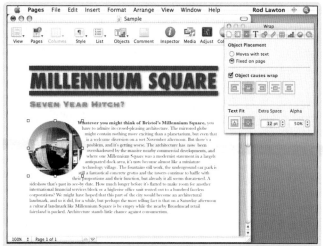

▲ **STEP 07 IRREGULAR WRAP SETTINGS** Now the masked photo's been moved into position at the start of the text block. The text wraps automatically around it. This is one of the beauties of Pages – it picks the right wrap settings by default, and these can be examined in the Wrap Inspector. If the wrapped text is too close or too far away, change the Extra Space value.

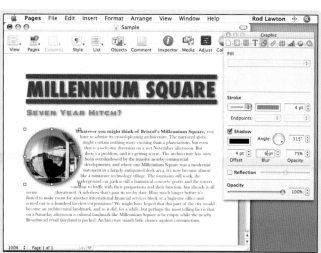

▲ **STEP 08 GRAPHIC EFFECTS** Pages looks simple, but it has unexpected depths. We can apply a Stroke to our masked photo and choose a thickness and a colour from the Graphic Inspector. A nice drop shadow is just a checkbox away and the finished layout in our main annotation on page 202 demonstrates the very attractive Reflection effect too.

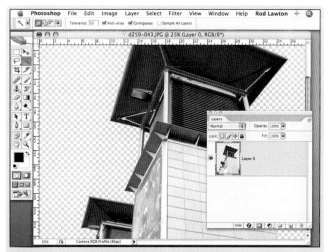

▲ **STEP 09 IMAGES WITH ALPHA CHANNELS** For our main image we want to use a cut-out shot of some modernistic towers, and while we could try to create a custom shape mask in Pages, it would be laborious and crude. Instead, we need to do a bit of preparatory work in Photoshop. We've simply promoted the background image to a layer and then deleted the sky.

▲ **STEP 10 PLACING THE MAIN IMAGE** Pages can import Photoshop files directly, so there's nothing more that needs doing. You don't have to actually create an alpha channel in Photoshop – simply erasing the unwanted parts of the image layer is enough. The photo's been dragged into Pages from the Finder and the text wraps automatically – simple as that.

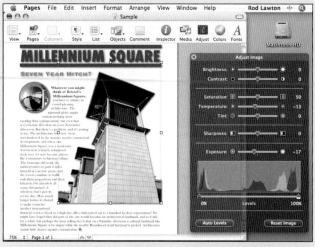

▲ **STEP 11 IMAGE ADJUSTMENTS** Not quite happy with the colours or the contrast or the sharpness? Clicking on the Adjust button opens up the familiar iPhoto Adjust palette. It's clever and surprising, and it might save you a bit of time and effort, but it's more likely you'll want to do all your editing separately, since the iPhoto adjustments are pretty crude and basic.

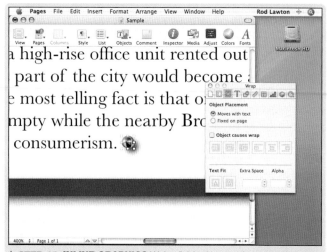

▲ **STEP 12 INLINE GRAPHICS** We've finished by creating a closing bullet from the circular photo used at the start by copying the image, placing the text insertion point at the end and pasting. The stroke was removed and the image resized to fit the line height. Be warned, though, that Pages doesn't resample photos when it resizes them, so file sizes can swell.

MASTERCLASS
Advanced charting in Excel

See the invisible and predict the future! And you thought Excel was just a spreadsheet? The right chart can reveal the meaning in your data...

Kit required Microsoft Office
Time 30 minutes
Goal Getting the best from Excel's charts
Skill level Advanced

Charts are a great way to prove a point. A graphical demonstration of a product's success or a department's contribution to company profits will always be instantly obvious in a chart, in a way that bare figures aren't.

But charts can do more than just convince other people of something you already know. Quite often, a chart can help you see something that would be impossible to grasp from simply looking at the numbers. Feeding a mass of seemingly random data to a scatter chart can show you quickly and visibly whether there's a correlation or not.

In our workthrough, we have created two sets of data. The first shows the monthly rental of a flat together with its distance from a mainline railway station. It's very hard to tell from simply looking at the figures whether there is a strong correlation or not but when the scatter chart is plotted, any correlation becomes very easy to see. This chart, therefore, can reveal invisible patterns in the data.

The second set of figures correlate the prices of petrol and biofuel over time. After plotting these lists of prices, we will use them to forecast what will happen to them using an Excel feature called Trendlines. These can take the existing data and extrapolate it into the future, using a variety of mathematical models to make the results much more than just guesswork.

INTERFACE

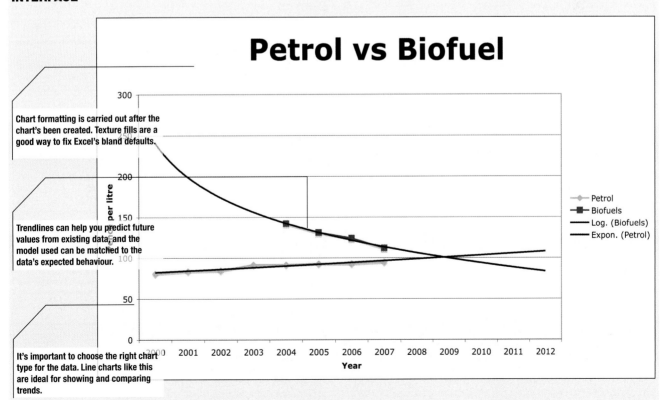

Chart formatting is carried out after the chart's been created. Texture fills are a good way to fix Excel's bland defaults.

Trendlines can help you predict future values from existing data, and the model used can be matched to the data's expected behaviour.

It's important to choose the right chart type for the data. Line charts like this are ideal for showing and comparing trends.

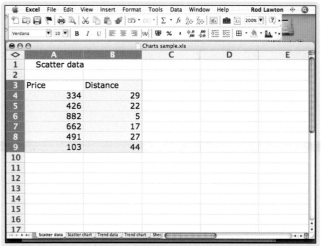

▲ **STEP 01 FORMATTING SCATTER CHART DATA** The secret to creating any chart is to arrange the data carefully before you start. You need contiguous data tables (no gaps) with labels at the top, at the sides, or both. Here, we've simply got two columns, one headed 'Price' and one headed 'Distance'. These cells and the data below have been selected.

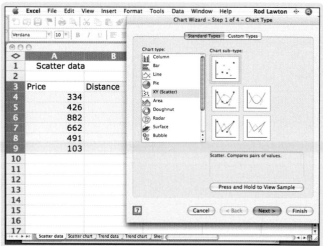

▲ **STEP 02 CHOOSE THE CHART TYPE** Now we click on the Chart Wizard button on the toolbar. The first step is to choose the chart type. We've gone for the 'XY (Scatter)' type. Scatter charts plot data points from two coordinates on the x and y axes. In this example, each property we look at has a 'price' (rental per month) and a 'distance' (from the station) value.

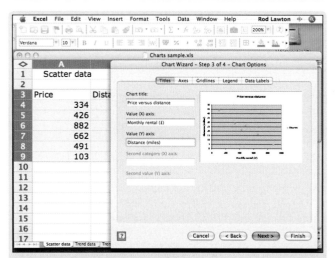

▲ **STEP 03 TITLE AND AXIS LABELS** Excel is pretty good at identifying data series and axis labels automatically from the data, but you will need to specify a title for the chart and the x and y axis labels. This is done in step 3 of the Chart Wizard. Here, you're just creating the necessary chart objects. Any formatting comes later, when the chart's been made.

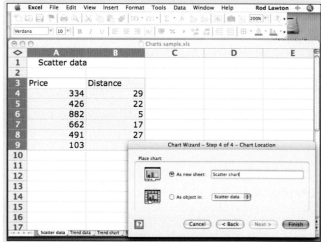

▲ **STEP 04 OBJECT OR SHEET?** The last step of the wizard asks whether you want the chart created as an object on the current sheet or on a separate worksheet of its own. The advantage of a new worksheet is that you can give it a descriptive name and go straight to your chart at any time in future just by clicking its worksheet tab at the bottom of the window.

▲ **STEP 05 FORMATTING THE CHART** This is the finished chart with the scatter points plotted. We've made a couple of other formatting changes too, because Excel's chart defaults look pretty grim. To change an object like the chart title or the plot area, select it and then click the Format button on the Chart toolbar. Here, we've given the chart area a texture fill.

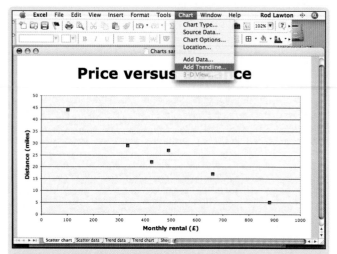

▲ **STEP 06 ADDING A TRENDLINE** Now it's clear just from looking at the scatter points that there is a pretty strong correlation. So can we use this data to predict prices for other distances (and vice versa)? Yes. We can get started by selecting the data series (just click on any of the points) and choosing Add Trendline from the Chart menu.

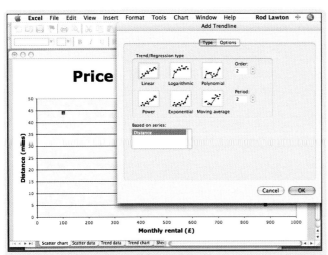

▲ **STEP 07 LINEAR TRENDLINES** Trendlines are a 'best-fit' line through the data, and they can be created with a variety of mathematical models. Our data is too limited in terms of the sample size to justify a complex trend analysis, though, so we're going for the Linear Trend/Regression type. This will just draw a straight line through the data points.

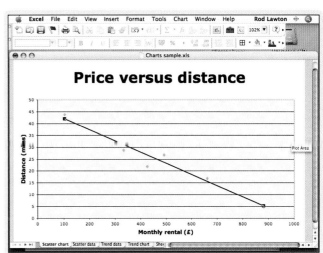

▲ **STEP 08 ASSESSING THE TREND** And the results actually look quite convincing. All of the data points are actually quite close to the line, so the correlation seems good. You could now use the Trendline to predict the cost of a flat at a given distance from the station, or set your maximum budget and see how close to the station you could afford to live.

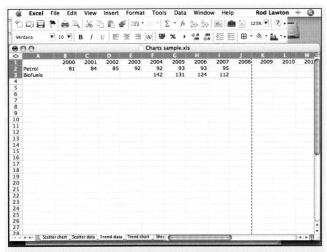

▲ **STEP 09 WORKING WITH TWO DATA SERIES** Now we're going to try something more ambitious. This time we want to make predictions rather than simply establishing a pattern. We've got two sets of data here – the prices of petrol and biofuels plotted against the year. However, our data is incomplete. We've got data up to 2007, but we want to plan for 2012.

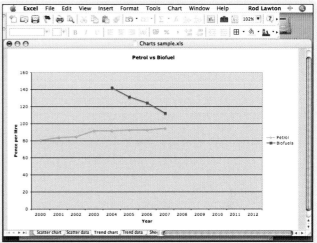

▲ **STEP 10 DUAL LINE CHARTS** We've used the Chart Wizard to produce a line chart from our two data series. Note, that although the bottom axis goes all the way to 2012, our data stops at 2007. We left the cells under the years 2008-2012 blank on purpose to make sure Excel produced a chart long enough to accommodate our predictions.

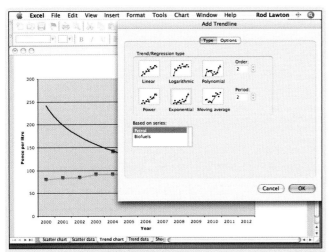

▲ **STEP 11 ADDING THE TRENDLINES** Here, simple Linear Trendlines seem just a bit too… well, simple. We expect the price of biofuels to start high, drop quickly and level out, and a Logarithmic Trendline will reflect this. Petrol prices, on the other hand, are likely to rise sharply as oil reserves fall and biofuels take over, and an Exponential Trendline will mirror this behaviour.

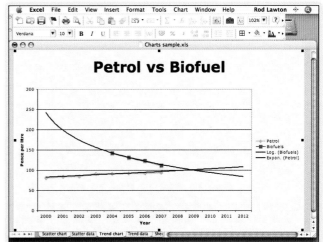

▲ **STEP 12 ANALYSING THE CHART** As you can see from the results, these Trendline types don't distort existing data into new shapes. Where the data points show a fairly linear progression, the Trendlines stick to it. But what our Trendlines can do is show us (a) when the petrol and biofuel costs are likely to be the same, and (b) a broad window of similar pricing.

MASTERCLASS
Filtering mail in Entourage

Every day we're bombarded by emails, the vast majority of which are time-wasting trash. If you've installed Entourage to bin the junk, here's how to ensure it does the job properly

Kit required Microsoft Office
Time 30 minutes
Goal Get your email sorted automatically
Skill level Intermediate

Entourage's junk filter does its best but it isn't really smart enough to figure out what we need to read and what we don't. Let's face it, any junk filter that fails to spot when our ISP's mail server inserts '*** SPAM ***' in the subject line can't be that bright. And there's always the worry that Entourage's junk filter' will chuck out messages it shouldn't – if you check the Junk folder now, you'll soon see that there's plenty to worry about.

In fact, it's easy to tell Entourage what isn't junk and stop it getting it wrong again. One option is to use mailing-list rules, which can automatically identify and file regular newsletters and bulletins – from there it's a short step to setting up your own custom rules that are just more advanced versions of the same thing. Rules intercept incoming mail and carry out specific actions depending on whether it meets the criteria.

Let's say you've an interest in *Coronation Street* memorabilia and you subscribe to dozens of possibly relevant mailing lists. You could set up a rule which checks messages for any *Corrie* reference and have them automatically flagged and filed. But do check that your rules really do work before letting them loose on your mail. And don't get so carried away that you create dozens of super-complex rules that you can't understand six months later when you've forgotten what you did and why.

Clever is good, but useful is better.

INTERFACE

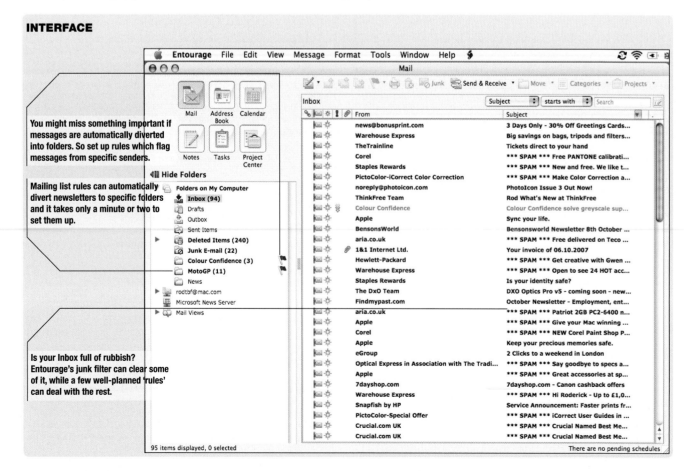

You might miss something important if messages are automatically diverted into folders. So set up rules which flag messages from specific senders.

Mailing list rules can automatically divert newsletters to specific folders and it takes only a minute or two to set them up.

Is your Inbox full of rubbish? Entourage's junk filter can clear some of it, while a few well-planned 'rules' can deal with the rest.

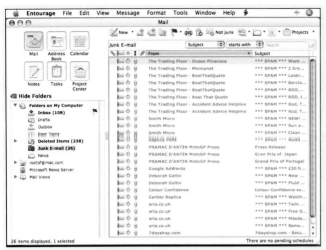

▲ STEP 01 **HOW THE JUNK FOLDER WORKS** Microsoft includes a Junk filter (called SmartScreen) in Entourage which automatically diverts what it thinks is junk to a special Junk folder. You're advised to check this folder now and then to make sure there's no 'real' mail in there, and you'd be wise to do so because the filter is far from perfect and often bins 'real' mail.

▲ STEP 02 **WHAT IF IT'S NOT JUNK?** If you find a message that isn't junk in the Junk folder you can select it and press the Not Junk button to return it to the Inbox. You'll also be asked if you want to prevent this happening again. Adding the sender's name to your address book is one solution – but creating a mailing list rule is a much better one…

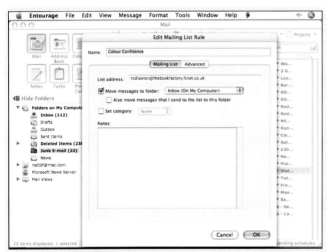

▲ STEP 03 **MAILING LIST RULES** Mailing list rules are useful for regular newsletters, and they're also a good introduction to user-defined rules, which we'll come to shortly. You can also create a mailing list rule using the Tools > Mailing List Manager option. This is the dialog you get but it must be filled in carefully. Don't just accept the defaults.

▲ STEP 04 **GET THE LIST ADDRESS RIGHT** It's the List address box you need to pay attention to. By default this will contain your own email address – the one the list is sent to. If you leave this as it is, the mailing list rule you create will apply to all your incoming mail. Instead make sure you insert the email address of the sender – you can get this from the message header.

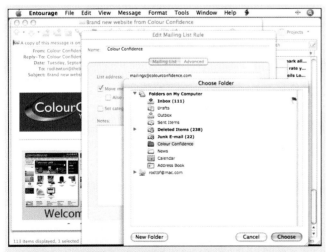

▲ STEP 05 **CHOOSING A FOLDER** The default action for mailing lists is to route them to a particular folder which you choose, using the pop-up menu under the List address box. This opens a dialog box where you can choose an existing folder or create a new one. Here, we're setting up a mailing list rule to divert a regular Colour Confidence newsletter to its own folder.

▲ STEP 06 **APPLYING RULES RETROSPECTIVELY** Any mailing list rule you create will apply only to new mail. Mail already received stays exactly where it is. But you can apply the rule to existing mail too. (It's probably best to apply it to a single message first to make sure it's working properly.) Select the message(s), Ctrl-click it and choose Apply Rule > All Rules.

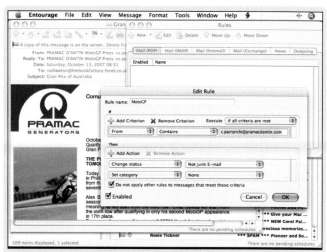

▲ **STEP 07 CREATING A CUSTOM RULE** Entourage doesn't distinguish between mailing list rules – they all come under the general heading 'all rules'. They're also limited to storing messages in specific folders. However, you can create much more sophisticated rules of your own (Tools > Rules) based on complex message criteria and producing more than one action.

▲ **STEP 08 CHOOSE THE RULE CRITERIA** This is a two-step process. First, you choose the criteria for identifying messages. Our MotoGP rule looks for emails from a specific email address, though you can also check subject or message content. It's possible to have multiple criteria and make the rule check for all of them or any of them in incoming mail.

▲ **STEP 09 CHOOSING THE ACTION** Next, you decide what you want to happen when specific incoming messages have been identified. Just as you have multiple criteria for identifying messages, you can set up multiple actions which you then want applied to the mail. Our first action here is to move the message from the Inbox to a different folder…

▲ **STEP 10 ADDING MORE ACTIONS** Our second action is to flag these messages. Typically you'd flag messages that you need to act on in some way but you can also use flags to prioritise messages to ensure you read the most important first. You could also display an Entourage 'notification', play a sound, forward the mail to another address and more.

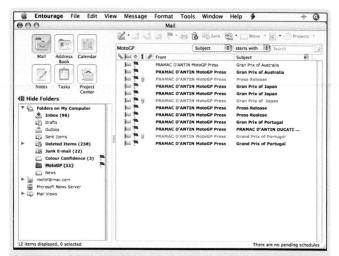

▲ **STEP 11 APPLYING RULES TO EXISTING MAIL** As with mailing list rules, you can apply these custom rules retrospectively, though do check them in individual messages before you apply them to the entire contents of your Inbox. This time when you open the Apply Rule menu, you'll see that any custom rules you've set up can be applied individually.

▲ **STEP 12 DOES IT WORK?** Our MotoGP rule has identified all existing mail from the Pramac D'Antin MotoGP press office, moved it to a folder of its own and flagged it. It'll now check incoming mail and do the same with any new messages. Just be careful when setting up rules that you don't make them so numerous and so complex that you forget what they do.

MASTERCLASS
Using signatures in Entourage

How many hours of your life have you wasted in manually signing off emails with your name, your phone number and your address?

Kit required Microsoft Office
Time 15 minutes
Goal Setting up signatures in Entourage
Skill level Beginner

Setting up signatures seems such a piffling little job that many of us simply never get round to it. Each time you sign off it just appears so much easier to type out a couple of lines of text manually than to ferret around in Entourage's entrails, looking for a way to set up a signature.

Okay, so it doesn't take long to type out your name. But what about your phone number or your mobile, your office address? A signature won't just save you time but it will also prevent you from making silly typing mistakes. Signatures also add a little polish and consistency to your messages.

They're a great way to promote the company that you work for, creating a subtly more businesslike impression. Without a consistent signature, it looks as though you're making it all up as you go along and if you work for a company, you may or may not be communicating on their behalf.

In fact, it doesn't take long to set up a few handy signatures. You can have one for friends and family, another for business colleagues and another for customers. All of these signatures are freely interchangeable between your email accounts – you just choose the one you want to use from a list at the top of the message window. Or you can pick a specific signature as the default for any given email account. There's even a good case for using Entourage's Random signature feature… Honestly.

INTERFACE

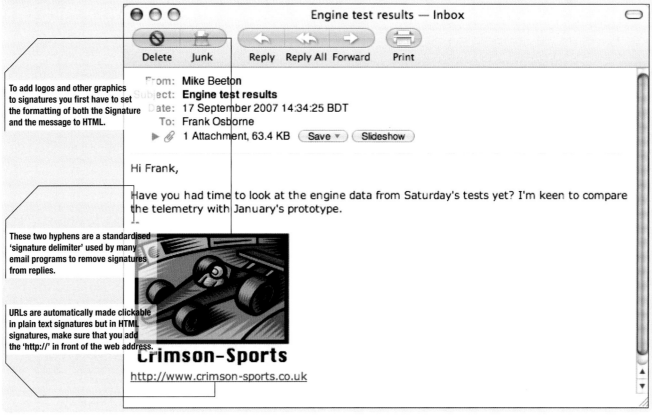

To add logos and other graphics to signatures you first have to set the formatting of both the Signature and the message to HTML.

These two hyphens are a standardised 'signature delimiter' used by many email programs to remove signatures from replies.

URLs are automatically made clickable in plain text signatures but in HTML signatures, make sure that you add the 'http://' in front of the web address.

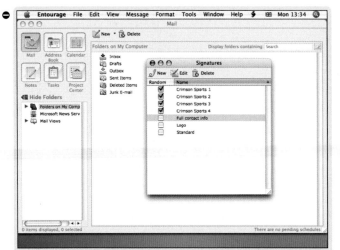

▲ STEP 01 **WHERE SIGNATURES ARE STORED** You can set up as many signatures as you like, any of which can be added to an outgoing message. To see your signatures, edit them or add new ones, go to Tools > Signatures. Note the checkboxes to the left under the Random column. Random signatures aren't such a crazy idea as they might sound, as you'll see.

▲ STEP 02 **INSERTING A SIGNATURE** This is straightforward. Write your message as normal, then look for the Signature pop-up on the toolbar at the top of the Message window. This displays a list of all the available signatures – the same list that you see in the Signatures window. When you choose a signature, Entourage inserts it on a new line.

▲ STEP 03 **ADDING WEB ADDRESSES TO SIGNATURES** You can use your signature to add your name, your phone number or your address. You can also use it to add the URL of your website. There's no need to add any special formatting – just type it in as you would in the address bar of your web browser. Don't worry that it's not highlighted as a link.

▲ STEP 04 **WHAT THE RECIPIENT GETS** If you send someone a URL as part of your signature, it arrives as a 'hot' hyperlink. When they click the link, it opens the site in their default web browser. (If you want to double-check that your email is arriving with a clickable link, just type your own email address into the Cc: field when you send the message.)

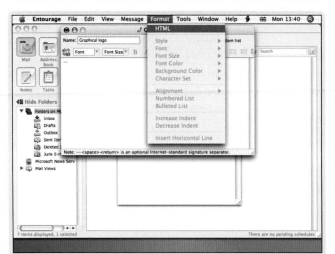

▲ STEP 05 **HTML FORMATTING** But what if you want to use your company logo in your signature? By default, Entourage sends plain text messages that don't support graphics; this also applies to its signatures. So when you want to create a signature with graphics, you first have to select the HTML option from the Format menu.

▲ STEP 06 **INSERTING A LOGO** There are two ways to add graphics. You can either use the Message > Insert > Picture command or open a Finder window and simply drag the image across. Ensure that you resize the image first, though, choosing dimensions suitable for on-screen viewing, because there are no facilities for resizing, moving or cropping images in this window.

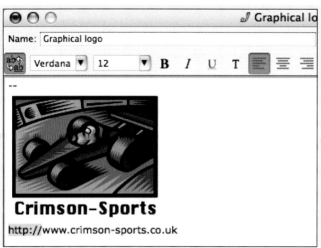

▲ STEP 07 **FIXING LINKS** There's one more thing you have to do. Bizarrely, Entourage will automatically make a URL 'hot' in a plain text signature but it won't do the same in an HTML signature, so that a link in this format won't work when it arrives with the recipient. What you have to do is insert 'http://' in front of it.

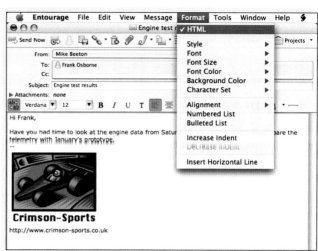

▲ STEP 08 **USING HTML SIGNATURES** Now here's another thing that can trip you up. You've created your HTML signature but when you try to add it to the end of a message, the graphics are missing. That's because the message itself is set to plain text format – here again you need to choose the Format > HTML option (or change the Entourage preferences).

▲ STEP 09 **WHAT THE RECIPIENT SEES** Assuming that your recipient has their email client set up to receive and display HTML-format messages, your signature should display correctly. This is how our message looks in Apple Mail. If some recipients complain it's not working, you'll have to design a plain text signature just for them.

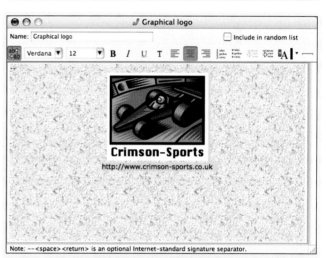

▲ STEP 10 **SIGNATURES WITH BACKGROUNDS** You can even add a background image. Entourage will tile this image repeatedly to fill the size of the message window, so bear that in mind when choosing graphics. Here, we've chosen a simple texture. Note that the background image doesn't just sit behind the signature – it will fill the whole message window.

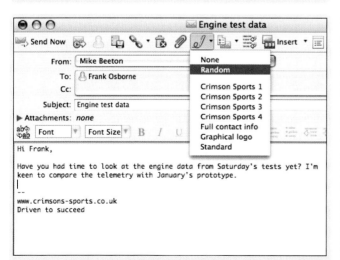

▲ STEP 11 **RANDOM SIGNATURES** Now what about these signatures? They might seem like a pointless novelty feature, but actually they can be useful. We've set up four signatures for our Crimson Sports company, each with a different slogan. If we insert a Random signature at the end of our messages, the recipients will get different slogans every time.

▲ STEP 12 **DEFAULT SIGNATURES** You don't have to choose signatures manually. Each of Entourage's accounts (Tools > Accounts) can be set up with a default signature – select the Options tab in the Edit Account window and choose a signature from the list. Now, whenever you create a message with that account, the signature is added automatically.

MASTERCLASS
PowerPoint's drawing tools

Given the state of most PowerPoint presentations, you might think its drawing tools date back to the Stone Age. We show you how to make a more modern show.

Kit required Microsoft Office
Time 30 minutes
Goal Get the most out of PowerPoint's drawing tools
Skill level Intermediate

It's PowerPoint's templates that are to blame. Whoever put them together didn't spend much time at design college and they certainly don't reflect the scope and the versatility of PowerPoint's drawing tools either. These are actually on a par with those from a half-decent vector-drawing program, and include fully-editable Bézier curves and transparency, together with extremely useful drafting tools, such as 'sticky' connector lines.

It's not really possible to demonstrate the full scope of PowerPoint's drawing tools in just 12 steps, but our workthrough does show a glimpse of their potential. We've based it on a typical business presentation – promoting a new product to the board or to potential distributors. The 30 minutes a slide like this might take to put together is easily justified if it tips a sale one way or the other. The main thing is to forget about the templates supplied with the program and start from scratch. If you're not a professional designer, just take inspiration from magazines or ads. The pro secrets are consistency and simplicity. Keep the number of fonts to a minimum, use just two or three colours and keep all the line weights the same.

The example seen here is a static slide, but don't forget that PowerPoint's animation tools can be used to build a slide like this an item at a time, giving the presenter time to introduce each item to the audience and add to the interactive feel.

INTERFACE

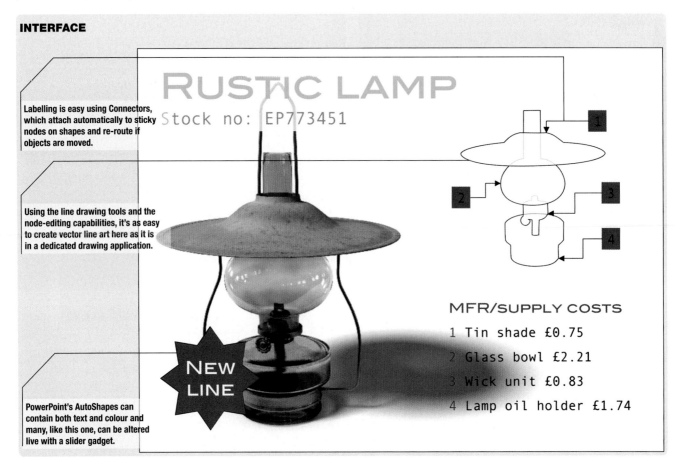

Labelling is easy using Connectors, which attach automatically to sticky nodes on shapes and re-route if objects are moved.

Using the line drawing tools and the node-editing capabilities, it's as easy to create vector line art here as it is in a dedicated drawing application.

PowerPoint's AutoShapes can contain both text and colour and many, like this one, can be altered live with a slider gadget.

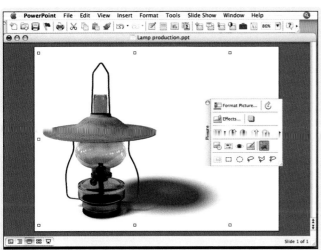

▲ **STEP 01 IMPORTING PHOTOS** When you insert a photo, the Picture toolbar will display automatically. This includes a Crop button that we can use to trim the white space around this image. To resize a photo, drag a corner handle, to reposition a photo, drag from the centre. Any vector art you insert is handled as a picture initially, but it can be converted into an editable object.

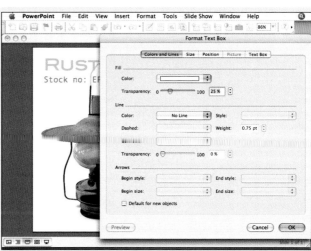

▲ **STEP 02 ADDING A TITLE BOX** Now we've added a title box for the slide and chosen the fonts and colours. But we need some way to dim the image behind the box, otherwise the text becomes illegible. We can do this by making the box background partially transparent. First, the fill colour is set to white, then the Transparency slider is set to 50% in the Format Text Box dialog.

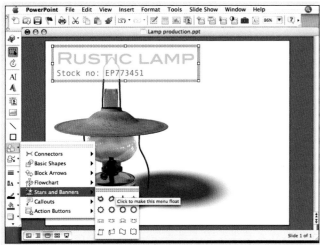

▲ **STEP 03 ADDING AN AUTOSHAPE** The next step is to add a flash advertising the fact that this is a new product. For this we can use one of PowerPoint's ready-made AutoShapes. This also demonstrates a neat bit of interface design – most of the pop-up palettes on the Drawing toolbar can be dragged off and floated on the screen, so they remain available all the time.

▲ **STEP 04 CHANGING AUTOSHAPE PROPERTIES** AutoShapes are more than static ready-made elements. Many of them can be modified quickly, like this eight-point star – look out for the yellow diamond-shaped gadgets. In this case, dragging the gadget changes the depth of the star's rays. The effect varies with the shape.

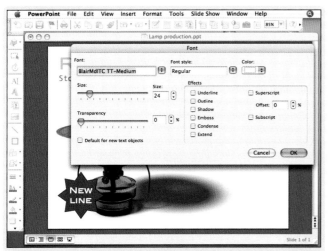

▲ **STEP 05 ADDING TEXT TO AUTOSHAPES** To add text to an AutoShape, control-click it and choose Add Text from the shortcut menu. Note that the AutoShape doesn't strictly act as a container for the text. If you make the AutoShape smaller, the text will simply overhang the edges. If you use the Format > Font command you can use a slider to adjust the font size live.

▲ **STEP 06 DRAWING LINES** The next job is to draw outlines for the main components of the lamp, and for this we need the Lines palette. Again, this can be torn off the Drawing toolbar and floated on the screen. The two most useful lines for this job are the Curve (bottom left) and Freeform (bottom centre) tools. One produces curved line segments, the other produces straight lines.

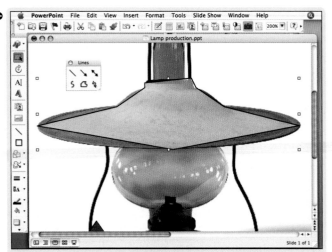

▲ **STEP 07 THE ROUGH VERSION** There's no need to be too accurate with this. It's easier to modify a small number of points carefully than it is to edit or delete a large number. To make the tracing job easier, the shape's fill has been set to white and the transparency to 50%. This means the photo shows through underneath, this makes it a lot easier to trace the outline.

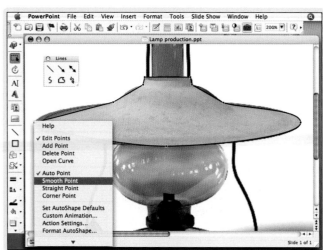

▲ **STEP 08 EDITING POINTS** To modify shapes, first control-click the shape and choose Edit Points from the shortcut menu. You can now move the points around individually. To change the point type, control-click the point and choose from Auto (the default – no handles), Smooth Point (a symmetrical Bézier node), Straight Point (asymmetrical Bézier node) and Corner Point.

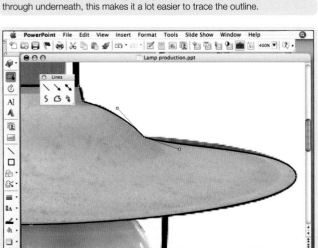

▲ **STEP 09 ADJUSTING CONTROL HANDLES** These control points are very easy to modify. The points don't highlight when you select them, but the cursor changes when you're over them and in practice there's no problem selecting points or their handles. In just a couple of minutes it's possible to produce a pretty good approximation of the lampshade.

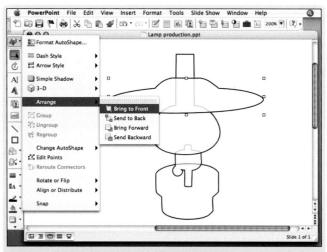

▲ **STEP 10 CHANGING THE STACKING ORDER** This is the result of tracing the other lamp components in the same way and then moving the shapes to the top right corner, where they're going to be used for labelled annotation. To give the required cutaway effect, each shape has a white fill set to 50% transparency. Then stacked in the right order with the Arrange pop-up.

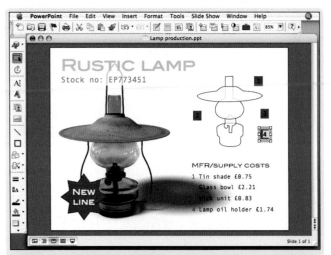

▲ **STEP 11 NUMBERED LABELS** The numbered labels are easy enough to do – these are simply text boxes with a solid red fill. It's best to create and format one box first and then duplicate it for the rest, rather than reformatting each new box individually. We could also have used an AutoShape with text inside it – that would be better if you wanted a circular shape, for example.

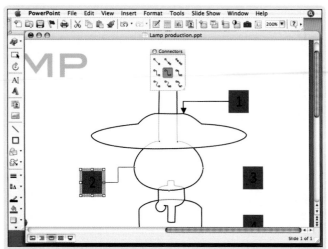

▲ **STEP 12 CONNECTOR LINES** Finally, we can add the Connector lines linking the numbered labels with the shapes. These Connectors have their own tear-off palette on the AutoShapes flyout. To use them, position the mouse pointer over the first shape and sticky blue nodes will appear. Now drag the line from one of these to connect with a sticky node on the other shape.

MASTERCLASS
Advanced animation in PowerPoint

Too many PowerPoint presentations are just dull and static screens of data. But they don't have to be when the built-in animation tools are so straightforward to use.

Kit required Microsoft Office
Time About an hour or so
Goal Discover PowerPoint's animation tools
Skill level Intermediate

If you've spent any time at all with PowerPoint you'll know that it comes with a wide range of slide transitions to liven up presentations. But there's a lot more you can do, and you may end up quite surprised by PowerPoint's capabilities.

Any object on a PowerPoint slide can be given an animation effect. The object starts off hidden, but then appears on the slide when the user clicks or when the previous animation effect has finished. This means that you can 'build' slides progressively, creating animated sequences that run on their own, or you can control this 'build' manually using the mouse.

Central to this is the Custom Animation dialogue, the hub of all PowerPoint's animation options. It looks complex, but it doesn't take long to get to grips with. PowerPoint on the Mac does have its limits (the Windows version, amazingly, even supports customisable motion paths), but there's still enough there to add some pizzazz.

We've only scratched the surface here, picking out just a couple of neat Entrance effects to work with. PowerPoint also offers Emphasis and Exit effects so that you can make an object appear and disappear too. Also, our workthrough only shows animation effects working one after the other, but they can also run simultaneously.

You can have a lot more fun with PowerPoint animations than you might have imagined.

INTERFACE

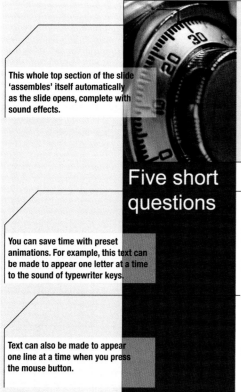

This whole top section of the slide 'assembles' itself automatically as the slide opens, complete with sound effects.

You can save time with preset animations. For example, this text can be made to appear one letter at a time to the sound of typewriter keys.

Text can also be made to appear one line at a time when you press the mouse button.

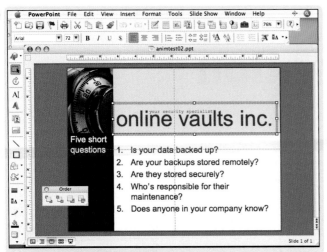

▲ **STEP 01 START AT THE END** It's tempting to try to assemble the finished slide one item at a time, animating as you go, but in fact it's much easier to start with the finished slide and work backwards. When all the objects are already in place, all that's left to do is work out how they get there and in what order.

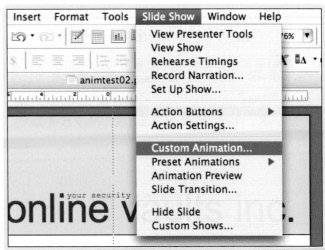

▲ **STEP 02 ANIMATIONS AND ACTIONS** We'll start by selecting the first object we want to appear on the slide – the close-up of the combination lock. The animation options can all be found on the Slide Show menu. You can use Preset Animations (we'll use one shortly) but for the moment we're going with the Custom Animation option.

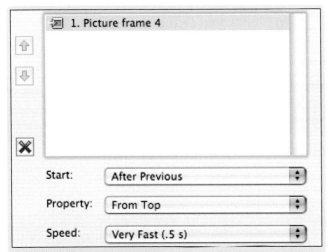

▲ **STEP 03 CHOOSE AN EFFECT** This opens the Custom Animation dialog. On the left is a list of the objects on the slide and below it is a small preview of the slide. Our photo (Picture Frame 4) is shown here as being selected. At the top right, we need to click the Add Effect button, then choose an Entrance effect from the list – we've gone for Fly In.

▲ **STEP 04 CHOOSE THE EFFECT SETTINGS** The animation effect is now added to the list on the right of the dialog, but we need to change its Start option. The default is On Click, but we want the animation to begin as soon as the slide is opened, so we change this to After Previous. We've also set the Fly In direction to From Top using the Property pop-up.

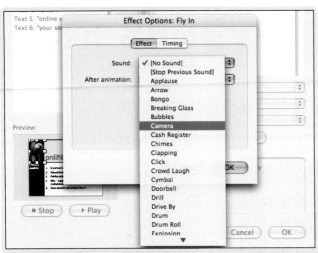

▲ **STEP 05 CHOOSE A SOUND EFFECT** The animation might look cool, but it's completely silent, which rather lessens the impact. You can add a sound to any animation by clicking the Effect Options button and choosing a sound from the pop-up. You'll need to try a few to find one that matches the duration of the animation – Camera works well here.

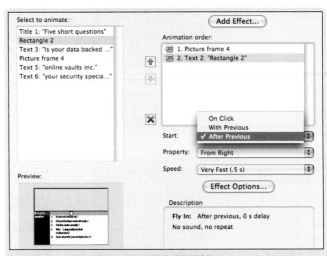

▲ **STEP 06 ANIMATING THE NEXT OBJECT** We want the blue-green box across the top of the slide to appear next, and it's the same procedure. Again, we've gone for the Fly In effect, and this time we've set the Property (direction) to From Right. We've also set the Start to After Previous so that it carries on automatically from the last animation.

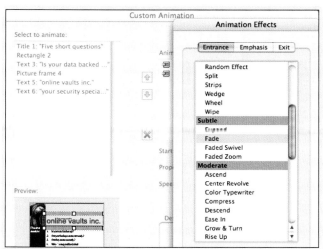

▲ STEP 07 **FADING IN THE TEXT** Next, we want the company name, Online Vaults inc, to fade in gently. It's good to introduce a little variety into your animations, but do stick to just two or three different styles and sound effects. It's like mixing fonts and colours in a design: one's not enough, two's good, but more than three is playing with fire.

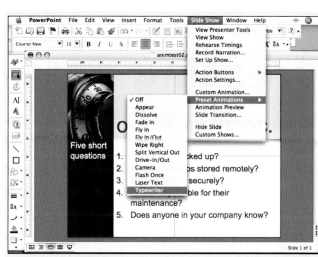

▲ STEP 08 **PRESET ANIMATIONS** Now we mentioned Preset Animations earlier, and here's a good opportunity to show them in action. Our company strapline is 'your security specialist', and we've used Courier, a 'typewriter' font, deliberately. PowerPoint's Typewriter preset makes the characters appear one by one to the sound of a typewriter.

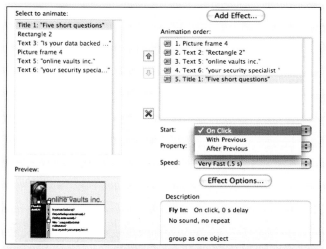

▲ STEP 09 **MANUAL CONTROL** That's the 'automatic' part of the slide taken care of. The elements assemble themselves neatly on the screen one after the other. Now, though, the presenter will want to control the pace of the presentation. The next item, the 'Five short questions' box, will Fly In from the bottom, but only On Click.

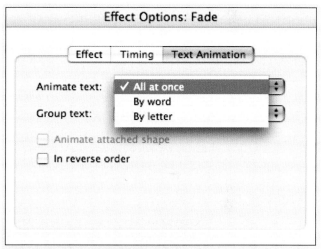

▲ STEP 10 **TEXT ANIMATION** Now for the box containing those questions. We want the questions to appear one at a time, so once we've chosen the animation effect (Fade) we need to click Effect Options and choose the Text Animation tab. What we don't want is for the text to appear a word or a letter at a time, so we set the Animate text pop-up to All at once.

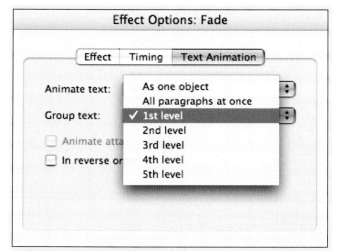

▲ STEP 11 **TEXT GROUPING** The Group text pop-up, directly below, controls how much text appears with each mouse click. If you're using one of the outline-style text boxes in PowerPoint's standard slide layouts, you'll see a list of heading levels – usually you'll want 1st level. If you've created a text box manually, 1st level will be the only choice.

▲ STEP 12 **THE FINISHED ANIMATION** That's it, we're done. The animations effects are listed in the window in the order we created them, but we can change that order by selecting any effect and using the up/down buttons to the left. All of the animation effects can be re-edited if necessary – it may take a few 'rehearsals' to produce a polished result.

MASTERCLASS
Creating a navigation bar in PowerPoint

How do you transform a tedious linear slideshow into an interactive multimedia resource? Well, a good place to start is to add a navbar.

Kit required Microsoft Office
Time 30 minutes
Goal Make navigation simpler in slideshows
Skill level Intermediate

PowerPoint presentations are designed for use by public speakers who talk and swap slides while the audience listens. This is fine for 'linear' presentations and, if necessary, the speaker can use the on-screen controls to backtrack to previous slides to revisit a particular point. However, this approach isn't much use when you want a presentation that users can work for themselves, and where they'll want 'random access' rather than a strictly linear tutorial.

What's needed is a 'navbar', a gadget that shows every slide in the presentation and lets you click on a button, or a thumbnail, to go straight to that slide. It's really quite easy to do, thanks to two key PowerPoint features. The first is the fact that you can add objects to every slide in the presentation by creating them on the Master slide. The second is that any object, even those on the Master, can be hyperlinked to a specific slide.

Our sample presentation offers tips on photographic composition, using six different photos, one for each slide. The navbar we create uses thumbnail versions of these photos, which we prepared in advance. And just to enhance it, we added a series of steps at the end that show how to animate slide objects so they appear one at a time rather than all at once. Although PowerPoint's pitched as a pretty dour business application, it's actually a half-decent multimedia authoring tool once you scratch beneath the surface.

INTERFACE

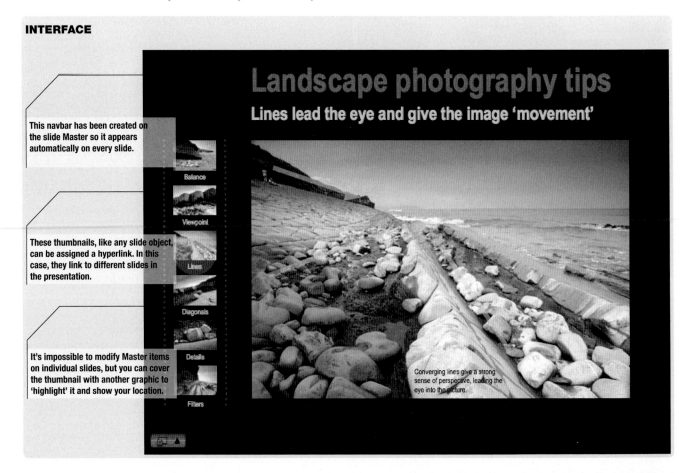

This navbar has been created on the slide Master so it appears automatically on every slide.

These thumbnails, like any slide object, can be assigned a hyperlink. In this case, they link to different slides in the presentation.

It's impossible to modify Master items on individual slides, but you can cover the thumbnail with another graphic to 'highlight' it and show your location.

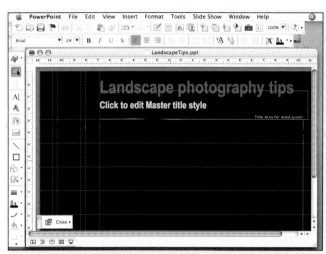

▲ **STEP 01 USING GUIDES ON THE MASTER SLIDE** We're going to create our navbar on the Master so it appears on every slide in the presentation. The navbar will be made up of six different thumbnails and titles arranged vertically, and we want to make sure they all line up. PowerPoint offers guides to help us. To create more guides, Alt-drag an existing one.

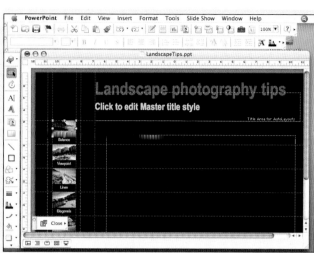

▲ **STEP 02 INSERTING THUMBNAILS** With the guides in place, it takes just a few moments to add thumbnail images (Insert > Picture > From file). We created a single text frame, and sized and positioned it below the first thumbnail, then duplicated for the others. The AutoLayout text boxes have already been repositioned at the top of the Master slide and restyled with our chosen fonts.

▲ **STEP 03 CLOSE THE MASTER** We can now Close the Master and start adding slides. This is easiest in Normal view, where we can click in the Outline pane, select anything already there and delete it. Next, in the Formatting palette, open the Add Objects section and click the Blank Slide icon. This adds a new, blank slide that shows only the items on the Master.

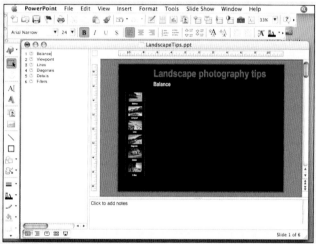

▲ **STEP 04 ADD THE SLIDE TITLES** In the Outline pane, we can start adding our slide titles. The Slide pane to the right shows the current background and all the slide titles we plan on adding. Once you've typed a title, press return to create a new slide. Keep typing in the titles, followed by return, until you have a slide for each thumbnail in the navbar.

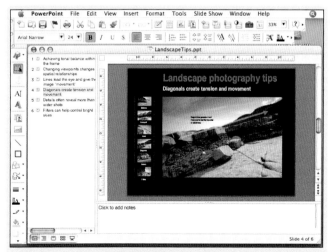

▲ **STEP 05 ADDING THE CONTENT** That's the basic structure of the presentation done. Now you can start modifying the content for each slide. We've started by extending the slide titles and, since this is a presentation about photography tips, we've added explanatory boxes and arrows. These can be left as they are or animated to appear in sequence.

▲ **STEP 06 RETURN TO THE MASTER SLIDE** Next, the whole point of a navbar, of course, is that it should provide push-button links to each slide. For this, we need to go back to the Master, where we click on the first thumbnail, and then open the Hyperlink section of the Formatting palette, open the On mouse click pop-up menu and choose Slide.

▲ **STEP 07 ADDING HYPERLINKS** The Hyperlink to Slide dialog shows not just the slide titles, but a thumbnail of each slide, making it easy to identify the right one. We simply go through each thumbnail in the navbar, linking it to the relevant slide. There's some redundancy, of course: if you click the thumbnail for a slide when you're already on that slide, it will simply re-open it.

▲ **STEP 08 TESTING THE PLAYBACK** Now is a good time to run the Slide Show to check it's behaving correctly and that every thumbnail links to the slide it's supposed to. There's no reason why you shouldn't add transitions for a little extra gloss, although that will slow down the navigation slightly, of course. Without transitions, PowerPoint displays new slides instantly.

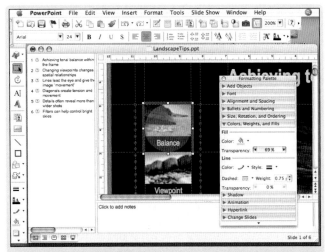

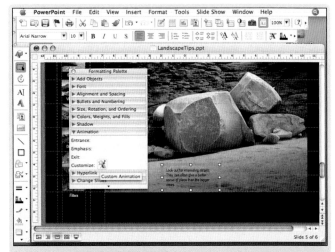

▲ **STEP 09 HIGHLIGHTING** From here on in, we're just going to add a little more polish to our presentation. The navigational structure is already complete. One flaw, though, is that the appearance of the thumbnail doesn't change to show you've clicked it. To get round this, we've created a semi-transparent circle that's simply placed over the relevant thumbnail on each slide.

▲ **STEP 10 ANIMATING OBJECTS** Next, we're going to animate the text and arrows used to explain the photographs on the slides. We want the text box to be invisible when the slide first opens, but to appear when we click the mouse. To do this, we need to open the Animation section in the Formatting palette and click Custom Animation.

▲ **STEP 11 MAKING TEXT 'APPEAR'** In the Custom Animation dialog, we click the Add Effect button at the top and choose Appear from the Animation Effects list. As the name suggests, this means the text box will simply appear when the user clicks the mouse button. There are plenty of other effects, but they're easily overdone and can become tiresome.

▲ **STEP 12 ADDING ARROWS** We can do the same with the arrows we've placed over some of the photographs to illustrate the compositional effects. When more than one object on a slide is animated, they appear as a list in the Custom Animation dialog so that it's possible to check the order in which objects appear. It's a very effective way to choreograph a number of objects.

MASTERCLASS
Using Hyperlinks in Keynote

Keynote isn't just for linear slideshows. With hyperlinks you can create interactive tutorials with non-linear navigation – quite apart from links to external websites.

Kit required iWork 08
Time 30 minutes
Goal Use hyperlinks for navigation in Keynote
Skill level Intermediate

Conventional Keynote presentations are all very well if you're standing at the front of the room and talking your audience through a set of arguments or points in a specific order. But there are times when you want to take a different approach. Maybe you want to use Keynote as an interactive learning aid for people to use on their own. Here, this conventional linear path isn't much use; your users will want to skip back and forth between topics to check things they didn't quite understand the first time around. Either that or jump past stuff that they know already to the things that really interest them. This is easy to do with hyperlinks. They disguise the linear nature of the slide show so that it behaves more like random-access multimedia.

Our workthrough's been kept simple just to demonstrate the basic principles but they'll also work with much more elaborate projects. In particular, Keynote's support for multiple Master slides means that you can create different sections within the presentation, each with its own navigational controls and layouts. For example, we could expand the presentation we've created here to include slides containing sample photos, together with a return button to get us back to the slide we were looking at. Hyperlinks are a very simple tool, with a great deal of potential. We used the instant alpha tool to produce the camera cutouts on our slides. For something so quick and simple, it's startlingly effective.

INTERFACE

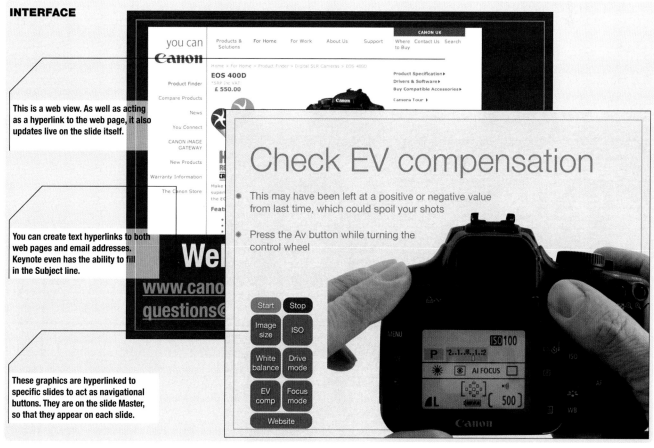

This is a web view. As well as acting as a hyperlink to the web page, it also updates live on the slide itself.

You can create text hyperlinks to both web pages and email addresses. Keynote even has the ability to fill in the Subject line.

These graphics are hyperlinked to specific slides to act as navigational buttons. They are on the slide Master, so that they appear on each slide.

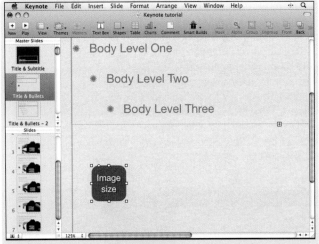

▲ **STEP 01 START WITH YOUR SLIDES** Our Keynote presentation is already complete as far as the content is concerned. It has an intro slide and six more that give specific information about camera settings. These are visible in the Navigator pane on the left of the screen. We need all the slides in place before we can start on the navigational hyperlinks.

▲ **STEP 02 EDITING MASTER SLIDES** There's no point in creating navigational buttons on every slide when we can simply create a single set on the slide Master. You can display Master slides using the View > Show Master Slides command. Our six main slides share the same Title & Bullets layout selected here for editing in the main window.

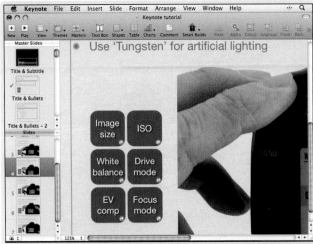

▲ **STEP 03 ADDING A BUTTON** We create our first button by choosing the round-cornered rectangle from the Shapes pop-up. These default to the current design theme's colours, though you can use the Inspector to change the colour if you want to. To add text to a graphic, just double-click and start typing, changing the text size if necessary.

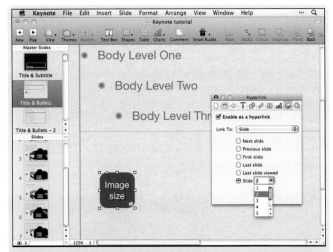

▲ **STEP 04 ASSIGNING A HYPERLINK** Any object you create in this way can be turned into a navigational button. Just select the object, open the Inspector (if it's not visible already) and select the Hyperlink tab second from the right. Check the Enable as a hyperlink box, select Slide from the pop-up Link To menu and choose the number of the slide you want to link to.

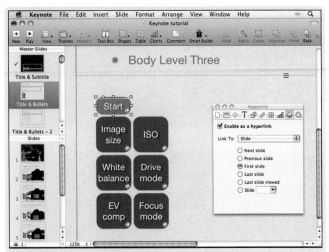

▲ **STEP 05 ADDING THE REMAINING BUTTONS** Here we've created buttons for all six slides, linking each one individually to the relevant slide. Remember that all this is being done on the slide Master, so the buttons will appear on every slide that uses it as long as you don't cover them up with anything (slide content will always overlay Master objects).

▲ **STEP 06 START BUTTON** We've added a green Start button at this point. This takes users right back to the first slide in the presentation in case they need to start again. We've linked to a Slide, using the pop-up menu in the Inspector but here we don't need its number – we just need to click the First slide radio button. You can also choose the Next, Previous and Last slides.

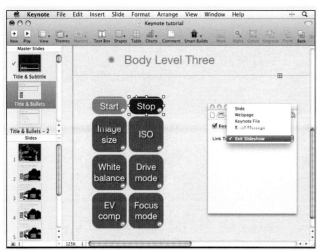

▲ STEP 07 **STOP BUTTON** This red Stop button exits the presentation. It's another one of the possible Hyperlink actions available in the Inspector. As you'll see from the list you can also link to other Keynote files, web pages and email addresses. We'll take a look at these last two options when we create a final links slide at the end of the presentation.

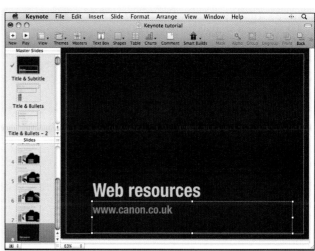

▲ STEP 08 **A FINAL SLIDE FOR LINKS** Here's our final slide. We've used a different slide Master for this because we don't want the navigational buttons appearing here. We've put the main heading low down on the page to make room for a graphic that we're adding shortly. Underneath, there's a URL that users should click on to visit a web page where they can find out more.

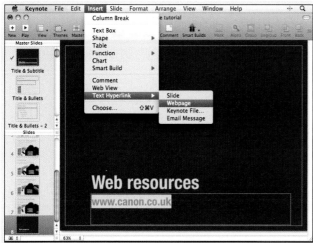

▲ STEP 09 **ADDING A TEXT HYPERLINK** Text hyperlinks are really straightforward. Just select the text and choose the Insert > Text Hyperlink > Webpage command. If the text itself is a URL, it will appear in the Inspector as the page that the hyperlink points to, so you don't need to do any more. If it isn't, you'll need to type the URL into the Inspector manually.

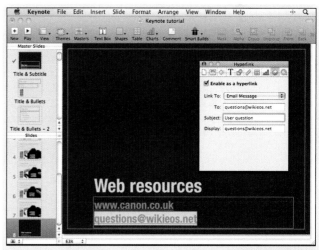

▲ STEP 10 **INSERTING AN EMAIL HYPERLINK** Email hyperlinks are just as easy. Here, you choose Insert > Text Hyperlink > Email message instead. Again if the text is already formatted as an email address, it will appear automatically in the Inspector. You'll notice here though that there's a Subject field – this automatically fills in the subject line in the email message.

▲ STEP 11 **ADDING A WEB VIEW** Now for one of Keynote's cleverer options. We would like to illustrate this final page with the web page that it links to and we can do this easily enough by opening it up in Safari, then dragging the page icon from the address bar on to the Keynote slide. This doesn't produce a static screen shot of the web page – it's a live web view.

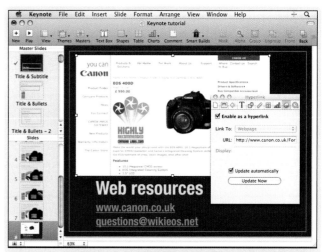

▲ STEP 12 **WEB VIEW PROPERTIES** You can click on these web view objects to adjust their properties in the Hyperlink Inspector. By default the web view acts as a hyperlink – clicking it opens that page in Safari (or whatever web browser you use). But there's also an Update automatically option. With this enabled, the page is updated whenever the presentation is viewed.

MASTERCLASS
Unscrambling a file that won't open

Occasionally, email attachments or web downloads arrive as unrecognised or incorrectly typed files. Accessing their contents needn't be complex.

Kit required TextEdit, StuffIt Expander (*bit.ly/Elt4F*), HexEdit (*bit.ly/3DreUz*), GraphicConverter (€29.95 from *bit.ly/102P02*), RCDefaultApp (*bit.ly/3o7dy*)
Time 20 minutes
Goal Opening a file that won't open in its intended application
Skill level Intermediate

Most of the time, email client applications and Mac OS X correctly identify the types of downloaded files, which means you can quickly process and open them. Sometimes, however, vital information is missing or incorrect, and you end up stuck with a file – most commonly an image – and don't know how to access it.

File types are recognised by a strict hierarchy of different information, including the filename extension, such as .jpg or .jpeg for Jpeg images, and .dmg for disk images to install applications and updates. This may have become removed, or could be incorrect. Sometimes, for example, files that have been compressed using GNU Zip are incorrectly labelled .zip instead of .gzip, which means they're not recognised.

It helps to know your way around different filename extensions. Email attachments and some downloads may be compressed into an archive using 'tar' (which has the .tar extension) and GNU Zip (both .gz and .gzip extensions), then encoded using BinHex (.hqx). Image files are commonly Jpeg (with .jpg or .jpeg), PNG (with .png), or Tiff (ending .tif or .tiff), but could be any of dozens of other formats with their own distinctive extensions, most of which are listed at dotwhat.net.

You can always change the application that opens a given document using the Finder's Get Info dialog box, but it's usually quicker and simpler to work directly with the file, changing its extension or using a conversion tool to eventually unscramble it and open it up.

INTERFACE

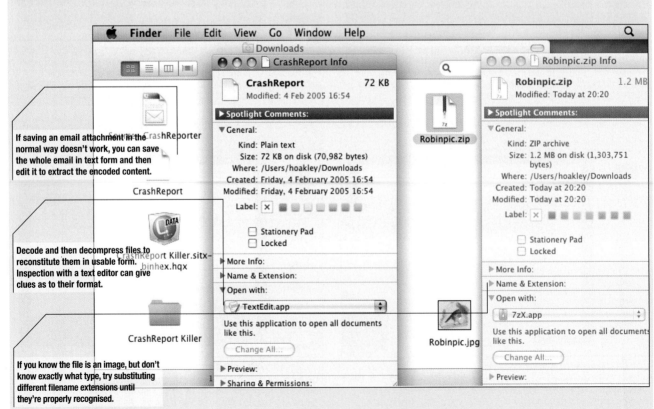

If saving an email attachment in the normal way doesn't work, you can save the whole email in text form and then edit it to extract the encoded content.

Decode and then decompress files to reconstitute them in usable form. Inspection with a text editor can give clues as to their format.

If you know the file is an image, but don't know exactly what type, try substituting different filename extensions until they're properly recognised.

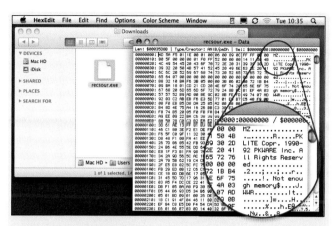

▲ **STEP 02 SAVE AND OPEN** Before trying to unscramble an attached or downloaded file, save it to its own folder, and save a copy. Next, try double-clicking the file in the Finder to see which default application opens it. Here, a Windows executable has been opened in a hex file editor, revealing that it was probably compressed using PKZip for Windows.

▲ **STEP 02 TRY CHANGING EXTENSION** To change the default application that tries to open a download, add or alter the filename extension. In most cases, there's a limited range of likely extensions. In the case of images received via email, the chances are that it's a Jpeg or Photoshop file, so change its extension to .jpg or .psd, then double-click on the file again.

▲ **STEP 03 PREVIEW AND QUICKLOOK** Recent versions of Mac OS X have better file preview capabilities. Leopard should display a preview of the contents of most image files in the right-most pane of the Finder. Images, movies and similar files that don't reveal a good preview are probably of a different type, so try a different extension.

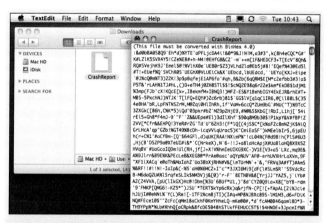

▲ **STEP 04 OPEN THE FILE IN TEXT EDITOR** If you're still struggling to identify the file type, open the file using a text editor such as TextEdit. You may see obvious clues as to the file's format. For instance, the first line of BinHex files reveals their type in plain English: either give it an .hqx extension or try running it through a decoder such as StuffIt Expander.

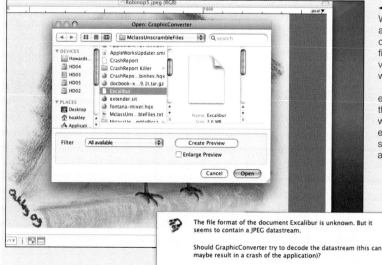

◀ **STEP 05 LET AN APP'S BUILT-IN CONVERTER GUESS** When you know or suspect that the file contains graphics, a movie, audio, or similar, try opening it from within an appropriate editor/converter application. The application may be able to recognise the file format from the contents. For instance, although Preview isn't very good at this, GraphicConverter can often detect the file type when you try to open an image file.

Opening a file blind to its type can overstress even the best editor/converter. GraphicConverter will work out its best guess from the content, then it'll present you with this information and ask whether you want it to try decoding the file. Before you do this, ensure that all work – in it and other applications – is saved and stable, because decoding unknown files can sometimes crash the application and may rarely result in a kernel panic.

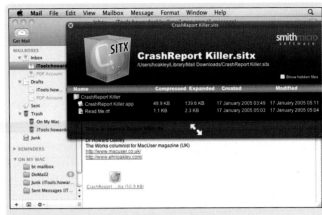

▲ STEP 06 **LOOK FOR OTHER CLUES** If GraphicConverter doesn't recognise the file format, the start of the file will be displayed as hexadecimal values and as text. This may give further clues as to the nature of the image. Click on the Try Raw Import button to give that feature a shot. Otherwise, return to your mail or browser to try to extract and convert the attachment.

▲ STEP 07 **IN-APPLICATION PREVIEWS USING QUICKLOOK** Mail version 3.5 (which comes with Leopard) supports QuickLook, which provides even better previews. Click on the QuickLook button on the line listing the attachment, and a floating semi-opaque window gives details of the file's contents. This feature can be extended by many applications.

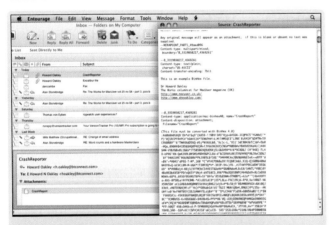

▲ STEP 08 **SAVE AS TEXT (ENTOURAGE)** Image files that are still encoded and/or compressed will prove impossible to open in Preview and GraphicConverter. Open the message that included the file and view its source. In Microsoft Entourage, use the Source command in the Message menu, or its equivalent in other applications, then save this source as a text file.

▲ STEP 09 **SAVE AS TEXT (MAIL)** To view the complete source of an email in recent versions of Mail, choose View > Message > Raw Source and the email's header will be expanded. To save the whole email to a text file, choose File > Save As > Raw Message Source. This creates a .eml file that contains plain text, so it can be read by a text editor.

▲ STEP 10 **CONVERT TO DECODABLE TEXT** Open the source in a text editor (here, BinHex, left, and Base64, right). Chop off the top and foot to leave the encoded content, and choose File > Save As and save to a new file in plain text format to retain the original copy of the email. You can now decode and decompress the source using StuffIt Expander or similar.

▲ STEP 11 **SET DEFAULT APPLICATIONS** If you have repeated problems with recognising downloads, change the way the system handles the file type using RCDefaultApp, which adds a new pane to System Preferences that gives you access to all the Mime types you may encounter. Select the file type, check it covers the right extensions, then set your chosen default application.

MASTERCLASS
Protect your portable USB drive from prying eyes

If you lose your USB drive or have it stolen then anyone can access the files on it. We show you how to encrypt the whole drive.

Kit required Disk Utility, TrueCrypt
Time 30 minutes
Goal Using TrueCrypt to protect files on your USB flash drive
Skill level Intermediate

Storing files on an online storage is handy, but USB flash drives are still popular. Modern offerings have huge capacities and they're more convenient than repeatedly uploading and downloading at different locations, and that's assuming that you even have Internet access to retrieve a file.

The convenience of flash drives is, however, dented by their lack of security. Some are incredibly small and are easily lost if they fall out of your pocket or bag, or if you leave them lying on a desk at work.

The trouble is that anyone can read their contents. Even if you know how to create a disk image that's encrypted and protected with a password, that file will still appear in the Finder and alert an intruder to the fact you have something valuable that you want to hide. TrueCrypt (*truecrypt.org*) is a free and open source tool, and it doesn't matter if you need to work on a PC or share files with a PC user at another location, as it's also available for Windows and Linux. Like the Disk Utility that Apple provides with Mac OS X, it's able to protect disk images, but it goes one better with the ability to encrypt entire drives.

It also allows you to create one area to contain files that aren't sensitive, or for others to use when sharing files, and another hidden area for your most sensitive documents. Powerful as it is, TrueCrypt doesn't have the prettiest interface, but it's worth persevering if you need to keep unwanted visitors away from your documents.

INTERFACE

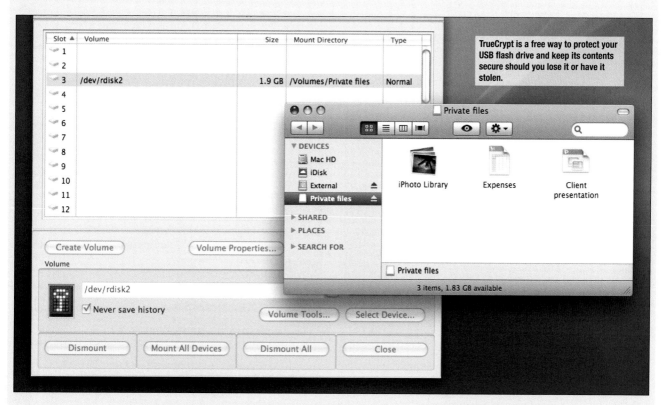

TrueCrypt is a free way to protect your USB flash drive and keep its contents secure should you lose it or have it stolen.

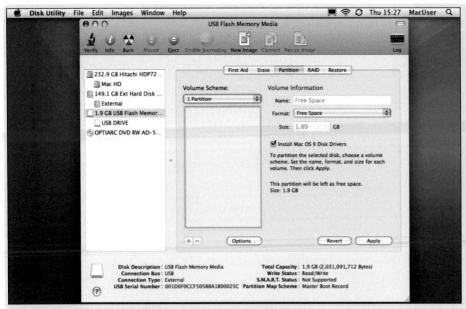

◀ **STEP 01 PREPARE YOUR FLASH DRIVE** TrueCrypt will complain if your flash drive contains any data, even if that means empty volumes. Back up any important files on your drive, then open Apple's Disk Utility and choose the drive in the left pane. Click on the Partition tab and set the volume scheme to contain a single partition. It defaults to a Mac format, but change this so that it says Free Space. Now click on the Options button and set the partition scheme to GUID or Master Boot Record; when we used Apple Partition Map, Disk Utility created an invisible volume that TrueCrypt will refuse to replace. Go back to the main window, press Apply and wait a few seconds for the drive to be wiped.

▲ **STEP 02 INSTALL TRUECRYPT** There are separate versions of TrueCrypt for Tiger and Leopard, so make sure that you've downloaded the correct one before installing it. Open TrueCrypt and it'll show a list of empty slots to mount encrypted files and volumes. Unlike double-clicking Apple disk images, you'll have to open TrueCrypt to access its files.

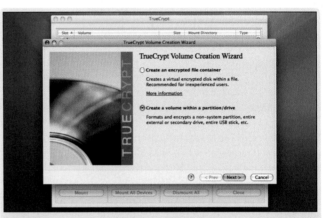

▲ **STEP 03 CREATE A VOLUME** With your USB flash drive connected, click on the Create Volume button beneath the list of slots and the Volume Creation Wizard will appear. The first question asks whether you want to create a disk image or file, or encrypt a whole drive. We're going to encrypt a whole drive, so choose the second option.

▲ **STEP 04 MAKE IT A HIDDEN VOLUME** When asked which type of volume to create, choose a hidden volume. This creates two volumes: an outer volume that you can use to fool someone if they guess or force you to divulge your password and, inside it, a hidden volume that isn't visible in the Finder. It's here you'll place your most sensitive files.

▲ **STEP 05 CHOOSE THE DRIVE TO ENCRYPT** Press Select Device and enter your administrator password. If the drive's capacity doesn't single it out, cross reference it in Disk Utility. Here, select the drive in the left-hand pane and click the Info button. The Disk Identifier's number matches the one shown in TrueCrypt, so disk1 is the same as /dev/rdisk1 in TrueCrypt.

▲ **STEP 06 CHOOSE AN ENCRYPTION METHOD** You can choose from several encryption and hash algorithms to encrypt your files. We've chosen AES, the same one used by Apple's Disk Utility, and TrueCrypt provides descriptions of the other seven that are available. For the hash algorithm, three are available. We've stuck with the default of RIPEMD-160.

▲ **STEP 07 CREATE AND PROTECT THE OUTER VOLUME** TrueCrypt prefers passwords of at least 20 characters. Don't use names of people, places or words from a dictionary. Use a cryptic format that's difficult to guess but means something to you, and make sure it contains a mix of numbers, letters and special characters – the # sign (Alt-3) is a good choice.

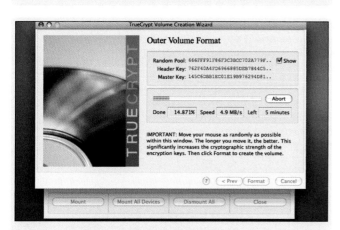

▲ **STEP 08 GENERATE RANDOM ENCRYPTION KEYS** As well as a password to authenticate access to files, you need to generate encryption keys. At the next step, move your mouse around the window and, in your own time, click Format to start creating a volume that's protected and encrypted using the details you just entered. This will take a few minutes.

▲ **STEP 09 CREATE AND PROTECT THE HIDDEN VOLUME** The inner volume is protected with its own details. When you choose which algorithms to use, they can differ from the ones chosen earlier. Set the size of the hidden volume, which is limited by the size of the outer volume. Leave enough space to hold some files that look like real work, but whose contents aren't sensitive.

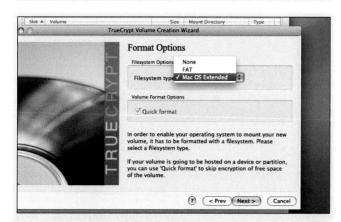

▲ **STEP 10 FORMAT THE HIDDEN VOLUME** The hidden volume needs its own password. The same advice on password strength applies as sensitive files will be stored here. When asked what format to use, stick with Fat to work on Macs and PCs, otherwise change it to Mac OS Extended. The final step once again requires mouse movement to generate random keys.

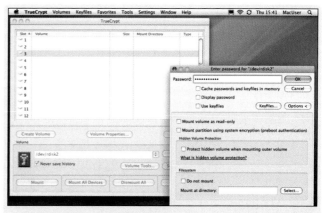

▲ **STEP 11 MOUNTING A VOLUME** The volumes won't appear in Disk Utility as their format is unrecognised. The drive can be erased but your files are obscured. Click an empty slot and press Select Device to mount a volume, and enter one of the passwords. Only one volume can be mounted at a time, so click Dismount then Mount to access the other.

MASTERCLASS
Creating cool photo cubes

Photocubes are a fun and different way to display your photos, so work your way through this tutorial and you'll be well on your way to getting all squared up.

Kit required iWork
Time No more than 20 minutes
Goal To understand image placeholders, and create customisable photo cubes
Skill level Beginner

One of the very handy but often overlooked features of the two applications in the iWork suite is the ability to drop pictures from your media libraries into predefined drop zones. Professional designers have been doing this for years – indeed, QuarkXPress and InDesign ostensibly insist on a target frame being drawn on the page into which you drop your graphic – but it's something that's new to the consumer end of the market.

Perhaps unknowingly, you've used this feature already, as any time you open a template in Pages or Keynote, and replace a placeholder photo with one of your own, you're using these drop zones. They're easy to define yourself, and by way of illustrating this, we'll show you how to create a template for a photo cube. Simply put, this is nothing more than a cube with a photo on each side, but they're very satisfying objects, and could be used for everything from a novel way to send pictures to friends and relatives, to a promotional unit, or even an oversized, personalised die if you feel like it.

You can expand on the principles outlined here to create complex layouts in Pages without having to resort to the pre-defined templates. You can also use the same techniques in high-end professional desktop publishing applications, making Pages the ideal first step for the budding designer.

INTERFACE

▼ Photo cubes are a cool and funky way to present your photos. Send them to friends and family, or create your own promotional material.

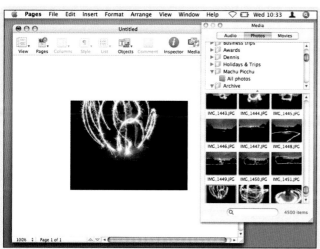

▲ STEP 01 **PLACE GRAPHIC** Launch Pages, and create a new, blank document. Click towards the edge of the page so that when you import a graphic, it will be placed as a floating graphic rather than inline as part of a block of text. The easiest way to insert images is from your iPhoto Library – just use the Media palette and drag a photo onto the page.

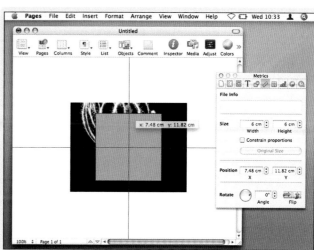

▲ STEP 02 **DRAW MASKING SHAPE** Now draw a square onto the page, accessible from the Objects menu in the toolbar. There's no need to alter the default fill and stroke colours or styles, as we'll simply be using this as a mask. Use the Metrics tab of the Inspector palette to alter the size – we're using a 6 x 6cm square in this example – and centre it on the page.

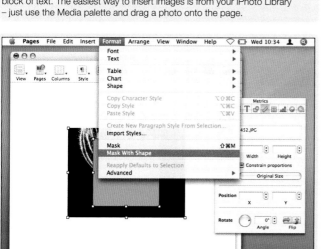

▲ STEP 03 **MASK GRAPHIC WITH SHAPE** With both the placed picture and the drawn shape selected, choose Format > Mask With Shape. You'll see that the image is now cropped within the boundaries of the drawn shape. This applies to any shape drawn within the iWork suite's applications, obviously, but it's the basic rectangle that matters to us for this Masterclass.

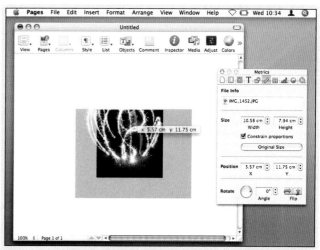

▲ STEP 04 **POSITION GRAPHIC WITHIN MASK** You may find that the image doesn't fit perfectly within the mask, but this is easily resolved. Simply double-click the image, and the original image that's being cropped will appear as a ghosted image. Resize, rotate, and move this image however you like; just click outside the graphic to confirm your changes.

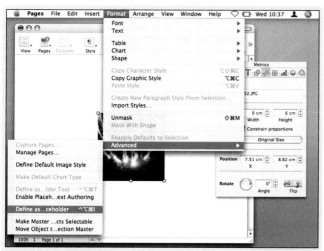

▲ STEP 05 **DEFINE OBJECT PLACEHOLDER** We want to make this template easily reusable, so select your masked graphic, and pick Format > Advanced > Define as Image Placeholder. Also, any rotations or effects applied with the Adjust palette are tied to the masking square, not to the graphic in that mask; drop in a fresh graphic, and the same effects will be applied.

▲ STEP 06 **FINISH AND SAVE AS TEMPLATE** Duplicate the square six times into a crucifix shape – using the Metrics palette to position pictures exactly – and, if desired, add tabs to show people where to have the cubes fasten up. Once you're happy with the design, choose File > Save as Template, which you can then share with friends, colleagues and magazine readers.

MASTERCLASS
Automatically resize images

If you're uploading a lot of images to a website and you need to change their dimensions then it can be a boring and repetitive job. Using the power of Preview and Automator can simplify and speed up the task.

Kit required Mac OS X 10.4 Tiger or later
Time 10 minutes
Goal To set-up a simple batch process tool
Skill level Beginner

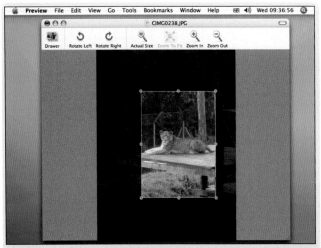

▲ **STEP 01 PREVIEW'S HIDDEN TOOLS** If you look at images in preview you'd be forgiven for thinking that it's nothing more than a fast tool for opening images and not much else. In fact, you can crop your images simply by clicking and dragging and saving a new image. If you want to resize your images, though, you have to be a bit tricky.

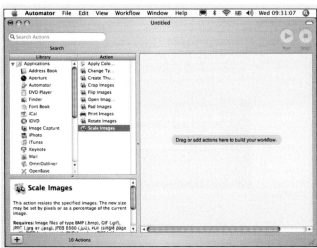

▲ **STEP 02 UNLOCK THE HIDDEN FEATURES OF PREVIEW** To get to some of the more interesting features of Preview you need to use Automator. Open the application and click on the Preview option in the Library pane. This reveals the options for Preview in the Action pane. Drag the Scale Images action to the workflow section.

▲ **STEP 03 SET THE SCALE** Once you've created your basic workflow, you can choose how to scale your images. You can select the exact pixel dimensions or just a percentage. If you want an exact percentage then click in the box and enter it. You can also use the arrows to give increments of 5% for each click.

▲ **STEP 04 SAVE THE ACTION** Choose Save As from the File menu, name your workflow and change the File Format drop-down menu to Application. Now all you have to do is drag and drop your images on to the application icon and they will be batch processed in seconds. And that's it – you've created a really fast tool that will save you lots of time resizing images.

THE ULTIMATE GUIDE TO GRAPHIC Design

£8.99

OVER 190 PAGES of help, advice, workshops, hints and tips to help you become a better designer.

- Killer Photoshop tips
- Smarter page layouts
- Jargon demystified
- Create maps with meaning
- Turn your photos into drawings
- Make stunning mono prints
- And much, much more...

OVER 190 PAGES!

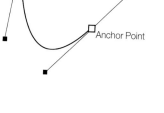

ISBN 1-906372-77-2

ON SALE NOW
To order direct call 0844 844 0053 or visit www.magbooks.com (Free P&P on all UK orders)

On sale now at: WHSmith BORDERS amazon.co.uk

ONLY £8.99

15 steps to better photos

Are your photos not living up to your memories? Well, with a few subtle adjustments in either iPhoto or Photoshop, you can really liven up lacklustre snaps.

It's 180 years since Nicéphore Niépce made the first photographic image; it was exposed onto a pewter plate covered with bitumen of Judea, a petroleum derivative. Until the advent of digital photography, anyone who wanted to improve their photos had to be more chemist than creative, but with software such as Photoshop and iPhoto, it's easy to turn lacklustre snaps into miniature works of art.

That's what we're here to help you do. Over the next five pages, you'll learn how to restore colour to faded photographs, produce stunning black-and-white images that leave the bland results of a quick Desaturate in Photoshop in the dust, create blemish-free skin and much more.

And the best bit is that you don't have to splash out on Photoshop to follow along. This flagship application of Adobe's may give you the most control and best results – and we'll be showing you how to best harness its power – but we'll also show you how to do the same task in iPhoto, which offers surprisingly sophisticated editing abilities, too.

What's more, it comes free on new Macs, so many of us can use the techniques described in this feature effectively without spending a penny.

Much of what makes a good photograph, though, happens before you press the shutter, not once you've imported it into an editing suite, so we'll also be showcasing essential tips to help you take good, novel, interesting and relevant photographs.

Put it all together, and you have *MacUser's* essential guide to getting the very best photographs possible. No longer will you have to worry about boring your friends and family with holiday snaps, or taking precious memories that don't capture the moment as well as you could.

TASK

Convert to monochrome

Many pictures can look much better in black and white. This is partly because we perceive differences in light and dark more readily than differences in colour, and partly because most colour photos actually display a narrow gamut of tonal variation. Converting to monochrome can make pictures dramatic and gives portraits an elegance that's difficult to achieve in any other way.

HOW TO IN iPHOTO

The first step is to convert your picture to greyscale, so bring up the Effects palette and click B&W, or click B&W in the toolbar at the bottom. The result looks insipid, so, if you're using iPhoto 6, click Boost Color. In either iPhoto 5 or 6, next drag the sliders in the Adjust palette to roughly match those shown here. You will need to tinker to suit, and you could try making the picture even more dramatic by dragging the left-most slider towards the right on the Levels control; avoid moving to more than 25%. In iPhoto 4, you're limited to brightness and contrast controls; move the former slightly leftwards and the latter a little to the right to punch up converted-to-greyscale images.

Cropping

We'd always encourage you to frame a picture properly before pressing the shutter. Occasionally, though, you may need to change format or alter the focus of the shot, or you may decide that your original framing was off, in which case, you can re-frame digitally. Remember that detail will be lost, and, particularly with compact cameras, you may not have enough pixels to allow you to crop in very far while retaining enough resolution to print successfully.

HOW TO IN iPHOTO

If you want to keep your picture constrained to the dimensions of normal photographic paper, pick one from the Constrain list; snaps are usually 4 x 6in. iPhoto will automatically select the maximum area to fit onto the chosen paper size; the proportions of many digital shots are different from those of traditional photographic paper. Move your cursor inside the selected area to move it around, or drag in the corners to change the size. By default, iPhoto will assume you want to keep the orientation the same, but an option at the bottom of the Constrain menu enables you to change the orientation for cropping. When you're happy, click Crop.

Correcting red-eye

Red-eye is caused by the camera's flash reflecting off the retinas of the photo's subjects, and is at its worst when the flash is positioned close to the lens. Many cameras now have a red-eye reduction feature that fires a pre-flash to contract the subjects' pupils, but even so you might find that some of your evening and night shots seem to be populated by demons.

HOW TO IN iPHOTO

In theory, this is very simple: just load up the photograph, click the Red-Eye tool and click in the centre of the affected eyes; in many cases, your job will be done. It's not perfect, however, especially where the pupils are small, either because the shot is relatively low resolution, or because the faces only take up a small area of the photo. In this case, if you have iPhoto 5 or 6, you can use an undocumented hack to dot out the red-eye manually. Select the Red-Eye tool, hold down Control and Caps Lock, and then tap 9 then Tab. Adjust the size of the eye-shaped target with the square bracket keys on your keyboard, then click on the pupil to correct.

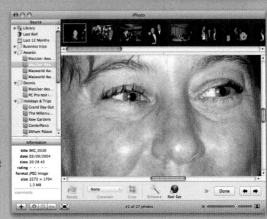

HOW TO IN PHOTOSHOP

This method is quite labour-intensive, so if you just want a quick-and-dirty mono conversion, convert your working colour space to Lab (Image > Mode > Lab Color) and choose Image > Adjustments > Desaturate. The results are much punchier than the insipid Desaturate command when in RGB. You can then convert back to RGB (or CMYK) for further work.

To do it right, convert your colour image to Lab and select the Lightness channel from the Channels palette. Now switch the Mode to Greyscale, which will use the information from the lightness channel to build the mono image. Command-click on the new Grey channel to select it, and then invert the selection. Create a new fill layer (Layer > New Fill Layer > Solid Color) filled with solid black, and adjust the opacity of the fill layer to tinker with the strength of this 'punching up'. You may also want to add another adjustments layer to control curves or levels, perhaps to control greyscale performance in shadows or highlights.

You can also 'crisp up' contrast to give your images a gallery feel. Duplicate the background by dragging it to the new layer icon at the bottom of the palette, and run the High Pass filter with a radius of about 10 for a 7-megapixel image. Change this layer's blend mode to Hard Light, and, again, adjust the opacity of the layer to change the strength of the effect.

Adding warmth to a pure monochrome image can make it look a little more human. You could either convert the colour space to duo-, tri- or even quadtone to achieve this, or you could simply convert to RGB and add a Photo Filter adjustment layer with one of the warming filters set to around 15%.

HOW TO IN PHOTOSHOP

Open the image and choose the regular rectangular marquee tool. If you just want to crop to your own proportions, simply select the area you want to crop and choose Image > Crop. To keep pictures cropped to aspect ratios of standard photo paper, simply change the framing style from Normal to Fixed Aspect Ratio, and enter the basic size of the paper onto which you want to print. Units are irrelevant, so you could enter 4 and 6 or 10 and 15 (inches and centimetres respectively, as it happens) for normal photographic paper. Once that's done, select the area you want to keep and choose Image > Crop. Enter the relevant dimensions in Image > Image Size.

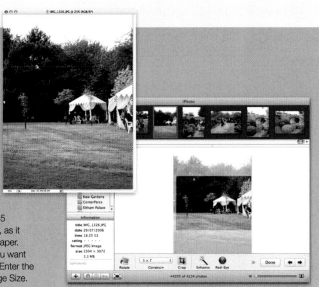

FRAMING TIPS

When framing your shots, you want to try to create the right balance of tension and harmony. Don't go too far either way – a portrait shot with the head in the exact centre of the frame is harmonious, but dull. Cropping off parts of the face introduces plenty of tension, but destroys the purpose of the piece.

Never position the horizon of a photograph exactly in the centre of the frame – you'll get a much more interesting image if you frame your shots so the horizon is around a third of the way up from the bottom of the picture. Many people rely on the idea of the golden ratio to help with framing; you can use the illustration at http://en.wikipedia.org/wiki/golden_ratio to get an idea of where you could focus a shot.

HOW TO IN PHOTOSHOP

If you have Photoshop CS2 or CS3, you do have a dedicated red-eye removal tool at your disposal. It's a bit hidden away – look in the fly-out tool menu for the Healing brush – but select it and you'll get a set of cross-hairs for clicking in the centre of the pupils. The default size usually works well for most photos, but the default 50% darken is a little strong and looks artificial in most snaps. Try reducing it to around 30%. If you want more control, though, or you don't have CS2 or CS3, you'll need the techniques described below.

Open your image and create a new layer. Switch the bend mode from Normal to Saturation, and select a brush that's a little smaller than the pupil you want to correct and just a little soft. Either use the eye-dropper tool to pick up a colour from the iris, or just stick with plain black, and begin to paint over the pupils. Remember that they're rarely perfectly circular, so avoid the temptation simply to dot a single spot of colour on top of the red-eye. Instead, gradually build up the shape of the correcting mask. Once you're done you can flatten the layers back down, and if you need to darken the pupils, a little subtle work with the Burn tool should see you right.

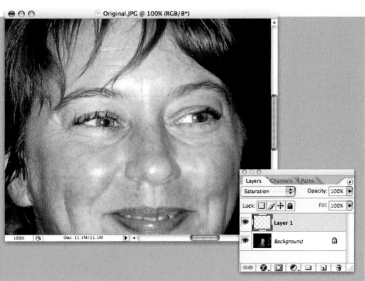

| TASK | HOW TO IN iPHOTO |

Refreshing old photos

Old, faded photographs do have a charm all of their own, but sometimes you want to restore them to something of their former glory. The techniques we'll discuss here are really only concerned with correcting the colours, not repairing damage – some of the techniques discussed in the Blemish-free skin section would apply here. The trick to this is to spot what colour shifts have taken place and compensate for them.

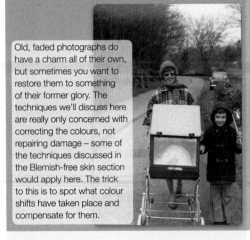

Most faded photos have a warm, orange cast. Correct this by dragging the Temperature slider towards the blue – not too much, but just enough to neutralise the colours. You may find you need to tint the picture with a little green. Most old photos benefit from quite drastic sharpening, so don't be afraid to really turn it up. Be very sparing with contrast increases – you may find that clipping in the dark slider for the Levels control does a better job.

With monochrome images, convert to greyscale, drag the Temperature and Tint sliders to the left, drag exposure to about -40, and bump up the contrast slightly.

Punch it up

It doesn't take much to spruce up humble holiday snaps, and these techniques simply add a little punch to your photos. Whether you've shot landscapes or people, a few seconds spent on each image can pay dividends. They can add drama to the most unassuming shot, but use them with care and print to check that the results aren't too extreme, especially if your system isn't colour calibrated.

HOW TO IN iPHOTO

The first step is normally to increase saturation – not too much unless you're deliberately going for a cartoonish finish. Next, try adjusting the Temperature slider: many landscapes benefit from a little warming up, so drag the slider to the right. A little sharpening doesn't usually go amiss here, either. Overexposing the picture a little often works wonders, and clipping the levels slightly at both ends can add contrast more effectively than the Contrast slider.

Blemish-free skin

One of the unpleasant side-effects of taking photos late at night is that people are often a bit sweaty or make-up has smudged, and the use of flash makes these problems worse. iPhoto's controls are a little coarse, but they do offer a way of removing the shine, and we'll show you a hack for iPhoto 5 and 6 to improve their Retouch controls. Photoshop offers finer controls, and we'll show you how to use a simple but effective technique.

HOW TO IN iPHOTO

If you're using iPhoto 4, click the Retouch tool and dab away at the shiny highlights to 'matte them out'. If you have iPhoto 5 or later, select the Retouch tool, hold down Control and Caps Lock, and then tap 9. Press Tab and you'll get a dotted circle with a figure below. Use the square brackets keys to adjust the size of this circle, and the curly brackets (Shift-square brackets) to adjust the strength of the effect. A large-diameter circle with low strength (about 0.25) works well for de-shining; use multiple clicks, dotted around the affected area.

HOW TO IN PHOTOSHOP

To improve photos, you usually have to do three things: remove a colour cast, increase the saturation and restore some contrast. We'll do all three using adjustment layers, so you don't destroy any detail from the original, and can tinker with all the settings at every step along the way. First, we'll deal with the colour cast, so from the control at the bottom of the layers palette (which looks like a black-and-white circle) pick Color Balance. You'll probably have to drag the top slider towards cyan, and the bottom slider towards blue, but adjust to suit your picture. Keep looking away from and back to your screen, as you can get 'colour fatigue' during this process, which clouds your judgement.

Next add a Hue/Saturation adjustment layer and bump up the saturation – a value between 25 and 35 is a good starting place. Now comes the magic – it doesn't make much sense, but your next step should be to add a new Curves adjustment layer; however, don't alter the curve. Instead, simply change the blend mode to Soft Light (or Overlay or Hard Light – experiment to find the one that works best) and adjust the opacity of the layer to alter the strength of the effect. You may at this stage have to make some adjustments to previous layers to ensure the best mix, and grouping all three will allow you easily to show and hide your total adjustments to suit. Remember that these are layer masks, so you can paint onto the mask to have each effect apply only to certain areas, and you can always create more than one of each adjustment mask.

HOW TO IN PHOTOSHOP

Begin by adding a new Hue/Saturation adjustment layer and bumping up the Master saturation a little. Next, add a Curves adjustment layer. Don't alter the curve at all, but change the blend mode of that layer to Soft Light or Overlay. The image will appear to have much richer shadows than before, and you can adjust the opacity of the layer to change how much this effect is applied.

Next, we'll add a Color Balance adjustment layer to correct any colour bias or introduce one to add to the sense of drama. In our picture, we've pushed the yellow a bit further than we would normally advise, but it brings out the colour of the brickwork and looks good. The colour of the sky is now a little insipid, so we've added another Hue/Saturation layer, switched from Master to Blues and increased the saturation. If it's mission-critical, you should mask off different areas using each adjustment layer's mask and apply different settings to each layer to ensure you keep as much detail as possible.

HOW TO IN PHOTOSHOP

Photoshop's controls are much more sophisticated. For starters, you can use the Clone and Healing brushes to remove obvious blemishes, after which you can begin to improve the overall skin tone. Much of the retouching work depends in part on the quality of the original photograph – particularly the lighting – so ensure a clean shot to begin with.

To remove blemishes such as spots, select a relatively soft healing brush, then Alt-click on an area to define the source for the repair. You should pick an area with similar texture to the section to be repaired; colour matching will be handled by Photoshop. Once you've defined the source, click on the blemish to remove it. Later editions have a Spot Healing tool, which can further streamline the process.

To improve overall skin tone, duplicate the background layer by dragging it to the new layer icon in the layers palette, and apply a fairly gentle Gaussian blur to this layer. Add a new Layer Mask – picking Hide all – and switch to the Brush tool. Ensure your foreground colour is white and then toggle the airbrush on (rightmost icon in the brush toolbar) and drop the opacity slider down to about 25%. Use a reasonably big brush for large areas such as cheeks, but keep changing the size and softness to suit where you're working. Next, following the contours of the face and working in broad sweeps, begin to reveal the blurred skin layer by painting onto the layer mask. Less is more – avoid the eyes and mouth completely, and don't push the effect so far that your subject starts to look plastic. Remember that you can simply re-paint the layer mask in black to reduce the effect of the clean-up.

Before you snap

Your Mac can work wonders in cleaning up and enhancing your shots, but it can only work with the source material you give it. Here's our handy guide to getting the best photograph before you even snap the shutter.

● TELL STORIES
In each shot, always have at the back of your mind a little voice asking you what story you want to tell with the photograph. While this sounds a little abstract, it has a real, tangible effect on your pictures. Say you're in a pub with some friends, and you want to take a picture of one of your more 'hilarious' mates doing something characteristically 'hilarious'. Is it more important to capture the party trick specifically – telling the story 'here's what a friend of mine does' – or the reactions of the audience – potentially telling the story 'my friend isn't as funny as he thinks'. The story can be simply aesthetic – 'this is a pretty flower' – but each picture has one, and identifying it will help you take more interesting shots.

ALWAYS SHOOT AT FULL QUALITY
Sure, you'll get more pictures on a memory card if you shoot at low quality, but they're much less flexible. Not only are you limited in the size at which you can print the shots, but if you later decide to crop in on a specific area, the compression or low pixel count will become more obvious and spoil the picture. Ensure that the resolution is set to its highest and compression to its lowest. Ideally, if your camera supports it, shoot in Raw mode for ultimate flexibility. Simply buy more or bigger memory cards if your settings indicate you'll only fit a few on at these settings – they're really pretty cheap, and what price pristine memories?

USE MACRO
Most cameras have a macro function to focus really close on a subject, and it's a great way of recording interesting textures, and to give context. If you're at a historic house, say, try hunkering down and taking a macro shot of some hanging blossom (you may need to hold your hand behind the bloom to give autofocus something to lock on to, then remove it before fully depressing the shutter) with the house blurred in the background. Much more atmospheric and evocative than a straight shot of the building at eye level.

GET CLOSER
Asked to take a snap of a group of people, most people will take a few strides back and fit everyone in from head to toe – with a fair bit of background thrown in for good measure. This results in the faces being little more than a few hundred pixels tall. Most pictures – especially group shots – benefit from being taken closer to the subject. Portraits often work well cropped in much more closely than you would normally imagine – force yourself to move the camera closer and you'll be pleasantly surprised.

CHANGE THE VIEWPOINT
Stand on chairs and walls, get down on your knees and generally make a fool of yourself to get the best picture. Most people just stand upright and lift the camera to their eye-line, resulting in mediocre pictures that don't tell the story well. Taking pictures of children? Hunker down to their eye-level; the context this gives tells a better, truer story. By all means take the normal, basic shot, but for each shot you take, force yourself to move up, down, sideways or upside-down and take another.

CONSIDER BACKGROUND AND FOREGROUND
The background is as important as the foreground. That's not to say each should be given equal prominence – using shallow depths of field to blur the background and draw the eye to the foreground subject is a time-honoured and useful trick – but one that you shouldn't just ignore. No busy backgrounds or bins in the foreground unless you're deliberately making a point about these.

TURN OFF FLASH
Most cameras' flashes just serve to wash out people's faces to blue-ish, pockmarked circles, and many have an effective range of no more than a couple of metres. Add in their ability to spoil photos taken through glass by reflecting back in to the lens, and they're often more trouble than they're worth. See 'Rest and use self-timer' for more.

REST AND USE SELF-TIMER
Turning off the flash means the camera has to keep the shutter open for longer to take the shot, so things can be blurred. Obviate this by resting the camera on a convenient flat surface (upturned glasses can be readily pressed into service in pubs) and taking the photo with your camera's self-timer activated. Many have a two-second self-timer as well as the more common 10-second variant, and even this provides ample time for the camera to stop rocking on its perch.

THE TWO-SHOT CHEESE
Most people, on hearing the command 'say cheese', will freeze their face into a rictus of agonised happiness but relax and share a genuine smile just after the shot has been taken. Use this to your advantage: count down to the 'official' photo, take it, but take another immediately after – everyone will look much more happy and spontaneous in this covert shot.

MASTERCLASS
Personalising Front Row

Front Row's interface may be elegant, but it's rather impersonal, so here's how to tailor its icons to better suit your tastes.

Kit required Front Row-equipped Mac + Photoshop
Time 20 minutes per icon
Goal To personalise Front Row's icons
Skill level Intermediate

▲ **STEP 01 LOCATE FRONT ROW** Open your hard disk, and from the top level, navigate to System/Library/CoreServices. There's a wealth of goodies in here you can use to personalise your Mac, but we counsel caution: a wrong step here could compromise your Mac.

▲ **STEP 02 LOCATE THE FILES TO EDIT** Right-click on the Front Row application, select Show Package Contents and dig through to /Contents/Resources. Turn on icon previews (from View > Show View Options) to find the four main Front Row icons. You could replace one wholesale, but here we'll edit the VideosIcon.png file.

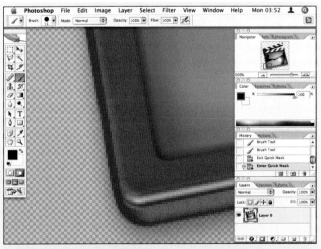

▲ **STEP 03 MAKE SELECTION** Copy the file to the desktop and duplicate it. Open the version that doesn't have the 'copy' suffix, and select the area where you'll add your own image. A combination of the Polygonal Lasso tool and the Paint Brush, used in Quick Mask mode, will work wonders and you can afford to be less precise than usual.

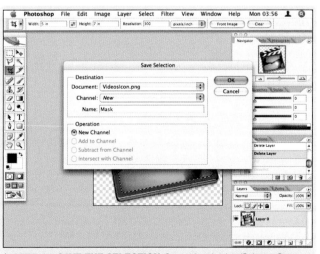

▲ **STEP 04 SAVE THE SELECTION** Save this selection (Select > Save Selection) for later use as a mask for your personalised image. It's always good practice to name your saved selections, even if you'll only be adding one to any given file.

○ **Although it lacks the TV tuner functionality** of Windows Media Center Edition, Apple's Front Row is by far a more elegant solution, and one that coexists very comfortably with the operating system proper.

It might strike you as a little impersonal, though, and so we'll demonstrate in this Masterclass how to replace the icons with ones that suit you better. In our example, we'll switch the blue hand-holding graphic from the iMovie-like icon used for the video section for one that is much more personal. Of course, there's nothing to stop you replacing the icons with different designs altogether – the principle is exactly the same – but for the purposes of this Masterclass, we'll focus on modifying an existing icon.

This technique could be equally useful in a corporate environment as in a home one. Just think about it: a Front Row interface decked out in your corporate colours or featuring your company logo would go a long way to helping maintain a strong brand identity.

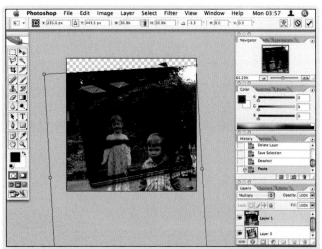

▲ **STEP 05 IMPORT NEW IMAGE** Paste the image you want to use on top of the existing image. Switch the layer mode to multiply so you can see the rough position and tap Command-T to bring up the Free Transform tool. This enables you to scale and rotate the image to suit. You can fine-tune these after you've applied the mask.

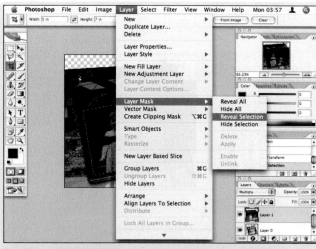

▲ **STEP 06 MASK IMAGE** Next, load the selection you created in step 3 and, ensuring you have the personal image layer selected, pick Layer > Layer Mask > Reveal Selection. Now you can switch the layer mode back to normal and fine-tune the position of the graphic.

▲ **STEP 07 FINISH AND FLATTEN** To give it a really polished look, add a subtle vignette. Merge the visible layers and save it out as a PNG. Keep the original file you duplicated on the desktop in step 3 in a safe place and copy the new VideosIcon.png back into Front Row's Resources folder. Authenticate as an admin and overwrite the original.

TAKING IT FURTHER
Although we've shown you just how to alter the videos graphic for Front Row, there's nothing stopping you altering all four icons, or even replacing them altogether with completely different graphics. If you want to do this, simply create any graphic to fit within a 500 x 500 pixel square; Front Row will take care of the reflection and drop-off you see when it's launched.

Although it seemed not to be necessary in our example, it's often worth pushing the colours and generally stylising photographs that will be included in Mac OS X screen elements. You could try boosting saturation and using the Noise and Scratches filter, as these help maintain the slightly artificial look of the Aqua interface layer. You could also try making the personal image dropped into the iMovie icon glossier by adding a masked brightness/contrast adjustment layer, as here.

MASTERCLASS
Make your own RSS screen saver

The RSS screen saver built into Mac OS X is a great way to display the latest news. It's limited to RSS feeds from Safari, but it's possible to build your own and change the display to suit you using Quartz Composer.

Kit Required Quartz Composer (free on install disks)
Time 10 minutes
Goal To make your own RSS screen saver
Skill Level Intermediate

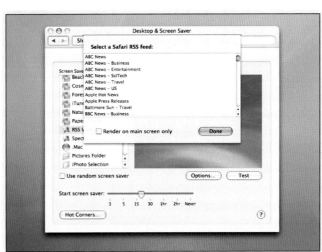

▲ **STEP 01 SCREEN SAVERS** You access the built-in RSS screen saver through the System Preferences control panel. It only gives you access to the RSS feeds you have in Safari, so you're stuck if you don't use the Apple browser to save your RSS feeds. To make matters worse, the design and colour scheme are static.

▲ **STEP 02 QUARTZ COMPOSER** Quartz Composer is a free application that can be found in the Developer Tools folder on your install disks. Open it and from the New Composition Assistant select Mac OS X RSS Screen Saver, which contains all you need to create your screen saver. First, you're taken to the setup screen and it's very simple to follow from there.

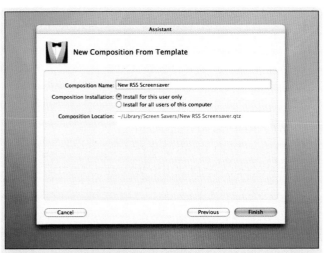

▲ **STEP 03 NAME YOUR SCREEN SAVER** The next step is to give your screen saver a name. This is how it will show up in the System Preferences control panel, so give it a memorable name. You can also choose to make the screen saver accessible to all the users of your Mac or just you.

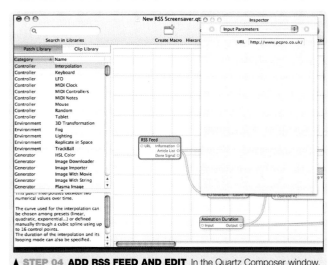

▲ **STEP 04 ADD RSS FEED AND EDIT** In the Quartz Composer window, click on the RSS Feed so it's highlighted and then on the Inspector, where you then select Input Parameters and put the RSS feed address in to the URL field. If you want to change the screen saver, select the element on the Quartz Composer window and change its settings from the Inspector.

- **FIRST FOR NEWS** – unlike other Mac magazines, MacUser is published fortnightly. Our readers get the lowdown on developments as they happen, not weeks after the event.

- **FIRST FOR REVIEWS** – with regular scoops, MacUser rates the latest products as they appear. A design classic, or a terminal disaster? You'll find out here first.

- **FIRST CLASS TUTORIALS** – from top tips and shortcuts to in-depth design workshops, MacUser's WORKS section and MASTERCLASS tutorials help you get the best from your Mac.

- **FIRST HAND KNOWLEDGE** – MacUser's lab tests put products through their paces. We pick the winners, enabling you to buy wisely.

ORDER ONLINE AT
www.dennismags.co.uk/macuser

SUBSCRIPTION OFFER MacUser

CLAIM 3 ISSUES FOR JUST £1

If you use an Apple Mac, then **MacUser** is essential reading for you. It is the UK's only fortnightly magazine with the very latest in Mac news.

Each issue is packed with **extensive reviews** of new hardware and software, the latest **industry news**, **expert comment**, tricks of the trade and much more.

FIND OUT MORE WITH 3 ISSUES FOR £1

Right now you can claim the next 3 issues for just £1! It's a **100% risk free** offer because if after 3 issues you're not completely satisfied you can write to cancel your subscription and you won't pay any more than the £1 already debited.

If you enjoy reading MacUser, your subscription will automatically continue at just £17.95 every 6 issues – a **saving of 25% on the shop price**.

OR CALL
0844 844 0063

using offer code **N0906MB2**

History of the Mac

'Apple ignited the personal computer revolution in the 1970s with the Apple II and reinvented the personal computer in the 1980s with the Macintosh. Today, Apple continues to lead the industry in innovation with its award-winning computers, OS X operating system and iLife and professional applications. Apple is also spearheading the digital media revolution with its iPod portable music and video players and iTunes online store, and has entered the mobile phone market with its revolutionary iPhone,' – positioning that appears at the end of all Apple marketing and press literature.

Apple, the company behind the Mac, was founded in California on 1 April 1976. Though it's never been confirmed, many believe it was named after Apple Corps, the Beatles' publisher; a poor choice of name that led to much legal wranglings over the years. Apple Corps dragged Apple Computer through the courts, made expensive financial settlements, and was assured by Apple Computer that it would keep out of the music business – a promise that was called into question with the arrival of the iPod, iTunes and online music store.

In retrospect, in a world where you can barely ride a train or bus without seeing a pair of distinctive white iPod headphones, it may have seemed a rash move to choose that name, but in 1976 the world was a very different place. Computers were primitive, the Internet was non-existent, and music came not on hard drives but flexible vinyl discs. That was the world into which Apple was born.

The two men we must thank for bringing us, over 30 years later, such masterpieces as the iMac, iPod and iPhone are Steve Jobs, the company's current CEO, and Steve Wozniak.

They met at the Homebrew Computer Club, a gathering of wannabe geeks in Silicon Valley. Despite the differences in their ages (Wozniak is almost five years older) the two men struck up a friendship, and started working on projects together. Jobs had spent some time as a programmer for Atari, then a leading light in video games production, while Wozniak had written a programming language and designed a circuit board for a brand new computer microprocessor. It was almost inevitable that the two men should found a computer company, along with friend Ronald Wayne, who we can thank for drawing the original Apple logo, which depicted Newton sitting beneath his famed apple tree.

The story of how they funded their first product – the circuit board Wozniak had designed and which they christened the Apple I – is well-known. Jobs had sold his camper van; Wozniak his programmable calculator. Finally they had start-up funding, but neither of them could have known that those few dollars they raised would be the foundations of a multi-billion dollar corporation.

If you look at the Apple I today, it doesn't look much like what any of us would consider to be a computer. It was quite literally a bare bones system that you had to put together yourself. Many of the photos that you can find of it on the Internet show it in a wooden case with the word Apple crudely sawn into the top, but this was a mere stopgap, and as such every Apple I would be unique.

The Apple II arrived the following year, and proved to be a revolutionary machine. For starters, it boasted colour graphics, and after initially shipping with a tape recorder for storage that was soon swapped out for a floppy disk drive. Despite this, it wasn't until VisiCalc arrived on the platform, allowing businesses to do their spreadsheeting tasks on a computer rather than squared paper, that it became a must-have machine.

By now, Ronald Wayne had already bailed out of Apple Computer and had sold his 10% stake in the company to Steve Jobs for a paltry $800; a move he should now be regretting, with its stock having accelerated to sky-high prices. Jobs had brought in a third partner, Mark Markkula, a one-time employee of Intel, who helped the company to secure funding to the tune of $250,000.

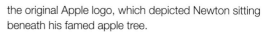

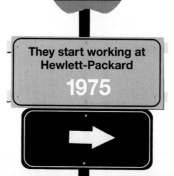

Steves Wozniak and Jobs meet
1971

They start working at Hewlett-Packard
1975

Apple Computer founded
1975

Illustration Chris Robson *chrisrobson.com*

Perhaps inevitably, the Apple II was followed by the Apple III at the start of the 1980s, and then the III+.

By then, though, Jobs had paid a visit to Xerox' research facilities at Palo Alto, the so-called Parc, where he saw the Alto Computer. This was a radical departure from the accepted norms of computing, as it eschewed screens full of text for a graphical interface, in which the three-button mouse was king. Jobs, and colleague Jef Raskin, were impressed by what they saw, and when they returned to Apple they started working on integrating a similar interface into two computers in its labs at that time: the high-end Lisa business machine, and the low-end consumer Macintosh, named in honour of Jef Raskin's favourite variety of apple.

Although the Lisa came out first, and was the first commercial computer to support a graphical user interface (GUI), it was hugely expensive, and didn't have the staying power of the Macintosh, which is the direct predecessor of today's Mac computers.

The Macintosh was finally sent to the shops in January 1984, and promoted with a memorable advert that aired in a break of the televised Superbowl that year. The ad, which cost a reported $1.5 million, portrayed a world not unlike that in George Orwell's book *1984*, which was brought crashing down by the appearance of an athletic saviour with a hammer, which she hurled through one of the iconic telescreens that are a central focus of the novel.

'On January 24th, Apple Computer will introduce Macintosh. And you'll see why 1984 won't be like "1984",' said the voiceover and on-screen legend. How true it was.

The advert itself was almost as revolutionary as the computer it promoted. Directed by Ridley Scott, who had just finished directing *Blade Runner*, it is held up as an icon of good advertising. Advertising Industry publication *Advertising Age* called it the best commercial of the 1980s and *TV Guide* names it the greatest commercial of all time, according to reports on CNN. It is much-quoted, reproduced in still photos and, at the time, received free replays by stations discussing its content, which would have gone a long way towards recouping the original cost of the slot in which it aired.

The advert was a dig at the growing influence of IBM – the largest computer company at the time – and the standards it had set with its PC, which still form the basis of all PCs sold to this day. Apple's advert portrayed IBM as Big Brother in Orwell's dystopian future, while it saw itself as the bright light that would free the world from IBM's domination.

Although Jobs loved the ad, and had even travelled to Shepperton Studios in the UK to oversee its week-long, $750,000 shoot in a studio filled with 200 British skinheads – not actors – the board was less keen and tried to offload the slots they had already bought in which to air it. Ad agency Chiat-Day, which had orchestrated the whole campaign claimed it was impossible at such a late stage, so the ad ran nonetheless.

Andy Herzfeld, a member of the original Macintosh team, recounts the board's reaction after the airing, and subsequent media interest on his site *folklore.org*: 'A week after the Macintosh launch, Apple held its January board meeting. The Macintosh executive staff was invited to attend, not knowing what to expect. When the Mac people entered the room, everyone on the board rose and gave them a standing ovation, acknowledging that they were wrong about

Apple I goes on sale 1976

Apple II hits the shops 1977

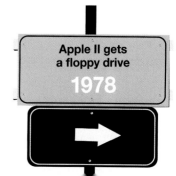

Apple II gets a floppy drive 1978

the commercial and congratulating the team for pulling off a fantastic launch.'

And so the 'affordable' Mac was born. It had a 9in monochrome screen, an 8MHz processor and 128KB of memory. Storage was limited to a 3.5in floppy drive. A hard drive would have been unimaginably expensive at the time. The machine came bundled with MacPaint and MacWrite.

Those specs may sound very conservative today – as indeed they are – but at the time they were enough to bring this machine to the interest of desktop publishing professionals. At $2495, it massively undercut comparative products, and the introduction of an affordable laser printer, and PageMaker layout software should perhaps be given credit for the Mac's continued success – to this day – in the field of design and print.

The Macintosh was revamped several times, but despite its success it was to be the ultimate author of Jobs' downfall at the company.

He had recruited John Sculley, one-time president of Pepsi, to act as Apple's CEO. He was a solid businessman, and found himself overseeing a company virtually split in two. The Macintosh team was proclaiming itself to be custodians of the company's future, while the Lisa team, selling its computers at $10,000 a pop, claimed it was the source of the company's income. Inevitably, the two didn't get on. Jobs' Macintosh team almost became a separate entity inside Apple, which was clearly something no CEO or board could condone.

Sculley and the board took the only course of action open to them; they stripped Jobs of his responsibilities. Jobs sold all but one of his shares in Apple and left to found NeXT Computer, a firm that developed extremely high-end machines, and a revolutionary operating system called NeXTstep.

Skip forward 10 years, and NeXT is doing well. Apple, though, less so. It had had a good few years, releasing a string of successful products, like the PowerBook and the Newton handheld computer. However, it had steadily lost market share to PCs running Microsoft Windows, and was valiantly trying to keep up the battle by licensing its own operating system to third-party hardware developers, while simultaneously running abortive projects to develop ever better versions, which never saw the light of day.

Nonetheless, it had the reserves to buy Jobs' new company, and in doing so bring him back into the fold, as a consultant. Now it was Jobs' turn to start bossing around the board. He ousted the current CEO at the time – Gil Amelio – and started to make immediate changes. He canned the failing operating system projects, terminated the Newton and cancelled the contracts with third-party developers to make Macintosh-compatible computers of their own. Apple was set to resume its role as the sole arbiter of both the hardware and software sides of its business.

Work started on porting the NeXTstep operating system from NeXT's own machines to the Mac, and it is that push that brought us to the Mac OS X environment that runs our Macs to this very day.

Almost straight away, Apple's fortunes were revived. Microsoft invested $150 million in the company and pledged to continue producing Microsoft Office for the platform, guaranteeing its continued viability in the business world. The following year, in May 1998, the most revolutionary product since the original Macintosh was unveiled by then interim CEO Jobs to an assembled crowd in San Francisco. It was the iMac.

Apple stock floated
1980

First Apple shareholders' meeting
1981

Apple releases the $10,000 Lisa
1983

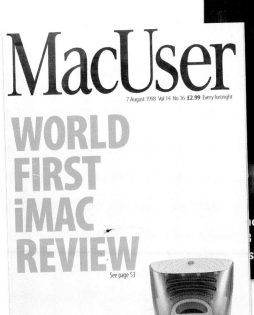

This machine was both a nod to the past and a pointer to the future. It was an all-in-one device, where the guts of the computer were built into the back of the monitor, and it sported a design like nothing that had gone before it. Out went boring beige boxes, in came translucent plastics in funky colours. Jobs had teamed up with young British designer Jonathan Ive to breathe new life into the computer world, and it had worked.

Suddenly Apple was back in the spotlight. It was the new darling of the computer world, and countless peripheral manufacturers jumped onboard. Printers, scanners, mice, keyboards… seemingly everything now incorporated a flash of colourful plastic in an effort to make PCs look as trendy and desirable as the iMac, but none of them quite pulled it off.

That original iMac went through several iterations, which saw it evolve from a simple home business/web browsing/emailing machine into a fully-fledged multimedia device with video editing tools. It was eventually joined by the iBook, which took its cues from the iMac, being moulded from similar translucent plastics (in tangerine and blueberry colours), and integrating a carry handle by the hinge (the iMac had a carry handle in the top). It was a love-it or hate-it product, which bore a striking resemblance to a plastic toilet seat. Fortunately this wasn't sufficient a problem to put off the countless users who bought one and it was particularly popular in the education market.

2001 and 2002 saw radical redesigns of these two product lines. In 2001, the iBook was given a more sober white casing, and lost its bulging curves. In 2002, the iMac swapped its TV-style monitor for a flat screen, with the workings of the computer now housed in a dome below, rather than behind the screen. Sales continued to rise. It seemed that the 'i' badged range of products was just what the world had been waiting for.

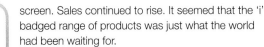

By now Jobs was officially back in control. He was no longer the interim CEO; he had the confidence of the board and he was breathing life back into a company that many, including Dell CEO Michael Dell, had pretty much written off.

New products followed, each one better than the last, and although not all seemed like logical additions to the range, such as the Mac mini, which looked good but was considered by some to be underpowered and over-priced in comparison to PC equivalents, it seemed that Jobs and Ive, between them, had an almost faultless understanding of their customers' wants and desires.

But then Apple hit something of a wall. It had put all of its eggs in one basket where processors were concerned. While most PC manufacturers split their ranges between chips from Intel and AMD, Apple was tied in to deals that saw it centre its designs on PowerPC processors from IBM and Motorola. They had served the company well for many years, but suddenly they seemed to top out. While customers clamoured for ever faster chips, the factories struggled to produce them. In a desperate attempt to sate public cries of frustration, it rigged up a Power Mac, one of its professional desktop computers, with a liquid-based cooling system that allowed the processor to be run at a faster speed than that for which it was designed. In true Apple style, it was an elegant implementation, but still it was something of a get around.

Next the notebook line-up started to suffer. PC competitors started to pull ahead with cooler, faster

Macintosh ships, and changes everything
1984

Steve Jobs leaves Apple; Apple's fortunes decline
1985

Steve Jobs returns; Apple's fortunes revived
1997

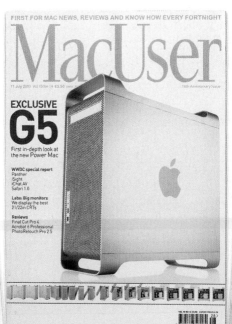

chips from Intel and Apple was starting to lag. A mobile edition of the G5 processor used in the latest desktop machines seemed as far away as ever and, taking the only course of action open to it, Apple announced in 2005 that it was to move away from the PowerPC processor, and standardise on the Intel platform, making its machines more like regular PCs than ever before.

This sent shock waves through the community. For customers it was great news; they'd finally have the speedy machines they were after, and perhaps at lower prices. For developers it was potentially terrible news. They had written their software to work with the PowerPC processor, and now they'd have to re-code it for an entirely new architecture.

Apple calmed their nerves somewhat by explaining that it would initially build in a compatibility routine to the operating systems on its new Intel machines. Called Rosetta, this would translate the instructions coming from the older software into the language understood by the new processors. It also demonstrated how easy it was to make the old PowerPC software natively compatible with the Intel chips.

However, the ease at which applications could be ported across depended entirely on their complexity. Simple tools like text editors could often be automatically re-encoded by the tools that translated the code from something humans would understand to the kind of low-level binary numbers understood by processors and memory. Other, more ambitious applications like Microsoft's Office Suite, or Adobe's Photoshop, required more serious surgery, and a lot of work and investment from their publishers.

Fortunately very few headline applications failed to make the move, so that by January 2008 order had been restored with every major Mac application, including Word, Excel, PowerPoint, Photoshop, InDesign, Dreamweaver, QuarkXPress and a host of other staples now running more happily and more efficiently on Apple's new Intel processors.

But of course the story of the Mac isn't just about products starting with 'i'. Over the years Apple has worked on first consolidating and later diversifying its product line up to include servers, ultra-light notebooks, consumer and professional desktop machines and media boxes that sit underneath a television to stream movies and music direct to the living room.

FUTURE OF THE MAC

So where does it go from here? That question could be answered in any number of ways, but it's almost certain that the correct answer won't involve the company licensing its operating system for use by third-party developers again. It tried that for a while, and it wasn't a success. Now, with Microsoft Windows in an even more dominant position, it can't afford to try it again.

Apple's financial outlook has never looked better than it does right now, thanks to a close-to-perfect fusion of hardware and software that couldn't possibly be maintained if it allowed others a modicum of control over the products on which its operating system is used.

Almost all of those products are based on various editions of its operating system. That means, beside its closely-integrated music and movie download businesses, Mac OS X has become the key to the company's future existence. It is one of the world's most advanced operating systems, and finally

increased sales are starting to do it justice. It has won plaudits from old hands and new arrivals alike, and it's getting rave reviews in the traditionally Windows-focused computer press. Meanwhile, the company is working hard to build it into an ever-increasing range of products, as it forms the basis of the iPhone and all recent iPods, apart from the shuffle. That's no mean feat, considering the system requirements of its competitors.

While brands like iTunes, iPhone and iPod remain the company's most visible icons, the word 'Mac' will live on for the foreseeable future for as long as Apple keeps on updating its operating system, and it's highly unlikely that it stop doing that. Microsoft is seeing its market share being slowly eroded and the best-placed company to benefit from this is Apple. That's not to say it will become the dominant player – it won't – but it offers great potential.

At the moment we are seeing more and more software applications move off computers' local hard drives and onto the web. Google is stealing a march with its highly competent online office suite, which gets better every day. Adobe is following its lead with Buzzword, an online word processor and, in early 2008, released a public test version of an online edition of Photoshop.

You might think that this is bad news for the Mac, but that couldn't be further from the truth. Once we're all running out software online, it won't matter what kind of computer we have or what operating system it runs, so nobody will be asking whether it will work with their computer – all they'll be interested in is how easy it is to get their Mac or PC online so they can use it. Here, the Mac has a trump card. It's supremely easy to get online, and it's just as happy running its

own browser, Safari, as it is with the cross-platform Firefox, which you'll find on as many PCs as Macs.

Apple, then, will continue to develop, improve and sell the Mac. That's a relief to many. With the arrival of the iPhone there was concern from some quarters that Apple had taken its eye off the ball where its computers were concerned. Developers were taken away from coding the latest release of Mac OS X and reassigned to the mobile phone project, much to the distress of faithful Apple computer users who saw the release date of their next software upgrade slipping back at a terrifying rate. When it arrived, though, Leopard was better than most had dared hope – a few grumbles aside – and it was clear that the delay was nothing more serious than a minor blip.

Apple is now making more money from selling computers than at any point in its history. It is gaining ground as one of the world's biggest manufacturers of notebook computers, trouncing the one-time big names of the industry. Investing in a Mac today gets you in at the ground floor.

However, there is one major sticking point for the Apple watcher, and that's what will happen to the company – and the Mac – once Steve Jobs moves on. He can't stay at the helm forever, and there is no obvious successor in place. Internal plans may be in place to handle this eventuality, but whatever happens and whenever it happens, Jobs' departure is sure to rock the company, its stock and its customers.

Right now Jobs seems as important to the company as its operating system and the Mac brand. After a brief brush with cancer a couple of years ago, Jobs has made the issue far more pertinent and pressing. Jobs is Apple, and Apple is Jobs as much as it is the Mac.

Mac OS X becomes the Mac's operating system
2001

Arrival of the iPod
2001

Apple drops 'Computer' to become Apple Inc
2007

Glossary

The Mac may be wonderfully easy to use, but the world of computing remains littered with technical terminology and acronyms, some of which is specific to the Mac, and some of which is in more general everyday use. A familiarity with these terms will greatly help in understanding and enjoying your Mac.

.Mac
Online service owned and run by Apple, has now been renamed MobileMe, but the service remains the same. (See MobileMe).

Apple TV
Small box-like device used to download TV shows and movies from the iTunes Store and play back the media on an HD television. It can also share music and video libraries stored on a Mac. First introduced in January 2007, it received a significant free software upgrade in January 2008, indicating that Apple sees media downloads as an increasingly important part of its future.

Boot Camp
Application shipped as part of Mac OS X 10.5 Leopard that allows you to run Microsoft Windows on Apple computers with Intel processors. It gives Windows full access to all of the Mac's internal hardware so that it can work directly with the processor, memory and storage. This delivers excellent performance making the Mac – surprisingly – one of the best computers on which to run Windows.

Click Wheel
The circular controller on the front of an iPod, under which four buttons arranged at the points of a compass allow you to skip backwards and forwards through tracks and navigate the menus.

Cover Flow
Feature found in iTunes and the latest generation of iPods and the iPhone, which allows you to flick through the covers of the albums in your music collection. With the iPhone and iPod touch, you can also tap the albums to access their tracks. A similar feature in Mac OS X 10.5 Leopard allows you to flick through files in the Finder in the same way.

Creative Suite
Series of application bundles from Adobe, comprising a combination of its most popular programs, including Photoshop, InDesign, Dreamweaver, Flash and Premiere. At present, Creative Suite is at version 4 and is a cost-effective way to buy more than one Adobe application at a time, as most bundles cost little more than two of the programs that make them up.

Cursor
Vertical bar used in word processors to indicate the point at which your typing will appear.

Dashboard
A hidden layer of Mac OS X 10.4 Tiger and 10.5 Leopard on which you can run mini applications called Widgets. These run like sections of web pages to perform specific tasks, such as tracking stock prices, reporting the weather or translating phrases.

Desktop
This is the graphical main area of the screen on top of which windows open and applications run. Its background can be customised to show an image of your choice, and it can also be used as a temporary storage area for files, although this is not to be recommended as it shows poor file management and can impact on your Mac's performance.

Dock
Translucent bar running along the bottom of the screen housing icons that are shortcuts to your most regularly-used applications. By right-clicking or Ctrl-clicking on the dividing bar in the right half of the Dock you can access its customisation menu, and from there move it to one side of the screen, change its size or have it automatically hide itself when not in use.

Double-click
To click twice in quick succession on the button of a mouse, the button in front of a trackpad, or the trackpad itself. This action when executed, rather than just selecting the item clicked on, will open a file in its associated application or launch a piece of software.

DTP
Acronym for desktop publishing that describes the process of designing pages on a screen rather than using molten metal, as was once the case with all printed matter. All magazines and newspapers, fliers and brochures are now designed using DTP software, which is a mainstay of the Mac platform. The two leading DTP applications are Adobe InDesign and QuarkXPress, although Apple Pages (part of iWork 08) and Microsoft Word offer similar tools tailored to home and small business users.

Exposé
Utility that reorganises your open windows to help you work more efficiently with your files. It is activated through the keyboard and can either display all active applications, split up active windows in the current application or clear the screen altogether to give you access to the Mac OS X Desktop.

Finder
The part of the Mac's operating system that handles navigation through files and folders. When you have no applications open, and are viewing the Desktop background you are in a pure Finder environment, as indicated by the word Finder at the left of the Menubar.

Font
Term usually taken to describe the visual look of a set of characters (letters, numbers and symbols). However, it can also be taken to mean more than just the style of the characters but also their dimensions, weight and other attributes.

Front Row
Media playback software found on Apple TV and Macs with Mac OS X 10.5 Leopard. It comprises large menus optimised for viewing on a regular TV screen, and is controlled by the Apple Remote, which can be bought for £15.

GarageBand
Home-user music creation application found in iLife in which songs are constructed by dragging pre-recorded musical clips, called Loops, into the working area.

GB
Abbreviation for gigabyte, which is 1 million kilobytes of data. A single gigabyte is enough to store about 250 music tracks on an iPod.

iBook
Consumer notebook that appealed to students and less demanding home users. It was introduced shortly after the original iMac and after several iterations Apple finally retired the product line in 2006. Its closest current equivalent in Apple's notebook range is the bottom-end white MacBook.

iCal
Calendaring application bundled with Mac OS X that lets you set reminders for upcoming appointments and track tasks that need to be completed. It uses industry-standard formats, allowing you to share appointments with people through a range of applications and operating systems, as well as publish your diary online.

iDisk
Web storage space that is included in a .Mac subscription. It can be made to work in exactly the same way as a local hard drive in Mac OS X, and will even show up in the list of drives in a Finder window. Certain applications such as iPhoto and iWeb can also use it as a place to publish photo galleries and websites.

iDVD
This is an application that is used to burn movies to DVD, complete with chapters and menus for use on a consumer DVD player and TV, or another computer. iDVD is found in the iLife suite.

iLife
Lifestyle suite produced by Apple, which comprises iTunes, iPhoto, iMovie, iDVD, iWeb and GarageBand. It receives an update roughly every 12 to 18 months, and can be seen as a creative companion to a regular office suite. It is included free with every new Mac.

iMac
An all-in-one computer, in which its inner workings are hidden behind the screen. The keyboard and mouse are the only external components. The current metal and glass iMac is the fourth generation of the machine, which started out as a semi-transparent computer in a curvy round case in a choice of colours, and is credited by many as being the computer that revived the ailing Apple's fortunes following its debut in 1998.

Inspector
A panel that is used in many software applications to examine the current attributes of an element. It is also used as a way of altering them. Examples include controllers for fonts and text sizes in a word processor, or the colour of objects in a graphics application.

Interface
The interface of any application is the collection of menus, buttons, text, graphics and panels that make up its on-screen appearance. In Mac OS X, this includes the menubar at the top of the screen, the Dock at the bottom (or on the left or right of the screen if you have changed its position), the windows containing files and applications and the icons that you click.

iPhone
Part pocket computer, part media player, part communications device, this is Apple's play for the mobile phone market. It sells itself on its cool looks and excellent software. It is only ever sold through one network in any country – in the UK, that network is O2 – and it attracts a high contract cost. This is somewhat offset,

● however, in that the contract includes unlimited use of the Internet and a generous allocation of bundled calls.

iPod
The world's best-selling music player, which is also made by Apple. There are four distinct varieties of iPod: shuffle, nano, classic and touch. In the past there has also been the iPod mini, but this was phased out when the nano arrived. All work with iTunes on either the Mac or PC.

iTunes
Free application for PCs and the Mac used for downloading and organising music and podcasts, as well as listening to Internet radio streams and uploading music to an iPod. It is also the home of the iTunes Store through which Apple sells music, movies and TV shows.

iWeb
Web design software included with the iLife. It can publish to regular web hosting space, but is designed to work primarily with the webspace included as part of Apple's .Mac online service. As such, it takes advantage of server-specific features that are not available as a part of third-party hosting packages.

iWork
Apple's own office suite, comprising Pages (word processor), Numbers (spreadsheet) and Keynote (presentation package). Each application uses its own file format, but it can also import and export Microsoft Office files for compatibility. Each application prides itself on the quality of its output, boasting many low-level desktop publishing-style tools.

Keynote
Presentation application used for creating slides, comprising text, images, sound, movies and transitions. It is not directly compatible with PowerPoint, although it can read and write those files.

MacBook
The family name for Apple's range of notebook computers. It comprises three different lines; the consumer MacBook, the high-end MacBook Pro and the highly desirable, ultra-slim MacBook Air. Together their screens range in size from 13in to 17in, while their prices span from less than £750 to almost £1900 in their standard configurations. Each has a built-in web camera, called iSight, in the lid and ships with the latest version of the Mac operating system, although as they feature the same Intel processors as you'd find in a PC notebook, they are also capable of running Microsoft Windows.

Mac mini
Small, consumer computer, about the size of a box of biscuits. Seen by many as the ideal media computer because of its integrated DVD drive and media playback software, combined with a compact chassis that makes it perfect for slipping under the TV, it seems likely that it is the Mac found in more living rooms more than any other.

Mac OS X
Apple's native operating system. The current edition is version 10.5, with each new release incrementing the number after the dot. Each one is given a wildcat-related codename in development, with the latest one being Leopard. This was preceded by Tiger, Panther, Jaguar and Cheetah. It was developed out of work done by NeXT, a company founded by Apple co-founder Steve Jobs, and later bought by Apple, hence bringing Jobs back into the company fold. It is based on a business operating environment called Unix, which makes it very secure and robust and less prone to infection from viruses and spyware than Microsoft Windows.

Mac Pro
Apple's professional-level computer. It ships without a monitor, in a drilled aluminium case. It is more powerful than an iMac or any portable computer Apple produces, but the primary reason for buying it is the expansion options it offers, with room for more memory and hard drives than Apple's consumer computers. It also ships with up to two processors, rather than just one, to crunch through intensive tasks more quickly.

MB
Short for megabyte, which is 1000 kilobytes. Old-style 3.5in floppy disks used to hold about 1MB of data, but these days even a simple Microsoft Excel spreadsheet can be many times this size. As such, fewer and fewer measurements in computing are expressed in terms of megabytes, with gigabyte measurements becoming more common usage to describe file sizes.

Menubar
Strip of drop-down menus found at the top of the screen. It performs the same function as the bar of menus attached to the top of every individual application in Windows, but as it's not attached to the application window itself it

instead tailors itself to feature only those options relevant to whichever application is foremost on the screen at any one time.

MobileMe
Online service owned and run by Apple. It offers remote storage of files, Hotmail-style webmail, photo galleries and web publishing. It is a paid-for extra, but as it is so well integrated into the Mac operating system and many of Apple's applications – in particular those in the iLife suite – it is a worthwhile investment for many users. More details can be found at *me.com*.

Multi-touch
Term used to describe hardware devices employed by Apple in the iPhone and various MacBooks that allow you to manipulate on-screen elements by sliding, twisting, flicking and pinching your fingers on a screen or trackpad.

Numbers
Apple's spreadsheet application, forming part of the iWork suite. It was introduced in 2008 and has its own file format, although it can import and export Microsoft Excel-compatible files. It has excellent design tools, which go a long way to making your spreadsheets look attractive and engaging, but its unique ability is to include more than one table on a single page. Excel can include only one.

Office
Generic term used to describe Microsoft's business applications suite comprising Word (word processor), Excel (spreadsheet), PowerPoint (presentation, and various email and database applications, depending on the year of release and whether it is a PC or Mac edition. Its native file formats have become something of a business standard adhered to by many rival applications.

Operating System
Software that controls the most fundamental hardware of a computer and passes instructions to it from the applications that they run. Mac OS X and Windows are both operating systems, but other popular alternatives include Linux and Unix.

Pages
Apple's own word processing application, found in the iWork suite. It boasts good home-user desktop publishing features, which were once to the detriment of its tools for regular plain text writing, although in later editions this imbalance has been redressed, making Pages a first-class text creation and editing tool.

Pointer
The on-screen arrow moved using the mouse or trackpad. In a spreadsheet such as Excel or Numbers, it is usually replaced by a cross when moving over the grid of cells in a table.

PowerBook
Now outdated notebook computer produced by Apple using its older generation of PowerPC processors. Physically it looked almost identical to the current MacBook Pro and, because of its build quality and the conservative demands on recent releases of Mac OS X, many are still in use.

Power Mac
The predecessor of the Mac Pro, once forming the upper echelons of Apple's desktop computer line and favoured by professional users, particularly in creative and design environments.

Preferences
Each application has a section dedicated to adjustable settings, called Preferences. You'll find it by clicking on the application's name in the menubar at the top of the screen, and then clicking on Preferences in the menu that drops down. More extensive settings used to control how the Mac works in general are found in System Preferences. Find this by clicking on the Apple icon in the top left-hand corner of the screen.

Processor
The brain of your computer, the processor is the chip that does all of the calculations that make it work. There are several processors in every machine, covering general system tasks and graphics. All recent Macs use the same kind of main processor as a PC, made by Intel, but older Macs use the so-called PowerPC processor line, and may be unable to run some of the latest software releases, including Adobe Premiere (professional video editing application) and FileMaker Bento (database for home-users).

RAM
Acronym for Random Access Memory; a series of fast chips used by the processor to temporarily store information while it is being worked on. All data stored in the Ram is lost when the Mac is turned off or rebooted. As such, files should be saved at regular intervals.

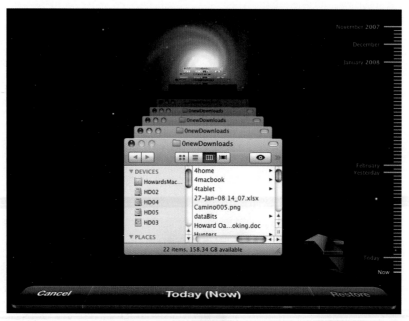

Right-click
Clicking with the right-hand button of a mouse to bring up a menu of options relevant to the item on which you have clicked. The mice that Apple used to ship came with only one button, so right-clicking was could be performed by holding down the Ctrl key while clicking to call up the same menu. Apple's current mouse offering, the Apple Mighty Mouse, can be configured for two-button use in System Preferences, while plugging in any two-button mouse works without any trouble.

Software Update
Small application found by clicking on the Apple icon in the top-left corner of the screen, which checks with Apple's servers for new and updated versions of the software on your Mac. It will automatically run every so often on its own, but if you notice it has not run in the last couple of weeks, it's worth invoking manually. This is the Mac equivalent of Windows Update and Office Update on the PC.

Spaces
Feature of Mac OS X 10.5 Leopard that allows you to have up to 16 virtual screens running on your Mac at the same time. This allows you to organise your active applications according to function, or run 16 of them in full-screen mode, rather than smaller windows.

Time Capsule
Hard drive with wireless features, allowing Macs and PCs to connect and use it for storage. It was designed specifically to work hand-in-hand with Time Machine. Time Capsule replaced a feature that was included in pre-release versions of Mac OS X 10.5 Leopard that allowed Time Machine back ups to be made over a wireless network.

Time Machine
Automatic backup system built in to Mac OS X 10.5 Leopard. Once you have plugged in an external hard drive and given Time Machine permission to use it, the application will copy changes made to your system every hour. Should you lose an important file or make changes that you should not have done you can then roll back through each hour of changes to find the file and return the data to its previous state.

Trackpad
Touch-sensitive area on a notebook computer, between the user and the keyboard. Sliding your finger across its surface will move an on-screen cursor, while tapping it will cause the pointer to select the item over which it sits. Usually accompanied by one or two selection buttons just beneath it to perform a similar task. Using two fingers on the trackpad of any MacBook-based notebook scrolls the contents of the current open window.

Trash
Found on the Dock, the Trash is where you drag files and applications when you want to delete them from your system. Other applications, such as iTunes, may also send files here when you delete them from within their own environment. Items sent to the Trash are not immediately deleted, allowing them to be recovered at a later date if deleted in error. Once emptied, however, the files are lost forever. The direct equivalent in Windows is the Recycle Bin.

USB
Universal Serial Bus; a port and cable combination that lets you transfer data to and from your Mac. It is used to connect almost every kind of device (hence the Universal part of its name) including printers, scanners, iPods and cameras.

Widget
See Dashboard.

Wifi
Colloquial term used to describe a wide range of wireless networking technologies. It can usually be taken to mean any kind of wireless connection over which you might browse the web or send and receive email.

Window
The container holding an application or an open file on the screen in any graphical operating system, such as Mac OS X.

Windows
Microsoft's operating system. The current edition is Windows Vista, but its predecessor, Windows XP, remains popular as some users have shown a reluctance to upgrade. It will only run on the Mac with the help of software built into Mac OS X 10.5 Leopard, or Parallels and Fusion from third-party developers (see page 98).

WWDC
Worldwide Developers' Conference held every summer at which Apple outlines its future strategy for Mac OS X and other key technologies, and makes an announcement for a high-end product or two.